CONFLICT
AND COMPROMISE

CLASS FORMATION IN
ENGLISH SOCIETY
1830–1914

CONFLICT AND COMPROMISE

CLASS FORMATION IN ENGLISH SOCIETY
1830–1914

A COMPARATIVE STUDY
OF BIRMINGHAM AND SHEFFIELD

DENNIS SMITH

Department of Sociology and Social History,
University of Aston

ROUTLEDGE & KEGAN PAUL

LONDON, BOSTON, MELBOURNE AND HENLEY

First published in 1982
by Routledge & Kegan Paul Ltd
39 Store Street, London WC1E 7DD,
9 Park Street, Boston, Mass. 02108, USA,
296 Beaconsfield Parade, Middle Park,
Melbourne 3206, Australia and
Broadway House, Newtown Road,
Henley-on-Thames, Oxon RG9 1EN.
Photoset in 10 on 12 Palatino by
Kelly Typesetting Ltd, Bradford-on-Avon, Wiltshire
and printed in Great Britain by
The Thetford Press Ltd, Thetford, Norfolk
© Dennis Smith 1982

Library of Congress Cataloging in Publication Data

Smith, Dennis, 1945–

Conflict and compromise.

Bibliography: p.
1. Social classes—England—Birmingham (West Midlands)—History.
2. Social classes—England—Sheffield (Yorkshire)—History.
3. Social conflict.
4. Birmingham (West Midlands, England)—Social conditions.
5. Sheffield (Yorkshire)—Social conditions.
I. Title.
HN400.S6S63   305.5'0942   81–21008

ISBN 0–7100–0969–0   AACR2

CONTENTS

CONTENTS

CONTENTS

TABLES

GRAPHS

PREFACE

This book explores the interplay between two contradictions in the development of English society between 1830 and 1914. The first is that the growth of industrial capitalism in England was favoured by and in turn threatened the existence of a decentralised state apparatus dominated by a commercialised country-house aristocracy. Industrialisation and urbanisation increased the relative power of urban businessmen, public officials and professionals and tended to shift the strategic sites of social and political management away from the localities and towards the national level. The second contradiction is that the fruits of ingenuity and labour were appropriated to a disproportionate extent by a relatively small class of property owners and their associates but the persistence of these arrangements depended upon the complicity of the many who were excluded from most of the benefits. As will be seen, these contradictions produced tendencies towards conflict and towards compromise between members of status groups and social classes which were themselves transformed in the process. The primary objective of the book is to identify and explain the dynamics of conflict and compromise in two strategically important cities. The processes of class formation which occurred in these decades are traced in a number of institutional spheres: primarily in the spheres of local government, municipal politics, formal education and industrial relations but also in the areas of commercial life, the professions, enforcement of the law, religion, leisure, charity, self-help, patterns of residence, property ownership and the family.

Each city is analysed in terms of its location within a hierarchy of mutually related levels of structural differentiation ranging from the domestic to the national level. Birmingham and Sheffield are distinguished from each other with reference to a number of structural characteristics. They include: the location of each city within the division of labour and network of communications, both regionally and nationally; the degree of structural weight borne by solidarities and institutions focused upon the neighbourhood, the municipality, county society and the national level and their relative significance compared to each other; the range and degree of structural differentiation and interdependence exhibited by each city, for example in its products and services but more generally in the social roles, forms of culture and varieties of experience offered within the urban social structure; and the forms of differentiation within the domestic sphere.

When researching this book, which was initially intended to be concerned principally with the education system, I became impressed by the fact that although both Birmingham and Sheffield were hardware towns surrounded by iron works and coal mines, class formation appeared to be occurring on very different lines when the two were compared. Sheffield had a strong and solidary working class confronted, before mid-century at least, by a weak and anomic bourgeoisie. By contrast, Birmingham had a working class whose structural defences in the industrial, political and religious spheres were relatively weak. It was faced by a bourgeoisie which was well-organised and confident. Furthermore, when investigation was carried forward into the 1860s it became apparent that the Sheffield working class was fundamentally divided, a split which manifested itself most clearly with respect to strategies of industrial bargaining. At the same time a deep division occurred within Birmingham's bourgeoisie with respect to strategies of managing public institutions. For about two decades from the mid-1860s competing segments of this bourgeoisie allied with each of the two wings of the pre-industrial order: the rural aristocracy on the one hand and on the other hand the merging social circles of the petit-bourgeois 'shopocracy' and the artisanry. By contrast, in Sheffield, under the new leadership of the large-scale steel makers the urban bourgeoisie threw its weight into the balance with the aristocracy and overwhelmed the parochial networks of craftsmen and petty traders. In the case of Sheffield a coalescence of agrarian and industrial capitalists occurred through county and metropolitan social circles, perpetuating a chronically weak municipal consciousness within the city and sharp class divisions. A similar coalescence occurred in the case of Birmingham but in this instance through municipal networks and in ways which tended to inhibit the expression of class divisions locally.

In Sheffield industrial production played a greater part in structuring class solidarities and conflicts than it did in Birmingham. This difference between the two cities is one expression of the fact that class formation in each city was fundamentally conditioned by the way it 'fitted into' structures focused at the regional and national levels. The relationship of the aristocracy to these towns was of far more than peripheral importance. Cultural and political capital in the hands of classes shaped by participation in the declining agrarian capitalist order was deployed in ways which determined important aspects of the forms of solidarity and fission within industrial capitalism. A qualification to that statement is necessary. By comparison with the gentry and aristocracy, skilled craftsmen and petty-bourgeois shop-keepers had little success in protecting their cultural and political (not to mention economic) interests in the face of industrial capitalism. This was largely due to the fact that they belonged to social networks coordinated at a sub-municipal level, that of the neighbourhood, whereas the increasing scale and complexity of urban industrial society was shifting the strategic sites of conflict and compromise away from that level and towards the national level where the aristocracy remained influential. It is not surprising that the educational and social theories of Herbert Spencer, who came from a provincial petty-bourgeois Dissenting background, should have had a much smaller impact in England than those of Matthew Arnold. The latter's social allegiance was to the ancient universities and the Church of England, institutions which had a special regard for the aristocracy and gentry. Spencer's major impact was in the United States where the petty-bourgeois values of pre-industrial society flourished under industrial capitalism. In England, the aristocratic-cum-clerical wing of the old order had particular success in shaping the new industrial society through the medium of formal education. In this sphere orientations deeply hostile to petty-bourgeois preoccupations with 'money-making' were inculcated. These orientations were compatible with advancing industrial prosperity only because Britain was favourably located within an even-more-encompassing structure, that of the international economy and system of states.

Potential readers' interests are likely to vary. Those particularly concerned with education should see chapters 5, 6, 8 and 9. An important sub-theme on the development of the professions runs through the book, especially chapter 6. A comparison of Birmingham and Sheffield with reference to mutually related levels of structural differentiation is carried out in chapter 2. The following chapter (chapter 3) focuses upon transformations within these structures and has a close relationship to chapter 10. Summaries will be found at the end of chapter 1, at the end of the second part of chapter 3, at the beginning and end of chapter 4, at the beginning of chapters 5, 6, 7, 8, 9 and 10, and in chapter 11.

Finally, I have some longstanding debts to acknowledge. Roy Downing pointed me in the right academic direction at an early age. I

owed much as an undergraduate to the teaching of Jack Plumb and
Quentin Skinner. More recently I have learnt much from my erstwhile
colleagues at the University of Leicester. In particular I have tested
ideas on Clive Ashworth, James Fulcher, Joe Banks, Sydney
Holloway, Terry Johnson, David Reeder, Philip Dodd, Val Riddell,
Roger Gallie and Philip Cottrell. Olive Banks supervised the thesis
upon which this book is based. Her encouragement throughout and
her perceptive editorial comments in the later stages were invaluable.
Richard Johnson and Colin Bell have both, in different ways, provided
great encouragement in the last phase and I have made a number of
small changes as a result of their timely remarks on the penultimate
draft. One of the pleasures of writing this book was meeting Mrs Joyce
Cadbury whose acute comments on Birmingham life, past and
present, were greatly appreciated. I also profited from the observations of Brian Simon, Bill Armytage and the late Jim Dyos although I
would not wish to implicate them in any particular aspects of my
argument or approach. Like the others mentioned here they bear no
responsibility for the book's inadequacies. In the later stages also,
Charlotte Kitson helped me to put some of the tables into shape and
Sue Massey endured the loneliness of the long-distance typist. My
thanks are also due to David Godwin of Routledge & Kegan Paul for
his unfailing courtesy and helpfulness. I also wish to acknowledge the
help towards the costs of research which I received from the Research
Board of the University of Leicester.

Immediately before commencing the final draft I spent several
weeks at Harvard as an Associate of the Centre for European Studies.
This lively and creative academic community provided an ideal setting
for research and reflection, just the right atmosphere for the ante-natal
author. During the long period of gestation Tanya Smith has borne it
all with patience and good humour. Edward, Susannah and Penelope
have been by turns curious and amused. Finally, if there are any merits
at all in this book then a great deal of the credit should go to my mother
and father who, in more ways than one, made it possible.

CHAPTER 1

'BUT HERE THE TOWNS ARE':

THE CHALLENGE TO THE OLD ORDER IN ENGLISH SOCIETY 1830–70

There are persons, no doubt, who regard our progress with horror: who, forgetting for a moment their doubled rentrolls, would rejoice to see Manchester and Birmingham brought back again to their condition of a century ago, with numbers a tenth of what they are at present.

But here the towns are: not indeed possessing any monopoly of ignorance and vice, but disfigured with deep scars from long continued neglect. We cannot revert to rural felicity, to green fields, to rough and manly and ignorant squires, to independent yeomanry, to ill-supported and superstitious and serf-like hinds.[1]

These words of 'a Birmingham manufacturer' written in 1869 introduce a central process with which this book is concerned: the confrontation between the class structures and institutional arrangements of a declining commercialised agrarian social order and a rising urban industrial order. The 'Birmingham manufacturer' was writing at a time when the outcome of this confrontation was not a foregone conclusion. To take one index, until the 1880s more than half of Britain's million-aires were landowners and not until the period 1880–99 did the number of manufacturers leaving private fortunes of at least £½ million draw nearly level with the number of merchant princes and financiers falling into the same category. Furthermore, in 1874 a quarter of English land was held by 363 landowners, mostly aris-tocratic. Over half of England consisted of estates of at least 1,000 acres, a size of holding generally regarded as being the minimum for membership of the landed gentry. No other European landed elite owned so large a proportion of the national territory.[2]

The term 'confrontation' oversimplifies matters. By 1830 an urban industrial order was emerging in complex interdependence with the rural agrarian order.[3] The distinction between the two was dramatised by the shift in social weight from the latter to the former in the course of the century. As this process occurred, elements that had been combined within highly localised structures in the decentralised society of 1830 and before were gradually and painfully wrenched apart. These elements were reshaped and combined in different ways within the more complex division of labour of the urban industrial nation-state. The disputes over the Factory Acts and the repeal of the Corn Laws are sometimes treated as great set-piece battles between 'the aristocracy' and 'the industrial bourgeoisie'.[4] However in order to trace the currents of social development of which these clashes were one aspect it is necessary to examine a multitude of local conflicts and accommodations involving a bewildering diversity of collectivities and social interests. Research has suggested that during the nineteenth century existing establishments in the metropolis were able to assimilate potential challengers such as newly-wealthy industrialists with apparent ease. The role of the public schools and Oxbridge in this process has been stressed.[5] However, less attention has been paid until recently to complementary processes, about which we still know and understand less, occurring in the English provinces during the same period. In a relatively decentralised society industrialisation and urbanisation presented their immediate challenge to provincial establishments.[6]

A recent commentator has argued that a debate which 'concerns all historians of nineteenth-century Britain, not just those interested in cities . . . is about why Britain came through a period of rapid industrialisation and urbanisation without the violent social revolution that was widely predicted and whose non-occurrence still disappoints so many'.[7] Investigation of this particular question ultimately requires international comparisons which should contribute to the larger quest of seeking to understand the sequences of structural transformation undergone by societies in the course of transition from commercialised agrarian polity to industrialised and urbanised nation-state.[8] The assimilation of business elites with 'traditional' elites at the national level in Britain might, for example, be compared with the development of elite relationships in Japan at this level in the late nineteenth century.[9] Processes of class formation within British cities could be compared with equivalent processes in the United States, France, Germany or Russia, and so on.[10] Studies confined to British (or in this case English) society may contribute to the broader enquiry indicated above.

2

In this study an attempt is made to delineate some aspects of the processes whereby distinctive institutional arrangements developed through which the production and distribution of material and cultural resources were managed in English society. It will be argued that such an investigation should be sensitive to the dynamic opposition between contradictory tendencies in class relationships and institutional orders. It should also be alert to the compromises made by men and women as they sought a degree of security and order while subject to conflicting constraints in their social relationships.

This book seeks to explain why three institutional orders, those of formal education, industrial relations and local government, developed in very different ways in Birmingham and Sheffield between 1830 and the First World War. The task is worth carrying out not least because the experience of the great provincial cities furnished a repertoire of institutional arrangements upon which central government was able to draw when confronting problems of educational organisation, the management of industrial conflict and the provision of public services at the national level in the twentieth century.[11] However, the book is primarily a comparative study of social development. It is argued that in the period concerned Birmingham and Sheffield followed quite dissimilar paths in undergoing the transition from being participants in a predominantly rural society under aristocratic leadership to being major centres within urban industrial society. In 1830 they 'fitted into' the national division of labour and their own regional power structures in very different ways while within the two cities different states of balance existed between the neighbourhood as opposed to the town as foci of social life. Transformations within these structures over the period 1830 to 1914 were, it is argued, dynamically related to processes of class formation of which changes in patterns of property ownership, control over industrial processes, residence, political activity, educational involvement and religious attachment were all, in part, an expression. Within this context, attention is paid to conflicts and accommodation between establishments among the better-off middle-class residents (or big bourgeoisie), within the ranks of shopkeepers and small businessmen (or petty bourgeoisie) and among the skilled working class. Particular regard will be given to the effect of these changing relationships on the three institutional orders mentioned. The values and practices expressed in the daily working of these institutions were a product of each city's particular trajectory of social development, tendencies within its class structure and the outcomes of struggles between competing industrial, political and religious establishments.

No city was typical of urban industrial society in England. If you take the six largest provincial cities in 1851 they fall into three categories. Liverpool and Bristol were centres of commerce and sea-trade with

3

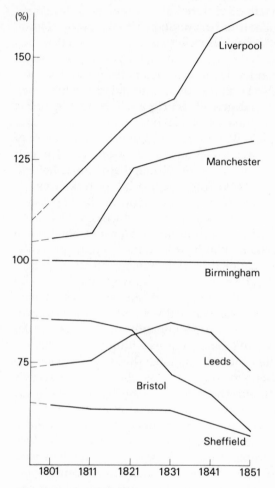

Graph 1   *Population size of various cities as percentage of population of Birmingham 1801–51*
Source: Mitchell and Deane (1962).
Note: 1851 borough boundaries are used.

warehouses, exchanges, mercantile companies and shifting cosmopolitan populations. Manchester and Leeds were manufacturing centres specialising in textiles production carried out in large mechanised factories.[12] Birmingham and Sheffield were manufacturing centres which concentrated upon metal work and engineering of various kinds carried out to a great extent in small workshops by skilled craftsmen. The patterns of demographic growth displayed by these six cities in the first half of the century may be contrasted by expressing the decennial series of census returns for each city as a percentage of Birmingham's

4

population (e.g. in 1801 Sheffield's population was 65 per cent as large as Birmingham's while Manchester's population was 106 per cent as large). Graph 1 shows that the leading part played by textiles in industrialisation during the early nineteenth century was expressed in the spectacular demographic advance of Manchester and Leeds, particularly between 1811 and 1831. Liverpool obviously also benefited from her position on the lucrative North Atlantic routes to and from the cotton plantations. Bristol, a city which had played a central part in the colonial trade of the eighteenth century, declined relative to the northern port and was overtaken in terms of population by Leeds. However, it is noticeable that by 1831 Manchester's rate of acceleration over Birmingham had slackened considerably and that between 1831 and 1851 Leeds fell back drastically compared to the Midland city. In sharp contrast, the demographic superiority of Liverpool increased at an even faster rate after 1831 under the impact of Irish immigration. Throughout this period the population of Sheffield was approximately 60 per cent that of Birmingham.

A similar graph may be constructed for the period 1851 to 1911, in this case taking the population within the boundaries of Birmingham as established in the latter date as the point of comparison for the whole period. By 1900 Birmingham had outstripped Manchester and Liverpool, becoming England's largest provincial city. Well before the First World War Sheffield overtook Leeds, her traditional Yorkshire rival.[13] This change of civic fortunes was one aspect of a major transformation within the industrial order. 'Between 1880 and 1900 British exports of iron, steel, machinery and coal doubled, to reach £95 million. The value of total textile exports fell absolutely during the same twenty years from £105 million to £97 million. The contrast in fortunes between these two sides of industry was remarkable.'[14] By focusing on towns specialising in metal-working and engineering and by commencing in 1830 this study catches in its early stages a wave of industrial and social development which was in full flood by the end of the century. Birmingham and Sheffield have been chosen not as being 'typical' but because of their increasing strategic importance within the developing national society.

Two assumptions which underlie the subsequent analysis will be briefly stated here. First, institutional orders such as education, industry and government are assumed to be particular and partial manifestations of complex networks of human interdependence. These networks are typically asymmetrical. In other words, within them the capacity to initiate activity, exercise authority and enjoy rewards are unequally distributed. These distributions are the outcome and continuing object of competition and conflict as are the guiding rules within institutional spheres.

Second, it has been found convenient to adopt a framework of

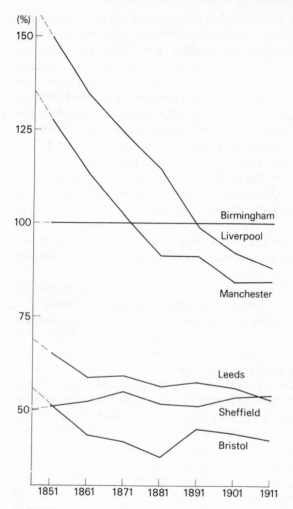

Graph 2 *Population size of various cities as percentage of population of Birmingham 1851–1911*
Source: Mitchell and Deane (1962).

analysis which distinguishes between different 'levels of integration'. These mutually-related foci of structural differentiation are the key sites within which processes of contradiction, conflict and compromise occur. It is possible to identify several such levels ranging from, say, the domestic level through the neighbourhood level and upward to the level of inter-societal relations. For present purposes four levels of integration are to be emphasised. They are the national level (locus of the central government, for example), the level of the county (with its characteristic social and administrative hierarchy led by the Lord Lieutenant), the municipal level (whose typical institutions include the

6

town council and the chamber of commerce) and the level of the neighbourhood.[15] In the early part of the period being studied the characteristic institutions of the neighbourhood were the local tavern and the vestry within which the parochial affairs of local inhabitants were discussed and largely decided. In the latter part of the period the neighbourhood became the single-class suburb; it asserted a smaller degree of control over its own destiny, its affairs became less important to many of its inhabitants and its relationships to other levels of integration were transformed.

THE CHALLENGE

Pre-industrial England had been dominated by landowning and mercantile interests whose interpenetration was well over two centuries old by 1830. As Harold Perkin points out, the peculiar relationship of this commercialised aristocracy to the state had created conditions favourable to industrialisation. In defence of its own interests it had used its power to guarantee personal liberty and property rights, and minimise central political controls except in so far as they provided protection from foreign competition.[16] Ironically, the appearance of unprecedented concentrations of capital and labour in the industrial towns placed an intolerable strain upon the very social system that had made this development possible. Industrialisation and urbanisation stretched beyond its limit the capacity for political management of institutions adapted to agrarian capitalism, small-scale craft production and local market trading. As these effects were increasingly felt, localised networks of kinship and patronage focused on the country house and the vestry gradually yielded up the tasks of government. They were taken over increasingly by more impersonal and universalistic institutions regulated by bureaucrats, businessmen and members of the old and new professions. Coordination and control tended to shift from the local level towards the national level.

In the 1830s the aristocracy effectively combined domination over a major economic resource (agriculture), control over the apparatus of political administration (in parliament and at Quarter Sessions) and the capacity to manipulate, interpret and enforce the ruling norms of the society.[17] However, the aristocracy and their institutions did not constitute an 'ancien regime'. That term would imply too much uniformity and cohesion within a decentralised society in which the county and the parish or neighbourhood remained the most important levels of integration.

The major political decisions with respect to county affairs were made and implemented through networks of clients, kin and friends

7

focused on the country houses of the aristocracy. Provision of justice, policing, administration, welfare and moral leadership were 'public' responsibilities of the leading dynasties, exercised both informally and through the ecclesiastical, legal and military bureaucracies.[18] A determination to maximise the privilege and influence flowing from each aristocratic household modified the commitment to the free market by the agrarian ruling class. One expression of this principle was the practice of strict settlement of estates upon male heirs.[19] Furthermore, within county society specialists such as physicians, lawyers, and academic tutors were constrained to recognise a subtle and strict hierarchy of status which regulated inter-personal contacts. They were placed in a clear position of inferiority vis-à-vis the aristocratic families which chose to patronise them.[20]

The relationship of the county aristocracy and gentry to men and women whose lives were centred within the more confined sphere of the parish with its little neighbourhood communities was symbiotic but vulnerable to outbreaks of hostility on both sides.[21] As late as 1830 in market towns and even large manufacturing cities such as Birmingham and Sheffield local affairs were to a great extent managed by shopkeepers, petty traders, agents and dealers of various kinds. Political influence was exercised, as at the county level, through networks of family and friends but in this case they ran through local taverns, parish vestries and bodies, often self-recruiting, such as highway boards, improvement commissioners and overseers of the poor.[22] Not far removed from this petty bourgeoisie in income and respectability were some of the skilled artisans, many of them organised in trade societies. Radical Dissent acquired much of its support from artisans and the petty bourgeoisie. Its condemnation of aristocratic 'tyranny' and 'anti-democratic' closed corporations reflected and drew upon their own experience.[23] George Eliot has portrayed the close but ambivalent relationship between the county and parochial forms of life in Felix Holt, describing the pervasive influence of kin and connection, the mediating role between the two levels played by the clergy and lawyers, the radicalism of some Nonconformist ministers and the subtle manipulation of 'the mob' by gentlemen and artisan demagogues.[24]

During the last two-thirds of the nineteenth century the burden of managing the human capacities of a rapidly expanding society shifted decisively onto urban structures. By 1851 the urban population had overtaken the rural and in 1881 town dwellers outnumbered those in rural areas by two to one.[25] The great industrial cities of South-East Lancashire, the West Midlands, the West Riding of Yorkshire, Merseyside and Tyneside grew up near and, in some cases, upon the estates of some of the wealthiest and politically most influential members of the landed aristocracy. Bateman's survey of great landowners, based upon parliamentary returns in the 1870s, tells us for example that apart from his 89,000 acres in Derbyshire the Duke of Devonshire had over 12,000 acres in Lancashire and another 19,000 acres in the West Riding of Yorkshire. Lord Derby was another major northern landowner, with 57,000 acres in Lancashire. The Duke of Portland owned 43,000 acres in Nottinghamshire, 8,000 acres in Derbyshire and 12,000 acres in Northumberland. This last holding was, however, overshadowed by the 180,000 acres held in that county by the Duke of Northumberland himself. Earl Fitzwilliam had a substantial rent from his 22,000 acres in Yorkshire, where the Duke of Norfolk also owned 19,000 acres of the West Riding. Both Fitzwilliam and Norfolk owned property in the city of Sheffield itself, making them urban landlords as was Lord Calthorpe in the Edgbaston area of Birmingham. North of that city, the influential Marquess of Hertford possessed a 10,000 acre Warwickshire estate and a county seat at Ragley Hall.[26]

The very size and concentration of the populations of the large manufacturing towns denied the possibility of controlling them through an indefinite extension of networks of personal influence, either 'across' from rural society or 'upwards' from the parochial level. How would these new urban configurations such as Birmingham and Sheffield, bursting at their seams, fit into the developing national society? How would the county hierarchies and urban regimes articulate with one another? Where would the social and political initiative lie? Which groups would wield the major sanctions? These were issues which were being fought out at all levels of society during the period under study. Social leadership, political management and economic influence in large manufacturing cities were shared (and to a great extent, in dispute) amongst groups of industrialists, aristocrats, gentry, Anglican clergy, Dissenting ministers and other professional men, not to mention members of the petty bourgeoisie and artisan communities. The balance of power and forms of solidarity within and amongst these groups varied considerably between cities and over time.

The institutions, attitudes and interests of 'old corruption' did not simply disappear in the period 1832–5 or shortly afterwards. Participants within the old and new orders were involved in bitter struggles at least until the 1870s in towns such as Birmingham and Sheffield. In the course of these struggles political and religious rhetoric was as common as reference to economic interest. However, if the quotation from the 'Birmingham manufacturer' with which we began is continued it reveals the latent hostility which existed between some industrialists and their longer-established rivals in commerce and land:[27]

In these towns, the manufacturers are the true leaders: for it is their enterprise and experience and capital which employ and

9

maintain the artisans; whose skilful labour produces the commodities the distribution of which enriches merchants and retailers.

The author goes on to lay about him at the expense of merchants and the aristocracy. Manufacturers and merchants, he argues, both have to 'perform the ordinary operations of buying and selling; but average common sense is enough for these. Unlike merchants, [manufacturers] . . . have all the processes of manufacture in their hands.' In order to compete with his rivals, the manufacturer 'requires a superior system of inspection . . ., a superior organization, and a judicious choice of managers. . . . Without lively and sound brains, a manufacturer is driven out of the field.' The manufacturer's intelligence and self-reliance, the writer clearly implies, place him above other classes. During the recent dearth of cotton as a consequence of the American Civil War 'there was no appeal to Parliament for Government aid, such as humiliated the rich landed proprietors, under the comparatively trifling misfortune of the Rinderpest. Our northern fellow subjects showed that in abilities and resolution they had not degenerated.'[28]

The challenge posed by the cities was not simply to do with the distribution of private wealth. Its full extent must be measured in relation to the position previously occupied by an aristocracy whose members had combined material opulence with control over the political apparatus (including its means of physical coercion) and close identification with the symbols of authority fashioned and transmitted through the ancient universities and the Church of England. In the course of industrialisation and urbanisation three changes occurred: the social configurations within which these means of power were to be exercised were profoundly transformed; the sum total of the means of exercising power increased greatly;[29] and a large proportion of these means became available to men outside the charmed circle of landed gentlemen and their close associates. Furthermore, definitions of fact and value underwritten by the authority of the Church of England were subject both to a new secular challenge and to an old religious challenge, newly strengthened.

The rise of the towns gave new power and confidence to Dissent, which was widespread amongst manufacturers and employees though far from having a monopoly within the urban populations or even amongst town-dwelling Christians.[30] Nonconformists, who were to be found in all classes, disagreed on much among themselves but shared a historiography which was deeply at odds with Anglican orthodoxy. A central theme in the Nonconformist view of history was that since the seventeenth century the righteous had been oppressed by the unjust. There was a widespread feeling among them that the influence and privilege of the Anglican church and the aristocracy should be diminished though there was disagreement about how powerful Leviathan should become and the extent to which the righteous could in turn oppress the unjust. Nonconformity provided a powerful and long-established legitimation for opposition to the class structure and institutional arrangements of the old order, one which drew upon values and perceptions shared by rich and poor, masters and men.[31] However, there was no strict coincidence of the lines dividing Anglicans and Nonconformists and the demarcations amongst 'economic' classes. For instance, the Birmingham manufacturer quoted above was an Anglican who in 1870 found himself at the head of opposition to the Dissenting interest on the Birmingham School Board.[32]

The political impact of Nonconformity has been nicely stated, in one respect overstated, by John Vincent:[33]

> The real corpus of thought uniting the middle class, or the Liberal section of it, was not a Benthamite, utilitarian, or natural-law view of the world, not American or economical principles, but something of a different order: a view or recollection of English history. The Dissenters above all, were formed in a historical culture of almost Judaic narrowness, and their political views were grafted onto an interpretation of seventeenth-century politics quite as much as those of the great Whigs were. One must think of the great Bicentenary celebrations of 1862, the revival of the cults of Cromwell and Milton, the woodcuts of Bunyan in Bedford gaol provided for readers of the Liberator – even John Bright reading his favourite Hallam aloud to his wife – to get some idea of the culture that the middle class could draw on to interpret their politics. The really important attitudes had nothing to do with the industrial revolution (sic!), much to do with the English Civil War.

To this may be added the comment that this historical culture was also available to men and women who were not 'middle class' but who read and discussed Bunyan and the Bible in Sunday school classes and mutual improvement societies.[34]

The increased scale and complexity of social life also encouraged the development of new skills in the manipulation of society and nature. Railway engineers, medical officers of health, industrial managers, and metallurgists are just a few examples of the host of professional and bureaucratic occupations brought into being.[35] Possession of the appropriate educational certification and recognition by national associations became increasingly common criteria by which 'experts' were identified.[36] Law and medicine, the established professions, and the nation-wide bureaucracy of the Church of England had for generations been delicately attuned to the subtle social rhythms of parochial and county life.[37] In this context genteel men of leisure were the social arbiters. However, the newer concerns of the large manufacturing cities and the metropolitan state apparatus offered, to old and new professions and to religious and secular bureaucrats, the chance for an expanded role and a new self importance. These were arenas where the interests of provincial landowners were in competition with those of urban businessmen and metropolitan statesmen.[38] Increasingly, debates about how to cope with the new tasks of an urban industrial society were conducted by 'experts' and 'specialists'.[39] The intellectual and practical initiative swung steadily in their favour. This growing 'clerisy' did not form a monolithic bloc. As will be illustrated, its development expressed the conflicts and contradictions of a rural society becoming urban, a localised society becoming more centralised and a face-to-face society acquiring the impersonal routines of bureaucracy and the market. However, it represented the advent of a source of authority, certified expertise, which could be tapped for different ends by competing interests. Its practitioners might be seduced by the lure of gentility, harnessed to serve the growing state bureaucracy or they might commit themselves to the open market. Prussia and the United States offered instances of the various ways in which 'experts' might be incorporated within a modernising society.[40] The education and organisation of such men, their disposition and allegiances, were of strategic importance in the developing nation-state.

It was suggested above that the old order of English society was adjusted to forms of life centred on the county and the local neighbourhood and that its management was mainly in the hands of the aristocracy in association with the 'old professions' and the petty bourgeoisie. This last category shaded imperceptibly into the artisanry on one side and the more substantial mercantile and manufacturing capitalists on the other. Implicit in the analysis has been a recognition that there were conflicts between social groups whose solidarity was focused at the parochial or neighbourhood level in urbanising communities and others closely tied in to the county networks of the aristocracy and gentry. Furthermore, market power, bureaucratic capacity and the possession of expertise as means of influence were held in tension with kinship and patronage at both these levels. Urbanisation and industrialisation transformed the context of these tensions and conflicts as a result of the increased significance which was acquired by the municipal and national levels of integration.

NATION, CITY AND NEIGHBOURHOOD

A radical disjunction appeared during the mid-nineteenth century between the disposition of institutions coordinated at the county and parochial levels and the social formations and social processes of the large manufacturing cities. For example, the strong tendencies towards residential segregation by class within the cities were an important manifestation of the working of the impersonal force of the market. New social formations took shape whose management was more susceptible to bureaucratic strategies, for example, through the provision of standardised educational facilities, than to strategies based on the manipulation of informal ties between kin, friends and clients. [41] The latter strategies had depended not only upon close inter-personal relations between men and women of different ranks but also upon a capacity to minimise or at least predict the effect of external influences upon each localised 'cosmos'. The management on a large scale of tasks such as installing drains, combating epidemics, instilling basic literacy and numeracy and improving communications was beyond their scope. [42]

The development of institutional orders coordinated at the municipal level of integration was encouraged by a number of factors. These included: aristocratic resistance to a growth in the power of central as opposed to local government;[43] the hostility of parochial interests to an extension of county influence over the city; the appear-ance of a new class of large manufacturers whose operations extended far beyond parochial limits; the scope offered to members of the professionalising occupations (such as medicine) by a large urban clientele which would enable them to reduce their dependence upon the aristocracy; and the added strength industrialisation and urbanis-ation bestowed upon a Dissenting tradition amongst artisans, the petty bourgeoisie and manufacturers, a tradition which furnished a powerful critique of the predominantly Anglican character of county and national government. In practice, large manufacturing cities developed during the nineteenth century in the context of complex interactions between solidarities integrated at the county, parochial and municipal levels, producing conflicts and accommodations which took varying forms between cities.

The situation became even more complex as the significance of the national level of integration gradually increased, especially during the second half of the century. The market and bureaucratic networks which tended to displace or swamp the old framework of social organ-isation were not bounded by municipal limits. The technical skills of bureaucrats, professional and 'experts' did not tie them to specific localities. Capital and labour were also mobile. Their fields of operation extended to the boundaries of the national polity and beyond. [44] Also, increasing international pressures upon the British state encouraged its managers in Westminster and Whitehall to take greater cognisance of the national stock of resources upon which it might draw and the national institutions through which these resources might be mobilised.[45]

Social classes were typically organised at more than one level of integration. As has been seen, the aristocracy dominated institutions coordinated at both the county and national levels. At mid-century, occupations such as medicine and the law were internally differentiated according to their practitioners' degree of commitment to weakening county and parochial orders or to the emerging municipal sphere.[46] Many of them were able to transfer their skills from the former to the latter and subsequently exploit the potential for national organisation. Many groups of artisans had skills whose value increased, initially at least, in the course of industrialisation. However, unlike doctors, lawyers and other occupational groups who provided specialised advice and services to clients on a personal level, the skills and autonomy of many artisans were quickly subject to the eroding effect of mechanisation and bureaucratic management. The responses of artisans to those opportunities and threats were organised at a number of levels; at the neighbourhood level (for example in the case of the Sheffield trade societies), at the municipal level (through the establishment of trades' councils) and at the national level (through bodies such as the Trades Union Congress and the National Association for Promoting State Colonisation).[47]

As the significance of parochial institutions declined, the petty bourgeoisie suffered a serious and increasing decline of influence. As Bechhofer and Elliott point out, the businesses run by this class were (and are) characterised by the combination, often within family concerns, of small amounts of capital, low levels of technology and a simple, unbureaucratised division of labour.[48] The growth of big business and the increasing bureaucratisation of municipal government simultaneously reduced their political influence and increased their rates. Opposition to these tendencies was expressed through ratepayers' parties active in town hall politics (especially during the 1850s and 1860s) and at the national level through the strident Nonconformist wing of the Liberal Party (from the 1870s) and subsequently through the Conservative Party.[49]

Whereas the petty bourgeoisie was the product of a parochial social order which was being slowly overwhelmed, the other major group within the lower middle class was prototypical rather than anachronistic. Its members were functionaries within the expanding bureaucracies of government and commerce, such as warehouse clerks, railway officials, foremen, policemen and elementary school teachers. Above them, but still marginal members of the middle class were some managers, accountants, engineers, surveyors, notaries and other specialists.[50] Like the semi-skilled and unskilled urban working class, this new lower middle class was a creation of the latter phases of industrialisation and urbanisation (from about 1850 onwards) rather than being an established class to whom these processes offered a series of challenges.

The dynamics of market competition and bureaucratic growth which helped bring these new classes into being also tended to distribute and segregate them spatially in suburbs of a single class character.[51] As *The Economist* recognised in 1857, this development had profound implications:[52]

> Society is tending more and more to spread into classes – and not merely classes but localised classes, class colonies; and nothing could have a more powerful effect on modifying our municipal institutions. It is not in London merely, nor as a matter of business and in consequence of the "division of labour" that this happens . . . there is a much deeper social principle involved in the present increasing tendency to class colonies. It is the disposition to associate with equals – in some measure with those who have similar practical *interests*, in still greater measure with those who have similar tastes and culture, most of all with those with whom we judge ourselves on a moral equality, whatever our real standard may be.

By mid-century the increasingly homogeneous suburb was beginning to displace the heterogeneous semi-urban, semi-rural neighbourhood. This had deep implications for the institutions of the parish. Parochial organisation had originally encompassed the class relationship between property owners and employees, both of whom had partici-pated in its institutions and resided within parish boundaries. In the 1850s, *The Economist* supported the proposal to establish unions of parishes jointly responsible for the care of their poor, since[53]

> [whole] parishes exist in which there are no poor, while all the work is done by neighbouring parishes in which there are almost no rich. . . . A rich district has its poor district in close superficial association with it, instead of distributed evenly through it. The labourers encompass the landlord – Chelsea touches on Belgravia, a zone of poverty encircles the zone of wealth.

The social formations in whose management parochial institutions had a share were increasingly subject to determination at a higher level of integration. By the end of the century, local patterns of residential segregation in suburbs were manifestations of status differences and class relationships which had a national basis. The urban working class and the new lower middle class who constituted the bulk of the suburban masses were to a great extent educated and employed within institutions which were increasingly subject to the influence of national agencies. Institutions focused on the municipal level were being overtaken, as parochial institutions had been earlier, by the increasing scale and complexity of social differentiation. The division of large cities in 1885 into several parliamentary constituencies encouraged this development, tending to emphasise the shared class interests of voters in similar constituencies in different cities.[54]

SOCIAL CONFLICTS

The birth of a new society in the womb of the old generated three kinds of social conflict. The first of these was the continuation under transformed conditions of the antagonisms which set the aristocracy planted in the shires against bureaucratic central government on the one hand, and against the highly localised parochial and neighbourhood circles of artisans and petty traders on the other hand.[55] The second kind of social conflict was between groups whose power and prestige were rooted in the norms and practices of the old society and other groups coming into being as a consequence of urbanisation, industrialisation and bureaucratisation. The third kind of social conflict arose from the response of participants to the unequal division of labour and distribution of rewards expressed through the new or transformed institutional orders which developed in the course of attempts to control and exploit the new resources and capacities of the urban industrial nation-state.

During the period 1830–95 all three kinds of social conflict were occurring simultaneously and influencing each other, a process expressed in complex and shifting alliances which varied between cities and regions. The significance of the first kind of social conflict during the early decades of the period, indeed until the 1870s, requires emphasis. Not until the 1880s did the third kind of conflict, with its characteristic 'modern' pattern of confrontation and bargaining between nationally-organised mass labour unions and nation-wide associations of employers begin to achieve dominance.[56] Mediating between these two kinds of conflict, interacting with both, was the second form of antagonism indicated above which will be elaborated further.

As urban industrial society became more complex and the significance of the municipal and national levels of integration increased, rights and responsibilities which drew their legitimacy from traditional values and local routines were challenged. Prominent in the new order were large joint-stock companies, central government agencies such as the Local Government Board and the Science and Art Department whose tentacles stretched deep into the provinces, and national professional associations such as the British Medical Association and the Institution of Mechanical Engineers.[57] Those who manned these new institutions could justify their influence and self-importance by referring to the social needs for their skills and their own merit as individuals, regardless of kinship or ties of patronage.[38] The protestant tradition of Christianity supplied a ready vocabulary of dissatisfaction with social evil and the need for rigorous self-examination according to the criterion of worthiness.

In analysing these processes, it is useful to distinguish between, on the one hand, personal or family assets which were exploitable in a very wide range of social contexts and, on the other hand, highly 'institutionalised' social and technical skills which retained their value only as long as the specific social configurations in which they were practised remained relatively undisturbed. The highest and lowest social strata were distinguished by their primary dependence upon the highly transferable assets of personal wealth and labour power, respectively. The unskilled labourer, probably already a migrant from the countryside, was able to transfer his muscle from place to place and job to job as the market dictated.[39] Since his status, market power and political influence were low, he had little to lose and possibly something to gain from such mobility. At the other end of the scale, rich manufacturers could apply their fortunes to building a position within aristocratic circles. From the middle of the century leading industrialists found their way into aristocratic society. Ennoblement was uncommon before 1880 but in Cheshire (for example) file manufacturers, cotton spinners and shipbuilders had been appointed to the county commission of the peace in increasing numbers during the preceding three decades.[60] By the 1860s businessmen were finding that a parliamentary seat was a useful qualification for directorships. Of the 465 Liberal MPs sitting between 1859 and 1874, 151 were businessmen. Only thirty-four of these could be described as radical.[61] At these commanding heights rich men were united by a common interest in managing their family fortunes rather than being divided by opposing commitments to an 'aristocratic class' and an 'industrial bourgeoisie'. Landed wealth could be applied to investment in mining and railway enterprises or used as security for loans drawing on the wealth of the towns.[62] The rapid development of credit and banking facilities assisted transfers of wealth between sectors.[63]

The second kind of conflict was most evident in the profoundly unsettled middle ranges of English society. Those under threat included many artisans living in close neighbourliness guarding the customs of their craft, lesser gentry whose standing depended upon their position within local chains of patronage, parish notables dominating vestry politics, the managers and beneficiaries of endowed charities from Oxford and Cambridge to small local grammar schools and so on. The atmosphere of 'old corruption' is conveyed in the following reminiscence of a man who in 1849 served as a church-warden at Kidderminster:[64]

> There were many charities connected with my office, and a large offertory to distribute, to say nothing of the trouble of writing out the rate books and collecting the rates. There was also a visitation held at Bromsgrove which I had to attend, and at which I refused to pay the visitation fees, as I considered that money drawn from the pockets of parishioners ought not to be paid to a number of hungry officials, who did nothing for it in return. . . . All the travelling, collecting, account keeping, and charity distributing were done for nothing, yet on the very first day after I was out of office, the old men and women, who used to touch hats and curtsey to me in the streets, suddenly lost their eye-sight, so far as I was concerned; the blessings of which they transferred to my successor.

The claims of customary privilege, grounded in law or tradition, were increasingly confronted with demands to eliminate waste, reduce injustice and increase national competitiveness.[65] During much of the nineteenth century a form of 'dual politics' was practised. On the one hand there were assaults (vigorously contested) upon closed corporate bodies, self-recruiting oligarchies and 'undemocratic' solidarities of all kinds; on the other hand antagonists sympathetic to both sides of these conflicts were busy making investments in the institutions of the new urban industrial order. Landowners under attack from the Anti-Corn Law League were heavily involved in the canal and railway booms and other aspects of urban growth. Faced with demands for disestablishment, Anglican clergy were building new churches in working-class neighbourhoods.[66] Oxford and Cambridge dons, confronted with appeals for a decentralisation of their endowments, established local examinations directed at the 'new' middle classes in the provinces.[67] The provision of education, the regulation of industrial production and the politics of local government were three spheres within which these conflicts were worked out, manifesting allegiances forged within the old society and creating solidarities which would help shape the new.

The next six chapters focus on the period between 1830 and 1870. Chapter 2 explores variations in the patterns of social differentiation in Birmingham and Sheffield, analysing inter-relationships between the national, county, municipal and neighbourhood levels of integration and also power relationships within families and between occupations and social classes. Chapter 3 opens with a discussion of the impact upon existing middle-class and working-class networks within the two cities of new norms and practices associated with 'modern' institutions such as municipal corporations and the mechanised factory. These processes are then placed in a broader urban context through a comparative analysis of demographic tendencies, shifts in the relationship of capital to labour, alterations in patterns of residence, and changes in the physical lay-out of the respective city centres. These transformations are related to changes in the urban status hierarchies and tendencies towards contradiction and conflict in the industrial sphere. The chapter ends by comparing two influential contemporary views about the tasks and functions which should be performed within communities and the kinds of institutions which should ideally be created to make this possible. These views are taken from the works of two ideologues, Isaac Ironside and George Dawson, who achieved fame and political influence during the late 1840s in Sheffield and Birmingham respectively.

The socio-political initiatives with which Ironside and Dawson were associated are in chapter 4 located within a comparative analysis of processes, under-way by 1830, whereby in each city members of establishments presiding over key institutions were subjected to challenges from competing groups. Following a period of approximately a decade from the early 1850s during which opposing social tendencies were in a state of approximate balance, the old establishments were overwhelmed, albeit not by the initial constellation of opposing groups. These changes are located within a broader regional and national context. Whereas in chapter 3 emphasis is laid upon patterns of persistence and change in norms and practices, in chapter 4 more attention is paid to the evolving strategies of competing social interests. In chapter 5 and chapter 6 developments in the sphere of formal education are discussed in terms of the preceding analysis, looking first at secondary and elementary schooling, subsequently at adult and professional education with particular reference to medical training. Chapter 7 examines the period of crisis and conflict in the late 1860s, focusing upon the investigations of the two royal commissions whose objects of attention were the Sheffield trade societies and the King Edward VI Foundation in Birmingham. The chapter ends by looking at the state of social relations and civic morale in the cities through the eyes of two prominent local men, writing twenty years after the visions of Ironside and Dawson had been first presented to their audiences.

CHAPTER 2

BETWEEN NEIGHBOURHOOD AND NATION

THE FRAMEWORK OF SOCIAL DIFFERENTIATION IN BIRMINGHAM AND SHEFFIELD 1830–70

> One has not great hopes from Birmingham, I always say there is something direful in the sound.[1]

Heaven knows what the snobbish Mrs Elton would have thought about Sheffield! In the social world which Jane Austen dissects in *Emma* such places were consigned to the fringes of consciousness. They were murky regions out of which there occasionally escaped upstarts such as Mrs Elton's former neighbours, the Tupmans, 'encumbered with many low connections, but giving themselves immense airs, and expecting to be on a footing with old established families . . .; and how they got their fortune nobody knows.'[2] By the third quarter of the century the 'degredation' and 'immorality' of manufacturing towns had become a major theme in fiction. Charles Reade for example, based *It is Never Too Late to Mend* (1853) on the report of a royal commission exposing corruption and cruelty in Birmingham gaol. The trade union 'outrages' in Sheffield provided material for *Put Yourself in His Place* (1870).[3]

There was another side to the picture which emerges in autobiography rather than the novel. F. Condé Williams, a vicar's son who made careers in journalism and the law passed through both Sheffield and Birmingham en route to high office.[4] In Sheffield he entered the literary circle of Alfred Gatty, vicar of Ecclesfield. Gatty had attended Charterhouse, Eton and Oxford before settling in Yorkshire.[5] Williams contributed to magazines run by the Gattys and made visits to the local theatre with 'the young men of the family – one of them now a dread functionary of the Heralds' College'.[6] Culture was apparently not quite dead in mid-century Sheffield, nor in Birmingham where artists such as William Hall and art dealers such as Charles Hawker were active in the formation of middle-class taste. Of the latter city, Williams wrote:[7]

> English art owed much to Birmingham, both in the sixties and before that period. It may not be too much to claim that Birmingham set the nation an excellent example in giving preference to the original works of modern English painters over copies and questionable originals of old masters, such as at one time almost held the field of artistic investment. . . . [Men such as] Charles Hawker and William Hall left their mark in the middle of the nineteenth century upon the taste of art patrons in Birmingham, and are to a great extent answerable for the fine collections accumulated at that period by manufacturing plutocrats of the district.

This is to answer contemporary critics in their own terms, to show that persons of sensitivity and taste were to be found in these apparently unpromising locales. However, broader issues are raised by the writings mentioned, such as the confrontation between old and new forms of public administration and economic organisation, the relationship between masters and men, the interplay among professional and business elites, the fashioning of popular taste and public opinion, and styles of local leadership. A systematic approach to these issues requires an analysis which sets each city in its regional and national context and locates neighbourhoods within the municipal framework.

THE NATIONAL CONTEXT

If you compare *White's Directory of Sheffield*, 1852 with *White's Directory of Birmingham*, 1850, you will find that of the 218 occupations listed for Sheffield thirty-seven are not listed for Birmingham.[8] Of these thirty-seven occupations the vast majority (thirty-one) are in cutlery and steel manufacture or closely related to them. However, you will also find that the Birmingham directory lists over 300 occupations which are not found in the Sheffield directory. These occupations are very diverse. Taking examples at random they include alkali manufacturers, artificial limb makers, bagatelle and billiard-table makers, bayonet manufacturers, case (card and cigar) makers, candle-stick manufacturers, dog-collar makers, door-spring manufacturers, ecclesiastical ornament makers, engineers (civil), ferrule makers, furriers, gilders, gun-barrel makers, handcuff makers, hook and eye makers, ink makers, ivory-bone toy and ornament manufacturers, japan makers, jewellers and gold-smiths, key-ring makers, letter-clip makers, lock manufacturers, mathematical-instrument makers, mould makers, net makers, optical-glass manufacturers, organ builders, pearl-button manufacturers, pencil makers, railway coach builders, Roman cement and plaster of Paris makers, scabbard manufacturers, sealing-wax manufacturers, teapot-handle makers, tulip-shovel makers, umbrella furniture makers, varnish makers, vice manufacturers, wedding and mourning ring makers, whip makers and zinc workers.

A comparison of the two directories suggests that the occupational structure was at least twice as highly differentiated in Birmingham as it was in Sheffield at mid-century. Degree of differentiation is not a mere function of population size. This can be shown if we compare the two cities in terms of relative population size and degrees of occupation differentiation (see Table 1). The comparison will be extended to include Leeds. White's 1847 directory lists 196 occupations in Leeds as

TABLE 1   *Population size and occupational differentiation: Birmingham, Sheffield and Leeds 1851*

	Birmingham	Leeds	Sheffield
Population size (1851)	100	73.8	57.9
Degree of occupational differentiation	100	37.2	41.4

Source: 1851 Census and directories.

compared with 527 in Birmingham (1850) and 218 in Sheffield (1852). In other words, although Sheffield was about six-tenths the size of Birmingham, the former city had an occupational structure only about four-tenths as complex as the latter. Leeds was nearly three-quarters as large as Birmingham but only four-tenths as complex in its occupational structure.[9]

The three cities may also be compared in terms of the proportions of their populations engaged in different types of occupation (see Table 2). The comparison will be extended further to include Bristol.[10]

Three initial observations can be made. First, when Leeds and Sheffield are compared they have a broadly similar distribution of persons among occupations with one major exception. Sheffield's occupational composition is very heavily biased towards engineering, toolmaking and metal working while in Leeds textiles are preponderant. However, in Leeds there are roughly two workers in engineering, toolmaking and metal work for every seven workers in textiles. By comparison, in Sheffield there is one textile worker for roughly sixty-two workers in engineering, toolmaking and metal work. In other words, although Leeds has a less complex occupational structure than Sheffield, this structure rests far less heavily upon a single branch of industry. Second, although Birmingham resembles Sheffield in the

TABLE 2   *Occupational distribution: Birmingham, Sheffield and Leeds 1851*

	Number occupied per thousand population, 1851			
	Bristol	Birmingham	Sheffield	Leeds
1 Engineering, toolmaking, metal working	21.1	165.8	187.6	41.2
2 Textile workers	11.7	5.5	3.1	146.1
3 Professional, literary, artistic	23.0	23.2	12.8	14.1
4 Mercantile occupations	10.1	9.1	6.3	4.6
5 Transport and communications	37.7	26.7	16.0	18.2
6 Liquor and victuals (wholesale and retail)	37.5	29.7	22.8	25.8
7 Domestic servants	74.7	43.0	33.6	31.0
8 Persons of independent means	14.3	4.3	4.4	4.2
9 General and factory labourers	30.9	17.4	14.3	14.8
10 National and local government officials (including police)	4.3	2.5	1.5	2.0

Source: 1851 Census.

predominance of the hardware trades, in other spheres there is much more activity in the Midlands city. For example, Birmingham supports nearly twice as large a proportion of persons engaged in or servicing the three 'old' professions, literary, artistic, theatrical and scientific activity, teaching, publishing and selling books. Also, the proportion of people occupied in mercantile activities (including for example bankers, brokers, salesmen, accountants and commercial travellers but excluding shopkeepers and lesser agents) is nearly twice as large in Birmingham as in Sheffield. Furthermore, transport and communications (a category of occupations involving for example rail, road and canal conveyance, warehouse provision and 'others employed about messages') commands a much greater share of personnel than in Sheffield. Third, in respect of the first two occupational categories just mentioned (professional, literary and artistic occupations and mercantile occupations) Birmingham strongly resembles Bristol and in respect of employment in transport and communications Birmingham stands midway between the very high ranking obtained by the south-western port and the very low ranking achieved by Sheffield.

These differences between Birmingham and Sheffield were, in part, manifestations of the manner in which each city fitted into the national division of labour and the national system of communications. In the period 1830–70, as in later times, 'made in Sheffield' signified high quality cutlery and high grade steel. An official report in 1865 noted of Sheffield that 'the manufactures of the district are far less miscellaneous than those of the Birmingham district.'[11] A high degree of local specialisation in a narrow range of products was encouraged by Sheffield's geographical isolation and the difficulties and cost of transport. By contrast, 'made in Birmingham' evoked a plethora of new-fangled contraptions coming out of the 'toy shop of the world'. The businessmen of Birmingham were located on a bustling regional and national crossroads and they provided a wide range of goods and services to consumers in an ever-changing countrywide and overseas market. A guide to Birmingham published in 1831 stated that the town possessed 'every convenience which can be desired in the way of public conveyances in every possible direction. It is, in fact, not so much in the *line of communication*, as itself the *centre* from which many routes diverge; the starting place for Coaches, Waggons, and Canal Boats without number'.[12] The Birmingham canal had been opened in 1770, half a century before Sheffield acquired its own waterway. By the 1790s the wharves in and around Birmingham were the hub of a national network of canals stretching out to Nottingham, Coventry, Oxford and Liverpool.[13] Birmingham's response to the railway from the 1840s onward was decisive and effective. In 1846 the city magistrates declared: 'Economy of transit should be carried to the greatest possible extent, *more particularly to a district so far inland.*'[14] The city centre was radically transformed by the construction of New Street and Snow Hill stations. A comparison of the impact of railways on Birmingham as compared with London, Glasgow, Liverpool and Manchester yields the following comment:[15]

> In many respects Birmingham provides a text book model for the
> impact of railways upon a great city. Its termini are central and
> provide underground through-transport beneath the city centre.
> The cross-town link railways, which caused such expense to
> shareholders and dissatisfaction to travellers in other cities in the
> 1860s and 1870s, were not necessary in Birmingham because large
> and early decisions were taken. Birmingham also emerged with
> the nearest approach in any of the main cities to a single Grand
> Central Station, when New Street was enlarged to fifteen acres in
> the early 1880s. Moreover, with certain exceptions . . ., the
> decisions on the siting and routes of Birmingham's railways and

24

termini in the mid-nineteenth century seem to have been taken, by the various interests concerned, in a manner which was not merely timely and rational, but was also peculiarly single-minded.

In view of this prevailing climate of opinion it is not surprising that the inventor of the penny post, which was inaugurated nationally in 1840, should have been a local man, Rowland Hill.[16]

Although both Birmingham and Sheffield were land-locked in England's centre, geography had been kinder to the former city which stood on elevated ground within easy access of the surrounding area. By contrast, Sheffield was skirted by hills and barren moors on three sides and by the often-flooded Don Valley to the east. Rotherham, 6 miles to the north-east, was favoured by navigation on the River Don whereas Sheffield had no suitable waterway to the sea until a canal from Tinsley was opened in 1819. Overshadowed by Hallam Ridge, Sky Edge and Pitsmoor, the only viable exit from Sheffield's claustro-phobic habitation was a half-mile-wide gap running south-west to north-east. Eventually a canal, two through railways, two goods termini, a mineral line and sidings, main roads, a gas works and several industrial plants were to be crammed into this narrow passage-way. Construction of turnpike roads and the canal was long delayed by the opposition of the neighbouring landowners and the difficulties of the terrain. The railway line to Rotherham was initially opposed by the Duke of Norfolk, the chief coal-owner in the region, probably for fear of its effect on coal prices. It was opened in 1838 but not until 1845 were the engineering problems of laying the line through to Manchester overcome. No direct rail connection to the Midlands and London existed until 1870. Unlike Birmingham, which was the scene of intense competition for its lucrative traffic, Sheffield had to force itself against considerable resistance onto the national network of communi-cations.[17]

Although it is an important conditioning factor, geography does not determine social development. For example, from the 1840s Sheffield became increasingly important as a centre for distributing foodstuffs throughout South Yorkshire, exploiting new rail links to the eastern counties and Manchester. This objective was deliberately sought by the Manchester, Sheffield and Lincolnshire Railway Company. It is significant that one of the directors of the Sheffield board of this company was Michael Ellison, the agent of the Duke of Norfolk's estates in Sheffield. Ellison's brother was on the Manchester board. Evidence such as this suggests that it would be fruitful to focus next upon the relationship of each city to its immediate hinterland within which the influence of the regional aristocracy was rooted.[18]

THE REGIONAL CONTEXT

The hardware trades of each town were complemented by iron works and coal mines which stood upon neighbouring landed estates such as those of Earl Fitzwilliam in the West Riding and Lord Dudley in Staffordshire. However, these economic and political similarities were aspects of social configurations which were developing in radically dissimilar ways. Birmingham was not only a centre of industrial production but also the entrepot of the Black Country and a flourishing market town, serving an extensive and well-populated region of industrial villages, rural hamlets and agricultural estates, all cheek by jowl. [19] George Eliot's picture of northern Warwickshire just before the first Reform Act applies well to Birmingham's regional setting:[20]

> In these midlands districts the traveller passed rapidly from one phase of English life to another: after looking down on a village dingy with coal-dust, noisy with the shaking of looms, he might skirt a parish all of fields, high hedges and deep-rutted lanes; after the coach had rattled over the pavement of a manufacturing town, the scene of riots and trades-union meetings, it would take him in another ten minutes into a rural region, where the neighbourhood of the town was only felt in the advantages of a near market for corn, cheese and hay.

Within 4 miles of Birmingham and gradually being swallowed up by it during the mid-nineteenth century were the settlements at Aston, Northfield, Erdington, Moseley, Castle Bromwich, Bordesley, Stetchford and Saltley. Like Birmingham they had a long tradition of hardware production and local market trading. Less than 10 miles away were the market towns of Solihull, Halesowen and Coleshill and other centres mixing agricultural and manufacturing activities. To the north-west in the Black Country stood the hardware town of Sutton Coldfield and also Walsall, built on coal and iron. West Bromwich and Dudley were close by in the north-east with their mines, quarries, brass foundries, brick works, glass works, railways and canals. Within a 20-mile radius were the market towns of Lichfield, Tamworth, Nuneaton, Coventry, Leamington, Warwick, Alcester, Droitwich and, 22 miles away, Worcester. The same area included the hardware town of Redditch and others in which manufacturers, farmers and merchants all plied their trade such as Bromsgrove, Kidderminster, Bewdley, Stourport, Stourbridge and the mighty Black Country metropolis of Wolverhampton.[21]

By contrast, apart from Rotherham, 5 miles to the north-east, there was no other major centre of population within 12 miles of Sheffield. Beyond this ring of desolation the towns of Chesterfield to the south, Barnsley to the north, Doncaster to the north-east and Worksop to the south-east formed a semi-circle of market centres, providing alternative locales for the region's trading activities, more accessible and pleasant than Sheffield. In the 1830s, an aerial photograph of the 10 miles around the junction of the River Porter and the River Don would have revealed a multitude of small villages and hamlets containing communities of cutlers, grinders and colliers. The parish of Sheffield was enormous, extending over 22,370 acres. It contained twelve villages and forty-seven hamlets within its area and was fringed by settlements at Dore, Totley, Norton, Greenhill, Woodhouse, Handsworth and Tinsley. The town of Sheffield itself was almost a geographical and demographic accident, the product of a confluence of rivers and valleys which provided water power and shelter for a dense cluster of small communities.[22]

There were important differences between the regional aristocracies with which the two cities were confronted as they grew. A glance at Sanford and Townsend's map of 'the great landowners of England' gives the strong impression that Sheffield was encircled by ermine. To the north-east just outside Rotherham was the seat of Earl Fitzwilliam at Wentworth House. His close neighbour was Lord Wharncliffe of Wortley Hall whose family, having made their money in the metal industry, was raised to the peerage in 1826. Fourteen miles to the south-west in Derbyshire was Chatsworth which had been the home of the Duke of Devonshire for three centuries. An arc traced around to the south-east into north Nottinghamshire passes through Welbeck Park and Clumber Park, opulent seats of the Dukes of Portland and Newcastle respectively. The Duke of Norfolk, whose principal residence was in Sussex, nevertheless held two-fifths of his estates in the West Riding of Yorkshire, and drew over half his rent from that region. The Norfolk interest in Sheffield radiated outward from his agent's offices in the corn exchange.[23]

The national influence of these men was immense. F. M. L. Thompson names Norfolk (the hereditary Earl Marshal of England), Fitzwilliam, Devonshire and Newcastle in his list of the eight most politically influential peers in the early 1830s. Wharncliffe was president of the Privy Council when Sheffield petitioned for its municipal charter in the early 1840s.[24] Not all of these peers were closely involved in the business of Sheffield. As far as the town was concerned, particular heed had to be paid to Wharncliffe who was an important organiser of the Tory interest in and around Sheffield, and to Norfolk and Fitzwilliam who owned extensive property within the city limits. In his *The Vital Statistics of Sheffield*, published in 1843, Dr G. C. Holland acknowledged the importance of the Ellison family, agents for the Norfolk interest in Sheffield and the 'great obligations' due from the town to Fitzwilliam and Wharncliffe. This powerful trio of West Riding interests, albeit divided politically, exercised great sway at three levels simultaneously: nationally, regionally and within Sheffield itself.[25]

A convenient way to identify the peers most closely associated with Birmingham in this period is to examine the presidential roll of the Birmingham and Midland Institute which was founded in 1854.[26] Nine of the first fifteen presidents were drawn from the local aristocracy. The wealth and property of their families, both locally and nationally, may be compared with that of the three leading South Yorkshire peerages as recorded in the early 1870s (see Table 3).[27]

TABLE 3   *Landowners in South Yorkshire and West Midlands*

| | Sheffield | | | |
| | Acreage | | Annual rent (£) | |
	Yorkshire	*Total*	*Yorkshire*	*Total*
Norfolk	19,440	49,866	'39,897'[a]	'75,596'[a]
Fitzwilliam	22,192	115,743	87,406	138,801
Wharncliffe	22,544	33,440	34,440	50,823

| | Birmingham | | | |
| | Acreage | | Annual rent (£) | |
	War./Wor. Staffs.	*Total*	*War./Wor. Staffs.*	*Total*
Lyttelton	5,907	6,939	9,170	10,263
Hatherton	14,901	14,901	23,196	23,196
Ward	19,428	25,554	117,005	123,176
Leigh	17,241	20,965	25,863	32,013
Wrottesley	5,785	5,785	11,021	11,021
Lichfield	21,433	21,530	41,560	42,042
Calthorpe	2,286	6,470	'114,608'[b]	'122,628'[b]
Dartmouth	7,316	19,518	16,356	58,657
Harrowby	5,165	12,625	7,728	20,291

Source: Bateman (1883).
Notes:
a An underestimate since this figure excludes the value of mines and shooting rights, Bateman (1883), 334.
b A gross overestimate, Bateman (1883), xxiii. By 1880 the Birmingham property of the Calthorpes was yielding a gross rental of nearly £30,000 which was over three-quarters of the Calthorpes' total income. Cannadine (1975), 729.

Although the largest West Midlands potentates recorded here could compete with Norfolk or Fitzwilliam in local rental (Calthorpe), local acreage (Leigh) or both (Ward, Lichfield) none had comparable national standing. Both Lord Ward (representing the Dudley interest) and Lord Lichfield were more dependent upon their Black Country holdings than were Fitzwilliam and Norfolk upon their South Yorkshire estates. Despite their influence in the West Midlands, the Staffordshire aristocracy were only bantam-weights at the national level.

Six of the nine peers recorded held their largest estates in Staffordshire which, acre for acre, had the second highest proportion of country seats in the nation. Of the remaining three, Lord Lyttelton represented the Worcestershire aristocracy, Lord Leigh the Warwickshire nobility, while Lord Calthorpe owed his influence to his position as landlord of Edgbaston, the salubrious middle-class neighbourhood which made up one-third of the area of Birmingham as incorporated in 1838.[28] Located on the meeting point of three counties, Birmingham was entrammelled in a much denser aristocratic mesh than was Sheffield. However, property and influence were not concentrated in the hands of a few families as was the case in South Yorkshire. John Bateman's survey, *The Great Landowners of Great Britain and Ireland*, contains data on individual landowners based upon parliamentary returns made in the early 1870s. Despite the acknowledged deficiencies of Bateman's compilation it provides a means of making a very crude comparison between estates in Staffordshire, Warwickshire, Worcestershire and the West Riding of Yorkshire.[29] Bateman records the acreage and rental of the estates held by owners whose total property in Great Britain and Ireland was at least 2,000 acres or which yielded at least £3,000 per year. There were 129 such estates in Staffordshire, 111 in Warwickshire, 84 in Worcestershire and 110 in the West Riding.[30] Each of these totals was distributed as indicated in Table 4, in percentage terms, with respect to acreage and rental.

The distribution of estates among the four quartiles suggests that the West Riding and Staffordshire supported the highest proportions of landlords possessing enormous acreage and gigantic wealth. It is notable that in its isolation Sheffield was more vulnerable to the influence of such men than was the rival city of Leeds which stood as the north-eastern bastion of a belt of textile towns stretching from Manchester.[31] Birmingham's relative independence was aided by the propinquity of the Black Country whose affairs 'soaked up' much of the influence of Staffordshire interests such as the Dudley estate.[32] Worcestershire and Warwickshire contained an aristocracy and gentry of more manageable proportions. As Lord Willoughby de Broke wrote of nineteenth-century Warwickshire, 'there was no great duke who owned half the county. The landowners were squires, one or two of whom happened to be also hereditary peers. There was no single estate of much more than 12,000 acres.'[33] As Bateman shows, the estates of Worcestershire were even smaller.

TABLE 4 *Distribution of estates by acreage and rental: South Yorkshire and West Midlands*

| | | Gross annual rent | | |
		£10,000 or less	over £10,000	
10,000 acres or under	Staffs	88.6	7.0	n = 129
	Warwicks	91.1	6.3	n = 111
	Worcs	94.0	3.6	n = 84
	WR of Yorks	79.9	9.1	n = 110
Over 10,000 acres	Staffs	00.0	5.4	n = 129
	Warwicks	00.0	3.6	n = 111
	Worcs	00.0	2.4	n = 84
	WR of Yorks	1.8	9.1	n = 110

Acreage appears on the left spanning the two groups.

Source: Bateman (1883).

The steep sides of Sky Edge and Hallam Rise effectively symbolise the vast social gulf which separated Wentworth House and Wortley Hall from the Sheffield cutler's workshop.[34] Up until the middle of the nineteenth century very small units of industrial production were typical of Sheffield. In 1846, for example, the forgers in the cutlery and allied trades occupied 2,535 hearths and were to a great extent self-employed or semi-independent.[35] Business enterprises were numerous but, as Holland wrote,[36]

> [the] merchants and manufacturers among us are not men of large capital, exercising immense influence. They are very far from treading on the heels of the aristocracy.

The residential pattern of Sheffield reflected the importance of the Sheaf, Porter, Rivelin and Loxley in providing waterpower for the grinding wheels of the cutlers and toolmakers. These streams, converging close by the loop in the River Don which marked the centre of old Sheffield, divided the townships of the borough from each other. The six townships of Sheffield were themselves merely collections of hamlets which gradually merged in the course of urban growth. For example, Eccleshall Bierlow, west and south-west of the town centre, contained the hamlets of High Field, Broomhill, Crooks Moor, Sharrow, Button Hill, Bents Green, Banner Cross, Abbey Dale and Whiteley Wood.[37] The difficulties encountered in getting into Sheffield were matched by the problems of traversing it. As late as 1936, a geographer could write:[38]

> From the heart of the town roads radiate outwards, mainly along the river valleys, but a few climb the steep ridges. Thus the branch roads diverge as they leave the city, and cross roads are few, winding and steep. There is no place for circular boulevards in the town. The circular bus routes afford the suggestion of switch-back railways.

Sheffield was, in effect, a collection of closely adjacent industrial villages. An official report from 1889 comments:[39]

> The population of Sheffield is, for so large a town, unique in its character, in fact it more closely resembles that of a village than a town, for over wide areas each person appears to be acquainted with every other, and to be interested with that other's concern.

Rather, Sheffield was made up of a number of villages. For example in the mid-nineteenth century,[40]

> the inhabitants of Upper, Middle and Lower Heeley were very clannish, and rarely associated one with the other, but kept themselves as much apart as if there were miles of space between each division.

The small industrial village, the large aristocratic estate and the interplay between them provided the framework for consciousness and action in South Yorkshire. Both social forms were intensely particularistic, the former built upon the strong solidarities created by common subjection to the dangers of the colliery and the grinding wheel, the latter exploiting ties of kinship and patronage in genteel society. On the side of the rural potentates the huge gulf between their world and that of the local workforce bred a tendency to regard the growth of the industrial population as a problem to be managed with an attitude of patrician disinterestedness.[41] The villages and towns were not a likely source of political allies or socially acceptable persons. On the side of the industrial population two tendencies were observable. The first was an intense conservatism and parochialism, a distrust of 'outside' agencies and a belief in self-reliance. The second was a responsiveness to political, religious and other 'solutions' offering an escape from isolation and insecurity. The interplay between these two tendencies helps explain why in 1843 Holland could claim that the proportion of artisans contributing to sick clubs in

Sheffield was probably 'far greater than any other manufacturing town' while at the same time the proportion of inns and beer houses per head of population was nearly 80 per cent higher than in Leeds. The great success of Methodism in South Yorkshire owed much to the contrast between its warm personal appeal and the distant authority of the Anglican church which was so clearly allied to the aristocracy.[42]

A radical and sometimes revolutionary political tradition persisted in this region throughout the early nineteenth century.[43] Within Sheffield, as will be seen, utopian politics had an anarchistic flavour. This was expressed in a desire to bring to account rogues who were mismanaging municipal and national affairs and a determination to keep power in the hands of the 'people' locally. These impulses were deeply traditional. Since at least the Civil War an ambivalent relationship had existed in English society between two kinds of solidarity, two networks of influence: between on the one hand the genteel landowning class integrated at the level of the county and on the other hand the small communities of producers and traders in villages and urban neighbourhoods.[44] In and around Sheffield, the links between the regional aristocracy and the metropolis were very close while the parochial and plebeian character of the industrial population was very marked. The underlying hostility between the two social worlds was the immediate stimulus for Sheffield's incorporation as a municipal borough. Local ratepayers who feared the woeful expense of a new corporation were frightened into it by the real threat that Lord Wharncliffe's newly formed West Riding Constabulary would take over the task of policing the town.[45] Not until the heavy steel industry developed in Sheffield after the middle of the century did new social formations develop which swamped these hostilities by transforming the urban class structure and altering the relationship between city and county.

Men like John Brown, Mark Firth, and Charles Cammell, owners of vast new steel works in Attercliffe and Brightside to the north-east of Sheffield's city centre, played a major part in mediating the relationship between Sheffield and its aristocratic neighbours after 1850.[46] By that date Birmingham's mercantile and professional class had been performing a similar function for at least a century. The gradient of status and influence climbed in moving from city to county was far less steep than in South Yorkshire and from 1754 country gentlemen had dined happily with Birmingham's leading citizens at the Bean Club. At the end of the eighteenth century its membership was described as including 'representatives of the Magnates of the County, the Gentlemen and Tradesmen of the town, and Clergy and officers from the Barracks, and the principal representative actors from the local theatre'.[47] John Money has argued that a distinctive 'Birmingham interest' was finding coherent political expression on some issues at least as early as the Warwickshire election of 1774. Birmingham's businessmen not only established their own pressure groups such as the commercial committee, active during the 1780s, but also exploited their connections with their neighbouring gentry and aristocracy to advance their interests in parliament.[48]

In Birmingham, merchants and bankers rather than manufacturers took the leading positions in public affairs. Birmingham's earliest members of parliament included Thomas Attwood and Richard Spooner (both bankers), Joshua and William Scholefield, P. H. Muntz and George Dixon (all merchants). Another prominent local banker, Charles Geach, bought the Park Gate Iron Manufacturing Company at Rotherham in the early 1840s, made a fortune out of the railway boom, served as mayor for Birmingham in 1847, helped found the Institution of Mechanical Engineers (at Birmingham) in the same year, and ended his career as member of parliament for nearby Coventry. Through railways, Geach spread his influence both nationally and internationally. He was, for example, not only an active promoter of the Manchester, Sheffield and Lincolnshire Railway but also one of the concessionnaires of the Western Railway of France.[49] Joseph Chamberlain, whose rise to political influence comes at the end of this period, was an accountant rather than a manufacturer. His brilliant financial operations helped to lay the foundations for what was to become the giant combine of Guest, Keen and Nettlefold.[50] Buccaneering bankers and bold financiers were not to be found in Sheffield. The banking enterprises of that city avoided overseas ventures and based themselves solidly upon small local businesses. After a number of bank failures in the early 1840s, financial conservatism increased further. The four local joint-stock banks had a scattering of branches in nearby villages and towns but very few in Sheffield itself before 1890. Commerce in Sheffield was a major aristocratic interest. One of the oldest banks, the Sheffield and Rotherham, was founded with the capital of a local iron-master and the Duke of Norfolk. Furthermore, Sheffield's very market place was controlled by the Duke, as lord of the manor, until 1899.[51]

In John Vincent's words,[52]

> In religion, politics, culture, wealth, there [was] almost no community of experience, no possible human solidarity, to unite the 'top ten thousand in Sheffield' with metropolitan 'good society', that is, with the world of Trollope, Thackeray, and Bagehot, with its extensions in the upper levels of Barsetshire society.

This was not true of Birmingham. The comparison of census data in 1851 has shown that employments associated with the old professions and with literary and artistic production occupied twice as many people, as a proportion of the total population, in Birmingham as in Sheffield. In actual numbers, Birmingham was over three times as well provided and was the centre of culture and entertainment for the region. The county flocked to Birmingham's triennial music festivals where they heard, for example, the first performance of Mendelssohn's *Elijah* in 1846. Birmingham men such as the lawyer Clement Ingleby played a leading role in the Shakespeare tercentenary celebrations at the Warwickshire market town of Stratford-upon-Avon in 1864.[53]

Political debate, like cultural activity, had a regional as well as a city audience, one fostered by the circulation of Birmingham's main newspapers, the *Birmingham Daily Post* and the *Birmingham Daily Gazette*.[54] Although at mid-century highly localised parochial conflicts were the staple of provincial politics, the constant movement of goods and people throughout the Midlands encouraged comparisons between particular disputes and the exploitation of specific local grievances in campaigns over general issues. The greater amount of sheer movement which occurred in and around Birmingham as compared to Sheffield is illustrated by the fact that the proportion of the population engaged in transport and communications was about 50 per cent greater in the former city. A commercial traveller such as George Griffiths, for whom a typical day's work in the 1830s included visits to customers in Stourbridge, Wolverhampton, Bilston, Dudley and Birmingham, was able to spice his business affairs with a long-running campaign against the abuse of educational charities. The subtle interplay between economic conditions and intellectual and political currents in Birmingham's hinterland is nicely conveyed in the title of his autobiography, *Going to Markets and Grammar Schools*.[55]

When contrasted with South Yorkshire, Birmingham and its immediate hinterland was characterised by a more complex division of labour, greater dynamic density (to borrow Durkheim's phrase), a stronger mercantile and professional element, and, instead of the gaping hiatus between county magnates and urban industrialists which existed in Sheffield, a much more balanced and open society in which no very small group of men could monopolise a resource, skill or activity.[56] Association, negotiation, argument and compromise were the stuff of politics and business in the West Midlands. Stationed on a great national crossroads within a social arena of this kind, people in and around Birmingham were especially sensitive to the flow and counterflow of ideas and the modalities of social exchange. This preoccupation was expressed in many ways: for example, in a readiness to adapt production techniques to shifts in popular taste (such as the decline in the fashion of wearing buckles), in sensitivity to design and presentation of wares, in the monetarist theories of Thomas Attwood and his followers, and in the confidence expressed by Joseph Sturge in the moral force exercised by currents of enlightened public opinion.[57] Having drawn some broad comparisons between the national and regional contexts of the two cities closer attention can now be paid to social formations at the municipal and neighbourhood levels of integration.

INDUSTRY, FAMILY, COMMUNITY

The skilled hardware traders of Birmingham and Sheffield had many similarities in the organisation of production and distribution but there were important differences between the two cities in the structure of power within industry. These dissimilarities in power structure were aspects of fundamental differences between Birmingham and Sheffield in the forms of bonding within and between groups and in the relative significance of the municipal and neighbourhood levels of integration.

The light trades of Sheffield were dominated throughout the period by the production of iron and steel goods, including joiners' and engineers' tools, agricultural equipment and cutlery. Typically, articles were fashioned initially by the forger on his hearth and anvil, passed on to the grinder to be smoothed and sharpened, and eventually delivered to the hafter or assembler who fitted the handles. It is less easy to summarise the Birmingham trades. In 1841 the borough of Birmingham gave employment to 3,056 brass founders and moulders, 2,888 people engaged in making buttons, 514 other founders, 964 glass makers, 1,781 gun and pistol makers, 631 japaners and lacquerers, 730 platers and 1,398 jewellers, goldsmiths, silversmiths and allied workers. No single kind of employment was dominant within the total workforce of some 7,000 people. It is possible, however, to make the following generalisations.[58]

Until the middle of the nineteenth century domestic industry and small-scale workshop production were common in both cities while factories were a comparative rarity. A typical figure was the 'garret master' who acted as the head craftsmen in a small work-team which included a few apprentices and members of his own family. Successful garret masters were able to extend their premises, usually around their dwelling places, and employ a greater number of craftsmen. The activities of large numbers of small specialised units of production were coordinated by 'factors' who performed a wide range of inter-mediary functions. For example, they supplied capital and raw materials, arranged orders and organised distribution. Manufacturers on a larger scale in some cases constructed purpose-built factory premises fitted with steam-driven machinery and took over them-selves many of the tasks performed by the factor. However, larger manufacturers were typically dependent upon a system of sub-contracting. Under this system responsibility for the processes of production was in the hands of intermediaries who were themselves the direct employers of labour. The sub-contractor reached an agreement with the factory owners on a price for the products and was himself responsible for paying the workmen. In times of expanded business additional contracts could be arranged with the owners of workshops and with garret masters outside the factory. Within such an industrial structure, rapid advancement was possible from the status of garret master to that of workshop-owner. A successful workshop might be extended in times of enhanced trade and even replaced by a specially constructed factory employing 100 workers or more. Movement in the opposite direction could occur with equal rapidity.[59] In 1830 John Parker was proud to claim that trade in Sheffield was 'as it ought to be, republican and not an oligarchy: it is in the town, and not in the hands of a few capitalists.' Just over a decade later, Charles Geach also commented that Birmingham's industry was not controlled by 'a few capitalists'.[60]

This general picture of industrial life in the period 1830–50 may be compared with the comments of, first a Birmingham industrialist and second, a Sheffield manufacturer in the mid-1860s:[61, 62]

> The manufacture of Iron Wood Screws . . . has, from its commencement, been carried on principally in Birmingham and the immediate neighbourhood, and now forms one of its staple industries. Its progress and the changes which have affected it, especially within the last sixteen years afford a good illustration of a revolution which is taking place in the principal hardware trades. . . . Almost all Birmingham trades have sprung from small beginnings and fifty years ago there were very few factories in the town of great size or importance. The business was carried on in some part of the dwelling house, or in small premises attached. The owner frequently worked himself, with his family and a few men; and these small manufacturers were more like the "chambermasters" of some London trades than the great mill-owners of Manchester or Leeds. Of late years, these factories have grown with extraordinary rapidity, the business has taken possession of house and garden, and the former occupant now lives out of town. Still, to this day, many of the largest works show their piecemeal origin; and the furniture of the old dwelling-house may frequently be seen in the counting-house or warehouse. The introduction of machinery and the universal employment of steam-power, has necessitated two changes: 1st the introduction of large capital into businesses which required little when hand-labour alone was used; 2nd, the construction of large mills,

especially adapted to the wants of each trade. These innovations have brought with them the factory system, and it is probable that the change, which is deplored by some, and which is certainly leading to the extinction of the small manufacturers, as such, and is finding them employment as overlookers, or foremen in large establishments, is really an almost unmixed good.

The chief branches of work carried on upon our premises are steel melting, converting and tilting, railway spring making, file making . . . also saw making . . . and the manufacture of small engineers' tools. . . . On the whole we employ more people off our premises than on them, particularly in file cutting. This is done chiefly at the houses of the workers, and it is this way that the greater part of the workers in the file trade are employed. In the Sheffield district, files are made by hand labour only. The forging, grinding and cutting could be done by machinery equally well, and at far less cost; but the jealousy of the workers on this point is so strong, that no manufacturer can venture to introduce machinery for the purpose. It would not be safe for him to do so; otherwise we could introduce machinery with great advantage. . . . The reputation, however of the Sheffield work is deservedly so great, and there are such advantages here for the manufacture of steel and steel goods, that in spite of the present impossibility of introducing machinery here, it is likely that the manufacture will continue to be carried on here on the present system on a very large scale, at any rate for a long time.

The first extract is from Joseph Chamberlain's contribution to *Birmingham and the Midland Hardware District*, a collection of reports on local industries produced for the British Association in 1866. The second extract is from evidence by Alfred Ibbotson contained in J. E. White's report of 1865 to the Children's Employment Commission. They describe extreme examples of tendencies which were present in the two cities during the period 1830–70. In Birmingham there was a movement towards increased mechanisation and concentration of the workforce within factories in which the firm of Nettlefold and Chamberlain played a leading role by taking over several local work-shops making woodscrews.[63] In Sheffield resistance to such a movement was powerful among the craft unions, especially those in the file trades.[64] Chamberlain's confident projection of his own industrial experience onto the whole of the hardware trades involved an exaggeration of the scale and pace of change. The factory returns of 1871 for Warwickshire distinguish between 'factories', establishments either using steam power or employing over fifty people, and 'workshops', establishments employing smaller numbers in handicraft trades. They show that factories were general in the production of iron, machines, glass and cartridges but workshops predominated in most of the gun trade and in the manufacture of files, saws, tools, buttons, gold and silver plate, jewellery and the 'miscellaneous metal trades'. The brass-finishing trades were divided fairly evenly between factories and workshops.[65] Similarly, Ibbotson's pessimism about the mechanisation of the file trade was, as will be seen, less justified with respect to some branches of the Sheffield light trades and hardly applicable to the rapidly expanding heavy trades.

Nevertheless, Chamberlain's optimism and Ibbotson's pessimism reflected important differences in the character of the artisan communities in Birmingham and Sheffield. These differences were reflected in the activities of craft unions in the two cities. Beginning in the 1820s and continuing during the 1830s and 1840s there had been an upsurge of union agitation in Birmingham, responding to a serious threat to artisan independence and living standards.[66] Faced with falling prices after the Napoleonic Wars, many employers increased the size of establishments, introduced machinery, attacked the institution of apprenticeship and reduced wages. By 1824 a local magistrate was asserting that 'combinations exist in every branch of manufacture'.[67] Over fifty strikes were recorded during the next quarter of a century, involving a wide range of trades. Confronted with the 'logic of the market' many groups of artisans organised themselves into trade societies to protect the traditional customs and usages of their occupations. Money alone was not at issue but a whole way of life. The old crafts, perhaps above all the gunmakers around St Mary's Church, were used to dictating their own pace of work. Saint Monday was frequently invoked to extend the weekend break. Tuesday was often canonised as well. The appeal to traditional norms was complemented by participation in radical political movements. For example, many trade societies took part in agitation for the Reform Bill and the Charter. In 1845 a central committee of trades was set up in Birmingham under the leadership of the Chartist John Mason, president of the local boot and shoemakers society.[68]

Despite these efforts, transformations within the means of production between 1830 and 1870 shifted the balance of industrial power away from skilled artisans. The tasks of organising (a largely unsuccessful) resistance and the increased scale of some industrial enterprises tended to encourage links between different trades, eventually leading to the establishment of the Birmingham Trades Council in 1866. The council's official historian later wrote:[69]

> The declared political policy of the Trades Council was alliance with the radical wing of the Liberal Party, and this was maintained until 1885 to the point of subservience. In industrial matters the counterpart of this alliance was arbitration and conciliation. In

1869 [its Secretary] William Gilliver read a paper to the Social
Science Congress suggesting that a permanent body of delegates
from the Trades Council and the Chamber of Commerce should be
the court of final appeal for industrial disputes. This attitude
dominated Trades Council policy till the end of the century.

Bargaining between masters and men over industrial, political and
other matters within shared or at least substantially overlapping
normative orders had been facilitated by the predominance of workshop organisation in Birmingham before mid-century.[70] By 1870 these
processes of bargaining were to a much greater extent focused upon
the municipal level of integration and took place through institutions
such as the trades council and the Birmingham Liberal Association.
Polarisation between some employers and their workforces had
occurred through the introduction of relatively large mechanised
factories in some industries such as glass manufacture.[71] However,
taking Birmingham's manufacturing population as a whole in 1871,
between a few large factory owners at one extreme and their unskilled
or semi-skilled labourers at the other extreme there stood a multitude
of people employing their capital and skills in small and medium-sized
enterprises. The municipal arena provided a forum which was not
sharply polarised between rich and poor, strong and weak. It was in
the interests of artisans whose control at the workplace was being
undermined with the advance of mechanisation to build as strong a
position as possible at the municipal level where they could adopt the
traditional strategy of reminding the masters that they had obligations
to fulfil within a shared moral order. Involvement in political movements alongside employers was part of this strategy.[72]

The *Trades' Union Directory* published in 1861 listed forty-two trade
unions at Birmingham. Sheffield, despite its smaller population, was
credited with sixty unions. Details of regular meeting times were
recorded in the directory for only seven of the Birmingham unions: two
met weekly, two fortnightly and three monthly. Meeting times were
listed for all sixty Sheffield unions. Half of their numbers were
recorded as having weekly committee meetings (in some convenient
tavern), a quarter had such meetings fortnightly and twelve unions
had an official on duty daily at a fixed time. This suggests a higher
degree of activity and closer communication amongst union members
in Sheffield than in Birmingham. The returns for Birmingham may be
incomplete but such slackness would be a further indication of the
lower level of union activity in that city.[73] Indirect evidence of the
greater capacity of the Sheffield unions to resist industrial changes of
the kind which occurred in Birmingham can be seen in three areas: the
adoption of steam engines, the employment of women and children,
and the fate of apprenticeship.

In 1835 when Birmingham's population stood at about 135,000, 169 steam engines averaging 16 horsepower were being used. Nineteen years later when Sheffield's population was over 150,000, only 109 steam engines (with a similar average horsepower) were in use.[74] In 1862, Pawson and Brailsford's *Illustrated Guide to Sheffield and Neighbourhood* quoted a file-cutter's recent poem:[75]

It's the wonder of wonders, is this mighty steam hammer,
What folks say it will do, it would make any one stammer;
They say it will cut files as fast as three men and a lad,
But two out of three, it's a fact, they are bad. . . .

So unite well together, by good moral means,
Don't be intimidated by these infernal machines;
Let them boast as they will and through the press clamour,
After all, lads, there's nothing like wrist, chisel, and hammer.

The attitude of these 'lads' was quite different from that of the smiths, founders and engineers of Birmingham whose efforts ensured that until the early 1850s far more patents for inventions were issued in that city than in any other place outside London. In Sheffield during the early 1850s Jelinger Symons was told by the bemused inventor of a magnetic guard and dust-receiving box that 'anything which tended to lengthen the lives of the grinders would be disliked by themselves, as tending to spoil the trade by enlarging the supply of labour.'[76]

A convenient way to trace the contrasting profiles of juvenile and female employment and the fate of apprenticeship in Birmingham and Sheffield is through the reports of inspectors to the Children's Employment Commission in the early 1840s and mid-1860s. Jelinger Symons and J. E. White found broadly the same pattern at Sheffield in 1843 and 1865. In White's words:[77]

Taking the manufactures of the district generally, the proportion of children to adults employed to them is small. It is in few that they are employed to any great extent under the age of 9 or 10, but from this age upwards they are employed wherever light work, and in some cases work which is not light, can be found for them. . . . [There] are few occupations at which females are employed to any large extent.

White's figures were imprecise but at the earlier date Symons identified about 4,000 persons under 18 years working for nearly 900 different employers as well as nearly 900 young persons of similar age employed at about ninety grinding wheels. The vast majority were reported as being over the age of 13. The biggest single form of juvenile employment was in hafting table and spring knives.[78]

Symons had found apprenticeship in full vigour, children being

40

'both apprenticed to and hired by the journeymen with whom they work, and not to manufacturers, except in some instances. . . . [In] most cases the apprentice leaves his parents, and boards and lodges with his journey-man master, who keeps, clothes and teaches him his business.' This practice was still widespread in 1865 though 'much declined, partly in consequence of the growing wish of the young for independence, and partly of the efforts of the trade societies to limit the number of apprentices allowed in each trade'.[79] In sharp contrast, R. D. Grainger found at Birmingham very few 'in-door' apprentices by 1843. There was local nostalgia for a passing system which was felt to have maintained standards of workmanship. He also found that '[in] Birmingham a very large number of children are employed in a great variety of manufacturing processes' and noted 'the system, which is prevalent in many branches, of substituting the labour of women for that of men'. In screw manufacture, for instance, some 80–90 per cent of the labour was female.[80] So widespread was this practice that in 1857 a local manufacturer, John Skirrow Wright, declared:[81]

> It has become one of our 'institutions', and the town of Birmingham owes its position to the ready supply of cheap labour afforded by women and girls, the suspension of whose industry, as at present carried on, would annihilate many of those trades for which Birmingham has been celebrated.

Pinmakers and button manufacturers consumed large quantities of child labour, averaging about 8 or 9 years old. By 1865 J. E. White was able to record that large numbers of boys were also employed in brass foundries and that at least 2,000 children under the age of 10 were labouring for wages in Birmingham. Grainger and White both record that child labour was broadly of two kinds: first, direct engagement of factory labour by employers, especially in the pin and button trades, and second, employment of juvenile helpers who were often their own children by the piece-workers themselves. Both inspectors found the second practice to be very extensive.[82]

The inspectors' reports thus suggest that child and female labour were employed to a greater extent in Birmingham than in Sheffield. These general impressions are strengthened by three other calculations. W. L. Sargant, analysing the *1861 Census*, provided figures which showed that in the age range from 20 years to 55 years, Birmingham had a substantial excess of women over men whereas in Sheffield the relationship was reversed. The census of 1871 recorded that whereas 71.4 per cent of females aged 20 years and above in Sheffield were 'wives and others engaged in household duties', in Birmingham the figure was only 58.9 per cent.[83] Finally, in a paper 'on the composition of the population of large towns' published in 1857, Thomas A. Welton computed the extent to which male and female adults and young persons aged 20 years and under were engaged in manufacturing in Birmingham and Sheffield.[54] His findings are shown in Table 5. As the table shows, over half the adult males of Sheffield were employed in manufacturing occupations, a degree of commitment to this sector which was well over ten times as great as that of their womenfolk. In Birmingham, only just over a third of adult males were so employed, a degree of commitment a mere four times as great as that of adult females. Although a Birmingham adult male was less than twice as likely to be in manufacture as a male under 21 years of age, his equivalent in Sheffield was over two and a half times as likely to be so employed.[55]

TABLE 5   *Rate of employment in manufacture per thousand by age and sex: Birmingham and Sheffield 1851*

	Birmingham			Sheffield	
	Male	Female		Male	Female
Over 20 years	349	83	Over 20 years	511	39
20 years and under	177	72	20 years and under	189	39

Source: Welton (1858).

Taking all this evidence together, it may be surmised that in Birmingham earning power was more widely distributed within families than in Sheffield. Very young children might be exploited by their parents as 'helpers' at the workbench. As they became older they could go into other branches of trade and so reduce the risks of a family being dependent upon a single income or·a single trade. This possibility was a result of relatively weak union control over the deployment of labour and must have taken some of the steam out of pressure for high wage rates. A committee of local medical men reported in the early 1840s:[56]

> The striking peculiarity of the manufactures of this town is the great variety and the division of labour. It rarely happens that all members of the same family work at the same trade; so that if one trade is in a depressed state, another may be in a thriving condition.

In Sheffield the overlap between the workplace and the household was exceptionally great, producing exceptionally strong control by the local community over its members. The authority of the father over his young was shared with that of the journeyman over his apprentice.

Women and children were to a much greater extent dependent upon adult male breadwinners than in Birmingham. Norms of masculinity within and outside the household must have been strengthened by the dominant position in local industry of the artisan controlling his labour and skills in conjunction with his fellows. As late as 1865, J. E. White noted that in spite of the increased use of steam-driven machinery in cutlery manufacture, '[the] workers even in factories keep much of the old independence of their master, in fact are more in the position of small manufacturers themselves.'[87]

The statement of an anonymous edge-tool maker, taken by the *Morning Chronicle* in 1851, neatly summarises many of these differences between the artisan communities of Birmingham and Sheffield:[88]

I left Sheffield to come to Birmingham about thirteen years ago, because work was slack there at the time. The strikes among the workmen are very numerous at Sheffield. In time of good trade a grinder will make three times as much at Sheffield as at Birmingham. They can make £3 a week there. A good deal of the heavy edge-tool trade has come to Birmingham and to Wolverhampton. I should think that the reason of this is, that iron and coal are cheaper here than at Sheffield, and also that the Sheffield unions are opposed to the introduction of machinery in the trade. . . . Machinery is much more extensively employed at Birmingham than at Sheffield, and the prejudice against it is so strong at Sheffield that I have known an instance of a man being obliged to leave that town because he substituted a bellows for the ordinary blow-pipe used for soldering. . . . Unions are much more general [at Sheffield] than at Birmingham. I was once obliged to leave a place in consequence of not belonging to the union of the trade in which I worked at the time; but it was not the trade to which I had been brought up, and the men took care to inform me that I was looked upon as an interloper. I had been out of work for some time before entering that business, but was obliged to leave it. I have seen nothing of that sort in Birmingham. There have been several attempts to form a union among the edge-tool makers in Birmingham and the neighbourhood since I have come here, but they have never succeeded. The men do not understand unions here so well as in the north, and the trade lies in a very large circle, so that the men cannot be often and readily collected together. In Sheffield I have known the children hoot a workman in the streets who did not belong to the union of his trade.

SOLIDARITIES AND SANCTIONS

In Birmingham during the first two-thirds of the century there were strong pressures for organisations representing skilled workers to focus more of their attention at the municipal level. Such pressures were not absent from Sheffield, as will be seen, but there was a powerful counter-pull. This was towards highly localised enclaves made up of fairly small groups of men and their families who earned their livelihood in similar ways. The workshop and public house were the centres of communal organisation and celebration. The beginning and end of apprenticeships, weddings, birthdays and Christmas were all attended with festive ceremony, as were fairs. Home-brewing followed by house-to-house visiting to taste the product was a customary prelude to such feastdays. Public houses were later the scene of drinking, dancing and singing. These outpourings of a vigorous local culture were praised in the works of Joseph Mather, 'poet of the filesmiths'. He died in 1804 but the tradition persisted in strength for at least another half century.[89]

The craft unions were one expression of these neighbourhood solidarities. These societies had been organised mainly during the late eighteenth century and early nineteenth century in opposition to the Cutlers' Company, dominated by the larger masters, which had sought to regulate apprenticeship and entry into the local trades throughout the Sheffield area. In 1814 the main provisions of the Elizabethan Statute of Artificers were repealed and the Cutlers' Company's powers of regulations were also abolished by a special act. In Birmingham subsequent attempts by trade societies to regulate apprenticeship and so control recruitment were widely opposed and circumvented by employers. For example, in 1826, the employers of silver-plate workers successfully united in a bond of £500 each to reduce wages and destroy apprenticeship control by the newly formed Silver Plate Workers Gift Society. By contrast, unions were by and large more effectively organised and employers less so in Sheffield than in Birmingham. In effect, over much of the light trades industrial regulation shifted to a lower level after 1814, into the hands of unions who believed that 'they were the rightful heirs of the Cutlers' Company'.[90]

The enclave mentality fostered by geography and residential patterns was increased by the effects of Sheffield's high degree of specialisation within the national economy. As so much of Sheffield's manufacturing production was in a narrow range of commodities, large numbers of men were in almost direct competition with each other, exploiting similar techniques and materials. Maintaining lines of demarcation was a basic strategy for securing livelihoods. There were, for example, ten different grinders' unions in 1861: edge-tool grinders, file grinders, fender grinders, fork grinders, jobbing grinders, pen- and pocket-knife grinders, saw grinders, scythe grinders, sickle makers and grinders and table-knife grinders. In 1867, Joshua Tyzack who was a saw manufacturer, acknowledged that a 'very important' cause of disputes within his firm was 'the different unions claiming the sole making of different kinds of goods'.[1] Sidney Pollard has summarised well the roots of union influence in Sheffield:[2]

> A determined and united trade society, in a branch whose members were easily assembled in one room and had the peculiar cohesion found in local specialised crafts, was difficult to resist. . . . [Experience] showed that well-organised trades did preserve high wages even during slack times, by maintaining men on the 'box', thus reducing the supply of labour, and since the demand for labour appeared to be well below unity, a policy of restriction could be very favourable to the branch. Furthermore, the effect of restriction on the bargaining position of a trade was cumulative: the limitations upheld by strong unions (eg most grinders' societies) made them stronger still; the unrestrained influx of labour into badly organised trades (eg the cutlers') weakened their unions further.

The strength of neighbourhood and occupational solidarities conjoining families dependent upon a common means of earning their livelihood was expressed in the widespread toleration of physical sanctions against anyone who disobeyed the norms of the local community. A typical reason for their use was the infringement of union rules, for example on the matter of apprenticeship, and they were directed against both workmen and employers. The most usual form was 'rattening', the covert removal of the grinders' bands which connected the grindstones to the revolving shafts. More serious measures were sometimes taken. During the 1850s and 1860s there occurred an attempted shooting (1854), a murder (1859), gunpowder attacks (1857, 1859, 1861, 1865, 1866) and several other serious assaults on persons and property. The grinders' unions were the most deeply implicated. That such attacks and the minor rattenings were expressions of collective rather than merely personal feeling is suggested by the difficulty of tracing offenders and the failure to elicit information by offering large rewards.[3] In 1867 the *Sheffield Independent* declared:[4]

> With regard to commonplace rattening it must be admitted that it is a branch of unwritten law, and it has been the system to enforce obedience by that sort of distraint. Very little interest attaches to that part of the subject. Outsiders may represent these things as something horrible and marvellous, but to those who know the usages of the Sheffield trades, there will not appear to be anything

more wonderful about them than in the executions put into force every week by the bailiffs of the County Court, except that the law of the land sanctions the one and forbids the other.

Within Birmingham neighbourhoods and occupations retained their distinctiveness but they merged into a city-wide network of inter-dependencies that was much more complex than in Sheffield. Artisans in Birmingham belonged to a moral order which was focused upon the city rather than the particular neighbourhood or specific occupation. Within such an order the regulation of particular relationships or tasks tended to be regarded as an expression of a set of general principles. There might be disagreement about these principles: for example, about the relative scope of the obligations and rights pertaining to private persons and public bodies. Disputes were also likely to take place about the particular application of widely accepted (though possibly ambiguous) general principles to novel tasks, relationships or situations. Such disputes were the daily bread of Birmingham Liberalism. Through their occurrence ambiguities were hammered out or glossed over, political commitments were re-charged, and opinion on the great 'strategic' questions of principle gradually given shape.[95]

The population of Birmingham, including its working men, were well used to public disputes of this character between contestants for their political support. Assessment of rights and obligations and the appropriate measures of political 'restitution' were carried out by the jury of public opinion. This included non-voting craftsmen and ware-housemen whose expressions of approval and disapproval weighed heavily in the minds of the shopkeepers and other property owners who enjoyed the franchise. Take the case of G. F. Muntz, Liberal MP for Birmingham. In 1847 Muntz refused to declare his support for William Scholefield who was the other local Liberal candidate during the General Election of that year.[96] Eliezer Edwards takes up the story:[97]

Matters stood thus when the meeting of non-electors was held in the Town Hall. It was a very hot afternoon, and the hall was crammed. The leaders of the Liberal party took, as usual, the right of the chairman, and filled the principal seats in front. Mr Muntz was conspicuous by his absence. The proceedings had gone on for some time, and on the name of Mr William Scholefield being proposed as a candidate, the whole audience rose enthusiastically, and the Town Hall rung with cheers, such as the Liberals of Birmingham know so well how to bestow on a Liberal favourite or a Liberal sentiment. In the midst of this demonstration, when the meeting was in a state of fervid excitement, George F. Muntz quietly came up the orchestra stairs, and took unobserved a seat upon a back bench, near the organ. I was within two yards of him. He wore a brown holland blouse, and had with him a paper bag, and as he placed his hat on the seat beside him, he emptied the contents of the bag into it. As he did so I saw that he had provided himself with half-a-dozen oranges.

In the course of the speeches that were made, much regret was expressed at the determination of Mr Muntz to stand aloof from the party in this election, and it was hinted that if the Conservatives should retain the seat, Mr Muntz personally would be to blame. Muntz heard it all pretty quietly, and at length, greatly to the astonishment of most who were there, who were not even aware of his being present, his stalwart figure rose, like an apparition, at the back of the gallery. Standing on a seat so as to make himself seen, he shouted out, 'Mr Chairman!'. The applause which greeted him was met with sober silence by Mr Scholefield's friends. He went on – I remember his very words – 'I was going into the Reform Club the other day, and on the steps I met Joe Parkes: you all know Joe Parkes. Well, he said to me, "I say, Muntz, you must coalesce with Scholefield." I said, "I shan't do anything of the sort; it is no part of my duty to dictate to my constituents who shall be my colleague, and I shan't do it." "Well," he said, "If you don't, I shall recommend the electors to plump against you!" Well, I gave him a very short and very plain answer: I told him they might plump and be dammed!' The uproar, the laughter, the shouts that ensued cannot be adequately described. In the midst of the din, Muntz coolly stooped, took a large orange from his hat, bit a piece out of it which he threw away, and then facing that mighty and excited crowd, proceeded to suck away in as unconcerned a manner as if no one were present but himself. When the noise had somewhat subsided, he commenced an elaborate defence of his conduct, and said he had been taunted with being too proud to ask for the votes of the electors. 'That's not the reason,' he said; 'I knew I had done my duty as your representative, and that I deserved your votes; and I knew that I should get them without asking; but if it is any satisfaction to anybody, I take this opportunity to ask you now, collectively, to vote for me. As for your second vote, that has nothing to do with me. Choose whom you may, I shall work cheerfully with him as a colleague, and I have no fear of the result.' This little speech was altogether characteristic of the man. It showed his stubborn wilfulness, his intense egotism, his coarseness of manner, and his affectation of eccentricity. But it exhibited also the fact that he thoroughly understood that he was liked by the bulk of the Birmingham people, and that he knew the majority of unthinking men would take his bluntness for manliness, and his defiance of the feelings and opinions of his political associates, for sturdy and commendable independence. He alienated many friends by his conduct on this occasion, but he won his election, coming in at the head of the poll.

By his skilful presentation of his rights and obligations *vis-à-vis* Scholefield and the people of Birmingham and by his assertion in this municipal arena of the principle of 'manly independence' which was central to artisan culture Muntz was an effective advocate in that 'court'. The ensuing election recorded Birmingham's assessment of the validity of his case.

CHAPTER 3

'THEIR BRUTAL, BLOATED, MINDLESS FACES . . .'

CLASS STRUCTURES AND INSTITUTIONAL ORDERS IN BIRMINGHAM AND SHEFFIELD 1830–70

The attempts by manufacturers to exploit the benefits of machinery in Birmingham and Sheffield were just one aspect of a multi-faceted process whereby members of middle-class establishments in business and the professions tested and sought to transform their relationships with the local working population. The complicity of the latter was the goal sought in the industrial and political spheres and in the realm of 'public order and morality'. The terms upon which it was obtained were very different in the two cities. However, a simple model of 'class conflict' or 'class bargaining' would be inadequate. As will be seen, not only were there deep divisions within middle-class and artisan establishments but the social configurations within which they sought to protect or advance their perceived interests were subject to transformations which were beyond the control of particular groups or social classes.

CLASS BONDS, CLASS BOUNDARIES

In 1855 a Birmingham man recalled, with a certain amount of romantic nostalgia, the old patterns of working-class work and leisure.[1]

> They lived like the inhabitants of Spain, or after the customs of the Orientals. Three or four in the morning found them at work. At noon they rested; many enjoyed their siesta; others spent their time in the workshops eating and drinking, these places often being turned into taprooms and the apprentices into pot boys;

49

others again enjoyed themselves at marbles or in the skittle alley. Three or four hours were thus devoted to 'play'; and then came work again till eight or nine, and sometimes ten, the whole year through.

R. E. Leader recorded similar traditions in Sheffield where the 'ale pot not infrequently stood on the idle anvil, and the men gossiped and drank instead of working.'[2] The patron of these artisan customs was Saint Monday, a day which was habitually kept in visiting the ale house and engaging in sports such as boxing and animal fights. A popular venue was Old Park Wood, 'the original fighting ground of Sheffield.'[3]

From about 1840 the traditional pattern so inimical to industrial discipline, particularly in large mechanised factories, came under pressure. For example, employers, the clergy and other local professional men sponsored 'rational recreation'. In Birmingham, cheap railway excursions began in the summer of 1841. The Botanical Gardens at Edgbaston, which had been founded in 1829 under the patronage of Lord Dartmouth and Lord Calthorpe were opened in 1845 to the working classes at a penny a time on Mondays.[4] Two years previously, the report of the Children's Employment Commission had noted that there were over 200 brothels in the town. A 'committee of physicians and surgeons' had stated that the lack of public walks drove mechanics to the skittle alley and the ale house.[5] However, two decades later, another witness declared:[6]

> I do not know . . . if there is as much drinking as there was. The cheap trains and the opening of the parks, & co., have undoubtedly a tendency to diminish it.

He continued,

> People . . . who go to parks and such places try to appear in as good and neat a dress as they can, which is good for themselves by increasing their self-respect, and also has a good influence on their neighbours in the yards in which many of them live, by shaming them into making themselves respectable too.

Rodger's *Directory of Sheffield and Rotherham*, 1841 recorded that botanical gardens had been opened by a proprietary company five years earlier and it reported the intention of the Duke of Norfolk, 'with the liberality for which he is distinguished', to offer some 50 acres in Belle Vue 'for the use of the inhabitants of Sheffield, to be laid out in plantations, lawns, promenades, &c'. Seven years later the Church of England ran a train trip to York, the first of its kind from Sheffield.[7]

A shift of control over habits of work and leisure away from the workforce was encouraged by the Saturday half-holiday movement.

This practice was being introduced by some Sheffield employers in the 1840s and became current in Birmingham after 1851, aided by the propaganda of the clergy and larger employers. In the words of a Birmingham master: '[The] half-holiday enables me still more strongly to insist on regularity, and say, "No, you have had your Saturday, and must be regular now."'[8] National legislation in 1867 insisted upon the Saturday half-holiday for females and juveniles, both more prominent in the economy of Birmingham than in Sheffield.[9] One reason for the undermining of traditional practices was, it has been argued, the appearance of a 'rift between artisans' dividing the supporters of Saint Monday from its opponents.[10] Old 'irregular' habits were undermined by the adoption of tighter discipline and control on the part of many artisans in their pursuit of higher living standards (becoming possible by the 1850s and 1860s) and more efficient industrial bargaining. For example, Thomas Wright, a journeyman engineer, poured scorn upon 'lushingtons' and 'loafers' in the Black Country. The secretary of the Scissors Grinders Union believed that 'half the men in Sheffield kept Saint Monday by their own folly.'[11] However, the parties to the 'rift' between artisans were not the same in Birmingham and Sheffield.

In Birmingham support for Saint Monday was characteristic of the declining trades such as sword-, nail-, and buckle-making and also prevailed among garret masters.[12] However, in Sheffield a vigorous defence of artisan controls over work practices attuned to long-estab-lished habits of working-class life was being conducted in the 1860s by strong trade societies such as the file unions which had benefited from an extended phase of recent prosperity.[13] By contrast, the Scissors Grinders Union had only acquired effective organisation in 1862 and it belonged to a branch of the light trades which had been among the earliest to feel the damaging effects of foreign competition.[14] There is 'evidence that Saint Monday in Sheffield lasted longer [than in Birmingham] as a workshop based observance.'[15] As will be seen, in Sheffield the rift within the light trades was not between 'lushingtons' and 'regular workmen' but between the supporters of two alternative strategies of industrial bargaining, one involving a great deal of cooperation with employers to the anticipated mutual benefit of both masters and men, the other entailing determined resistance to the dilution of the artisan community's capacity to regulate its own affairs. Both strategies required considerable discipline and organisation.[16]

The working people of Sheffield shared a culture which was less penetrable and manipulable from above than that of Birmingham's population. The difference was long standing. In 1791 Anglican and loyalist magistrates, including the vicar of Aston, had encouraged a Birmingham mob to burn down houses belonging to radical supporters of Joseph Priestley, crying 'destruction to the Presbyter-ians, Church and King forever'.[17] By contrast, in the same year

51

Sheffield's vicar and chief magistrate had his own house destroyed by a crowd incensed at local enclosures and the desecration of a graveyard in order to widen Church Street. The crowd were 'inflamed by one of Mather's fiercest diatribes' against 'the old Serpent', Rev. James Wilkinson.[18]

In 1835 a Sheffield mob attacked the local school of anatomy in anger at the work of the 'resurrection men'. Meanwhile, the administrators of Birmingham School of Medicine were peacefully collecting all the paupers' corpses they required for dissection with the cooperation of the Guardians and Overseers of the Poor.[19]

When they are speaking of the labouring classes in the early 1840s the difference in tone between leading citizens in Birmingham and Sheffield is striking. On the one hand pained disapproval mixed with a paternalistic regard for the welfare of those needing moral regulation; on the other hand a grudging respect, tinged with anxiety, in response to the fierce independence of the artisan population, including their children. Theophilus Richards, a Birmingham manufacturer, suggested that many children in employment would benefit from being lodged in homes 'under the inspection of visiting committees and resident superintendents. The committee might consist of 6 gentlemen, 6 master manufacturers, and 6 steady respectable workmen with families.' A library could be attached to each boarding-house and occasional lectures given.[20] The medical men cited earlier were sympathetic in their assessment of the social causes of 'improvidence and thoughtless extravagance':

> The improvidence of which we speak is to be traced in very many instances to extreme ignorance on the part of the wives of these people. The females are from necessity bred up from their youth in the workshops, as the earnings of the younger members contribute to the support of the family. The minds and morals of the girls become debased, and they marry totally ignorant of all those habits of domestic economy which tend to render a husband's home comfortable and happy; and this is very often the cause of the man being driven to the alehouse to seek that comfort, after his day of toil, which he looks for in vain by his own fireside. The habit of a manufacturing life once established in a woman, she continues it, and leaves her home and children to the care of a neighbour or of a hired child, sometimes only a few years older than her own children, whose services cost her probably as much as she obtains for her own labour.

This committee recommended the provision of not only public walks but also public kitchens, public baths and 'the better education of females in the arts of domestic economy'.[21]

In the evidence collected in Birmingham for the Children's

Employment Commission in the 1840s, the dominant emphasis is upon deprivation and the lack of stable family life or regular employment as the root causes of the sorry state of many juveniles. Benjamin Ride, a Birmingham police superintendent, suggested that thieving by juveniles working in the hardware trades was due to the large number of young people employed, the irregularity of employment, the low rate of wages and the 'lamentable state of ignorance, moral and intellectual; the total absence of education of every sort'. He believed that 'many of the prostitutes had been driven to this kind of life by distress caused by want of employment.'[22] Another police inspector stated that prostitution was often due to 'the vicious habits of the parents. Sometimes from the drunkenness of the father; sometimes from the second marriage of the mother, leading to disputes and strife'. He continued:[23]

> In the low lodging-houses many boys and girls are admitted to sleep; the usual charge is 3d a night each. They change about, sometimes they sleep at one place, and sometimes at another; it is not unusual for them to sleep in barns, and outhouses, or at brickhill fires; and in the summer under hayricks &c. Some years ago a farmer living about a mile and a half from the town made a complaint of the annoyance to which he was subjected; witness went and found in a hovel about 8 couples of 'little lads and wenches', the eldest of whom did not exceed 16.

Evidence of this kind focuses heavily upon the juvenile poor but reveals general attitudes respecting the labouring population as a whole. It is noticeable, for example, that although Birmingham had recent memories of the Chartist riots of 1839 and Sheffield of a revolutionary conspiracy the following year, anxiety about the threat of violent acts appears much more frequently in the Sheffield evidence.[24] The vicar of St Mary's in Sheffield told of beer houses in which 'companies of . . . youths, eight or ten in number not infrequently conspire in committing depredations, and robberies'. He believed that there had 'been a perceptible and unfavourable change in the character of the children in our Sunday-schools since the prevalence of Socialism'.[25] George Mason, a police officer, also believed that young people were 'getting worse, independent of the growth of population'. He continued:[26]

> I think the cause is, that the system of apprenticing them, the masters paying them something per week, even if they lodge with their parents, gives them too much liberty, and makes them feel independent. . . . I remember the Chartist attack on Sheffield last winter; I am certain that a great number of very young lads were among them, some as young as fifteen. They generally act as men.

Depravity rather than deprivation, corruption rather than improvidence are the underlying themes of the Sheffield evidence collected by the commission. The young are seen to have parental acquiescence in their wicked ways. Like his subordinate, Sheffield's superintendent of police believed:[27]

> That the system of apprenticeship, and the uncontrolled state of the children removed from their parents after their work is done, is a great cause of the juvenile depravity which prevails. . . . The great bulk of the men habitually spend their evenings in the beer houses, which is a great cause of the loose life of the younger branches of these families. Numbers of the apprentices are not even lodged with the journeymen who employ them, but are put out to board and lodge at houses where they are taken in, and where no control is exercised over them, and where their morals will not be improved. They are at best half-educated—numbers cannot read who say they can. Parents generally are very proud, and won't send their children to school unless they can go well dressed: but the general feeling is that they attach no importance to education. Witness is confident that the morals of children can not be so bad in Manchester and Leeds because the factory system prevents them running wild in the same manner.

Jelinger Symons concluded that 'as regards habits, hours, education and religious instruction, children are their own masters before fourteen years of age in the generality of instances.'[28]

An extreme statement of the fears of middle-class people, conscious that they had little control over the thoughts and ways of Sheffield's labouring population, came from Ebenezer Elliott, arch-opponent of monopolies:[29]

> Let any stranger, who happens to have formed a high opinion of the intelligence and morality of the workmen of Sheffield, take a walk on a Sunday morning through the Old Park Wood, or visit the lands and footpaths adjoining the town, and he will be surprised to meet group after group of boys and young men playing at pitch-penny, or fighting their bull-dogs, and insulting every decently-dressed passenger. Our Mechanics Institute has not on its list of members *one* physical-force Chartist; no, it is among the dog-fighters that physical-force orators, and other hirelings of monopolists, find applauders. They are the parties who, in the eve of Saint Monday, shoulder the white cravats from the causey, or extend a leg to throw down the passer-by to the disgust and astonishment of foreigners. The horrid words of the incipient sage and legislators; their ferocious gestures; their hideous laughter; their brutal, bloated mindless faces appal and

amaze the stranger; and in their looks throughtful men see a catastrophe, which is too probably destined to cast the horrors of the first French revolution utterly into the shade.

There is a significant clue in Elliott's repeated reference to the surprise which people from outside Sheffield would feel at these things. The 'problem' was not that working-class Sheffield was spectacularly dis-organised and chaotic but that to a great extent it regulated itself, through institutions from which middle-class Sheffield was largely excluded, and in ways which denied Sheffield's more substantial citizens those means of eliciting deference and exercising influence which were available more readily to their counterparts in many other towns. Ironically, to belong to the 'civilised' upper region of Sheffield society was in a sense to be 'disenfranchised'.[30] Dr Arnold Knight perceived a deep communications barrier:[31]

> far too little is done by the middle classes to entice and allure the
> working classes from their vices and errors; we ought to meet their
> feelings in our efforts to improve them; there is much which is not
> reached at all by many institutions; we are too wise and
> philosophical in our modes of approaching and instructing them;
> something more must be done to meet them and adapt our efforts
> to their tastes.

Symons unwittingly acknowledged the existence of a 'restricted code'[32] which excluded his kind in his description of a major Sheffield institution:[33]

> The great bulk of the public-houses . . . appear much more like
> private houses externally, at least at night, the only outside
> indication of their character is a painted window blind, merely
> coloured in a pattern, and without any letters or announcement
> on it. In these a large body of the workmen habitually spend their
> evenings.

In 1851 there were 359 beer-shop keepers in Sheffield compared to 716 in Birmingham, representing a slightly greater provision per head of population in the latter city. However, although Sheffield's population was only six-tenths as large as Birmingham's, it gave employment to more innkeepers: 108 as opposed to 95. The census count of inn-servants (366 in Sheffield, 565 in Birmingham) suggests that such places of liquid refreshment were on average larger in Birmingham, many of them providing comforts for the 'carriage trade' whereas in Sheffield a host of cosy locals were catering for a neighbourhood clientele.[34]

Although by 1851 the vast majority of the urban population were not churchgoers, places of 'spiritual refreshment' provided centres of leadership and organisation which rivalled the taverns. The comparative strengths of the religious denominations in Birmingham and Sheffield is presented in Table 6.[35]

TABLE 6 *Church membership Birmingham and Sheffield 1851*

	Birmingham (%)	Sheffield (%)
Church of England	47.9	30.8
Roman Catholic	6.9	10.1
Wesleyan	10.5	25.1
Other Methodist	5.0	13.6
Congregationalist	9.4	10.8
Baptist	10.9	6.0
Presbyterian	1.0	—
Unitarian	3.7	2.8
Quaker	1.2	0.6
'Isolated congregations'	3.4	0.3

Source: Hennock (1973).

Two points which emerge from the figures in Table 6 are, first, the stronger position of the Anglican establishment in Birmingham compared to Sheffield, and second, the dominance of Methodism in the latter city. Within Methodism, distinctions may be made between the conservative and ministerialist strand of Wesleyan Methodism, shaped by the authoritarianism of Wesley and Bunting, the more democratic strand of the Methodist New Connexion, and the more plebeian tendency of Primitive Methodism.[36] Measured by the same methods used to produce the figures in Table 6, support within Methodism was distributed as shown in Table 7. In effect, nearly a third of the membership of the major denominational grouping in

TABLE 7 *Methodism in Birmingham and Sheffield 1851*

	Birmingham (%)	Sheffield (%)
Wesleyan Methodism	69.2	64.7
New Connexion	9.7	14.6
Primitive Methodism	7.4	17.6
Other	13.7	3.0

Source: 1851 Religious Census.

Sheffield worshipped at chapels with a distinctly 'democratic' or 'plebeian' flavour as opposed to the well-heeled respectability which pervaded Wesleyan Methodism. In Birmingham, Methodism could claim only a third of the support enjoyed by the Anglican church and within Methodist ranks only one in six gathered at the chapels of the New Connexion or the Primitives.[37] The denominational pattern just examined illustrates in a particular sphere the general point that in Birmingham the means of exercising cultural influence over the working class, from 'outside' and 'above' it (for example, through the Anglican clerical hierarchy), were more highly developed than in Sheffield. In the latter city habits of self-regulation were more fully and widely institutionalised. Again, the conclusion is not so much that Sheffield was a very much less regulated society than Birmingham as that the means of exercising control and their class location were different.

Had Sheffield's more substantial citizenry been in great fear of their lives and property in the early 1850s one might have expected a larger police force to have been in existence than was recorded. In 1852 from his office in the town hall the superintendent of the police force commanded (in day time) an inspector, a sergeant, a clerk, twenty-eight constables and a detective force of four men. At night Sheffield was policed by an inspector, three sergeants, six patrol sergeants, seventy-three watchmen and an office-keeper.[38] Birmingham's force was, in proportion to that city's population size much larger. It also had a much more complex organisation. In 1850 there were three police stations, a 'section house' and a separate office for the detective force. The chief superintendent of police directed the work of one chief superintendent, five inspectors, six sub-inspectors, twenty-two sergeants and 282 constables.[39]

In a paper read before the British Association in 1865, J. Thackray Bunce compared the judicial statistics relating to Birmingham and other large towns, including Sheffield. He included a table based upon the Home Office statistics relating to 1864 (see Table 8).[40] The figures in Table 8 should be approached with considerable caution but an interesting point which emerges is that Sheffield which had the lowest proportion of police to population among the examples listed, also had the highest rate of arrests relative to crimes reported, viz., an arrest rate of 94.6 per cent compared to 84.7 per cent in Leeds and 79.5 per cent in Birmingham. The rates for Liverpool and Manchester were 49.1 per cent and 21.2 per cent respectively. It seems likely that in Sheffield indictable crimes would be readily reported to the police when they infringed the moral code of a significant part of the local community involved. In such circumstances apprehension of suspects would be relatively easy. When giving evidence to White on the possibility of legal regulation of child labour, two table-knife hafters were of the

TABLE 8   *Indictable offences in various English cities, 1864*

	Offences	Apprehended	Discharged	Convicted	Police to population
Leeds	489	414	77	337	1 in 787
Sheffield	351	332	120	212	801
Birmingham	752	598	157	431	785
Liverpool	4326	2125	1213	912	431
Manchester	6623	1407	775	632	504
All England	51058	28734	8700	20004	906

Source: Bunce (1865).

opinion that there were 'plenty of people here who would let it be known if the law was being broken'.[41] However, 'rattening', which had the support of many unions, was a different matter. The Sheffield Outrages Inquiry heard from a workman that 'recourse is seldom made to the police to recover property so taken away, but application is almost always made to the secretary of the union.' An employer, himself a magistrate, also commented that 'we as manufacturers had learned not to go near the bench with [trade cases].'[42]

In Sheffield, solicitude for the condition of public morality was mightily tempered by concern for the state of the private purse. This was true also of important sections of Birmingham society but the greater strength of the latter impulse in South Yorkshire is illustrated by the history of attempts to establish courts of quarter sessions in the two cities. Birmingham successfully petitioned for such a court in 1839 and it was duly established as 'the natural complement to the Charter of Incorporation'.[43] Two years later Lord Wharncliffe, president of the Privy Council and a man who presumably knew his Sheffield asked for some assurance that the town would petition for a court of quarter sessions (and a recorder to go with it) before advising the Queen to grant a charter of incorporation. After Sheffield had been duly incorporated the matter of the court was half-heartedly discussed by the town council in 1846 (when they preferred an increase in the county bench), in 1864 (when they pleaded a lack of 'adequate cell accommodation'), in 1869 (without action), in 1873 (deciding to 'postpone the consideration for six months') and in 1874 when they set up a special committee to look at the issues involved. Four years later the committee was discharged without having presented a report. Finally in 1880 the council took its courage in both hands and successfully petitioned for the court. Justification of a kind was received in 1882 when the borough accountant stated that by having the court of quarter sessions, the town council had saved over £3,500 on its rates bill. Such was Sheffield's craving for effective judicial administration.[14]

The resistance of the town council and Sheffield's ratepayers to extending the duties and expense of official government implied a grudging tolerance of the less respectable, legitimate and public institutions through which much of the labouring population managed its own affairs. One rare instance of a limited but more positive alignment of interests was the issue of the new Poor Law. Hostility to the new 'bastilles' was expressed by middle-class Tories, some local philanthropists such as Samuel Roberts and by the trade unions.[15] In 1841 widespread economic distress drove only 632 people to seek indoor relief at Sheffield. Eight years later, rather than put any of its members 'on the parish', the filesmiths union paid more than £4,000 to its members over six months. The trade societies of the edge-tool grinders, Britannia-metal smiths and file hardeners all employed their surplus labour on farms.[16]

Mutual tolerance between important sections of the labouring classes and their 'betters' in Sheffield was made easier by shared assumptions expressed, for example, in the language of Methodism and a common thriftiness. However, the spirit of enthusiastic collaboration in the management and use of common institutions shown in the Birmingham Committee of Non-Electors, the Complete Suffrage Union, the Birmingham and Midland Institute and the fund-raising organisations of the Birmingham hospitals was much less weakly developed in Sheffield.[17] The Sheffield Savings Bank provides one illustration. Its first chairman was James Montgomery who had printed Samuel Roberts's attack on the state's treatment of paupers in his *Sheffield Iris*.[18] In 1840 G. C. Holland analysed the occupations of the 5,022 depositors. Prominent among them were tradesmen such as butchers (24), dressmakers (75), victuallers (26), tailors (54), grocers (15), confectioners (10), millers (22), book-keepers (80) and black-smiths (35) along with occupations such as men servants (153), female servants (650), labourers (201) and housekeepers (84). Holland was disappointed at the low proportion of artisan investors (relative to the numbers employed in each trade), finding the highest participation among the better-paid such as forgemen (24), edge-tool makers (25), steel smelters (38), scythe makers (45) and saw makers (34). He blamed this upon 'an impression in the minds of many, that these institutions originate with Government, and are instruments in their hands for purposes not yet apparent.' In his investigation of friendly societies and sick clubs, Holland also encountered considerable 'prejudice and suspicious feeling'. He found that the principal means of distinguishing them was in terms of '*the greater or lesser respectability of the members*. Some clubs are composed exclusively of artisans, and others have a large proportion of master manufacturers, shopkeepers and persons of independent property. This is an important distinction.'[49]

The reluctance of artisans to associate with more substantial manufacturers and others with greater social pretensions is shown again in the history of land societies in Sheffield. The provincial movement of freehold land societies had received great stimulus from James Taylor's pioneering enterprise in Birmingham. Following the recent election of G. F. Muntz and William Scholefield as Liberal MPs for Birmingham extension of the franchise and political cooperation between different classes were popular causes in that city. Taylor had taken an active part in temperance and building societies in Birmingham. Described as a 'working man', he 'soon found influential supporters' in support of his double object which was 'that of creating county votes and of promoting the welfare of the working classes, by stimulating them to save their money and invest it in allotments of land or in cottage-houses'. Muntz and Scholefield were both presidents of the Birmingham Freehold Land Society, and its members included manufacturers such as W. H. Blews and J. S. Wright.[50] The example of the Birmingham Freehold Land Society was soon followed by the establishment of similar societies in Sheffield. Significantly, the forerunners of the Sheffield societies were not exercises in inter-class cooperation as in Birmingham but independent initiatives taken by trade societies: specifically, the acquisition of farms by the edge-tool grinders and the Britannia-metal smiths mentioned above.[51]

So far, it has been argued that the network of working class institutions in Sheffield was more resistant to transformation by penetration and manipulation 'from above' than its equivalent in Birmingham. More briefly, how did the network of institutions through which the more genteel and bourgeois sections of urban society manage their affairs in the 1830s respond to the establishment of the municipal corporations?[52] Just as new strategies of industrial management threatened Saint Monday and the pattern of life which accompanied it, so new modes of civic administration presented a challenge to a host of settled arrangements built up piecemeal over the preceding decades.

When the town councils of Birmingham and Sheffield were set up, no existing institution of any significance was actually abolished, nor willingly gave up any major powers. The councils had to shoulder their way onto the municipal stage against considerable resistance, both active and passive. The 'state of play' in Birmingham by 1849, just over a decade after incorporation, is conveyed in part by the report of Robert Rawlinson, inspector for the Central Board of Health.[53] Among the governing bodies of the borough he listed, apart from the municipal corporation, the Birmingham guardians of the poor, the street commissioners for Birmingham (with powers of paving, lighting, cleaning and regulating streets, markets etc., in Birmingham parish), similar commissioners for Deritend and Bordesley, another set of commissioners for Duddeston and Nechells, and three groups of highway surveyors for Deritend, Bordesley and Edgbaston respectively. He commented:[54]

> There are eight distinct and separate governing powers within the Parliamentary borough of Birmingham, and consequently eight separate sets of officers have to be paid to do the work which may be done by one efficient staff. These establishments act in opposition to each other.

Apart from the aforesaid, account has to be taken of the water works company, the two gas companies, Queen's Hospital and the general hospital, a long list of charities headed by the very wealthy King Edward VI Foundation (which ran the town's grammar school), the county and borough magistrates, and the large clerical establishment which accrued to a large and long-established market town whose borough boundaries included three parishes. Rawlinson might complain about the state of the town's drains but this tangled forest of institutions offered a splendid terrain for prolonged political battle.[55]

Sheffield also had its gas and water companies, a rather shorter list of charities (mostly administered by the Cutlers' Company), the general infirmary and an endowed grammar school whose management was one of the functions of the church burgesses.[56] Apart from the Guardians of the Poor, the other principal bodies outside the town council in the late 1840s were the town trustees (in existence since 1297), annually-elected highways boards, and the improvement commissioners.[57] The last-named were established in 1818 and included among their number the town trustees themselves, the master and wardens of the Cutlers' Company and some eighty others. Overshadowing them all were the Fitzwilliam and Norfolk estates, especially the latter. Norfolk's ancestor had given the town trustees their original charter and his legal agent dominated the Court Leet, whose principal function was to regulate the local markets.[58]

In both Birmingham and Sheffield the social composition of the town councils in their early years was heavily biased towards small businessmen and away from the established urban elite. Hennock notes that although twenty-eight of the thirty-four street commissioners stood as candidates only eleven of these found their way onto the town council in Birmingham. He shows that in 1842 large businessmen and gentlemen accounted for 14 per cent of the membership of the town council in Birmingham; ten years later large businessmen and lawyers made up 20.3 per cent of the membership. Over the same period the share of representation taken by small businessmen was 46.9 per cent and 37.5 per cent respectively.[59] In Sheffield forty-two councillors were elected to serve alongside fourteen aldermen, including the mayor. Only two town trustees – William Vickers, an iron founder (who resigned from the council in 1845) and J. W. Hawksworth, merchant and manufacturer – were elected to the town council in 1843. Three had stood for election. William Fisher who came top of the poll in Brightside refused to serve. Five years later, Hawksworth and Henry Wilkinson, a silver-plate manufacturer, were the only men serving on both bodies. In 1853 there was again an overlap of only two, John Carr (surgeon) and T. R. Baker (white lead manufacturer).[60] In the course of its first decade, the council attracted an increasing proportion of small-scale agents, dealers and petty traders partly at the expense of manufacturers in the heavy trades (steel manufacturers, including men in the allied file, edge-tool and saw trades) and employers in the light trades such as cutlery and silver-plating (see Table 9).

TABLE 9 *Sheffield Town Council membership 1843–53*

	1843	1848	1853
Heavy trades	9	12	9
Light trades	11	8	9
Smaller manufacturers, agents and dealers	18	24	25
Total council members	56	56	56

Source: J. M. Furness (1893) and Sheffield directories.

In spite of these very broad similarities in the composition and situation of the two councils there were some remarkable differences in the careers of the two institutions. In the case of Birmingham, the issue of incorporation arose in the context of intense competition between Radical and Conservative parties for municipal influence. The sponsors of incorporation were overwhelmingly Radical lawyers and businessmen. Its opponents were Conservatives from a similar range of occupations. At the highest level, incorporation was opposed by men such as Lord Wharncliffe, who later supported the granting of Sheffield's charter, and, closer at hand, by the Earl of Warwick.[61] In its favour were the political skills of Joseph Parkes, the Birmingham lawyer who may also have had a hand in drawing the municipal ward boundaries so that the Tories were disadvantaged.[62] Once in being, the Birmingham town council was from the start fighting for its legal existence. After the Bull Ring riots of 1839, the government took away the council's police powers which were not restored until 1842. The Conservatives, who captured control of the Poor Law Guardians in 1840, challenged the validity of the Charter of Incorporation, and (through the lawyer, J. W. Whateley) the right of the council's appointee as coroner to exercise his powers. The county justices of Warwickshire also disputed the council's powers. The Overseers of the Poor resisted the borough rate in 1841. Four years later, the street commissioners prepared a bill (followed by another one in 1849) which would have given parliamentary sanction to an extension of their own local powers.[63]

Despite all this intense pressure, by 1851 the Birmingham Town Council had successfully sponsored an improvement bill against the initial opposition of 'the Street Commissioners, the Duddeston Commissioners, the Governors of the Grammar School, the Gas and Water Companies, and the representatives of other public and private interests which were supposed to be affected by the provisions of the bill'. The powers of the street commissioners were added to those of the town council and the former bodies ceased to exist.[64] Following a period of relative quiet during the 1850s and early 1860s the town council spearheaded an attack on the exclusivity of the King Edward VI Foundation, eventually obtaining representation on its board of governors. In the 1870s the council made a successful assault on the gas and water companies, which became municipal enterprises under council control.[65]

Contrast the progress of the Sheffield Town Council. Brought into being by reluctant ratepayers in order to prevent the county justices from having greater police powers over the town, the council was largely preoccupied in its early years with expressing radical or 'progressive' attitudes while taking care not to exceed its limited powers and budget.[66] The flavour of the council's business may be tasted in a list of some of its decisions during the late 1840s and early 1850s. In 1847 they decided not to try to purchase the Duke of Norfolk's manorial rights (12 May) but asked him, unsuccessfully, to stop keeping game on his estate near the town (8 December). In 1848 they encouraged the formation of a local medical sanitary association (26 January) but deprecated the centralising powers of the Public Health Bill (15 March). They kept a weather-eye on the projected local railway and canal bills 'but no cost on the Borough Fund to be incurred for that purpose' (12 April). They also asked, successfully, for a borough commission of the peace to be established, supplementing the county magistrates (9 August). The following year, the council petitioned for parliamentary reform and the closing of the post office on Sundays (9 May) and sent a deputation to the Paris Peace Congress (8 August). They worried about the water supply in Attercliffe (12 September) and 'ill-conducted public houses' (10 October). They established in 1850 a scale of fees for the magistrates' clerk which was 'lower than is allowed . . . in other towns' (13 March) and petitioned for parliamentary reform, the extension of the County Court Act, reduction of stamp duties and Fox's education bill (10 April). A sardonic smile is appropriate when reading that in 1851 they authorised the spending of £25 'for the better heating of the Council Chamber' (12 March).[67]

Their one very limited success in advancing their powers at the expense of local rivals was in applying pressure on the church burgesses, a body of Anglicans much weaker than the King Edward VI Foundation in Birmingham. The council proposed in 1852 that the burgesses' powers should be transferred to themselves. In the event the attorney-general approved a scheme which slightly increased the proportion of the burgesses' revenue which was to be spent upon elementary education. This occurred a year after the dismal failure by the town council to obtain an improvement bill which would have considerably increased its responsibilities. Not until 1864 was such a bill obtained and the powers of the improvement commissioners and the highways boards vested in the council.[68] However, the town trustees continued to exercise their functions and the Cutlers' Company substantially increased its influence after 1860.[69] Although Fitzwilliam gave up control over the Ecclesall manorial rights in 1866, the water company survived enormous unpopularity following the Dale Dyke dam disaster of 1864 and only yielded to municipal control in 1888. The gas company retained its independence and was vigorously expanding as late as 1924.[70]

The evidence of this section suggests that the networks of working-class and middle-class institutions already established by 1830 in Sheffield were much more resistant than in Birmingham to manipulation and erosion through the activity of 'modern' institutions. The progressive undermining of spheres of artisan independence in industry at Birmingham over the whole period contrasts with the pattern in Sheffield where a relatively high degree of artisan autonomy and strength was maintained through the craft unions until there occurred (as will be seen) a relatively effective attack upon their power in the last decade of the period.[71] Turning to the two municipal corporations, the town council in Birmingham went through three stages in its relations with (principally hostile) outside bodies. During the 1840s it was subject to intense attack; this opposition had been beaten off by 1851 and the subsequent dozen years were a period of comparative quiescence; from the mid-1860s, the town council went onto the offensive in its turn, initially (as will be seen) taking on the King Edward VI Foundation.[72] By contrast, during the first two decades of its existence the Sheffield Town Council and its institutional rivals maintained an uneasy truce. This was broken by occasional sorties on the part of the council which did little to alter the *status quo*. Not until the mid-1860s were the powers of the town council significantly increased. However, the trajectory of its ambition was far lower than its counterpart in Birmingham.

URBAN-INDUSTRIAL TRANSFORMATIONS

The institutional tendencies noticed so far will now be located within a broader analysis of urban-industrial transformations between 1830 and 1870. The most obvious alteration in the conditions of existence in both cities was the increase in population (see Table 10).

TABLE 10   *Population growth: Birmingham and Sheffield 1801–71*

				Population (000's)				
	1801	1811	1821	1831	1841	1851	1861	1871
Birmingham	71	83	102	144	183	233	296	344
Sheffield	46	53	65	92	111	135	185	240

	Decennial rate of population increase (%)						
	1801–11	1811–21	1821–31	1831–41	1841–51	1851–61	1861–71
Birmingham	16.9	22.9	41.2	27.1	27.3	27.0	16.2
Sheffield	15.2	22.6	41.5	20.7	21.6	37.0	29.7

Source: Mitchell and Deane (1962).

During the first three decades of the century both cities grew at a similar rapidly increasing rate, culminating in the heroic ingestion of people during the 1820s. Subsequently, they diverged sharply. Birmingham settled down to an almost constant rate of growth for three decades, increasing in population size by just over a quarter every ten years. The decade of the 1860s witnessed a retardation of this rate of growth. Sheffield also grew steadily after 1830 but at a slower rate than Birmingham and for two decades, not three. During the 1850s Sheffield experienced a massive demographic surge which rivalled in size the earlier wave of the 1820s. The onslaught abated somewhat during the 1860s but still amounted to a rate of increase nearly double that of Birmingham during the same decade. The demographic 'gear changes' (down in the 1830s, up in the 1850s) were much sharper in Sheffield than in Birmingham. They were related to structural transformations, for example in industry and residential patterns, which inflicted sharp reverberations upon the main body of Sheffield society. In Birmingham, the effects of transformations in these spheres were to a great extent 'cushioned' within the social structure, in ways to be explored, and in any case were more readily apparent on the fringes of the city rather than within the borough itself. This latter point is suggested if we look at the rates of population increase since 1841 in the

Greater Birmingham area, created in 1911 by addition of districts on the outskirts of the existing borough (see Table 11).

TABLE 11 *Decennial rate of population increase: Birmingham and Sheffield 1841–71*

	Decennial rate of population increase (%)		
	1841–51	1851–61	1861–71
Birmingham	27.3	27.0	16.2
Greater Birmingham	30.7	32.2	21.1
Sheffield	21.6	37.0	29.7

Source: Mitchell and Deane (1962).

The figures in Table 11 suggest that the rate of growth was increasing, fairly steadily, in the Birmingham area during the 1840s and 1850s, but that the burden was carried disproportionately by populations outside the borough itself. In any case, the rate of demographic growth slowed down both in and around the borough of Birmingham during the 1860s, dropping to rates well below Sheffield.

Industrial and urban developments followed contrasting courses in the two cities between 1830 and 1870. Sheffield will be considered first. During the 1850s and 1860s, huge markets developed for heavy steel forgings of many kinds, especially in railway construction, ship-building, armaments and machine tools. Sheffield firms such as Sandersons, Jessops and Naylor, Vickers and Co., had been engaged in steel production since the late eighteenth century but the bold venture of building large new plant on the extensive flat land north-east of the town centre in Attercliffe and Brightside was first undertaken by Charles Cammell, a newcomer to the industry. In 1845 he opened the Cyclops Works on the line of the Midland Railway going towards Brightside.[73] By 1862, a local guide was able to report:[74]

> Mr Cammell was followed by Messrs Spear and Jackson; by Messrs J. Beet and Son (now Peace, Ward and Co), Agenoria Works; Messrs John Brown and Co; Atlas Iron, Steel and Spring Works; Messrs Thomas Firth and Sons, Norfolk Works, who carry on a large steel trade, manufacture heavy ordnance, and also send out files, edge tools, and Messrs Moses Eadon and Sons, President Works; Mr Bessemer, who carries on the manufacture of steel by his own process; Messrs Wilson, Hawksworth, Ellison and Co, Carlisle Works; Messrs Sybray, Searls and Co; and others. Indeed the advantages of the locality are so apparent, that all the new steel manufactures are being built in this direction. The large extensions . . . contemplated by Messrs Naylor, Vickers and Co

are on land further outside the town near Brightside, and on the estates of Earl Fitzwilliam. The other manufacturies mentioned are on land belonging to the Duke of Norfolk. Some idea of the extent of the works in this locality, may be formed from the fact that, on the estates of the Duke of Norfolk alone, about 50 acres have been taken for manufactures, and about 70 acres more for dwellings for the workpeople, while upwards of ten miles of roads have been made. These figures refer only to this one particular locality, there being other extensions within the same township of Brightside.

When in 1856 Bessemer told the British Association that steel could be made quickly and potentially in vast quantities by blowing cold air through liquid pig iron in a convertor, he received several applications for licences to exploit this technique. None came from Sheffield, an indication of the strength of local conservatism.[75] Bessemer took the technique to Sheffield himself in 1859 and repaid the initial capital outlay of his partners eighty-one times in the first fourteen years. By 1864, both John Brown and Charles Cammell had established limited companies, each with a nominal capital of £1,000,000, to exploit the Bessemer process and, subsequently, the open-hearth process invented by C. W. Siemens. An army of labour was needed to man these new operations. The workforce of John Brown increased from 500 in 1856 to 5,000 in 1872. Cammell's payroll numbered 3,000 in 1865.[76] The transformation wreaked upon the labour market by heavy steel production in the second half of the century is shown in Table 12.[77] The expansion of the heavy steel industry was to a considerable

TABLE 12   *Employment in the light and heavy trades of Sheffield 1850–91*

	Light trades	Heavy trades
1850–1	21,350	5,200
1891	32,100	21,384

Source: Pollard (1959).

extent fuelled by immigrant labour and immigrant capital. During the demographic surge of the 1850s and 1860s roughly half the increase was accounted for by net immigration, although this understates the amount of actual immigration since considerable numbers were also moving away from Sheffield, particularly to the United States.[78] However, the mid-1860s were also the culmination of a lengthy period during which the Sheffield light trades with their proud local traditions and dependence on local capital had expanded and dominated international markets in tools and cutlery. At a point when foreign competition was beginning to throw traditional techniques and forms of organisation in the light trades into question, the north-eastern part of Sheffield was rapidly being colonised by a modern, highly mechanised industry organised on an Olympian scale. Within the new works of Attercliffe and Brightside, with the exception of the engineers, the labour force was not strongly unionised. It was subject to the stricter managerial discipline made desirable by the technology of high volume steel-making.[79] In other words, during the 1850s and 1860s in Sheffield, two modes of capitalist production – the older one reaching and passing its peak of strength, the newer one enormously powerful but still becoming institutionalised – existed side by side. Contradictions between the two modes of production were sharply experienced in firms which combined steel production with a trade in files, saws and edge-tools. One such firm was Ibbotson Bros whose spokesman, Alfred Ibbotson, complained to the Children's Employment Commission of 1865 about his men's resistance to mechanisation.[80] Another firm was Thomas Turton and Sons, under the direction of F. T. Mappin, which was acknowledged to be 'at the head of the file trade' and whose Sheaf Works were 'very large'.[81]

Contradiction and conflict in the industrial sphere was complemented by a strong centrifugal tendency in the sphere of housing. The central area of Sheffield had become very crowded by the early 1840s. Speculative house construction, much of it carried out by small builders, contributed to a movement outwards to the west, south and east. Working-class back-to-back terraced housing mushroomed around the old town, for example on the Norfolk Park Estate to the east. Those families who had their own transport or who could afford to ride on the horse-buses moved further out.[82] G. C. Holland wrote:[83]

> All classes, save the artisan and the needy shopkeeper, are attracted by country comfort and retirement. The attorney, – the manufacturer, – the grocer, – the draper, – the shoemaker and the tailor, fix their commanding residences on some beautiful site and adorn them with the cultivated taste of the artist. . . . As an illustration of the proof of one part of this statement, we may mention, that in this town there are sixty-six attorneys, and generally men of high probity and respectability, and of this number, forty-one live in the country, and generally in the most costly mansions; and of the twenty-five remaining in the town, ten have been in practice only about five years.

Over the next thirty years Upper Hallam and Ecclesall to the west and south-west benefited greatly from this tendency. In 1865, sites were advertised on Earl Fitzwilliam's estate in the Dore and Totley districts as being 'admirably adapted for villa residences, the air being salubrious and clear of the smoke of Sheffield.'[84] The number of inhabited houses in Dore and Totley increased by 50 per cent between 1861 and 1881.[85] They were on the south-west fringe of Sheffield, about as far away as it was possible to be from Attercliffe and Brightside in the north-east. These latter were the scene of vast new working-class housing developments during the same period, much of it on Norfolk land. The population of Attercliffe, for example, rose from 4,156 in 1841 to 16,574 in 1871, an increase of almost 400 per cent in thirty years.[86]

In sum, not only was the localised, artisan-controlled mode of production in the light trades being challenged by the industrial organisation of the new steel works but the cantonal pattern of close-knit neighbourhood communities in 'old' Sheffield and on its rural fringes was also being eroded and diluted by the development of class-based residential segregation within the rapidly growing city. The expansion of Attercliffe and Brightside with their vast new population of immigrants recruited to serve in the heavy steel industry dramatised the close relationship between changes in the industrial and residential spheres.

Between 1830 and 1870 Birmingham's industry became more mechanised and the average size of the unit of production increased. However, at both the beginning and the end of the period the same groups of products were prominent, notably guns, buttons, brassware and jewellery.[87] Instead of developing a sharp dichotomy between two radically different modes of production orientated to very different products and markets, Birmingham's business life continued to present a wide range of variation in scale and technique of production within its staple industries. Differentiation occurred within existing industries rather than by adding new ones.[88] A comparison of entries under different types of businesses in Birmingham directories for 1777, 1830 and 1860 yields the following comments:[89]

Although Birmingham attracted new business appropriate to the nascent engineering age from 1830 to 1860, by number of businesses top industrial trades scarcely shifted position even by 1860. Among industries jewellers, buttonmakers, coal dealers and brassfounders were predominant, betraying only slight differences from rankings in 1777 and 1830, and thus traditional lines continued to offer opportunity to new entrepreneurs. Although eighty-three percent of the entries in the 1860 directory were absent from the 1830 directory, new categories were often simply more specialised versions of established industries. For example, in 1830 the gun industry comprised nine different types of business but expanded to thirty-five types in 1860. Among the nine, the thirty-one firms in the category of gun lock and furniture forgers and filers later broke into twenty-one gun lock makers, seven gun lock filers, five gun lock polishers and twenty-nine gun furniture manufacturers. Thus, continued growth in familiar trades prompted much dynamism among business institutions.

The gun trade was centred in the district around St Mary's Church, north of the city centre. Localisation was also a feature of the jewellery trade which expanded greatly and developed a much more complex division of labour in the course of the period. As producers sought larger premises, the centre of the trade shifted from the Newhall Estate around St Paul's Church northwards beyond Great Hampton Street. Both trades were subject to the gradually-increasing impact of mechanisation. In 1854, at the time of the Crimean War, machinery was introduced on a large scale into the gun trade through the government factory built at Enfield. Eight years later the Birmingham Small Arms Company established works on 26 acres of land near the canal and railway at Small Heath, south-east of the city. A decade afterwards, Witton to the north-east of Birmingham had become the site of a large cartridge works. However, as late as 1866 J. D. Goodman could write that '[till] within the last few years, [gun] locks were entirely the production of hand labour.' Nevertheless, he continued, '[at] the present time the steam hammer and stamp are superseding the forge, and milling machinery is doing much of the filer's work.' In the jewellery trade, expansion occurred largely through the proliferation of small concerns, many set up by men who had originally been apprentices or workmen. It was reported in 1866 that there were 'few large manufactories' although such establishments were being encouraged by the increasing use of dies and machinery.[90]

Mechanisation rather than skilled handicraft work was the dominant feature of the highly-populated button and steel-pen trades, the latter being a new industry in 1830. Both trades had an indirect but strong symbiotic relationship with the gun and jewellery trades. Of the 6,000 workers in the button trade, two-thirds were women and children in 1866. They were drawn heavily from working-class families living in the traditional gun and jewellery quarters which formed a useful reservoir of cheap labour. Although it employed a great number of workers, there were few large factories in the button trade and many small shops and outworkers. By contrast, in 1866 the steel-pen trade was employing about 2,400 workers (of whom 360 were men) in only twelve establishments. A total of 330 horsepower was being applied by that date, indicating easier working conditions than the button-makers' sweatshops. It is significant that the leading steel-pen manufacturers, Joseph Gillot and Josiah Mason should have located their works in the jewellery quarter and the gun district respectively.[91]

The existence of the button and steel-pen industries, both dependent upon female and child labour, softened the contrast between skilled handicraft work in small shops in the jewellery and gunmaking quarters, and the highly mechanised factory production which was developing in, for example, the brass trade and the making of iron woodscrews. Joseph Chamberlain's description of the spread of factory production in the last-named industry was quoted in chapter 2. By 1850, screw production was spread among some thirty-seven manufacturers employing many women as machine minders. However, over the next decade and a half J. S. Nettlefold in association with Joseph Chamberlain and his father introduced American automatic screw-making machines, set up a large factory at Smethwick and increased their rate of manufacture until this firm was responsible for about 70 per cent of local screw production. The change in technology and the shift of location to the outskirts of the city were accompanied by an increased dependence upon male mechanics rather than female machine minders.[92]

Between 1831 and 1861 employment in the brass trades increased by nearly five-fold. Male workers were traditionally predominant and only about a quarter of the labour force were women and girls. As the industry expanded new plants were built in Moseley, Islington and Bordesley towards the south, south-west and south-east of the city. Housing grew up around the brass works creating new working-class areas.[93] Factory construction outside the built-up city centre towards the south and, a little later, the north became an important movement in the 1860s but it did not produce such a radical or swift transformation of the urban social environment as the expansion of heavy steel production in Attercliffe and Brightside; nor was it focused upon one industry and a clearly defined set of neighbourhoods. Factory construction outside Birmingham's built-up city centre had been occurring as early as the 1840s, when Arthur Albright began making phosphorous by the Worcestershire canal at Selly Oak. Even further back, Matthew Boulton's brass foundry at Soho to the north-west of the city had been employing over 800 workers in 1770.[94]

The building of new housing for factory workers as the city's industry developed meant that residential segregation by class became increasingly evident in Birmingham as in Sheffield during this period. For example, Ladywood to the west of Birmingham's city centre was a new working-class district which grew rapidly. Its population was 8,787 in 1841, rising to 42,774 by 1871, an advance of about 500 per cent.[95] However, there were four major differences between the structural contexts within which these processes occurred in the two cities. First, in Birmingham, unlike Sheffield, increasing residential segregation by class did not coincide with the emergence of a giant new industrial sector which divided the city by challenging the influence and assumptions of an independent and well-entrenched artisanry. The second difference is indicated by the fact that immediately adjacent to

Ladywood was the immensely salubrious suburb of Edgbaston, owned and developed by the Calthorpe family as a leafy middle-class neighbourhood with low density housing. Sheffield had no equivalent of 'Birmingham's Belgravia', in close proximity both to the local working class and to the city centre which was approximately a mile from Edgbaston.[96] When the Duke of Norfolk had essayed a similar development at Alsop Fields in the late eighteenth century it had failed to prosper.[97] Sheffield's wealthiest and most prestigious citizens took flight to the western slopes while Birmingham continued to offer an acceptable quarter in the city's midst. In 1881 the first issue of *Edgbastonia*, almost the house journal of Birmingham's civic elite, described this suburb as 'the favourite place of residence for the professional man, merchants and traders of the busy town which it adjoins with a population more wealthy than those of other suburbs'.[98]

The third difference between the cities is suggested by the comparison of inhabitants' occupations in 1851 and 1871 (see Table 13).[99] Taken together the proportional increase in domestic servants, labourers and persons of independent means in Sheffield compared to a proportional decrease in Birmingham implies a tendency towards increasing polarisation in status differences in Sheffield and decreasing polarisation in Birmingham. This impression is strengthened by

TABLE 13 *Occupational distribution: Birmingham and Sheffield 1851, 1871*

	Number occupied per thousand inhabitants (aged 20 years and over)			
	Birmingham		Sheffield	
	1851	1871	1851	1871
1 Engineering, toolmaking, metal working	206.4	199.4	258.7	264.2
2 Professional, literary, artistic	28.1	27.3	19.6	22.2
3 Mercantile	13.6	18.0	9.9	11.7
4 Transport and communications	29.2	37.2	17.0	27.1
5 Domestic servants	45.7	42.1	32.7	34.4
6 General and factory labourers	28.3	27.2	24.0	34.1
7 Persons of independent means	7.7	6.7	7.9	9.2

Sources: 1851 Census, 1871 Census.

the proportional rise of about one-third in persons occupied in mercantile activity at Birmingham compared to a proportional rise of only about one-fifth in Sheffield. As a result, Sheffield had a smaller proportion engaged in this sphere in 1871 than Birmingham could boast twenty years earlier. Since mercantile occupations were the heart land of the new white-collar lower middle class, these contrasting patterns of growth suggest that Birmingham had a much more substantial wedge of warehouse clerks, office workers, bank officials and so on than Sheffield. Members of these occupations, respectable but not wealthy, filled out the middle ranges of the urban status hierarchy and so blurred the distinction between rich and poor, strong and weak, master and man.

Finally there were very great differences between Birmingham and Sheffield in the development of their respective city centres. At the time of its incorporation in 1838, the town of Birmingham was largely restricted to the eastern half of the parish of Birmingham. During the next three decades, outward expansion coincided with a vigorous restructuring of the old town, transforming it into the nucleus of a large city. The functional segregation of public administration and trading activities had begun in 1834 when the town hall was opened about half a mile west of the Bull Ring which was a major shopping and market place. The street commissioners who managed much of Birmingham's civic business until 1851 had their public office in the Bull Ring. However, the land around the town hall became the main civic centre and was gradually occupied by public buildings such as the council house (opened 1879). Meanwhile the city's markets became increasingly concentrated in the area adjacent to the Bull Ring. The street commissioners had leased the market rights from the Lord of the Manor in 1806, later acquiring them outright. In 1834 a covered market hall was opened in the Bull Ring complementing the new town hall to the west. The wholesale slum clearance entailed in the construction of New Street and Snow Hill railway stations opened the way for the development of Colmore Row, New Street and the land in between as commercial and shopping centres.[100]

In sharp contrast, throughout this period Sheffield was characterised by a very low degree of functional segregation in the city centre. Lacking a bustling hinterland and being highly specialised industrially, the impulse towards developing a distinct commercial centre was very weak. Not Council Hall (seat of Sheffield's town council) but Cutlers' Hall and the corn exchange were the major centres of influence within municipal life. By 1860 the Cutlers' Company had been reformed to make it representative of all local steel-making and steel-using firms. The third Cutlers' Hall had been built in 1832 on the existing site in Church Street, a few hundred yards from the corn exchange just off Sheaf Bridge. From the Ellisons' office in the corn exchange the Norfolk interest cast its influence over the development of the adjacent market facilities, prohibiting their expansion into the suburb of Ecclesall early in the century, developing them after mid-century in order to exploit Sheffield's potential as a regional distributive centre for foodstuffs. Between Cutlers' Hall and the corn exchange and in the shadow of these two heavy-weights lurked the town council housed in its makeshift accommodation, the old assembly rooms on Norfolk Street.[101] No imposing colony of public buildings magnified its importance in the manner that Victoria Square announced the crescent glory of Birmingham Corporation.

Elements of 'modern' urban industrial capitalism, such as the widespread use of machinery in industrial production, the establishment of large factories and the appearance of single-class suburbs, were coming into existence in both cities, especially after 1850. However, not only were these elements related to each other in different ways in Birmingham and Sheffield, but they were associated with dissimilar tendencies in occupational recruitment, especially in the new lower middle class and working class, and in the topology of the city centres. These differences were due in part to the massive impact in Sheffield of the rapid establishment of a heavy steel industry. However, the nature of this impact was a consequence of the character of the urban and regional social structure within which it was planted. In the previous chapter these structures were compared in Birmingham and Sheffield with respect to the forms of social differentiation and bonding within networks of human interdependence. It was seen that Birmingham exhibited a more highly differentiated structure encompassing a wider range of occupations. It was also seen that the municipal level of integration was increasing in importance as a focus of solidarity and influence for social groups and as the site of institutional activity at the expense of both the neighbourhood and the county. By contrast, Sheffield offered a cantonal pattern of neighbourhood solidarities. The institutions and solidarities of two foci of the older capitalist order, the aristocratic landed estate and the parochial sphere of the town-dwelling artisanry and petty bourgeoisie, were articulated in different ways in Birmingham and Sheffield. One manifestation of these differences was the respective situations of wealthier middle-class people, members of the big bourgeoisie in the two cities: the larger manufacturers and merchants, doctors, lawyers, ministers, clergy and leisured gentlemen.[102]

In Birmingham, municipal life revolved around the alliances and disputes of the people mentioned previously. As will be seen, some of them reached out into the county for wider social and political support; others found allies within the ranks of the city's skilled craftsmen, shopkeepers, and commercial clerks. In Sheffield the position was reversed. The great landed estates, with tentacles reaching deep into urban life, and the neighbourhood communities of grinders, forgers, small stores and beer-shops constituted the framework of class relationships and political life. Sheffield's larger businessmen and urban professionals were full members of neither the aristocratic networks nor the artisan solidarities; they were marginal to both. In both cities, middle-class men and women were connected through family ties and their joint participation in voluntary associations and public bodies. They were also divided and set against each other through their distinct occupational, ideological and economic commitments. The dynamic relationship between these two tendencies worked itself out in different ways in the two cities between 1830 and 1870. Various aspects of these processes will be examined in the course of the next few chapters, first with respect to the conduct of politics (though paying attention to the religious and industrial spheres), and subsequently with respect to formal education. However, the considerable divergence between the directions in which development was tending in Birmingham and Sheffield can be shown rather dramatically by contrasting the ideas of Isaac Ironside and George Dawson.[103]

ISAAC IRONSIDE AND GEORGE DAWSON

In 1846 Isaac Ironside became the chief spokesman of Sheffield's Chartists (or Democrats, as they called themselves). The following year George Dawson became minister at the Church of the Saviour in Birmingham. Each man's ideas acquired considerable prominence in his own city during the late 1840s and 1850s, a prominence which flowed in each case from the congruence between the message preached and existing tendencies within the urban social structure.

Ironside had been born in 1808 at Masbrough, near Rotherham, a major centre of Dissent and when his family moved into Sheffield he attended the Congregational chapel in Queen Street.[104] He acquired a deep conviction that by giving ordinary people knowledge through education they would become truly enfranchised, politically and morally. Above all, education should occur through direct involvement in public affairs at the level of the neighbourhood. In the early 1850s, when his influence was at its height, he wrote:[105]

> Local and self-government cherishes and develops every moral and intellectual faculty and gives each of them in every man full scope for action; it humanises and elevates and kindles every kindly charity.

Ironside was a disciple of Joshua Toulmin Smith whom he tried, unsuccessfully, to promote as MP for Sheffield in 1852.[106] Toulmin Smith's ideas were outlined in his book *Local Self-Government and*

Centralization which had been published the previous year. He abhorred 'centralization' which he described as 'that system of Government under which the smallest number of minds, and those knowing the least, and having the fewest opportunities of knowing it, about the special matter in hand, and having the smallest interest in its well-working, have the management of it, or control over it.' The contemporary tendency to centralisation was expressed in such measures as the Sturges Bourne Act of 1818 which gave larger property owners multiple votes in vestry elections, the Poor Law Amendment Act of 1834 which created the Poor Law Boards, the Public Health Act of 1850 which established a Central Board of Health, and state intervention in the provision of education. Toulmin Smith proposed a return to what he saw as the old English tradition of 'local self-government': 'that system of Government under which the greatest number of minds, knowing the most, and having the fullest opportunities of knowing it, about the special matter in hand, and having the greatest interest in its well-working have the management of it, or control over it.' The appropriate model he argued, was the Anglo-Saxon 'folk note', a regular meeting of local inhabitants at which attendance was compulsory. At such meetings 'all and any subjects can, at any time, be brought under discussion by any persons; are fully discussed; and – having been discussed – the result of that discussion is carried out by an organised and regular machinery.'[107]

Between 1846 and 1849, successes in municipal elections gave Ironside's party twenty-two out of fifty-six seats on the town council. During the early 1850s, Ironside sought to take power back, as he saw it, to the people. He promoted the 'science of direct legislation' by instituting 'ward-motes' in Nether Hallam, Ecclesall and the wards of St Philip's and St George's. In these little local parliaments citizens were encouraged to discuss matters as varied as the state of the drains and the status of the new regime of Louis Napoleon. According to Ironside, 'the decisions of a properly convened vestry for the common good would hold against King, Lords and Commons.' Acting upon the 'authority' of ward meetings he engineered the election of seven 'people's aldermen', laid a set of deep drains in central Sheffield, mounted an onslaught upon the directors of the Midland Railway and established for a brief period a Sheffield Consumers' Gas Company.[108] That such an extraordinary series of events could occur is some indication of the relative strength of the neighbourhood as a focus of solidarity and a potential political base in Sheffield.

It is revealing to compare Ironside with a Birmingham ideologue who achieved a similar degree of local fame during the same period. George Dawson, who drew inspiration from transcendental philosophy, attracted a large and faithful congregation of Birmingham's leading citizens to the Church of the Saviour. His sermons and prayers acquired national renown. Like Ironside his primary concern was the education of the local community. The architecture of his church was modelled on a lecture theatre in the University of London. However, the focus of his preaching was not the parish but the city as a whole. Municipal affairs, he argued, should be approached with the sense of duty and altruism appropriate for the family itself. The cultivation of personal grace, so characteristic of Evangelicalsm, should be extended to a practical concern with public business. Men and women should embrace an ever-widening sphere of responsibility, reaching out from the home to the city and, still further, to national and inter-national affairs. It was Dawson who invited the Hungarian patriot, Kossuth, to Birmingham in 1851 and sat on the box of the carriage while Charles Geach rode inside.[109] However, he repeatedly told his audience that their immediate work lay in the city of Birmingham itself. Writing soon after Dawson's death in 1876, R. W. Dale recalled this preoccupation:[110]

> For many years – as long indeed as I can remember – he maintained, though for some time without much effect, the vital importance of securing for municipal offices the wisest, the most upright, and the most able men in the town. He strengthened his teaching by his example. He let men see that in his case intellectual culture and literary enthusiasm did not make a man too fastidious to fight for a good candidate in a municipal contest; and that, while he was interested in European revolutions, he was resolved to do his best to get a good town council for Birmingham.

Unlike Ironside, Dawson wished to see the powers of the town council increased, not diminished. As Hennock has shown, Dawson and other prominent members of his church such as E. C. Osborne, Robert Wright and William Harris campaigned vigorously for the local adoption of the Public Libraries Act, the Birmingham Improvement Act of 1861 and the discrediting of the petty-bourgeois regime which ran municipal affairs from the mid-1850s to the late 1860s.[111] The philosophy of Dawson was given its most memorable expression at the opening of the Birmingham Reference Library in 1866. That library, he declared, represented[112]

> the first fruits of a clear understanding that a great town exists to discharge towards the people of that town the duties that a great nation exists to discharge towards the people of that nation; that a great town is a solemn organism through which should flow, and in which should be shaped all the highest, loftiest, and truest ends of man's intellectual and moral nature.

The organic analogy is clear. In Dawson's eyes, public institutions of ever-advancing scope and complexity offered increasing opportunities for the exercise of men's duties and obligations towards one another. By contrast, Ironside perceived such institutions as a massive and alien imposition which increasingly frustrated the capacity of men to exercise their right to have their interests as members of local communities directly and fully represented. Dawson's ideas assumed a highly differentiated society within which there existed a broad consensus over means and ends. It offered a vast executive function to a civic elite. Ironside's ideal assumed a cantonal arrangement of small neighbourhood communities, each able to satisfy its major wants within its little cosmos. It minimised the distinction between the representative and executive tasks and abhorred elites of any kind. Dawson lived to see his vision acquire substance, in part at least. The ghost of Ironside, a man doomed to disappointment during his lifetime, may have taken some cold comfort from the radical programme of the Sheffield Workers' Committee in 1917.[113]

CHAPTER 4

FROM CONFLICT TO EQUIPOISE

POLITICAL, INDUSTRIAL AND RELIGIOUS CONFLICT IN BIRMINGHAM AND SHEFFIELD 1830–64

Within South Yorkshire and the West Midlands the development of large manufacturing cities was associated with decisive shifts in the equilibrium of social, economic and political power during the period 1830–70. However, the dominant tendencies were different in the two regions. In the West Midlands the shift was a lateral one, away from the county hierarchies of Staffordshire, Warwickshire and Worcestershire and towards the municipal regimes of the cities, especially Birmingham. In Sheffield the disposition of power and initiative shifted away from the neighbourhood level of integration and towards the national level.

The manifestations of these processes in the political, religious, and industrial spheres will be discussed in the course of this chapter which is divided into three parts. In the first part, the structure and political dispositions of Sheffield's municipal establishments during the 1830s and 1840s are described. During this period they confronted industrial, religious and political challenges to their authority (and indeed to all centralising authority) from movements based at the neighbourhood level. The dynamic interplay between municipal and neighbourhood establishments was increasingly superseded after mid-century by the development of new social formations associated with the heavy steel industry which was to a much greater extent oriented to regional and national levels of integration. In the second part it is argued that in both Sheffield and Birmingham the period between about 1854 and 1864 may be understood as an 'age of equipoise' during which contrary social tendencies were in approximate balance. Four axes of social differentiation and conflict are identified in terms of which the two cities are distinguished. In the third part, the sharpening confrontation between a rurally-oriented Anglican establishment and a predominantly Dissenting urban-oriented establishment in Birmingham is analysed. During the 'age of equipoise' the interplay between these establishments produced a relatively inactive town council regime whose torpor was to throw into sharp relief the energetic municipal enterprise of Joseph Chamberlain at a later date.

SHEFFIELD

During the first two decades of the period 1830–70 Sheffield's municipal affairs, as opposed to the neighbourhood concerns which preoccupied the majority of its inhabitants, were largely managed by members of two establishments. One, Tory and Anglican (or Wesleyan), was broadly satisfied with the distribution of power and prestige in pre-1832 England. The other, more liberal and including both Anglicans and Dissenters, was prepared to respond more positively to demands for 'reform' in the interests of the 'people'.[1] Up until the 1850s the latter group had the political and social edge within Sheffield, being represented by families such as the Rawsons of Wardsend, long-established in business, and the Parkers of Wood-thorpe, a legal and banking family.[2] Tory activists were to be found among the local Anglican clergy, the Wesleyan ministry, among the church burgesses and in the commanding heights of the Cutlers' Company. The Ellins, knife manufacturers, and members of the Creswick and Younge families (both in silver-plating) were notable local Tories. Their political weakness is shown by the fact that the local Conservative candidate polled only 665 out of 4,827 votes during the 1837 General Election.[3]

Both establishments tended to look to rural society for leadership. The county bench of magistrates was a point of contact between city and shire. In 1841 the three leading families were represented on the bench by the Lords Fitzwilliam, Wharncliffe and Howard and also the Hon. J. Stuart Wortley. Hugh Parker was there, along with W. J. Bagshaw. The latter two men were among the proprietors and trustees of the Tontine Inn, the centre of pre-Reform Bill politics.[4] Significantly, the Anglican clergy upon the bench were not from the town. The Church of England in Sheffield offered fewer pickings to clergymen hoping to live in style than did Birmingham. While the latter city was intersected by three parishes and offered a fair number of reasonably attractive livings Sheffield consisted of a large single parish which was divided in 1846 into a vicarage district and twenty-four perpetual curacies. This measure reduced the vicar's income to about £500 per annum compared to £1,048 that John Cale Miller was drawing in at St

Martin's in Birmingham. Miller's colleagues at the churches of St George, St Thomas, St Mary and St Bartholomew were all pocketing stipends of £500 or over. As has been seen, under a third of Sheffield's worshippers were Anglican compared to nearly half in Birmingham. The relative weakness of the church's authority in Sheffield was manifest in the very swift settlement of the issue of church rates. Sheffield's Dissenters had won the right to avoid these payments as early as 1818 but Birmingham was still divided by the question two decades later. Parliamentary representation in the two decades after the Reform Bill of 1832 also reflected the local disposition of political interests. Sheffield sent to Westminster one moderate reformer (John Parker) drawn from the professional and business classes and one radical (from 1849 J. A. Roebuck) who was popular among the artisans.[5]

The town trustees provided a base for the more liberal and reforming establishment. Thomas Asline Ward, as town collector, suggested that G. C. Holland carry out the survey published in 1843 under the title *Vital Statistics of Sheffield*. Ward, a Unitarian cutlery merchant, worked closely with three Anglicans (James Montgomery, journalist and poet, Samuel Roberts, silver-plater and Rowland Hodgson, gentleman) in a variety of philanthropic causes encompassing plantation slaves, chimney sweeps, aged females and the poor.[6] They have been described as a 'mild and ladylike set, with their tea-parties, their verse-writing, their respectable domesticity'.[7] Ward had his finger in many pies. Somehow, in the gaps between philanthropy and money-making he squeezed politics. His chief allies amongst local Liberals were a Quaker banker, two lawyers (one Congregationalist, one Unitarian), a Unitarian merchant, two more Congregationalists (a stove-grater manufacturer and a newspaper proprietor) and an Anglican colliery owner.[8]

The relative weakness of Tory and Anglican interests within Sheffield's urban population discouraged formality and continuity in the organisation of Liberal and reforming politics. Also, the over-lapping responsibilities and jurisdictions of the magistrates, town trustees, church burgesses, improvement commissioners and high-ways boards encouraged a relaxed atmosphere which was fostered by the mediation of legal agents such as James Wheat who not only was a trustee of the Tontine Inn but also served as clerk to both the town trustees and the church burgesses.[9] Furthermore, Sheffield's leading Liberals had much more in common socially with their Tory 'oppo-nents' than with the petty bourgeois and working-class leaders who were to an increasing extent attempting to seize the initiative from them. This challenge from below had industrial, religious and political expressions and threatened Tory and Liberal establishments alike.

Before the 1850s (and, in all but the first respect, after the 1850s also)

Sheffield lacked large manufacturing enterprises, a powerful Anglican hierarchy, a substantial professional and mercantile establishment and well-developed public bureaucracies. It is not surprising that the political opportunities opened up by the rapid growth of the manufacturing city should have been seized first by leaders whose constituents were the artisans and traders of Sheffield's tightly-knit neighbourhood communities. Nor is it surprising that they should strongly resist centralising and bureaucratising tendencies which would in the names of 'efficiency', 'progress' and 'discipline' take power away from the local community. The increased power of the trade societies, achieved at the expense of the Cutlers' Company, has already been mentioned.[10] A second movement, whose centre was amongst tradesmen and shopkeepers but which drew in some of the more 'respectable' artisans, took a religious form.

Following Wesley's death Methodism was riven by a conflict which Robert Currie describes as being between[11]

> Wesley's search for Christian Perfection or Scriptural Holiness, and the Methodist people's search for a religious democracy. Christian Perfection was born of an authoritarian personality. It vitalised a severe and demanding ethic. It was imposed by a drastic system of authority and control. It sought to create on earth a heaven of saints. The ideal of a religious democracy emerged in the conflict between the interests of local communities created almost incidentally in the search for perfection, and the demands of a disciplinarian hierarchy. This ideal required a religion of liberty, community and personal responsibility. It sought to create on earth a heaven of brothers.

On the one hand there was the conference, dominated by Jabez Bunting in whose eyes 'METHODISM was as much opposed to DEMOCRACY as to SIN'.[12] Itinerant ministers and an 'aristocracy' of wealthy laymen tended to support this position. On the other hand there were the lay ministers, the class leaders and the local preachers who resented the cost and power of the hierarchy. Sheffield was one of the most powerful centres of the democratic tendency in Methodism. Alexander Kilham's revolt against conference in 1797, which led to the foundation of the New Connexion, drew very heavy support from Sheffield. Kilham led his 'Tom Paine Methodists' from Scotland Street Chapel in that city till his death in 1798.[13] The New Connexion chapels, and even more so the Independent Methodist chapel in Bow Street gave expression to what John Livesey, the incumbent of St Philip's, recognised in 1840 as the Sheffield artisans' 'feeling of English Independence . . . which leads them to desire a place which they can call *their own*'.[14] When Wesleyan Methodism split over the issue of democracy in 1849, one of the three expelled 'martyrs' was James

Everett who had been a minister at Sheffield and retained close local connections. By 1851, the number of Wesleyan Methodists (supporters of conference) in Sheffield had dropped by over a third. Only sixteen of the sixty-two local preachers supported the conference.[15] The temper of this reform movement is shown in the inscription on the foundation stone of the first new chapel, built at Grimesthorpe. The stone was laid[16]

> in the presence of an assembled multitude who [had] unjustly been deprived of church membership simply because they could not conscientiously contribute their money to support a system of priestly intolerance and irresponsibility which has shaken our beloved Methodism to its centre, and bids fair . . . to vie with the Apostate Church of Rome.

The financial reference is very typical. Sheffield Methodists wanted control over their investments whether material or spiritual.

A third movement, equally contemptuous of centralising authority, also burst into local prominence in the late 1840s and early 1850s. Its spokesman was Isaac Ironside whose party had by 1849 captured nearly half the seats on the town council. Ironside's early political experience had been gained through the affairs of the Sheffield Political Union which had campaigned for parliamentary reform before the 1832 Reform Act. The union was initially a movement of artisans whose leadership was captured by moderate businessmen and professionals, headed by Thomas Asline Ward. Despite his popularity amongst the unenfranchised in Sheffield, Ward failed as a candidate in the 1832 General Election and serious riots followed. From the late 1830s artisans and small shopkeepers were drawn towards Chartism while moderate reformers such as the manufacturer William Ibbotson, with more to lose, supported the Anti-Corn Law League.[17] This was the immediate background to the success of Ironside's Chartist or Democratic Party in municipal politics. As has been seen, the town council offered a new arena of public representation to the petty bourgeoisie. Ironside was an accountant and his close followers were agents and tradesmen in a small way of business. They included a plumber and glass merchant, a surveyor, a grocer, an auctioneer, a merchant, a table-knife manufacturer, a saw manufacturer and a cabinet-case maker.[18] In 1851 Ironside challenged the informal management of Liberal politics by founding a Central Democratic Ward Association with a formidable apparatus of committees and delegates.[19] Robert Leader, whose newspaper spoke for moderate Liberals issued a warning:[20]

> The middle classes are not very likely to furnish the sinews of war for political agitation for the benefit of the unenfranchised, when it

is made a boast that they are excluded by 'democratic triumphs' from most of the wards of the borough, and efforts are being made to turn them out of the rest.

Despite his party's spectacular advances on the town council, Ironside's position was severely weakened by his failure to establish strong links with the industrial and religious movements against centralising authority. In 1839 a meeting of the 'Sheffield Organised Trades' decided, in the wake of police harassment of Chartist meetings, that it was impolitic to support that cause 'in the capacity of Trades' Union Societies'. Most local trade societies also refused to join in the wave of strikes in support of Chartism in 1842.[21] This rigidly apolitical stance of the organised trades continued throughout the period. Well-to-do artisans might support Ironside's Democrats as voters and attend their meetings but their trade societies kept strictly to industrial affairs. A similar distinction between the opinions and actions of individuals and of the organisations to which they belonged may be applied to the Methodist denominations, particularly Primitive Methodism. Wickham has 'no doubt that Primitive Methodism embraced more of the artisan class than any other church (in Sheffield) in the second half of the century'. He also points out that although Primitive Methodism provided early training for many working class leaders it was also 'the most pietistic, otherworldly [and] politically-passive working-class religion'.[22]

Ironside also encountered a serious contradiction between the Democrats' advocacy of speedy and effective reform of urban conditions and his own insistence on the importance of ward-motes, which were based upon local neighbourhoods. Having acquired great influence on the town council, he used this in 1851 to oppose an improvement bill which would have increased the council's powers to provide municipal services. The following year he unsuccessfully sponsored the candidature of his hero, Joshua Toulmin Smith, in the parliamentary election at a time when moderates such as Hoole and Dunn were divided over support for J. A. Roebuck. Meanwhile he used the highways board, whose members were sanctified by election through vestries, to promote a gas consumers' company in opposition to the existing gas company whose directors included opponents of Ironside such as Hoole and Montgomery. Acting without parliamentary licence, the new company's men dug their trenches by day while the old company sent its workforce out to fill them up again by night. Ironside's adventure was terminated by the amalgamation of the companies in 1855, with three council nominees being appointed to the company board.[23]

The Central Democratic Association ceased to exist in 1854, a date which marks the termination of a serious political challenge from below. During the subsequent decade the balance of power and initiative over Sheffield's affairs shifted away from the neighbourhood level of integration. However, it did not swing decisively towards establishments whose influence was primarily vested at the municipal level. Rather, the decade from 1854 to 1864 is characterised by a complex and unstable equilibrium between competing social tendencies. For example, although Ironside had been pushed off the town council he continued to exercise influence as chairman of the highway board which was elected through the vestries until its abolition in 1864. Furthermore, the informal management of parliamentary elections by the Liberal moderates ceased to function smoothly in the mid-1850s and a local Conservative, the lawyer William Overend, narrowly missed victory in the General Election of 1857. This was an early indication of a secular trend towards increased Conservatism in the upper ranks of Sheffield society which was hastened by the Crimean War.[24]

The conflict with Russia accelerated the growth of the Sheffield steel industry which won massive government contracts to supply armour plating for the British navy. Thomas Turton and Sons installed a Naysmith hammer in March 1855. The following year John Brown concentrated his business at the huge Atlas Steel and Spring Works. In 1858, with the help of J. D. Ellis and William Bragge, Brown built the new forges, rolling mills and convertors demanded by the Bessemer process.[25] This surge in activity was reflected in the representation of the new generation of steel manufacturers on the town council. During the five years 1848–53, in Ironside's heyday, the leading steel and file manufacturers of the day had drifted away from the council. In 1848, Turton and Sons, large-scale file manufacturers, had been well-represented, having T. B. Turton, J. Turton and W. A. Matthews in the chamber. Samuel Butcher, Edward Vickers, Charles Peace and John Marsh had carried the flag of the established steel firms. Charles Atkinson, Adam Knowles and Samuel Jackson represented Attercliffe and Brightside.[26] Between 1848 and 1853 the proportion of seats held by leading industrialists in the heavy trades fell by a quarter.[27] However, following the demise of the Democrats the newer steel manufacturers began to arrive on that body in greater force. Mark Firth arrived in 1855 and John Brown in 1856. Robert Jackson (of Spear and Jackson) and George Beardshaw were elected for Brightside and Attercliffe respectively in 1856 and were joined by Charles Cammell (Brightside) and S. S. Brittain (Attercliffe) in 1857. Alfred Beckett, a steel and file manufacturer, also joined the council that year. The arrival of the new steelmen in municipal politics was confirmed by the selection of John Brown as Sheffield's mayor in 1861 and 1862. By the following year large-scale manufacturers in the heavy trades still only held ten seats out of a total of fifty-four but the mayor was Thomas

Jessop, senior partner of W. Jessop and Sons.[28] This firm had steel works in the Park, Soho and Brightside and was described in 1862 as being 'the most extensive engaged solely in the steel trade, [with] branch establishments or depots in Manchester, Paris, Canada and at no less than six of the principal cities of America'.[29]

With the council secured by ballast such as this it was safe to transfer to it the powers of the improvement commissioners. This body was duly abolished in 1864. The Dale Dyke disaster preceded this decision by a few weeks and dramatised the issue of municipal control over public services. This event no doubt stiffened the resolve of councillors to accept the financial burden of hiring a borough accountant and borough surveyor (if only part-time). One compensation was the chance to be rid of Ironside's remaining base, the highways board.[30]

The town council did not rise in public esteem to the same degree that the new steel masters rose in private wealth and industrial influence. Instead, it suffered much criticism in the mid- and late 1860s for its failure to deal with the trade union 'outrages' (of which more below). Following its reform in 1860 to encompass the new steel industry, the Cutlers' Company offered a more congenial social circle and a more satisfying array of honorific offices. John Brown was Master Cutler in 1865 and 1866, being succeeded for each of the next three years by Mark Firth.[31] By 1868 the number of steel manufacturers on the town council had fallen to seven and in 1873 there were only nine such men although the number of council members had increased from fifty-six to sixty-four.[32]

The new men moved rapidly out to mansions in private parks on the western and south-western outskirts of Sheffield, to Endcliffe, Ranmoor and Tapton. This path had been blazed during the 1830s and 1840s by George Wostenholme, one of the first large-scale cutlery manufacturers, who was responsible for the development of the Kenwood Park Estate at Sharrow.[33] During the 1860s the movement reached its peak. John Brown built Endcliffe Hall in 30 acres of ground and probably employed about fifty servants. Mark Firth was rumoured to have spent £60,000 on Oakbrook in 1867.[34] Valerie Doe points out that such houses[35]

> were the active centres of social and political life as well as the
> tangible expression of the achievements of self-made men. These
> heads of large business concerns played a part in their
> communities not dissimilar to the part played in theirs of the
> landed elite, and they too needed a place which worked in a
> similar way to a country house as a centre of influence.

Elsewhere she describes the Victorian suburban mansion house as 'an urban branch of the great country house tradition' which persisted for an unusually long period in Sheffield as compared to other towns.[36]

> In Sheffield . . . the wealthy businessmen were loyal to the city,
> and many of them lived out their lives in the houses they built in
> prosperous middle age. In other towns, such houses were an
> anachronism almost before they were finished, to be superseded
> by real country houses on real country estates.

'Loyalty' to the city in terms of physical residence on its surrounding hills was complemented by entry into county society. For example, John Brown was appointed deputy lieutenant of the West Riding in 1867 and was knighted the same year.[37] Like their aristocratic neighbours, Firth, Cammell and Brown were responsible for the management of massive economic enterprises employing large amounts of capital and labour. The fact that many of the steel works were planted on land owned by Norfolk and Fitzwilliam and that both estates were suppliers of coal served to strengthen the bonds of interest between the steel masters and the local aristocracy. Thomas Jessop was able to acquire very large estates on the Yorkshire Wolds where he went shooting and fishing.[38] Charles Cammell bought the manor of Norton which had previously been owned by the Shore family and was resident in Norton Hall, some 4 miles south of the city, by 1852. He subsequently took 'advantage of every opportunity that presented itself . . . to purchase land in the neighbourhood'.[39] The opulent residents of Endcliffe, Tapton and Ranmoor did not in fact need to become extensive landowners in order to acquire effective insulation from the murky sources of their wealth. Attercliffe and Brightside were on the other side of the city; the Derbyshire moors were on their doorstep; and they benefited from an extensive *cordon sanitaire* of detached houses on estates for the not-quite-so-opulent middle classes many of which were planned by the same architects who had designed their own magnificent residences. Furthermore, a man did not need to worry overmuch about worming his way into county society if county society, and indeed metropolitan society, came to him. When he was prime minister, Lord Palmerston visited Brown at Endcliffe Hall and in 1875 Mark Firth played host to the Prince and Princess of Wales for nearly a whole week. On the first evening Firth's dinner table was graced by not only the Archbishop of York but also the Duke of Norfolk, the Earl and Countess Fitzwilliam and Lord John and Lady Manners.[40]

The gravitational pull away from municipal concerns towards regional and national networks of power and influence was increased by the transformation of a number of the leading steel firms into limited companies drawing on capital from outside Sheffield. This process strengthened the links of local manufacturers with financiers in other parts of the country, particularly in the Manchester area. An important agent of company formation was the Manchester accountant, David Chadwick, whose firm acquired a London office in 1863 or 1864. Chadwick's allies, many of them merchants and manufacturers from the Manchester area, normally became directors of the companies he helped to organise. These men formed a major interlocking management block in the iron, steel, coal and engineering industries during the 1860s. The enormous expense of the Bessemer process made Chadwick's propositions attractive to Brown and Cammell in 1864 and Vickers likewise in 1866 following a period of financial difficulty. Sheffield was very early in the field with respect to the formation of joint-stock companies which were relatively rare in industry until the 1880s.[41]

As a consequence of the changes outlined above, by the mid-1860s the moderately reforming and Liberal Sheffield establishment associated with the Parkers of Woodthorpe and Thomas Asline Ward was being strongly challenged by the predominantly Anglican and Conservative steel manufacturers.[42] Local Conservatism had also acquired the powerful voice of W. C. Leng, editor of the *Sheffield Telegraph* from 1864. The division between the old establishment and the incoming industrial regime was manifest in the many clashes of opinion between Leader and Leng through their respective newspapers during the mid- and late 1860s.[43]

The penalties for the new steel masters of this division within middle-class Sheffield were minimised by two circumstances. First, the influence of the old establishment over the labouring population, as opposed to its capacity to draw upon its political support by sponsoring electoral candidates, had been relatively weak since the early 1830s. The career of Ironside had damaged those links that did exist. During the Crimean War, while middle-class Liberals supported Roebuck's movement for administrative reform which he headed as chairman of the Sebastopol Investigation Committee, Ironside had thrown his lot in with David Urquhart, who was sympathetic to Toulmin Smith's emphasis on the priority of local institutions. The Sheffield Foreign Affairs Committee and the *Sheffield Free Press* (acquired by Ironside in 1855) led a virulent campaign, supported almost entirely by working men, against Russian imperialism and the government of Lord Palmerston.[44] It cannot have been pleasing for men of property to learn of Karl Marx's articles in the *Free Press*, even though their turgidity caused Ironside to complain that 'Dr Marx's articles were entombing the newspaper'.[45] The second circumstance which aided the industrial magnates of Attercliffe and Brightside was that they were not recruiting their labour force from Sheffield's old staple trades. Until the 1880s most of their workers came from country districts or other iron-working areas rather than from the local light trades.[46]

To summarise: in the period before 1854 a municipal establishment of professionals and businessmen, largely integrated through personal ties, confronted a powerful political challenge from local Chartists which drew upon the support of artisans and tradespeople whose interests were focused upon neighbourhood communities. However, Sheffield's Democratic Chartists, led by Ironside, failed to harness the organisational power of the trade societies or the more plebeian Methodist chapels. Nor did its leader overcome the contradiction between the intense parochialism which his ideology sanctioned and the difficulties of promoting urban reform in England's sixth largest provincial city through institutions focused at a level of integration below the municipality. The period from 1854 to 1864 had three dominating characteristics. The first was rapid and drastic structural transformation associated with the expansion of the heavy steel industry. The second was continuing prosperity in both the light and the heavy trades.[47] The third characteristic was the persistence of an unstable and shifting state of balance between contrary or competing social tendencies. For example, the light trades were experiencing good trading conditions at the same time as the new steel works were being established; the influx of new large-scale steel manufacturers onto the town council in the late 1850s coincided with Ironside's continued agitation from bases outside it; the Liberal establishment maintained its grip on the management of parliamentary elections but faced a serious challenge from the Conservatives in 1857. The third period, after 1864, was characterised by a strengthening of regional and national networks of influence at the expense of municipal institutions and loyalties.[48]

EQUIPOISE

During the second half of the 1860s the period of unstable equilibrium came to an end. A series of overt conflicts were fought as a result of which it is possible to identify victors and losers reasonably clearly, although both victory and defeat were far from complete. The immediately preceding period from the mid-1850s to the mid-1860s coincides, give or take a couple of years, with the decade and a half which W. L. Burn has labelled 'the age of equipoise'. He argues that the dates 1852 and 1867 mark the approximate beginning and end of a 'generation in which the old and new, the elements of growth, survival and decay, achieved a balance which most contemporaries regarded as satisfactory.'[49] He describes the period as follows:[50]

> Something of the passions, of the ingenuous and romantic emotions, which had found expression in Chartism, in Tractarianism, in the bitter controversies over the corn laws and

the sugar duties, in dozens of utopian schemes, had abated. . . . [There] was less of that single-minded vehemence which had characterized and perhaps nearly destroyed an earlier England. But in 1867, though there had been tremors and vibrations [*The Origin of Species* appeared in 1859 and *Essays and Reviews* in 1860] the surface of things could be seen as almost intact. The England of the School Boards and the highly-organised parties, the upper-middle class England where the purchase of commissions had ceased and the highest ranks of the Civil Service were recruited by open competition and talent counted for rather more than birth or connection, was still a little distant. Although there was a great deal of talk about the middle classes the government of the country was still aristocratically directed; local government of the country was still markedly and in some respects chaotically local; France rather than Prussia or Germany was the enemy to be feared; the labouring classes were still, for the most part, subordinate to their betters and their employers.

The above quotation is inevitably based upon a broad overview of processes in a number of institutional spheres and in different parts of the country. However, it is noticeable that when citing examples of mid-Victorian businessmen in his first chapter, Burn turns straight away to William Lucas Sargant of Birmingham and that in the second chapter, when noticing a few individual careers as illustrations of his theme his first two choices are Joseph Parkes, Birmingham's radical lawyer and Matthew Davenport Hill, the recorder of Birmingham.[51] It will be argued in the second part of this chapter that the period from 1854 to 1864 was indeed one of 'equipoise' in Birmingham and that equilibrium was accompanied by a substantial degree of equanimity since that city did not experience the traumatic structural changes which were inflicted upon Sheffield's population. In fact it is fascinating to discover that the central meaning of Burn's equipoise thesis is applicable, though in rather different ways and with different nuances, to both Birmingham and Sheffield. In both cities it is possible to divide the period from 1830 to 1870 into three broad sub-divisions. Before the early 1850s members of establishments presiding over key institutions in the two cities faced new or strengthened challenges from competing groups. During the subsequent period of 'equipoise' challengers and challenged were on approximately equal terms and opposing social tendencies roughly balanced out. However, by the late 1860s rising interests were able to seize the initiative and seemed set for domination. These changes were aspects of transformations within the broader regional and national configurations to which the cities belonged. In Sheffield, power and initiative shifted in a vertical direc-tion, away from members of social networks focused upon the neighbourhood and towards regional and national establishments. The municipal level of integration, with its civic institutions, networks and loyalties, remained relatively unimportant. By contrast, in Birmingham the shift which occurred was predominantly lateral or horizontal: away from the county hierarchies and towards establishments whose primary focus and commitment was the municipality.

Within each city four axes of conflict are identifiable in the period from 1830 to 1870. The first is the conflict between Tories or Conservatives on the one side and Whigs and Radicals on the other. The former, whose heartland was in the shires, were broadly satisfied with the disposition of authority and privilege in pre-1832 English society and sought to defend as much of that structure as possible, incorporating the newly wealthy where necessary and adopting fresh means of inculcating habits of deference among the lower orders in the big cities. The latter were prepared, with varying degrees of conviction, to allow the expressed wishes of the articulate and organised middle and lower orders to be recognised and realised in the new institutions of urban industrial society. The second axis of conflict was between Anglicans and Dissenters, the latter being largely excluded from the choicest prizes in public and professional life in the earlier part of the century.[52] The third axis of conflict was defined by the steadily increasing differentiation between the owners or controllers of industrial capital and the providers of skilled and (increasingly important) semi- and un-skilled labour. The fourth axis of conflict divided the executives and beneficiaries of public authority (in government, the law, chartered companies and elsewhere) from 'radicals', strongly represented in the petty bourgeoisie, who were deeply suspicious of 'corrupt' and 'exclusive' monopolies which, they believed, diverted public money and abused public responsibility for narrow and private purposes.[53]

In Sheffield as has been seen, the latter two axes of conflict were predominant. Opposition to centralising authority at all levels above the workplace, tavern and chapel was a motif common to Chartism, Methodism and trade unionism in the city. The failure of these movements to combine their organisational strength was to have an ironic historical sequel in the coalescence of the interests of Anglicanism, Conservatism, large-scale capital and national government through the emergence of the staunchly Tory steel-masters of Attercliffe and Brightside bolstered up by massive government munitions contracts. These axes of conflict were less prominent in Birmingham. Radical opposition to 'corrupt government' in that city was split during the 1830s between the supporters of Thomas Attwood, whose characteristic appeal was upward to the crown for help against 'borough mongers' who perverted the currency, and the colleagues of Joseph Allday, a small trader whose targets were more varied and predominantly local.[54] Furthermore, the organisation of new trade societies in

Birmingham was a response to employers' tactics in the 1830s and 1840s whereas in Sheffield such societies were much more deeply entrenched. The latter's very presence inhibited and delayed innovation, eventually leading to a direct and radical confrontation which was avoided in Birmingham.

The first two axes of confrontation between Tories/Conservatives and Whigs/Radicals and between Anglicans and Dissenters were much more central in Birmingham, as will be seen in the next section. Two other important distinctions between the cities may be noticed here. First, to a much greater extent than in Sheffield, the four axes of conflict cut across each other in Birmingham, producing a complex pattern of shifting alliances. Second, and related to the previous point, in Birmingham there was a much more pronounced tendency for organised interests (defined, for example, by occupation, religion and political persuasion) to negotiate with each other and throw their weight into the balance in a calculated manner in order to seek maximum tactical or strategic advantage as situations unfolded. The politics of Birmingham were more sophisticated and less atavistic than the politics of Sheffield.

BIRMINGHAM

The Free Grammar School Bill sponsored by the governors of the King Edward VI Foundation in 1830 included the proposal 'that no person shall be elected a governor who is not a member of the Established Church of England.'[55] This attempt to formalise a practice that had grown up over preceding decades was an early and unsuccessful move in a process of shoring up the defences of the powerful Anglican-Tory establishment against attacks from many quarters.[56] This establishment belonged both to Birmingham and the surrounding county areas. It had to adjust to the secular drift of power and influence towards the city, compounded by the demographic surge of the 1820s and the constitutional changes of the 1830s. By 1847 new lines of communication and avenues of influence had been established. In that year, a rigorously Anglican constitution was foisted upon Queen's College and C. B. Adderley founded an Anglican teacher training college at Saltley. Although Richard Spooner, Birmingham's Tory MP, lost his seat that year, he almost immediately found another one in North Warwickshire, evidence of the close ties that had been forged between city and county amongst Tory political managers of post-1832 politics.[57]

A key figure in Birmingham's Tory politics was John Welchman Whateley, secretary to the governors of the King Edward VI Foundation and himself a governor of the general hospital.[58] When examined before a parliamentary committee on the Free Grammar School Bill of 1842 he was asked whether it was not the case that the foundation had 'been a tory trust ever since you were acquainted with it?' His answer was: 'Yes; and there are other trusts in the town equally exclusive in their character.'[59] It was not entirely clear whether he meant other 'tory trusts' but it was bitterly pointed out two years later that of the twenty governors of the foundation, eighteen were also governors of the general hospital and that seven of the hospital's officers had connections with the grammar school.[60] The leading hospital governors at that time included Lord Dartmouth, Lord Calthorpe, the manufacturers Robert Winfield, J. O. Bacchus and Charles Shaw, the banker James Taylor and Rev. J. Garbett of St George's, the rural dean. Winfield and Bacchus were prominent Evangelical churchmen, lay members of a movement which became strong in the city after 1830. Its centre was Elmdon Hall, home of William Spooner, rector of Elmdon. The Spooner family was related to the Calthorpes and the Wilberforces. Richard Spooner's son Isaac was vicar of Edgbaston. Informal and family ties gave added strength to the Church of England Lay Association which was founded in 1839 with Lord Dartmouth as president and James Taylor as treasurer.[61]

The politics of reform were far more difficult to organise in Birmingham than the politics of conservatism. The Birmingham Political Union was founded in January 1830 on the basis of an unstable alliance between extreme Tories who hankered for a return to a pre-seventeenth century natural order and Radicals who wished to move forward to the new kind of society envisaged by Tom Paine.[62] Thomas Attwood's promise of currency reform as a universal panacea appealed to marginal merchants and manufacturers unable to cope with the immense pressures of economic and social change. His allies such as George Edmonds, a Baptist attorney's clerk, offered Birmingham's artisans a more direct and effective influence on the politics of the unfolding urban industrial society.[63] Parliamentary reform was a cause which held them together for a while. In the months before the 1832 Reform Act the union had the enthusiastic support of the crowds who gathered at Newhall Hill and the far more cautious and pragmatic backing of the professional and mercantile men whose petition in favour of reform was delivered to Attwood by Joseph Parkes in May 1832. The involvement of the latter group ceased once the limited reforms of 1832 were passed, as did that of the local shopkeepers who no longer felt a common interest with the labourers who were left as the major constituency of the union.[64]

Radical Dissenters such as Edmonds, with the support of Parkes, turned their attention to opposing the levying of church rates by the Anglican establishment. The issue caused considerable local political excitement but its unintended effect was to stimulate more effective organisation by the city's Tory Party. In 1834 the Birmingham Loyal and Constitutional Society was founded. Its most active agent was J. B. Hebbert, a solicitor who later helped in the prosecution of G. F. Muntz after a church rates riot at St Martin's Church. Hebbert 'became the recognised agent and representative of the Tory party, both in the county and the borough'.[65] Although church rates were not levied successfully in Birmingham parish after 1831 they were collected in Aston parish until 1843, and in Edgbaston parish until 1853. Another consequence of the church rate dispute was the propulsion of Richard Spooner, Attwood's banking partner and one-time supporter, into the opposing camp.[66]

However, Tory influence among the enfranchised ratepayers was insufficient to win them representation on the new town council in 1838. The Birmingham Political Union, revived in 1837, had lost the support of the shopkeepers but it had the benefit of what the organis-ation's most recent historian describes as 'a new political front in Birmingham, a coalition between the unionists [i.e. the Birmingham Political Union] and the leaders of the trades' societies, organisations of skilled labourers which had 13,000 members in the city'.[67] Backed by the *Birmingham Journal*, the Birmingham Political Union captured all the seats on the town council and appointed all the officers. The first mayor was William Scholefield, son of Joshua Scholefield, the union's former deputy-chairman. Although Thomas Attwood and William Scholefield had founded the union and entered parliament as advocates of action by national government to reform the currency, the union's most solid achievement was local: the successful compaign for municipal incorporation and the subsequent capture of the town council. It may be significant that very soon after this local political base had been constructed and occupied, the union ceased to exist.[68]

The immediate prelude to the union's demise was the National Chartist Convention in Birmingham, during which the union com-peted for leadership of the Chartists with the London Working Man's Association and Feargus O'Connor's 'physical force' movement. In 1839, as in 1832, Attwood's organisation provided a temporary focus or meeting point for disparate interests. However, on neither occasion was Attwood able to harness the energies of his apparent allies in support of his own programme. The events of the decade created a myth of Birmingham's centrality in furthering political democracy within the nation. Ironically, the decade ended with local Whigs, Radicals and Dissenters in utter disarray, with Joseph Parkes cursing the town council's 'aristocratic Bourgeois propensities' and the Tories cock-a-hoop at achieving a virtual walk-over in the Poor Law elections of 1840.[69]

Between 1839 and 1847, while the town council was under sustained frontal attack from resurgent Conservative interests in county and borough, the old leaders of the union fell out on the issues of the suffrage and (to a lesser extent) free trade. Joseph Sturge, the Quaker corn factor, took a radical position on both questions. In 1842 he founded the Complete Suffrage Union, dedicated to middle- and working-class cooperation in pursuit of a wider franchise. His supporters included Henry Hawkes (an associate of Joseph Parkes), Henry Smith (a Unitarian manufacturer and street commissioner) and James Baldwin (another Dissenting manufacturer).[70] When Joshua Scholefield died, Sturge competed with William Scholefield for the vacant parliamentary seat. The latter, who had been mayor during the Chartist riots of 1839, was less radical than Sturge. The split between them at the subsequent by-election of 1844 let in Richard Spooner as Birmingham's first Tory MP, with G. F. Muntz serving as a Liberal. This Tory success was matched in the town council. Between 1844 and 1846 Tory representation there increased from nil to eight. However, during the General Election of 1847, William Scholefield adopted a position more clearly in favour of greatly widening the franchise. Spooner was defeated and the Tory advance was at last slowed down.[71]

The late 1840s were a minor watershed in Birmingham's political and religious life as they were in Sheffield's. The radical anti-centralising tendencies of Sheffield's Chartists and Methodists were powerfully expressed in those years, strengthening the organisational barriers to close cooperation between leading local businessmen and professionals and the lower middle and working classes. In Birmingham, by contrast, these years witnessed a new determination by the more prosperous Whigs and Dissenters of Birmingham to cultivate their links with skilled artisans and the middling commercial classes coming into existence. The willingness of artisans to cooperate in this political alliance is likely to have been increased by the signal failure of their own attempts to resist erosion of their traditional customs by industrial action. For example, following disputes in the glass industry in 1846 and 1848 the local bench found for the employers and imprisoned the offending workmen. In both cases the magistrate was the prominent local Tory, Charles Shaw, later described by one of his friends as 'the *hardest* man in Birmingham'.[72] The liberal strategy of cooperation was aided by previous experience of collaboration between leaders of political and industrial organisations in the later days of the Birmingham Political Union. The campaigns of the union and the Dissenters had also been thoroughly intertwined during the long dispute over church rates. This complex interplay between political, industrial and religious movements had been lacking in Sheffield.

Discontent with the exclusive practices of the Anglican establishment reached into the upper ranges of Birmingham society. As a long standing and thriving market and manufacturing centre, Birmingham was well-stocked with prosperous members of old Dissenting congregations. The Quaker and Unitarian families were the most distinguished, by and large, the former strong in commerce and manufactures, the latter tending to gravitate towards the professions. The Congregationalist and Baptist congregations were less wealthy and 'genteel'.[73] Prominent among the Unitarians were the Kenricks, Rylands and Beales while the Society of Friends boasted the Cadburys, Bakers, Barrows, Goodricks and Sturges.[74] George Goodrick was a political ally of Joseph Sturge and a close friend of many Chartists.[75] However, deep involvement in radical politics was not a necessary precondition for the creation of grievance. The Quaker industrialist Richard Tangye tells in his autobiography that the 'road locomotive' which his firm developed was effectively prohibited by parliament because the 'squires became alarmed lest their horses should take fright'.[76] The Congregationalists produced fewer political radicals although their number included the jewellery manufacturer Henry Manton who founded the Birmingham Sunday School Union in 1842. Sixty-one years later he was remembered as a 'true and earnest Liberal of the old Birmingham School'.[77]

The Baptists, on the other hand, included not only George Edmonds but also the solicitor William Morgan who had been active in opposition to church rates and who became town clerk in 1852. A close friend was another Baptist, the manufacturer William Middlemore. The Middlemores were an ancient Birmingham family and William Middlemore acquired leading positions in several local companies. Another ardent Baptist was John Skirrow Wright who had his goods distrained on several occasions for non-payment of church rates.[78]

Memories of ancient wrongs were still sharp. The Unitarian solicitor, H. W. Tyndal, was a descendant of the sixteenth-century Protestant martyr. Richard Tangye collected relics of his hero, Oliver Cromwell. William Sands Cox owned the chair upon which Charles I had sat during his trial at Westminster Hall.[79] However, the presence of old Dissenting congregations was not in itself a sufficient condition for the emergence of a strong civic establishment, actively identified with the prestige of municipal institutions and politically engaged with Conservative interests. It has been calculated that of the eight largest boroughs outside London in 1851, Birmingham had the largest proportion of Unitarians and Quakers amongst adherents to religious denominations. Between them, they accounted for a 4.9 per cent of all worshippers. However, the second highest proportion of Unitarians and Quakers combined – amounting to 3.4 per cent – is to be found in Sheffield where the 'civic gospel' was very undeveloped throughout this period.[80] Although this comparison does not take account of members of Dawson's Church of the Saviour, which had the support of many Unitarians, it emphasises the need to relate tendencies in the religious sphere to other aspects of social structure. Ties of religious affiliation, interwoven as they were with business, professional and kinship ties, made an important contribution to a political strategy which also, however, owed a great deal to the balance of power along three axes: between urban and rural interests, between the Tory establishment in Birmingham and its opponents, and between the professional and business elites of Birmingham and their labouring and clerical employees.

The urban estates of Calthorpe, Gooch, Colmore, Adderley and Inge 'had not reached their high money-making point in the 1830s'.[81] Although the growth of the city was to increase the riches of these genteel interests it did not magnify their political influence within Birmingham itself. The inactivity of the town council during the 1850s offered much scope for private munificence by the Calthorpes, amongst others, but the latter did not seek to exercise political leadership.[82] C. B. Adderley offered the council land for a park in 1857 but he was turned down. When the following year he obtained an injunction against the council to try to stop it fouling the river close by his home at Hams Hall, Adderley indirectly helped to stimulate a slow revival of municipal activity which would ultimately swamp the county influence around Birmingham.[83] In 1839 Lord Hatherton, a leading peer in South Staffordshire, had still been confident that political affairs in the county at least could be managed between himself and Lord Ward: 'he and I could keep the county quiet,' he wrote. However, in 1853 he was telling his diary:[84]

> The patronagage of the seats for the Southern Division is passing into the hands of the trades in the chief towns. In my earlier days they neither thought of it – or were thought of by others. The chief county families settled the matter among themselves.

He was no doubt thinking mainly of the coal and iron masters but the general tendency benefited Birmingham, and not only Dissenting manufacturers. For example, when in 1849 the Bishop of Worcester tried to send a diocesan inspector into the elementary schools run by the King Edward VI Foundation, the headmaster, Rev. E. H. Gifford, tartly refused to permit it.[85] The underlying shift of political weight away from the county and towards the city meant that although the Tory interest in Birmingham and its rural hinterland had been able to exploit Whig and Radical disarray in the borough during the 1840s, the urban constituency was steadily increasing in significance. As has been seen, institutional barriers to manipulation from above such as protected Sheffield's artisans were less well-developed in Birmingham. Despite their many failures, the careers of the Birmingham Political Union and the Complete Suffrage Association had provided the Tories' opponents with valuable experience in political negotiation with local artisans. This experience was exploited.

James Baldwin, who had worked in the Complete Suffrage Union, founded the Birmingham Political Council in 1848. His allies included the Chartist shoemaker John Mason, who declared the following year that 'the strength of democracy consists in reconciling the various classes of society, and inspiring every man with a just confidence of public order and security.' Baldwin was proud to be a self-made man as was John Skirrow Wright who was an active member of People's Chapel which he helped to found in a working-class district in 1848. Political debate was as common as religious worship in the chapel and Wright helped to organise Sunday school teaching, penny banks and clothing clubs among the congregation. He was an enthusiastic supporter of the Birmingham Freehold Land Society, being the twenty-sixth member and the first allottee on the first estate purchased by the society.[86] The new lower middle class was also fished with this net of unpatronising patronage. In 1846, George Dawson presided over a meeting at which the Birmingham Clerks' Association was founded to campaign for early closing. Two years later, Baldwin spoke at a meeting of the clerks and assistants during which they declared for universal suffrage. By 1853 a Professional, Commercial and Manufacturing Clerks Association was in existence.[87] The political relationship between the Liberal leaders and their artisan and lower middle-class supporters depended upon the cultivation of an atmosphere of mutual respect and good humour, as was exemplified by Muntz's appearance before the non-electors in 1847, described in chapter 2. During the 1850s and 1860s the alliances forged in the late 1840s were strengthened: for example, through the meeting of electors and non-electors to adopt John Bright as Liberal candidate for parliament in 1857, through the work of the Birmingham Reform Association (founded 1858) which embraced 'men of all shades of liberal opinion, enfranchised middle class and non-electors', through meetings of the Radical Reform League (from 1861) and through the work of the Birmingham Liberal Association (from 1865).[88]

By the early 1850s Tory and Liberal establishments in Birmingham were in approximate balance with each other, the former sustained by gradually weakening county hierarchies, the latter by gradually strengthening artisan and lower-middle-class organisations within the city. The collapse of the resistance of the street commissioners to the town council's improvement bill enacted in 1851 reflected the increased weight carried by a Liberal Party which was building up a solid lower-class constituency. However, during the 1850s the town council did not greatly expand its activities; nor did it follow up the demise of the street commissioners by attempts to supplant other competing bodies. In 1855, for example, a plan to buy out the water company was defeated and two years later Piggot Smith, the nationally-renowned borough surveyor inherited from the street commissioners, was sacked. Schemes for road-building and improving sanitation came to a virtual halt. When a government inspector pointed out that the borough needed 100 more policemen, a derisory fifteen were appointed. The city's reliance on voluntary efforts of various kinds to provide public services continued. Facilities for popular recreation were provided by the Botanical and Horticultural Society and Calthorpe Park, the latter being opened to the public in 1857. To the services provided by the Birmingham General Hospital and the grammar school were added those of the Birmingham and Midland Institute, founded in 1854.[89]

The foundation of the Midland Institute illustrates the state of delicate equilibrium which had been reached by 1854. The institute's most active sponsor was Arthur Ryland, a prominent Unitarian lawyer who had served with Sturge's old ally Henry Smith on the Street Commission. Although Ryland had initially resisted the abolition of that body he had ultimately cooperated in the transfer of powers and became a councillor in 1854. Ryland, who was prominent in the Birmingham Law Society, was to be remembered among other things for his labours to amend the act disqualifying practising solicitors from the county bench but in founding the institute he cooperated wholeheartedly with the county establishment. The first president of the institute was Lord Lyttelton and, as has been seen, his immediate successors were drawn from the neighbouring shires. *Ex officio* members of the first council included Rev. E. H. Gifford, who had resisted the Bishop of Worcester's demands to inspect the grammar school in 1849 and J. T. Law, the chancellor of the Lichfield diocese, who had helped impose an Anglican regime on Queen's College two years before that.[90] The institute's council also included the mayor and four town councillors but they were swamped by thirteen other elected governors headed by local gentry such as Sir Francis Edward Scott and William Mathews. Active Tory politicians were represented by Richard Spooner and J. B. Hebbert. They sat beside more radical men such as Henry Hawkes, Charles Sturge and John Jaffray. The institute's auditors were R. L. Chance, a glass manufacturer whose family had extensive political influence in Staffordshire and Worcestershire, and the merchant George Dixon, who was to be an ardent advocate of municipal interests.[91] The institute was organised into a general department, providing culture for the upper ranks of Birmingham society and an industrial department, offering useful knowledge to Birmingham's artisans and clerks.[92]

As in Sheffield, 1854 or perhaps slightly earlier marks the beginnings of a brief period of 'equipoise' lasting until the middle of the 1860s. One of its manifestations was the cooling of sectarian rivalry between

Church and Dissent during these years. For much of this period John Cale Miller was the rector of St Martin's Church. Relations between Miller and John Angell James, the Congregationalist minister of Carr's Lane Chapel were close enough for an informed observer to write of an 'underground connexion' existing between the churches. Controversy over issues such as the 'papal aggression' and Sunday observance did not divide Church from Dissent but set liberals against Evangelicals within each. By the time of the Crimean War, the local Tories had joined the Liberals in support of free trade but the latter subsequently divided on the war itself. John Bright, who sat for Birmingham from 1857, drew the support of anti-Palmerstonian Radicals such as James Baldwin and Henry Hawkes. Whigs, such as Van Wart drifted towards the Tories.[93]

Throughout this period, a potent source of disagreement within city and county, church and chapel was the question of the proper limits of state activity, both locally and nationally. Education was a focus of such disagreements. Among the prominent local landowners were C. B. Adderley (later Lord Norton) who became vice-president of the Committee of Council on Education in 1858 and Sir John Pakington whose resolution in the House of Commons that year led to the Newcastle Commission.[94] Adderley's friend and neighbour, Lord Lyttelton had presided over a national conference in Birmingham on industrial and reformatory schools whose object was to stir up public opinion in favour of legislation.[95] The high churchman Adderley found a strong ally in M. D. Hill, the recorder of Birmingham who, although an Anglican came from a family of strict Dissenters. However, Anglican opinion ranged from Adderley's enthusiasm for state involvement to the more cautious conservatism of George Lea, vicar of Christ's Church. Hill's positive approach to government action was counterbalanced by the militant voluntarism of the Dissenting minister John Angell James.[96]

These disagreements amongst the leaders of Birmingham society in conjunction with the temporary stalemate in power relationships opened up a political corridor through which an Economist party could advance to influence on Birmingham Town Council in 1855. Its leader was Joseph Allday who had been the principal rival of Attwood during the early 1830s for the support of Birmingham's shopkeepers and small tradesmen. Some of Allday's activities recall Ironside's campaigns against lapses by government. Allday stirred up public opinion against clerical abuse of the church rates, mismanagement at the Court of Requests and corruption in Birmingham gaol. This latter crusade had inspired Charles Reade to pen his novel *It's Never Too Late to Mend*.[97] In his *Personal Recollections of Birmingham and Birmingham Men*, Eliezer Edwards described the visits of 'the mighty and omniscient Joe Allday' to the Woodman Tavern in Easy Row. On these occasions[98]

the discussion sometimes became a little more than animated, the
self-assertive Joe making the room ring . . ., as he denounced the
practices of those who ruled the destinies of the town. Here one
night, lifting his right hand on high, as if to appeal to Heaven, he
assured his audience that they 'need not be afraid.' He would
'*never* betray the people of Birmingham!'

Both Ironside and Allday distrusted the motives and competence of
public officials who spent ratepayers' money. However, Ironside's
advocacy of ward-motes was foreign to Allday whose constituency
was 'the people of Birmingham'.

The social composition of the Economists was similar to that of the
Sheffield Democrats. Allday's party was led by a draper, a cabinet
maker and a vestry clerk. It is significant that the dominance of both
Ironside and Allday within municipal politics was effectively ended by
their opposition to improvement bills. Having fought bitterly against
the introduction of the Improvement Act of 1861, Allday retired from
the town council in disgust. During the 1860s Allday's successors such
as Thomas Avery, appropriately enough a scale manufacturer, were
preoccupied with keeping borough expenditure in balance with a
modest income from the rates.[99] However, slowly and grudgingly they
were prepared to concede the necessity for council control to be
extended over essential services like the water supply. The gradually
increasing influence of a more generous conception of the town
council's role is indicated by the fact that William Harris, a disciple of
George Dawson and later a colleague of Joseph Chamberlain, worked
closely with Avery in the late 1860s.[100] However, by that time
Birmingham's 'age of equipoise' had come to an end.

To summarise: in contrast to the vertical shift of political influence in
Sheffield, away from the neighbourhood and towards the county and
national levels, in Birmingham a lateral shift occurred which benefited
the borough at the expense of the surrounding counties. Although
kinship and private connections were important in Birmingham as in
Sheffield, the greater structural complexity and 'dynamic density' of
the former city encouraged a greater reliance on formal organisations
in the political arena. Also the interplay between political, religious
and industrial issues and organisations was much greater. The spirit of
Birmingham's public life in this period is nicely conveyed by John Cale
Miller, who wrote in 1851 that in all '*politico-religious* questions a
Minister is not only justified in giving, but is bound fearlessly to give,
expression to his opinion, and to influence, by all fair and legitimate
means, the opinions of others.'[101]

Tory interests, well-placed in prestigious institutions such as the
grammar school and the general hospital, had been able to respond
quickly to the new constraints of post-1832 politics and by the mid-

1840s they held the initiative. However, the Tory alliance between urban professionals and businessmen and country gentry was by the end of that decade being increasingly counterbalanced by a strengthening of the links between, on the one hand, Liberal professionals and businessmen and, on the other hand, members of Birmingham's artisanry and lower middle class. From about 1854 a state of approximate equilibrium existed between county and borough and between Tories and Liberals. Internal divisions on matters such as the relative influence appropriate to state institutions and voluntary associations produced conditions for the establishment of a regime of Economists on Birmingham's town council. Although their social composition and attitudes towards public spending were reminiscent of Ironside's Democrats, the Economists sought their victories on the council, not in ward-motes.

In the wake of the decade of 'equipoise' Birmingham's big bourgeoisie of businessmen and professional men was divided by a conflict, running through all its major institutions, between a county-oriented establishment and an establishment closely identifying itself with the concerns of all Birmingham's citizens. By its creed, expressed in 1861 through the words of George Dawson, the latter defined itself in opposition to traditional institutions:[102]

> It was the tendency of old associations, old corporations, old churches and the like, to go to ruin and to serve no longer the objects which in bygone days they were established for. . . . But while the old guilds and the old corporations had declined, we had found a new plan of forming ourselves together more in accordance with the thought and feeling of the time, and capable of bringing about a better union of classes.

The city itself was to undertake the task of caring for its inhabitants since[103]

> a great town exists to discharge towards the people of that town the duties that a great nation exists to discharge towards the people of that nation.

The new civic establishment was largely successful in winning the support of Birmingham's artisan population as well as making significant headway among the new white-collar lower middle class. As it re-acquired the aggressive strain of Nonconformity which had been expressed three decades before it also offered a congenial focus of allegiance for Dissenting shopkeepers and related elements of the old petty bourgeoisie.

In chapter 3 it was argued that the institutions and solidarities of Birmingham and Sheffield could be understood in terms of the relations between the big bourgeoisie and the two foci of the older capitalist order centred respectively on the landed estate and in the social networks of artisans and the petty bourgeoisie. In Birmingham, the big bourgeoisie divided into two sections, each establishing an alliance with a major wing of the old order. Birmingham's artisans and small traders were inheritors of norms and practices belonging to an age before mechanisation and bureaucracy although both had been constrained to adapt, the former through the paternalistic but forceful insistence of employers and the latter through the painful learning experiences of men like Allday and Avery. A complex interplay between a yearning for old ways and a modernising dynamism, between pressures to harry ancient enemies and a growing fear of new social dangers was to characterise the movement which Joseph Chamberlain was eventually to lead.[104] The division of Birmingham's business and professional leaders between the two wings of the old order is worth emphasising since it throws into sharp relief the contrasting pattern in Sheffield. In that city, as has been seen, the big bourgeoisie was acquiring great wealth and influence and a new set of leaders with the rise of the heavy steel industry. This new establishment did not divide between the two wings of the old order but threw its weight decisively onto the side of the great landed magnates in opposition to long-entrenched artisan and petty-bourgeois solidarities whose manifestations had included the trade union 'outrages' and Ironside's democratic political movement.[105] As will be seen, the division within Birmingham's middle-class leadership was paralleled by a serious split within Sheffield's artisan population. An exploration of these two schisms, which had important consequences for the subsequent development of class relationships and institutional orders in Birmingham and Sheffield, will be carried out in chapter 7. Before that, however, the emergence of a distinctive pattern of provision in the sphere of formal education in each of the cities will be described.

CHAPTER 5

'THE TRAINING UP OF WELL-EDUCATED, SOBER, LOYAL AND OBEDIENT SERVANTS'

ELEMENTARY AND SECONDARY EDUCATION IN BIRMINGHAM AND SHEFFIELD 1830–70

The most important fact about education in the period 1830–70 is that it was provided and consumed almost entirely by volunteers. This was particularly the case in Birmingham and Sheffield which were practically untouched by the provisions of the Factory Acts. In 1851 less than 3 per cent of children attending school in the two cities were (at the behest of the guardians of the poor, employers or magistrates) attached to workhouse, factory and industrial schools. Endowments subsidised the education of less than 10 per cent of pupils. Government money, entailing the threat of increased central direction, began to flow more freely in the late 1850s but compulsory attendance at elementary schools was not generally required until after 1870.[1]

Members of all social classes participated as sponsors or clients of educational institutions, giving the time, money and energy needed. Because of this formal education provides a sensitive indicator of differences between cities with respect to the social fissures and alignments that occurred as the growing manufacturing city impinged upon the old order. In order to capture in some degree of fullness the way formal education participated in the development of local class structures it is desirable to consider together institutions catering for a wide range of middle-class and working-class groups. In this chapter secondary and elementary education are discussed. In the following chapter adult education and medical schools are examined.

There are two strands of argument interwoven within these chapters. First, a number of persisting structural characteristics of formal education in each city are interpreted as particular aspects of the forms of social differentiation analysed in chapters 2 and 3. For example, it is argued that the pattern of secondary education which developed in each city was an aspect of: the level of commercial and professional activity; the relative social power of professional as opposed to commercial families; and the relative influence of traditional status norms emphasising classical learning (as opposed to the market in business occupations) in regulating the relations between schools and clients. In Birmingham the schools of the King Edward VI Foundation acquired a central position within the city's array of civic institutions and became a major object of political conflict. The foundation served as an institutional nexus closely linking together the schooling of professional and business families in an educational context which preserved the supremacy of classical learning. These schools greatly diminished the potential middle-class clientele of the private sector locally and, along with the Edgbaston Proprietary School, were for many an acceptable alternative to boarding public schools. In Sheffield secondary education was dominated by private provision oriented to vocational, particularly commercial studies. Boarding school was a much more attractive option for professional and business families.

As will be seen, the pattern of elementary education in each city was greatly influenced by the level of demand for juvenile labour and the vigour of apprenticeship as a form of industrial training under the control of the trade unions. In both cities working-class clients of educational institutions expressed a combination of motivations with respect to schooling. Among these were the desire to obtain marketable skills (such as literacy and numeracy) and the wish to express 'respectability'. In both cities also, middle-class sponsors had mixed motives. These included: the struggle for relative advantage between competing middle-class establishments, in part expressed as a contest between Anglicans and Dissenters; the attempt to maximise their influence over the socialisation of working-class youth; and, linking the two, the Evangelical mission to save souls and cultivate a Christian morality within domestic and class relationships. However, the relative priority of these different motives and their means of expression differed between the two cities. For example, it was more difficult in Sheffield than in Birmingham, especially at the beginning of this period, for working-class people to obtain marketable skills through formal education without a loss of 'independence'. The paucity of private schools for members of their class and the bureaucratic regimentation of the public day schools made Sunday schools a more popular source of instruction than in Birmingham where private provision was more abundant at this level.

Similarly participation in adult education in Sheffield entailed either subjection to a stifling middle-class morality or an assertion of self-government by artisans in their 'own' institutions. In Birmingham, by contrast, a less tense relationship between the classes was maintained within adult education. This reflected the weakness of autonomous artisan institutions in that city and the more relaxed disposition of members of the big bourgeoisie towards their employees. In these conditions the conflict between evenly-balanced civic elites within this bourgeoisie acquired great prominence and structured the provision of elementary day schooling in the public sphere. By contrast, in Sheffield a 'truce' developed whereby Dissenters maintained pre-dominance in the sphere of Sunday schooling and the Church of England was allowed to build up a leading position in the sphere of weekday schooling. In this city the major axis of conflict was not horizontal, within the big bourgeoisie, but vertical, between members of that class and the labouring population. It was expressed, for example, in the hostility of Anglican clergy towards apprenticeship.

The second strand of argument refers to the participation of formal education in the transformation of class structures and related aspects of social differentiation as analysed in chapters 3 and 4. Between the 1830s and 1850s the provision of education in Birmingham was one aspect of a broader process which had three aspects: conflict occurred within a divided big bourgeoisie; there was a steady expansion of the network of civic institutions especially in the educational and cultural spheres; and the independent influence of working-class inhabitants within both the educational sphere (as clients of private schools) and the industrial sphere (as members of trade unions) was weakened. By the mid-1850s conflict within the big bourgeoisie was being dispersed or contained. Birmingham's labouring population were becoming tied in to a complex network of institutions through which inter-class control and intra-class bargaining took place.

Two examples may be mentioned. First, the progress of the King Edward VI Foundation was greatly affected by the conflict within the big bourgeoisie. Its tentative movement in the direction of the public boarding schools was halted during the 1830s by opponents of the Anglican establishment. However, subsequent expansion of the foun-dation's local educational provision strengthened its influence over the lower middle class. Second, during the 1830s and 1840s the Church of England, having been under attack on the issue of church rates, succeeded in greatly extending public day school provision for working-class children at the expense of private schooling. Their efforts were matched by their Dissenting opponents. Jointly, the progress they made before mid-century in 'coralling' working-class children within their schools was paralleled by the steady erosion of artisan privileges in the sphere of industrial production.

Meanwhile, as will be seen, the development of medical education in Birmingham was affected by conflict between, on the one hand, lawyers and clerics strongly connected to county society and, on the other hand, doctors whose influence was increasing in the course of urban industrial growth. By contrast, in Sheffield urban professional men measured their success not by their capacity to resist the old rural order but by the extent to which they were accepted by it. There were parallel differences between the cities in the development of elementary education although in this case the most powerful constraints in Sheffield derived from the neighbourhood level rather than the county. Before 1870 the provision of public elementary day schools made comparatively little headway against the contrary assertions of neighbourhood autonomy expressed through Chartism, plebeian Methodism and the trade societies. More specifically, in contrast to Birmingham, elementary education was in competition with the structures of control in the industrial sphere rather than complementing them. A decisive transformation in social relationships occurred at Sheffield during the two decades after mid-century. The growth of the heavy steel industry had three effects with important implications in the educational sphere. First, the relative influence of the trade societies and their apprenticeship rules was greatly reduced. Second, a considerable growth occurred in a section of Sheffield's population whose offspring were subject to the control of neither the trade societies nor clerical educationists. Third, a new elite of steel manufacturers was formed whose members had the political and economic capacity to construct a more extensive system of elementary and secondary education. However, little was done before the 1870 Education Act, a state of inactivity which reflected the weakness of either cooperative or competitive impulses in the public sphere in Sheffield.

Two other general points should be made. First, it will be seen that strong links were already developing between the different sectors of education in Birmingham by the 1850s, forming one part of the complex web of institutional bonds meshing together establishments and social classes in that city. Sheffield's educational enterprises were far less closely tied to each other and to other institutional orders within the city. This was one expression of a deep-seated revulsion in many parts of Sheffield society against participating in extended networks of interdependence and thereby increasing the elements of vulnerability and uncertainty in social life. By contrast, Birmingham's educational institutions tended to be legitimated by their sponsors in terms of their responsiveness to a wide range of demands from different sectors of society. They tried, of course, to channel this demand for their own purposes but it was the comprehensiveness of the service on offer which they stressed before their public. By contrast, educational schemes in Sheffield tended to be either efforts by special interests to look after their own exclusive concerns or speculative attempts at drilling through the gritty barrier protecting labouring communities against intrusion from above. The Church of England broke many a bit in this endeavour. The code words of Birmingham education were 'responsiveness', 'encouragement' and 'comprehensiveness'. In Sheffield the code words were 'exclusion', 'inhibition', 'discouragement', 'rescue' and 'salvation'.

Second it should be emphasised that solidarities focused upon the municipal level of integration in Birmingham exercised, through their complexity and aura of self-confidence, an increasingly strong gravitational pull on local neighbourhoods and the county. By contrast, in Sheffield the city's middle class were hemmed in between the confident patrician culture of the country houses and the vigorous 'rough' culture of Sheffield's streets and woods. Schoolrooms and lecture halls were irrelevant to the latter.[2] When he first came to the town, Mr Ashley of the Lancasterian school had been shocked 'by the dog-fighting exhibitions on Sundays, in the vicinity of the town':[3]

> Such a concourse of young men and boys in the field on the Sabbath, struck me as being a peculiar feature in the manners of the people; and, as I saw them only at a distance, I at first supposed that pugilistic contests were the occasion of these assemblies, till their number and frequency convinced me that it must be some more popular amusement that could congregate such numbers so constantly, and I soon learnt that these cruel and barbarous scenes were peculiarly interesting to the youth who systematically train a great number of dogs for the purpose.

By the 1840s, such sports were anachronistic in Birmingham. In 1841 the rector of All Saints remarked of part of his flock[4]

> The population of Nineveh is much behind the rest of Birmingham in moral, religious, and intellectual habits. Bull-baiting was only given up two years ago, being kept up longer than in any other part near Birmingham.

It remains to provide evidence to support the generalisations set out above, beginning with secondary education.

SECONDARY EDUCATION

In 1552, Edward VI endowed a free grammar school in Birmingham with lands yielding £21 per annum. In 1603, Thomas Smith endowed a free grammar school in Sheffield with lands worth £30 per annum. By the time of the Schools Inquiry Commission the King Edward VI Foundation was worth over £12,000 per annum, an income greater than the combined total receipts of the other thirty-nine endowed grammar schools in Warwickshire, Worcestershire and Staffordshire (excluding Rugby School). At the same period Sheffield Grammar

School could scrape together a mere £200 a year. The headmaster of King Edward VI Grammar School proposed to the members of the Schools Inquiry Commission in 1865 that this school should stand alongside Rugby, Harrow and Eton at the head of a national system of endowed public schools.[5] By contrast, the assistant commissioner in Sheffield reported:[6]

> The general character of the institution is that of a secondary or commercial school of a high class rather than of a purely grammar school. . . . [It] leaves one great want, that of a high or classical school, still unsupplied.

Birmingham's endowed grammar school had reaped the benefit of its favourable location in a thriving centre of commerce and on the crossroads of national communications. The foundation's income had risen four-fold since 1824 and was increasing further as leases fell in and property values moved upwards. A huge debt had recently been settled by sales of land to the London and North Western Railway Company.[7] The equivalent institution in Sheffield, marooned in its isolated collection of manufacturing communities, had been starved of funds and clients.

The career of Birmingham's grammar school up to the 1850s is woven into the broader conflict between municipal establishments for control of the city's institutions described in chapter 4. In 1842 the town council expressed the opinion that the revenues of the King Edward VI Foundation 'if duly husbanded, would amply suffice to furnish the means of sound instruction to every family in the borough'.[8] The foundation was in fact in the middle of a programme of expansion which between 1837 and 1852 provided four elementary schools, each placed in one of the four quarters of the town complementing the grammar school which was at the town centre in New Street. By the latter date over 1,000 boys and girls were receiving instruction in these schools which, like the grammar school, charged no fees and admitted pupils on the recommendation of the twenty governors of the foundation. The term 'elementary' is misleading in so far as it suggests that the schools were patronised by the poor. The school registers show that from the beginning almost all the children were the sons of tradesmen and artisans, shopkeepers, clerks and small manufacturers. These schools were under the general superintendence of the headmaster of the grammar school and their curricula included geography, history and the casting of accounts. By the 1860s Latin was being taught in one of the schools.[9]

Three major complaints were directed against the foundation. The first was that its rapidly growing revenues were under the close control of a narrow clique of Tories, with the solicitor J. W. Whateley at the centre. The second was that the funds of the foundation were not being used to help the 'poorer classes, to whom it is in name and, in substance, ought to be principally devoted'. The third was that the grammar school concentrated upon classical studies to an intolerable extent in a large manufacturing city. Before mid-century the main attacks came in two waves. When in 1830 the governors applied to parliament for permission to build a new classical school on the outskirts of town (with the promise of a new commercial school only when this was completed), opposition was led by middle-class Radicals such as the lawyer Joseph Parkes. The deputation to the House of Commons in which he served was backed in its protests by petitions from 7,000 artisans, the Birmingham Cooperative Society and the board of guardians. In effect, the governors, who also wished to increase the number of boarders at the grammar school, were hoping to make the establishment more like a public boarding school. However, they agreed to keep the school in the city centre, begin work on new classical and commercial departments simultaneously, and establish the 'elementary' schools described above. In 1842, the second attack came, this time at the hands of the newly-established town council. On this occasion the curriculum and clientele of the foundation schools were secondary issues. It was a battle between rival corporations – one Tory and Anglican, the other with a Dissenting and Radical stamp – who were competing for control over a strategic and increasingly valuable resource. Although the town council pressed for the governors to be given powers to extend the provision of elementary schools their main demands were that they, the town council, should appoint five additional governors and that the borough auditors should examine the accounts of the foundation on a regular basis. They were completely unsuccessful.[10]

From 1837 the grammar school received competition from the Edgbaston Proprietary School. The new school was sponsored by a number of prominent Dissenting businessmen in reaction to the Anglican bias, old-fashioned classicism, cramped conditions and harsh pedagogic regime of the grammar school at that time. However, its principal propagandist, himself a manufacturer, insisted that the school's founders could not 'be accused of making sacrifices to a barren utility'.[11] From the start its daily curriculum consisted of English, Latin, Greek, mathematics and French with German and drawing as occasional subjects.[12]

> After twenty years' adherence to this course, they reaped their
> reward: for on the establishment of the Oxford Local
> Examinations, the school, in the first year, stood at the head of all
> the competing schools in the kingdom.

The same year that the Edgbaston Proprietary School opened its doors, the foundation obtained an act which allowed it also to intro-

110

duce modern languages, English literature and other branches of the arts and sciences into the classical school. However, the new commercial school (which became known as the English department) was described by T. H. Green as a 'crowded and ill-ventilated' place which 'towards dusk on an autumn or winter afternoon . . . became a mere bear-garden'. Although most of the students passing through the grammar school (in both its classical and English departments) were destined for some kind of commercial occupation, Green found least to criticise when discussing 'the most careful and effective' teaching of the classics in the upper school. There was, he thought, some truth in the accusation that the grammar school 'turned out a great many bad clerks and accountants for the sake of turning out a few very good scholars'.[13]

Having survived the onslaughts of 1830–1 and 1842 and modified the curriculum, the governors and headmaster of the grammar school were by mid-century apparently in a secure and dominant position within Birmingham education. The *Gentleman's Magazine* caught the prevailing mood in 1855:[14]

> The Birmingham school is an important example of the good administration of an old foundation under timely change, which has raised it from insignificance to splendour, instead of the revenues being sacrified to a job.

When the British Association held its inaugural meeting at Birmingham, E. H. Gifford, the headmaster of the grammar school presented figures which were apparently intended to emphasise the wide range and judicious balance of the foundation's educational provision. Of 465 pupils, 250 were in the classical school and 215 in the English school. Sons of professional men accounted for about a quarter of the former total but did not figure in the latter. Offspring of manufacturers were almost equally divided between the two schools. About six-sevenths of the pupils in the English school were the sons of manufacturers, clerks and tradesmen. The elementary schools drew upon 'small tradesmen and respectable artisans'. Anglican pupils had a preponderance of about five to one in the classical school and three to one in the English school. In the elementary schools the ratio was only about two to one. Finally, Gifford remarked with satisfaction that the elementary schools 'do not interfere to any considerable extent with the parochial schools, as three-fifths of the boys and more than four-fifths of the girls have never been in any other public elementary school'.[15] Complementarity with other institutions rather than competition, openness to 'legitimate' educational aspirations rather than 'arbitrary' exclusiveness: these were the latent themes of Gifford's paper. By the 1850s, the foundation was emphasising its close identification with the educational needs of Birmingham while continuing to

111

give effective pre-eminence to the prestigious classical curriculum. These values were shared by the leading spokesman for the Edgbaston Proprietary School:[16]

> Now for commercial pursuits, a boy may acquire by the time he is thirteen all the rudiments which are necessary; and if he is intended to be a clerk he may well leave at that age. If however, he is to come into an established business with the expectation of becoming a principal, he may well complain in after life, if he is removed so soon. He will find afterwards that he is at a great disadvantage when he gets into the company of educated men. He will frequently not understand what they are talking of, or their illustrations and allusions: a Latin quotation in a book, or a Latin name in a museum, abashes him: let him be the severest democrat imaginable, he finds that there is such a thing as intellectual rank, and he feels that his place is a low one. He may get wealth and outward consideration, but he cannot pass over into the class of the educated.

The foundation thoroughly dominated middle-class education in Birmingham, pushing private enterprise at this level to the fringes. In the mid-1860s T. H. Green noted 'the want of good preparatory schools now felt by the more educated class'. Private schoolmasters had to compete with the free provision offered by the foundation. The existence of the foundation was responsible for a 'degredation of the private schools of the town'.[17] The *1851 Education Census* showed that recorded attendances at private day schools were in both Birmingham and Sheffield just over 40 per cent of all day-school attendances.[18] However, such attendances were distributed between 'middling' or 'superior' private schools for middle-class children and 'common' or 'dame' schools for the children of poorer parents. A basis for comparing the two cities in terms of this distribution is provided by two investigations carried out in 1838, one in Sheffield by Thomas Sutton, vicar of Sheffield, and one in Birmingham by J. R. Wood acting on behalf of the Birmingham Educational Statistical Society (see Table 14).[19]

The data shown in Table 14 are obviously not strictly comparable in all respects but even within their limits they suggest that 'superior' schools commanded a larger share of the private market in Sheffield than Birmingham. Although the Sheffield figures exclude local boarding schools, their inclusion would possibly have increased the bias in Sheffield's favour. White's directories for 1849 list twenty-five private academies offering boarding accommodation in Sheffield and only twenty-six such institutions in Birmingham despite its greater size. Green complained that the 'number of boys attending schools of any kind, public or private, professing to be of the "middle" kind, in

TABLE 14   *Private schooling in Birmingham and Sheffield 1838*

| | Sheffield | | |
Private or general day schools	Schools	Scholars	(%)
Superior	31	1273	28.5
Middling (day and evening)	22	1019	22.9
Common (day and evening)	27	1130	25.3
Dame schools	46	1037	23.3
Total	126	4459	100.0
	Birmingham		
Schools supported solely by the scholars			
Infant schools (Private)	3	68	0.7
Dame schools	267	3900	37.4
Common day schools	177	4280	41.1
Superior private and boarding schools	97	2166	20.8
Total	544	10414	100.0

Sources: Holland (1843); *Birm. Stat. Soc. 1840.*
Note: Sheffield figures refer to enrolments. Birmingham figures refer to average attendance.

Birmingham and its suburbs, seems much smaller than it should be.'
At Sheffield in 1838, though not in Birmingham, such schools had been sufficiently numerous and distinct to merit a separate classification.[20]

Whereas in Birmingham the foundation dominated secondary education through the strong vertebral link it created between the most prestigious local schools for professional families and the schools most favoured by the lower middle class, in Sheffield the sector was regulated by the market mechanism. This had important consequences for curricular patterns. In Birmingham, as Green noted in the 1860s, 'the professional class' were 'the first element in the constituency of the classical school'; 'probably four-fifths' of the local medical men had passed through that department.[21] Businessmen aspiring to enter 'the class of the educated' accepted the values propagated there. In Sheffield, however, the strategic determination of curricular emphases within middle-class education resided in the broad band of commercial and manufacturing occupations. Vocational relevance was the key selling point for enterprising schoolmasters. They peddled their wares in a fickle market to a clientele who had to be convinced of their utility. Rather like eighteenth-century physicians vying for aristocratic patronage, some of them offered to the local middle-class ambitiously-framed systems of educational diagnosis and treatment which would make their children fit for the struggle of life.[22] Cosmologies abounded, eclectic mixtures of Pestalozzian and phrenological principles.[23] An example will illustrate the character of these enterprises. In 1839 H. C. Flory of Myrtle Spring House was claiming to teach only 'what is practicable and practically useful'. This included English grammar, composition and elocution, French, German, Italian, Spanish, Dutch, Anglo-Saxon, Latin, Greek, Hebrew, accounts, mathematics, history, geography, drawing, singing, and 'lectures on all branches of Moral and Natural Philosophy'. A few weeks later he also advertised 'Pestalozzian gymnastics with riding, swimming, fencing and dancing'. Flory in effect provided counting-house skills as a staple diet, adding a variety of side dishes to catch as wide a range of customers as possible. His competitors, such as Rev. H. H. Piper at Norton Academy adopted a similar strategy. Samuel Eadon and J. H. Abraham were other well-known local pedagogues. Apart from the market mechanism, a degree of informal coordination between the leading private schools arose from their masters' participation in organisations such as the Sheffield Literary and Philosophical Society and the part played by a few schools such as Abraham's Milk Street Academy in training men who later founded schools of their own.[24]

Green found that in Birmingham the wealthier businessmen, especially those 'whose wealth is of longer standing, generally send their sons to boarding school' or, if Dissenters, to the Edgbaston Proprietary School.[25] It is likely that patronage of boarding schools was at least as pronounced, if not more so, in Sheffield. Although both the Sheffield Collegiate School (to be discussed below) and the Sheffield Grammar School had some professional support, they could provide no equivalent to the foundation's classical school.[26] One Sheffield chronicler recalled that in the 1850s 'well-to-do people in Sheffield were sending their sons to Germany for educational purposes. Saxe Meiningen being a favourite place.' Herbert Bramley, a prominent solicitor who became Sheffield's town clerk, had an 'elaborate education' in that locale, for example.[27] J. G. Fitch, reporting in the 1860s, believed that 'an unusual proportion of parents in the middle and upper ranks of life probably send their children out of the town to be educated.'[28] In a sample of British steel manufacturers in 1865 drawn from more than one region but over-representing Sheffield, Charlotte Erickson found that roughly half had attended local schools and half had been sent away to boarding schools. Erickson found that an 'increasing proportion of the steel manufacturers in each subsequent period was educated at independent boarding schools away from home.'[29]

Standing between the boarding schools outside Sheffield and the private adventure schools, many ephemeral, within the town there were three more substantial enterprises which sought to provide a broadly-based middle-class education. Apart from the grammar school, there were the collegiate and Wesley College, both founded in the 1830s presumably with the hope of tapping an expanded clientele conjured up by urban growth.[30] Their respective fates are instructive. Wesley College, founded by a subscription of shares in 1837, was the most successful. Its curriculum in the mid-1860s was described as follows:[31]

> 'Fancy Classics', as they are sometimes called, are discarded. . . . Classics and mathematics furnish the groundwork of the mental training, but are turned earlier (than in the ordinary grammar school) to account as instruments of general culture.

The students of Wesley College were overwhelmingly boarders: 197 out of 227 students in 1864. The day boys were 'chiefly sons of manu-facturers'. Wesley College did not depend upon Sheffield for its success but drew upon 'the upper ranks of Methodist Society' over a wide area. Backed by the Wesleyan Methodist Society it could keep its fees low and its classrooms full.[32]

The collegiate was founded in 1835 as an Anglican classical school under the presidency of Lord Wharncliffe. Unfortunately, many shares remained unsold, no dividend was ever paid, and from 1843 successive headmasters ran the collegiate as 'essentially a private school'. In 1862 Rev. G. B. Atkinson, the headmaster, established a 'School of Practical Science' at the collegiate which was to offer prelim-inary instruction in engineering or 'any manufacturing or constructive art'. The Duke of Devonshire visited Sheffield to inaugurate the venture. This enterprising effort to boost student numbers failed miserably. By 1864 Atkinson and his eight staff were teaching only seventy-one students, of whom twenty were boarders. In 1872 the collegiate came within a hair's breadth of closing down altogether.[33]

The Sheffield Grammar School had introduced a commercial cur-riculum in the 1840s. So far from dominating local education was this establishment that in 1823 it had even lost control over the Free Writing School which the church burgesses had founded in its grounds a century before.[34] The steady decline of the Sheffield Grammar School, stubbornly resistant to resuscitation, contrasts forcibly with its name-sake in Birmingham. In 1863 the headmaster of the latter was dreaming of establishing scholarship links with the local public elementary schools and in this way giving his own school 'the position of a University, fostering and improving all the educational establishments of this neighbourhood'.[35] At this point it is convenient to turn to the sphere of elementary education.

The rest of this chapter is organised into four sections. First the motivations and realms of influence of working-class clients and middle-class sponsors of elementary education are discussed. Second, the character and significance of the development of Sunday schools in Sheffield and Birmingham are considered. Third, some aspects of the Evangelical movement in the two cities are analysed with particular reference to the provision of public day schools. Finally, the developing relationship between the institutional orders of formal education and industrial production is examined for each city, especially after 1851.

SPONSORS AND CLIENTS

I should say that the greater part of parents are indifferent to the education of their children though occasionally I have met pleasing instances to the contrary. It is the opinion of most people connected with the welfare of the poor, that each church should have its day-school as well as a Sunday-school; and I trust the spirit is now abroad which considers this measure to be necessary. As to the schools of the Dissenters I know nothing, having the privilege of belonging to the Church of England; and I am fully persuaded church schools, attached to each church, and overlooked by the minister, would be the best means Government could adopt for the training up of well-educated, sober, loyal, and obedient subjects.

Member of the Visiting and Bettering Society, Sheffield 1843[36]

I've been married 18 years. I've eight children, five girls and three boys; the ages of the girls are respectively 18, 16, 9, 6, and 1½ years; and of the boys, 14, 12, and 4. The youngest that works is the boy of 12 years old . . . he works with a table-knife hafter, who gives him 2s.6d a week. The boy of 14 works with his father, who is a table-knife hafter. . . . The two eldest girls are spoon-buffers. . . . Buffing is men's work; it's very hard work . . . they work about 12 hours a day at buffing; the boy of 12 works twelve hours a day. Sometimes when my husband has work, my eldest son and he will work from 8 in the morning to 10 at night; my son has been accustomed to do so from the first. My husband thinks it better to work a little later at night than to get up early in the morning, for it would disturb the neighbours, as he works from home. The work tires my sons very much; they have to turn a glazer frame with the foot. We are all tired at night; I can hardly get up the stairs myself sometimes at night, my bones ache so. The boy that works out, works with a religious young man, who treats him well. They are not unhealthy children, but we are obliged to

116

give them emetics and physic sometimes, for the dirt gets down their throats and makes them poorly.

The only one of my children who has been to school is my eldest son, who can read; he was taught to read at the poorhouse. The others can't read; they may tell their letters. The three eldest have been at Sunday-schools, but they don't go now, for want of clothes; therefore one only can read, and none of them can write. We sent one of the little girls to one of the large day-schools, where she went for four months, but didn't learn her letters; we can't afford to do more for them in the way of learning. On Sundays I make a fire upstairs, and keep them in the house as much as I can; I always try to keep them out of the streets, and the oldest boy reads sometimes.

There are great numbers of children who do run about the streets on Sunday. In many workshops there is great cursing and swearing; but the children are not forced to learn the habit. Some are well-behaved and some are not.

There are not two girls anywhere who are better behaved than mine, though they neither go to church nor chapel. I can't write myself; I could write when I was 15 years old. Children, in a general way, forget after they go to the [work] shops what they learned at school.

Harriet Ashton, 40 years of age, 1843[37]

The lady from the Visiting and Bettering Society would probably not have considered that Harriet Ashton was one of the 'pleasing instances to the contrary' of the maxim that most Sheffield parents were 'indifferent to the education of their children'. After all, Mrs Ashton's three eldest had only been in intermittent attendance at Sunday school, a daughter had been taken away from day school after a mere four months, and it was only thanks to the poorhouse that one of her sons could read. In juxtaposition the two quotations indicate many aspects of the encounters between middle-class and working-class people which took place through the sphere of elementary education. The lady visitor was asserting the claim of the Anglican church to take responsibility for educating the labouring classes against the rival claims of Dissenters and the government. The 'elementary school contest' between Anglicans and Dissenters was much more pronounced in Birmingham than Sheffield. It was informed by resentment against the rule of squire and cleric built up over several generations in the old lower middle class of shopkeepers and tradesmen.[38] There is evidence suggesting that although denominational enterprise in Birmingham was dominated by wealthy businessmen and leading professionals the lower middle class may have been better represented in Dissenting organisations.[39]

The first quotation reflects the Anglican preference for day schools rather than Sunday schools. The latter sector, which relied heavily upon unpaid teachers, was dominated by Dissenting congregations.[40] A day school implied the employment of a paid teacher and emphasised the clergyman's continuing responsibility for educational work.[41] The monitorial system, still in fairly widespread use during the 1840s, relied upon the services of the more literate children as 'monitors'. In the Sunday schools, dependence upon the voluntary efforts of students drawn from among ex-students was even greater. Many of them were little more than children themselves. The detailed management of the Sunday schools, especially those run by the Dissenters was often in the hands of the teachers. Furthermore, Sunday schools drew an important part of their income from the donations of chapel congregations while day schools were to a significant extent dependent upon the schoolpence supplied by parents. The private schools also offered a degree of competition. In sum, the clientele of elementary schools were in a position to exercise a great deal of *de facto* influence over what occurred within them. The master of Pinfield Street National School went so far as to admit that 'if he was not very careful, the monitors would generally be bribed'.[42]

Harriet Ashton epitomises the attitude towards education of the 'respectable' working class, a category which is not defined by income (since the Ashton family had clearly known hard times) but by a pride in sober, disciplined and 'moral' behaviour. These values were not the product of attendance at church and school.[43] On the contrary, such attendance was one expression of respectability: the major inhibition against going to Sunday school was 'want of clothes'; that is, respectable clothes. The next best thing was to keep the children indoors and off the streets. Literacy and the opportunity for self-improvement were benefits which could be purchased at the expense of time, energy and money through attendance at school. In this case, a four-month trial of 'one of the large day-schools' (the apparent indifference to denominational colour is noteworthy) did not produce a result which justified the outlay. For many, Sunday school was a cheaper alternative. In Sheffield, Symons found that Red Hill Sunday School owed 'its popularity chiefly to its excellence as a *writing* school, for which it is still noted'. Allen Street Sunday School had a similar reputation.[44] As late as the mid-1860s in Birmingham, a manufacturer observed: 'I have found on inquiry that many of our people go to the Quakers' Sunday schools (which is strange, seeing that this is not the national religion), for the sake of the writing, and because they are systematically taught, and not merely confined to the Testament.'[45]

SUNDAY SCHOOLS

It is possible to make crude distinctions among types of schools providing elementary education according to the degrees of influence upon their daily management which was exercised by, respectively, their predominantly middle-class sponsors and their predominantly working-class clients. Private schools, which had to survive in the market, were most subject to the whims of consumers. Public day schools, whose paid teachers were to a great extent responsible to managers, trustees, particularly clergymen, and to an increasing extent government inspectors, exemplified a higher degree of 'sponsor power'. Sunday schools stood at various points on a continuum between high client power and high sponsor power. Responsibility for their management was shared between teachers, many of whom were drawn from ex-pupils, and subscribers with a special regard for the interests of the sponsoring church or chapel.[46]

The distribution of children among the three forms of educational establishment may be roughly assessed by comparing once more figures drawn from the two surveys conducted in 1838. The context of these surveys will be briefly explained. The Birmingham Educational Statistical Society was formed in 1838 with the support of 'a considerable portion of the clergy . . . as well as others not connected with the establishment, and gentlemen around'.[47] The regular agent of the Manchester Statistical Society carried out the survey, street by street, in a manner that appears to have been very thorough. He obtained enrolment figures for Sunday schools and figures of average attendance, which he thought were artificially low, for day schools.[48] The same year Thomas Sutton carried out his own survey of enrolments in Sheffield schools and 'subsequent enquiries in 1840–1', almost certainly by G. C. Holland were reported by the latter to have 'exhibited no material alteration in the facts'. The latter survey, which computed the 'number of children on the books' in Sunday schools and public day schools, produced slightly higher figures for Sunday schools and slightly lower figures for public day schools compared to Sutton's enquiry.[49] The relevant findings of the surveys of Wood and Sutton are set out in Table 15.[50] Wood computed a figure for average attendance at Birmingham's Sunday schools of 12,224 which is 72.9 per cent of the enrolment figure. In the early 1840s Symons showed that in fifteen public day schools '26.47 per cent of the whole are continually absent', implying an average attendance of not more than about 73 per cent. Symons also calculated that nearly a quarter of enrolled pupils were regularly absent from Sheffield's Sunday schools.[51] If the above figures for enrolment in both cities are uniformly reduced by 27 per

TABLE 15 *Enrolment and attendance at Sunday schools, public day schools and private day schools: Birmingham and Sheffield 1838*

	1838	
	Birmingham	*Sheffield*
Sunday schools	16,757 (enrolment)	11,212 (enrolment)
Public day schools	3,834[a] (attendance)	6,100[b] (enrolment)
Private day schools (ie Common day schools and Dame schools)	12,014 8,180 (attendance)	8267 2,167 (enrolment)

Sources: Holland (1843); *Birm. Stat. Soc. 1840.*
Notes:
a Excludes scholars of King Edward VI Foundation.
b Original figure of 6,188 reduced to exclude Sheffield Grammar School.

cent the distribution of average attendances obtained is shown in Table 16. The figures in Table 16 suggest that in Birmingham the Sunday schools attracted about the same number of students as the day schools in 1838 but that in Sheffield the Sunday schools were about a third more successful than the local day schools.[52] Undoubtedly there was some overlap in attendances since, for example, denominational day schools sometimes attempted to make attendance at Sunday school obligatory.[53] Private schools accounted for about two-thirds of day school attendances in Birmingham but only about a quarter of day school attendances in Sheffield.

TABLE 16 *Average attendance at Sunday schools, public day schools and private day schools: Birmingham and Sheffield 1838*

	Birmingham		*Sheffield*	
Sunday schools	12,224		8,185	
Public day schools	3,834	12,014	4,453	6035
Private day schools	8,180		1,582	
Number of private schools	444		73	
Average size of clientele in private day schools	18.4		21.7	

Sources: Holland (1843); *Birm. Stat. Soc. 1840.*

The relatively high popularity of Sunday schools compared to day schools in Sheffield cannot be explained with reference to a market for juvenile labour during the week since, as has been seen, this was much more pronounced in Birmingham.[54] The pull of the labour market may, however, have contributed to the fact that attendances at all types of school drew a smaller proportion of the juvenile population in Birmingham than Sheffield, according to the *Education Census 1851*, as shown in Table 17. In fact the paucity of work for young people in

TABLE 17   *Levels of school attendance by juveniles: Birmingham and Sheffield 1851*

| | 1851 | |
| | Birmingham | Sheffield |
	%	%
Total juvenile population (20 years and under)	106020 (100.0)	62220 (100.0)
Total Sunday school attendances	21406 (20.2)	14919 (24.0)
Total private day school attendances	9151 (8.6)	6284 (10.1)
Total public day school attendances	13032 (12.3)	9333 (15.0)

Source: 1851 Census.

Sheffield is likely to have tended to increase attendance at school during the week. In 1841 the master of Sheffield's Lancasterian boys' school commented that:[55]

> while nothing is so provoking to the teacher who is anxious to do good, yet nothing is more common than the following expression which is uttered by the parents when they apply for the admission of their children to the public school. 'Sir, I've brought my boy, if you'll have him; for I thought he might as well come here till he's fit to earn a trifle, as it will keep him from running the streets and getting into mischief, for we don't know what to do wi' him at home.'

The effect of the labour market on attendance seems to have been most pronounced, as would be expected, in the case of girls in Birmingham (see Table 18). The rate of attendance at public day schools among juvenile girls was about 35 per cent higher in Sheffield than in Birmingham. By comparison, the rate of attendance among Sheffield's male juveniles was only about 12 per cent greater than among their peers in Birmingham. Rev. Thomas Nunns of St Bartholomew's ran a day school for boys and girls in Birmingham. He commented in 1841:[56]

TABLE 18   *Levels of school attendance by juveniles, distinguishing by sex: Birmingham and Sheffield 1851*

| | 1851 | |
| | Birmingham | Sheffield |
	%	%
Male juvenile population (20 years and under)	52640 (100.0)	31108 (100.0)
Male Sunday school attendance	10906 (20.7)	7380 (23.7)
Male private day school attendance	4377 (8.3)	2992 (9.6)
Male public day school attendance	7508 (14.3)	4986 (16.0)
Female juvenile population (20 years and under)	53380 (100.0)	31112 (100.0)
Female Sunday school attendance	10500 (19.7)	7539 (24.2)
Female private day school attendance	4774 (8.9)	3292 (10.6)
Female public day school attendance	5524 (10.4)	4347 (14.0)

Source: 1851 Census.

> The number attending the day school is about 150 boys and 60 girls. The age of admission is about 6 years. The average age of those attending is about 10; at 11 years the boys are generally withdrawn, because they can earn so much that the parents will not allow them to remain longer. Many of the boys are withdrawn to help in manufactures at an earlier age, some as young as 8 years. The girls are much less regular in their attendance, being called away by various causes, especially to nurse and take care of the family while mother is at work, washing &c. Many little girls also go out as servants to small shopkeepers. From these combined causes, the education of the girls is infinitely more neglected than that of the boys.

To some extent, Birmingham's young female population did make up for educational neglect during the week by attendance at Sunday school. It is noticeable that in both cities female attendance at private day schools was higher than male attendance. This probably reflects the prevalence of schools offering 'refinements' to young ladies from middle-class families of which there were a great number in both Birmingham and Sheffield.[57]

To return to the issue raised above: how is the relatively high popularity of Sunday school attendance at Sheffield compared to Birmingham in the late 1830s to be explained? A lack of places in the public day schools is unlikely to have been the cause since, as a local Wesleyan minister noted in 1843, 'in this town there is provision for more than are receiving instruction, – several schools not being full.'[58] Perhaps part of the answer lies in the relatively small availability of private schools for working-class children in Sheffield. Nineteenth-century Birmingham had inherited a strong regional tradition of private schoolmastering from the previous century which ensured a ready supply of pedagogues, of varying degrees of ability and levels of aspiration, to set up dame schools and common day schools.[59] Sheffield was a less attractive site for anyone with literary or scholarly inclinations and those who made the journey from outside may well have preferred to fish the potentially more lucrative pond of middling-wealthy families in the market for commercial training. The two surveys of 1838 recorded 444 private schools offering services to working-class clients in Birmingham but only seventy-three such schools in Sheffield.[60] As a consequence, it was relatively more difficult in Sheffield to obtain training in literacy and numeracy for moderate fees as a straight market transaction. Some of the attractions of such an arrangement are suggested by the findings of J. G. Fitch in his survey of Birmingham's day schools later in the period.[61] One private-school teacher said that parents liked his school because the boys were not knocked about as in the '2d National Schools'. By paying slightly higher fees parents might buy for their children a less strict regime and be free from tiresome enquiries about the regularity of their attendance. Their children might even be addressed as 'Miss' and 'Master'.[62]

Sunday schools, especially those run by Dissenting chapels, were less subject to the control of middle-class subscribers, trustees or clerical watchdogs than either the denominational schools or the endowed charity schools. Given the paucity of private schools and the size and bureaucratic regimentation of the large Lancasterian and national schools in Sheffield, Sunday schools may well have been a favoured alternative.[63] The evidence of young people to Symons in the early 1840s suggested that attendance at private school followed by visits to Sunday school when full-time work commenced was con-sidered an acceptable pattern of education:[64]

> I was two years at a private day-school before I went to work; and now I go to St Paul's Sunday school, and to Queen Street evening school twice a week.

> I was at a private day school a year before I went to work, and now I go to Red Hill Sunday school. I don't go to chapel always, but I always go to school.

> I go to Red Hill Sunday school now: I was at a private day school a

year before I began to work. I can't write but I'm learning at Sunday school: they teach me to spell a little too.

I went to Mr Meakin's private school. I can write and read; I have gone as far as fractions and arithmetic. I attend Mr Farish's church and Sunday School; and am a teacher there.

I was at a private school before I commenced work. I can read and write. I know as far as interest in arithmetic. I have not learnt geography. I go to a Wesleyan chapel and used to go to Sunday school.

In 1838 fifty-six Sunday schools were recorded at Birmingham and eighty-three at Sheffield. This implies an average clientele of about 100 pupils per school in Sheffield's Sunday schools and roughly twice that number in Birmingham. The *1851 Education Census* also suggests that the average size of the Sunday gatherings was smaller in Sheffield than Birmingham.[65] It thus seems likely that Sheffield's Sunday schools were smaller and more intimate, catering for a multitude of face-to-face neighbourhood communities like the inns and beershops with which they were in competition. The Sunday schools of Sheffield were attuned to the wishes of many inhabitants of these communities for moral emancipation, independence and a means of expression, inclinations whose other manifestations were the support given for Ironside's Chartists and the democratic movement in Methodism during the 1840s. However, these different movements and the independence of the trade societies were not concerted expressions of a 'united working class'. Exponents of the Sunday schools were engaged in a struggle with their very own neighbours for the soul of Sheffield's local communities. The battle with the beershop was crucial in the eyes of ministers and clergy alike.[66] It was interwoven with other conflicts: between parents and children, masters and employees, workmen and their juvenile helpers. A 12-year-old warehouse errand boy told a government inspector[67]

> I don't go to Sunday School, because they don't larn me enough; I am going to another, a better one. . . . My father used to teach me a little sometimes on Sunday; he doesn't now. I go out walking in the country on Sundays, or sometimes go to church; I don't know how to play at pinch. When I get the 4d for coming here I shall give it my mother; my mother won't make me, but I shall give it her myself.

Representatives of a stove-grate manufacturer were reported as saying:[68]

> No 'saint-mondays' are kept on their premises. . . . They have taken a great deal of pains with the morals of their work-people

and believe them to be very good. No ale is ever permitted to come on the works; the men drink nothing but water. Those who are the sons of workpeople brought up here have such education as Sunday schools give. It is the general practice for them to go. There is a club in the works for sickness; and there are also fines for swearing, &c. None of the workmen . . . are permitted to belong to trades' unions.

A table-knife hafter[69]

> attributes bad morals, in a great degree, to the boys not being bound. . . . Wishes it to be made penal to employ a boy in any trade without indentures; and would like it to be made imperative on the master to send him either to a Sunday school or a place of worship.

The success of the Nonconformist Sunday schools was not lost on Sheffield's clergy. Rev. Livesey of St Philips noted that 'of young people engaged in work only a small proportion attend Sunday schools connected with the church. In Dissenting schools, where writing is taught on Sundays, I am informed the number is greater.' He wanted the church day schools to tap similar sources of support:[70]

> It is my decided conviction that if, instead of congregating many hundred children in large central schools, smaller and more numerous schools were opened in the most convenient localities, many children might be brought under a sound system of instruction. . . . Also many additional subscriptions might be obtained from shopkeepers and other residents.

Thomas Booth, a Sheffield iron master had similar views:[71]

> I encourage private or small schools in preference to large public establishments, where education is carried out on the Lancasterian plan, for reasons which it would be superfluous in me here to state.

However, Livesey's colleague at St Mary's, Rev. Farish, implicitly acknowledged the tendency for Sunday schools to express rather than mould currents of feeling within the communities they served:[72]

> There has been a perceptible and unfavourable change in the characters of children in our Sunday schools since the prevelance of Socialism, though I think we feel it much less now that our national school for boys has been for a few months open.

Jelinger Symons believed that the main value of Sheffield's Sunday schools was that they kept 8,000 children off the streets during the Lord's Day. He thought that the religious instruction imparted was 'very deficient: signally so where writing is taught'.[73] By contrast, R. D. Grainger noted deficiencies in the Sunday scholars' 'practical knowledge of religion' in Birmingham but made a point of criticism the fact that 'in Sunday schools of the Established Church, and in those of some dissenting congregations, reading in the Scriptures or religious books is the only instruction given; consequently the children who have attended no other school than these . . . have no knowledge of writing or accounts.'[74] The difference in tone suggests that in Birmingham there was less fear than in Sheffield of the Sunday schools acting as a focus for a working-class culture relatively independent from, and perhaps hostile towards the culture of the larger employers and professional men. Indeed, Grainger quoted at length the Report of the Birmingham Statistical Society which declared:[75]

> As a moral means, the value of Sunday schools cannot be too highly appreciated. . . . They have been the means of infusing the most powerful moral checks into the consciences of tens of thousands . . . [and] . . . on the whole, the Sunday schools in Birmingham must rank higher than those of any other place which has been subject to a similar investigation.

EVANGELICALS AND INDUSTRIALISTS

The patterns of weekday schooling may be examined further from the 'supply' side, particularly with respect to the public sector. The relative lack of enterprise in providing day-school education for working-class children in Birmingham before the 1830s was not simply a reflection of the thriving private market in schools or the demand for juvenile labour.[76] It was also a reflection of the structure and disposition of potential sponsoring groups. The Evangelical movement in Anglicanism and Dissent alike stressed education of the poor as one means of saving their souls.[77] Not until the 1830s did the movement make a sizeable impact in the upper reaches of Birmingham society, at least a generation after it had become dominant in Sheffield. It is true that by the first decade of the century the Congregationalists led by John Angell James at Carr's Lane and the Baptists at Cannon Street were both strongly influenced by the missionary impulse to spread scriptural truth at home and abroad.[78] However, their congregations were of a lower social standing than the Unitarians at the New Meeting, whose minister Samuel Bache was a Conservative, and the Quakers at Bull Street who did not feel the new spirit with any real force until the 1830s.[79] Even more important, the Church of England, by far the most numerous and influential religious organisation in Birmingham, lacked effective local leadership before the end of the 1820s. For much of that decade the rectors of St Martin's and St Philip's were absentees, the latter until 1844. W. F. Hook of St Philip's disliked the Evangelical tendency and was the hero of the Tory *Birmingham Argus*. In Aston parish, high church sentiments reigned at least until the 1850s. However, the foundation of the Birmingham Clerical Society in 1825 indicated the new influence of Evangelicalism in the city. Henry Ryder, the Evangelical Bishop of Lichfield frequently visited Birmingham after his appointment in 1824. During the late 1820s two local Evangelicals, William Spooner of Elmdon and George Hodson of Christ Church, were made archdeacons.[80]

The next stage in the infiltration of the movement into Birmingham's Anglican hierarchy was roughly contemporaneous with the halting career of the Birmingham Political Union. The chief agent of Birmingham Evangelicalism was Thomas Moseley who in 1829 was appointed rector of St Martin's, the central church of Birmingham parish. Moseley was vilified by local radicals for his attempts to collect church rates but the effort to enforce taxation was in part a response to the Church of England's enlarged sense of its local mission for which it had meagre funds. Pastoral efficiency was increased by an informal division of much of Birmingham parish into smaller districts in 1829 and by the creation of three new churches as separate rectories early in the following decade. In 1830, visiting societies composed of lay members of Anglican congregations were established to organise the distribution of charity and Evangelical propaganda. Since the Nonconformist churches tended to be in the more respectable areas, the Church of England had a fairly open field of work amongst the impoverished. Moseley had the help of colleagues such as John Garbett at St George's and J. G. Breay at Christ Church. Breay built new schoolrooms at Pinfold Street where he ran a national school for boys, a female school of industry, a Sunday school and a provident institution (the last founded in 1836). Garbett was similarly active.[81] While the late 1830s witnessed the collapse of the Birmingham Political Union, its chief activists finding a new base on the town council, the same years saw the institutionalisation of Evangelical predominance amongst their opponents. In 1837, leading local Evangelicals set up a trust to ensure 'a succession in perpetuity of holy and devoted Ministers'. The trust exercised effective control over appointments to four out of the five rectories in Birmingham parish.[82]

By contrast, church affairs in Sheffield had since 1805 been dominated by the vicar of Sheffield, Thomas Sutton, 'a strong evangelical churchman [who] . . . was responsible for a long sequence of evangelical clergy in the parish'.[83] The survey of educational facilities in 1838 was one indication of Sutton's concern to provide schooling for working-class children, chief among whose vices he listed 'insubordination to all authority'. His greatest enemy was the beershop and his best hope that in all social relations 'the directions of Scripture' would be adhered to. These aspirations found strong support among Wesleyan ministers such as John Henley who believed that a 'thorough scriptural education of the rising race would doubtless do much to improve the morals of society, and promote the national welfare'.[84] The work of 'redemption through education' was carried out with little interdenominational rivalry. Public provision was dominated by the two Lancasterian schools, the first of which had been founded in 1809. Although Dissenters were predominant in its management many of its earliest pupils were Anglicans. In 1838 the two Lancasterian schools contained nearly 20 per cent of all children being educated in the public sector. Between them they had an enrolment of 1,140 pupils.[85]

Two complaints recur in counterpoint within the comments of the tiny band of clergy, ministers and laity engaged in the sponsorship of Sheffield's public day schools for working-class children. The first is that the wealthier part of Sheffield was not sufficiently involved in the sponsorship of education:[86]

Very few of the upper class give themselves with any heart to this work, which is much to be regretted . . .

many wealthy and benevolent persons have thought they have done sufficient for the education of the poor in supporting Sabbath schools, and have been very indifferent about day schools. . . .

The great indifference of Christian churches, to which the [Sunday] schools respectively belong, in not taking oversight of their management . . .

those who are better qualified to teach, or to suggest the best methods of teaching stand aloof, or nearly so, from such self-denying engagements.

The other sore point was the independent spirit of the pupils and their families:[87]

A son of hers, merely because he was dressed as a member of the Society of Friends, was grossly insulted and pelted with dirt in the street. . . . The parents make it quite a favour to send their children to school. Pride is a great and very prevailing vice among them; the least thing said to a child at school is taken as an offence.

The denominations felt they were fighting a battle with precious little help from those in other spheres who shared their interest in discipline and order, notably manufacturers. As Symons pointed out in 1843:[88]

Manufacturers . . . are not the employers of children in Sheffield, with a few exceptions. There is no school attached to any of their establishments, nor do they, *as manufacturers*, take any part in promoting education, though many subscribe liberally to existing schools.

Samuel Earnshaw, who was assistant minister at the parish church from 1847, repeated the complaint in the 1850s.[89] He was clear that the school was in competition with industrial employment. Earnshaw wrote that in Sheffield 'boys are generally apprenticed to their fathers or to a workman'. Where piecework prevails, apprentices can in times of good trade make high earnings which allow them to follow their masters 'into habits of drunkenness'. Absence of parental restraint breeds an 'American notion of liberty' for which 'children naturally long; and are themselves anxious to leave school and begin work that they may at once "become men" and imitate the folly and vices of those that are grown up.'[90]

As has been seen, in Birmingham the Anglican hierarchy had the active cooperation of factory owners such as J. O. Bacchus, William Chance and R. W. Winfield. The latter two men both established factory schools. The church also had the support of the Church of England Lay Association. Through the Spooner family, the local Evangelicals penetrated into the centre of borough and county politics and into the Clapham Sect in London. During the mid-1840s Evangelical strength in the clergy was increased by the arrival of Grantham Yorke, son of the Earl of Hardwick, G. S. Bull, the old ally of Oastler in the latter's campaign for factory reform, and John Cale Miller.[91]

By comparing data from the surveys of 1838 and the *1851 Education Census* it is possible to assess in broad terms the degree of proportional shift between private education and publicly-provided education between the two dates in Birmingham and Sheffield (see Table 19). Table 19 includes all forms of schooling recorded at the two dates, that is, for both the working-class and middle-class children. Sunday schools are not included.

In Sheffield the public and private sectors expanded at roughly the same rate during the 1840s but in Birmingham the public sector made considerable strides at the expense of the private sector. Table 14 (see p. 113) suggested that common day schools and dame schools accounted for about half the private provision being used in Sheffield but well over three-quarters of private provision at Birmingham in 1838. The King Edward VI elementary schools were built between 1838 and 1852 and their impact on the middle and the top end of the private market in conjunction with the grammar school itself has been noted. It is likely that the private sector was hit even harder by the opening of national schools such as those attached to St Matthew's (opened 1841),

TABLE 19 *Support for public and private schooling: Birmingham and Sheffield 1838, 1851*

1838	Public	Private	Total
Sheffield[a]	6188 (58.1)	4459 (41.9)	10647 (100.0) (%)
Birmingham[b]	4066 (28.1)	10414[d] (71.9)	14480 (100.0) (%)
1851	Public	Private	Total
Sheffield[c]	9333 (59.8)	6284 (40.2)	15617 (100.0) (%)
Birmingham[c]	13032 (58.8)	9151 (41.3)	22183 (100.0) (%)

Sources: Holland (1843); *Birm. Stat. Soc. 1840; 1851 Education Census.*
Notes:
a The 1838 figures for Sheffield refer to enrolments.
b The 1838 figures for Birmingham refer to average attendance.
c The 1851 figures for both cities refer to attendances on Census Day.
d This total includes some boarding provision.

St George's in Great Russell Street (1842), St Philip's (1842), St Mark's (1843), All Saints' (1843), St Peter's (1844), St Paul's (1845), St Mary's (1846) and St John's (1848).[92] On Census Day in 1851, 6,220 children were attending twenty-six Anglican day schools. However, by that time other denominations in Birmingham claimed 3,726 children in twenty-three schools.[93] The latter included, for example, the New Meeting Street school, erected by the Independents in 1844.[94] The extent of denominational provision in the public sector by Anglicans and non-Anglicans in Birmingham and Sheffield in 1851 is demonstrated in Table 20.

TABLE 20 *Public day schools supported by denominations: Birmingham and Sheffield 1851*

	Anglican		Others		Total	
	Schools	Scholars	Schools	Scholars	Schools	Scholars
Birmingham	26	6220 (62.5)	23	3726 (37.5)	49	9946 (100.0) (%)
Sheffield	18	5814 (77.2)	7	1716 (22.8)	25	7530 (100.0) (%)

Source: 1851 Education Census.

The bulk of Birmingham's public provision had been established since 1830.[95] The climate of competition between Church and Dissent during the next two decades had stimulated a wave of new foundations on both sides. In Sheffield, interdenominational competition was far less marked and the Anglican superiority in day school provision probably reflects the lack of enterprise by Dissenting congregations who apparently preferred to rest on their laurels in the realm of Sunday school provision. This is shown in Table 21. In Birmingham, resurgent Anglicanism had increased its harvest of Sunday school pupils from just over a quarter to about four-tenths. In Sheffield, the Church of England had only advanced its strength from about one-quarter to under a third of all attendances.[96]

TABLE 21   *Level of support for Sunday schools in Birmingham and Sheffield 1838, 1851*

	Anglican	Others	Total
1838[a]			
Sheffield	2758 (24.6)	8454 (75.4)	11212 (100.0) (%)
Birmingham	4565 (27.2)	12192 (72.8)	16757 (100.0) (%)
1851[b]			
Sheffield	4524 (30.3)	10395 (69.7)	14919 (100.0) (%)
Birmingham	8911 (41.6)	12495 (58.4)	21406 (100.0) (%)

Sources: Holland (1843); *Birm. Stat. Soc. 1840*; *1851 Education Census*.
Notes:
a 1838 figures for Sheffield and Birmingham refer to enrolments.
b 1851 figures for Birmingham and Sheffield refer to attendances on Census Day.

During the two decades after the *1851 Education Census* the rates of population growth in the two cities diverged sharply. By 1871 Birmingham's population had increased by less than half but Sheffield's population had grown by over three-quarters. During the decade 1861–71 the rate of population growth in Sheffield was nearly double that of Birmingham (29.7 per cent as compared to 16.2 per cent).[97] During the late 1860s, J. G. Fitch carried out investigations of school provision for 'the poorer classes' in both cities.[98] His findings suggest that in both cities public provision had made ground against private provision since mid-century (see Table 22). It seems likely that

TABLE 22   *Distribution of working-class pupils between private and public sectors: Birmingham and Sheffield 1868–9*

	Private	Public	Total
Birmingham (1869)[a]	8424 (18.1)	38113 (81.9)	46537 (100.0) (%)
Sheffield (1868)[b]	2584 (18.3)	11516 (81.7)	14100 (100.0) (%)

Sources: Fitch (1870); *SIC* (1868).
Notes:
a Birmingham figures refer to pupils enrolled.
b Sheffield figures refer to pupils 'in attendance'.

in the private sector, dame schooling continued to bulk larger in Birmingham than in Sheffield. In 1869 Fitch noted that in Birmingham well over 5,000 children were attending establishments in private houses most of which were 'mere dame schools . . . and scarcely profess to be places of instruction'.[99] The general standard of the lower private schools in Sheffield seems to have impressed Fitch a little more favourably. He commented:[100]

> It is singular that a considerable portion of the children of the class usually found in National schools are in Sheffield taught in private adventure schools, of which there is a large number of a humble kind. . . . [Some] of the humbler private schools are of unusual size, several of them containing upwards of 100 scholars.

As has been seen, Sheffield's middle-class establishments had few channels through which to exercise influence over the labouring population. Public day school education provided by the denominations had to bear a very large share of a burden which was in Birmingham shared among a wider range of institutions, especially industrial and political. In the sphere of working-class education in Sheffield, the weakness of interdenominational rivalry bred a readiness to allow the Anglican clergy to carry the heaviest part of the responsibility for running the schools. After mid-century the scale of the task increased enormously. To the recalcitrance and independence of working-class parents and children was added the difficulties of catering for the growing army of labouring families resident in Attercliffe and Brightside. Samuel Earnshaw had suggested a solution to the former difficulty in 1857. It was:[101]

> To make apprenticeship illegal until a certificate has been obtained of ATTENDANCE at an approved school a certain number of days (say 500 *whole* days, *rejecting halves*) after the age of 6 years.

Investigations into Sheffield's steel industry carried out by the Children's Employment Commission in the 1860s found some blatant cases of the exploitation of child labour.[102] The dilemma in which revelations such as this placed the local clergy, who felt themselves almost alone in educational work amongst the lower classes, was expressed in 1865 by Rev. W. Wilkinson, a manager of one of Sheffield's larger schools:[103]

> [If] education is to be made compulsory, I ask, when are the schools to be founded? Who is to provide them? If the whole burden of raising funds and working schools is to be thrown on the clergy, the temptation to them will be to say – 'We withdraw, and confine ourselves to our spiritual work; we leave the management of the schools to others, only taking care that the word of God is carefully taught.'

The note of distaste running through the words of Earnshaw make a sharp contrast with the appeal of Birmingham educationalists to values shared between masters and men. These values were to be cultivated by a strategy of kind inducement and benevolent paternalism. For example, Rev. Nash Stephenson, in an open letter to the manufacturer R. W. Winfield suggested that the prospect of prizes was likely to be a more effective means of moulding behaviour than the fear of penalties. He had been a pioneer in the development of the Birmingham Prize Scheme and the Coventry Archidiaconal Prize Scheme. The main feature of such schemes was the award of prizes consisting of cash, prayer books and Bibles to children who were regular in attendance, of good character, attentive to their religious duties and successful in annual examinations in secular and religious subjects. [104]

In Birmingham the 'barbarism' of the workshop was tempered by the more Christian spirit evinced by J. Fawkener Winfield who wrote in 1857 of the [105]

> noble efforts of our friends the Bagnalls, and the Chances, and others in our district, in furthering the education of their children, the glorious results which have attended these efforts, the self-denying labours of Messrs Wilson at Price's Candle Company – men worthy of the highest honour – these and many, many other such instances might be brought forward.

Apart from the pleasures of self-congratulation, Winfield derived other benefits from his factory schools: [106]

> Your people become attached to you. They serve you from a love to you, because they feel you care for their best interests. They are not eye-servants. We have no strikes, no disorder. I have our lads at my house under perfect control; we can trust them, and look upon them as members of our own family.

Evidently, Evangelical zeal was regarded as having a measureable effect on levels of production. However, this economic motive was part of a larger concern to establish a harmonious social order in which all had their Christian duty to perform. A similar tone runs through John Thackray Bunce's description of Birmingham's 'feeding schools and evening schools' for the poor. There was, he believed, 'a large class of children who can only be *enticed* to school'. One means of enticement was the provision of a square meal. [107] Another was the creation of an atmosphere of mutual respect: [108]

> The pupils should be taught to consider themselves as members of a family rather than merely as scholars: and above all . . . nothing should be done to check, but rather everything to foster that spirit

of independence, self-respect, and self-reliance, by which our best artisans are so favourably distinguished, and without which schoolmasters, clergymen, and teachers, may labour in vain to advance the *real* education of the working class.

The positive stress placed by Bunce on artisan independence antici-pates the later political division which would place him in the Liberal camp in opposition to the Conservatism of the Winfields.[109] However, the relaxed attitude towards the labouring population of both men is quite distinct from the frustration and resentment of Earnshaw.

In 1857 Rev. Sydney Gedge, a master at the King Edward VI Grammar School offered a 'balanced view' of the relationship between education and industry.[110] Gedge noted the general opinion that 'the improvement in the quality of the education in the schools under inspection (by Her Majesty's Inspectors) had been accompanied by an average shorter attendance of the children at those schools.' However, he thought it probable 'that the children are in many cases deriving more benefit in the shorter time' and recognised the 'necessity laid upon working-men, as a class, to supply the demands of the manufactury, whatever they are, for juvenile labour'.[111] He added:[112]

> The truth is, that we are at present in this position: either we must cease to congratulate ourselves on our increasing trade, or we must submit to the stern necessity of having more children as well as more adults employed.

Gedge believed that the introduction of the Factory Act to Birmingham would hamper factories at the expense of the 'house-shop' and believed that the best immediate strategy was not only to inculcate 'sound principles' and 'good habits' in school but also 'to carry the spirit of a good school into the manufactury'. Gedge con-tinued:[113]

> A school of good or evil it certainly is – not, I venture to think, under any circumstances, of unmixed evil, unless the children are weighed down by a pressure of labour beyond their power to bear – not, I say, of unmixed evil, because a boy of even ten years of age, on entering a manufactury is, at all events, placed under a certain kind of discipline. He must learn something of an honest occupation. He can scarcely fail to acquire habits of punctuality, alacrity in duty, submission to just authority, and willingness to oblige those about him in the workshops. He sees many incentives to industry, and he may have an honest satisfaction and not improper self-respect in the consciousness that a widowed mother, or both parents of a large family are assisted by his earnings.

Gedge saw formal education as acting in harness with other institutional orders as a means of ensuring harmonious class relationships in Birmingham. He believed there were grounds for optimism:[114]

> [Partly] from the direct efforts made for their improvement by employers, ministers of religion and other friends to the working-classes; partly through the reflex influence of schools through their children; from the better literature placed within their reach; from the absence, I venture to add, of political excitement, while there has been a growth of political knowledge; from connexions with provident societies, savings banks, and other institutions of the same kind; as well as from other causes, not easily traceable, but perhaps more influential because less directly so, many of the working-classes are rising in the scale of moral worth, and learning to measure themselves by the standard of Holy Scripture.

In 1850 the Birmingham School Association was founded. It sent a deputation, including William Harris, to the conference which established the National Public School Association. The object of the Birmingham School Association whose members included William Scholefield, Charles Geach and William Middlemore, was 'the introduction of a free, secular, and compulsory system of National Education supported by local rates'.[115] It was an unpropitious time to start a radical movement in education at Birmingham. Following the dying down of 'political excitement' in the 1850s, the initiative in the sphere of elementary education rested firmly in the hands of staunch Anglican paternalists amongst manufacturers and clergy. The Birmingham Educational Association founded in 1857 had amongst its most prominent members the merchant J. D. Goodman, the manufacturer J. F. Winfield, Rev. William Gover, principal of Saltley College (founded by Adderley), and J. T. Bunce (like the others, an Anglican).[116] The main achievement of the association was a survey of education among Birmingham's labouring population conducted by the Anglican clergy which demonstrated that levels of attendance were far short of the accommodation available.[117] Nevertheless, trade was good and there was little sign of popular discontent.[118] It is true that the most popular preacher in Birmingham was not a churchman but the nationally-renowned George Dawson at the Church of the Saviour. However, in 1858 this famous Liberal Nonconformist was faced with a strike by his own workers on a newspaper he had tried to get under way in the city.[119] In the same year Sir John Ratcliff, Wesleyan mayor of Birmingham, appointed as his chaplain Rev. Isaac Spooner, the well-born Evangelical churchman who was also vicar of Edgbaston.[120] That a degree of complacency should develop in Anglican circles was not surprising. It spread even to Dissenting radicals such as John Skirrow Wright who in 1862 told the Social Science Congress in London about

Birmingham's 'comparative freedom . . . from crime', the good relations between masters and workmen, the general 'spirit of independence and self-reliance' and the fact that '[as] regards education, the facilities for obtaining it are so great that no child or young person need be without the elements at least.'[121]

CHAPTER 6

MECHANICS AND MEDICAL MEN

ADULT EDUCATION AND MEDICAL SCHOOLS IN BIRMINGHAM AND SHEFFIELD 1830–70

The pursuit of 'improvement' by adults in their leisure time was a minority activity but one which revealed clearly the different forms of solidarity and division which were developing within the class structures of Birmingham and Sheffield. A broad distinction may be made between two kinds of enterprise: associations of professional men, businessmen and gentlemen of leisure for the discussion of literary and scientific topics; and gatherings of 'intelligent working men' (and youths) seeking 'mutual improvement' through their own efforts or with the guidance of men associated with the former kind of enterprise.[1] In Birmingham the two categories of enterprise merged together between the mid-1840s and mid-1850s. In Sheffield, despite efforts to integrate the different kinds of enterprise during the same period very strong tendencies towards fission and segregation predominated.

Implicit in the forms of education indicated above was an encounter between middle-class culture and working-class culture and the form this took depended greatly upon the confidence and vigour of each. In Sheffield, reaction to the 'pagan' traditions of the Sheffield Sunday (and Monday) dominated middle-class and working-class enterprises to enlighten the artisan population. At the same time, the genteel meetings of the Sheffield Literary and Philosophical Society represented a rather desperate attempt to show that recruits to the thin red line of literati defending the outposts of civilisation in South Yorkshire were capable of justifying the words of James Montgomery:[2]

We know of nothing in the soil of Hallamshire that will prevent it from growing philosophers, artists and poets equal to those of Greece.

So insecure were these sentinels of civilisation that when Ebenezer Elliott, who despite his radicalism yielded to none in his revulsion from revolutionary upheaval, applied for admission in 1839 he met with a refusal.[3]

SCHOOLING THE WORKING CLASS

Sheffield's 'respectable' working class were awkwardly placed between a vigorous 'rough' working-class culture and a weak, snobbish and insecure middle-class culture. Association with the former compromised their respectability and contact with the latter carried a cost in loss of independence. Retreat into the sanctuary of the home or an attempt to create an alternative working-class culture were the other perceived options. Birmingham's working men and women did not face these choices. Masters and employees could associate without loss of dignity on either side. The strength and confidence of professional and business establishments in Birmingham permitted them to admit labourers into close association without either side feeling threatened. The Society of Friends in Birmingham were particularly successful in managing this relationship. An early student at the Severn Street First Day Adult School recalled that he had looked forward to his weekly visits 'so that I might have the pleasure of meeting with men far superior to myself, who were always ready to make me their equal for the time being'.[4] This school, in connection with the Bull Street Quaker Meeting, was teaching eighty-four students in 1847. Eight years later, it had subdivided into several classes containing 646 youths and adults. In 1862 John Skirrow Wright gave accommodation to a Severn Street School class at his People's Chapel in Hockley. By 1870, approximately 20,000 students had passed through the classes and received lessons in reading, writing, arithmetic, grammar, geography and elementary science.[5]

Some Anglican clerics followed suit. Grantham Yorke promoted 'self-improvement' at the St Philip's Literary Institute. This was opened in 1846, the year that John Cale Miller took up his post as rector at St Martin's. Miller established a workingmen's association and in 1854 offered a prize for the best essay on the subject of 'cooperation of the working classes and the other classes of society for the elevation of the former'. He found it 'pleasant to see the working men of the parish, not standing alone in a class distinct from the others but going hand in hand with the higher order'.[6] Like Sturge and Wright, Miller drew no sharp division between his religious and political involvements. The subtle weaving together of education, religion and politics was also exemplified in the relationship between the Church of the Saviour and the lower middle class. When the drapers' and grocers' assistants formed a mutual improvement association in 1845, George Dawson was one of its first speakers, delivering a lecture on poetry. The following year he was in the van of the campaign of the clerks and assistants for early closing.[7]

At Sheffield, in marked contrast to Birmingham, establishments for educating the working population were rigidly separated into three compartments: those which gave strict priority to scriptural education; those whose sponsors recognised the validity of discussing 'politico-religious questions'; and those which were sternly utilitarian in their intent, emphasising the need to train artisans in occupationally-relevant skills.

The reluctance of Sheffield's leading citizens to participate in any of these enterprises is ironically recognised in a resolution passed at the meeting to establish the Sheffield School of Design in 1841:[8]

> That notwithstanding the neglect of the leading men of the town in not meeting, it is the duty of those who are assembled, amounting to *three*, to persevere till the great object be accomplished, aware from history that much greater revolutions have been accomplished and begun by much more incompetent means.

A little more enthusiasm had been shown for the Sheffield Mechanics' Institute, founded in 1832. Many of its committee members were drawn from participants in the Sheffield Literary and Philosophical Society, in other words from the thin layer of 'public' professional and business leaders which included Montgomery, Ward and medical practitioners such as Arnold Knight and Charles Favell.[9] Like the Sheffield Literary and Philosophical Society, the Sheffield Mechanics' Institute had an ideology which stressed utility. Its object was to supply to the labouring classes 'instruction in the various branches of Science and Art' which were 'of practical application to their diversified avocations and pursuits'.[10] The institute's predecessor had been the Sheffield Mechanics' Library, founded in the early 1820s. In both cases, the initiatives had come from artisans but the establishment of the institutions had been managed and monitored by the town's middle-class leaders: again, Montgomery, Knight, Ward, other businessmen and a sprinkling of Dissenting ministers and Anglican clergy. In line with its philosophy, an ambitious programme of scientific instruction was attempted and experimental apparatus purchased. However, by the 1840s the mechanics' institute was attracting only a few dozen students to its classes.[11]

During the late 1830s the mechanics' library and the mechanics' institute were both under attack. The former was accused of making available books which would tend to 'deprave the minds, injure the morals, and weaken, if not subvert the religious faith of the great majority of readers'. [12] The latter was seen as narrowly secular. Many of the Anglican clergy, whose prominent role in the provision of basic schooling has already been noted, were deeply opposed to the mechanics' institute. In 1839 they established the Church of England Instruction Society, claimed by its supporters to be 'among the first of its kind in the country'. [13] It was intended to provide a continuing education for graduates of the Sunday schools and an alternative to the streets for young apprentices. In its curriculum it placed a very heavy stress upon religious indoctrination. G. C. Holland noted in 1843 that the object of the society was [14]

> to afford general knowledge to the artisan, and at the same time to produce religious impressions, a prejudice being entertained against the Mechanics' Institute, from the latter being altogether excluded from the scheme of instruction.

Another denominational enterprise was the Quaker adult school, inspired by the example of Birmingham. However, its founder, the banker J. H. Barber was a different kind of political animal from Joseph Sturge. Barber was a 'strong Liberal' but lacked the common touch. This 'singularly undemonstrative' man devoted himself to commerce and good works, not the hustling, bustling world of popular politics. [15]

The complaint of the denominations against the mechanics' library and mechanics' institute was the lack of positive provision within them for the inculcation of 'orderliness' in moral (and, consequently, social and political) behaviour. The attack from within was on different grounds. Early participants in the mechanics' institute had been the Nonconformist minister R. S. Bayley and the maverick Chartist Isaac Ironside. Bayley objected strongly to the strait gate of practical instruction through which working men were to be herded in the name of 'education'. [16] His People's College, founded in 1842, offered a more humanitarian vision. [17] Like its rivals, the People's College aimed to provide an alternative to the education of the street. Its curriculum aspired to give instruction in geography, history, philosophy, Latin and Greek. Science and natural history were also included but were by no means dominant. Students were not to be drilled into 'suitable' moral positions but encouraged to debate the issues arising from 'the history and science of politics'. Not surprisingly, financial aid from the wealthy part of Sheffield society was almost completely absent at the inauguration of this venture. A democratic atmosphere was inculcated drawing on both the model of the Nonconformist chapel and the ideal of a 'college' of scholars pursuing understanding. Its president in 1849 was a shoemaker, Thomas Rowbotham. When Bayley left Sheffield in

1848, sixteen of the students took over People's College and ran it as a self-governing institution supported to a considerable extent by the fees of its scholars.[18] Nearly twenty years later, John Wilson, a prominent Sheffield artisan was proudly stating its virtues before the Social Science Congress. He told his audience:[19]

> How the schools are to be maintained, is the problem to be solved.
> My present experience inclines me to the principles of the
> Sheffield People's College – 'Self-support and self-government'.

Isaac Ironside fell out with the committee of the Mechanics' Library, of which he was secretary, in 1839. The committee had been applying a trenchant policy of censorship since the library's foundation, sixteen years earlier. Sir Walter Scott, and indeed all novels and plays, were considered dangerously subversive. In 1839 Ironside was faced with the dire accusation that he had allowed the plays of William Shakespeare and works with a socialistic leaning most dangerous to Christianity to be placed on the library shelves. He was ejected from his position as secretary and immediately transferred his abundant energies to the Hall of Science, opened in March that year by Robert Owen. To an even greater extent than in People's College, the encouragement of open debate on controversial political issues was the object of Ironside's Hall of Science. For example, the socialist G. J. Holyoake delivered a series of lectures in 1841, including a talk on 'the advantages and disadvantages of trade unions'. Through this institution Ironside was putting into practice his conviction that the broadest possible cultivation of working men's intellectual and critical faculties was an essential step towards political emancipation. Like People's College, there was more than a little of the 'chapel' in the spirit of the enterprise. In 1840 Ironside claimed that the hall was a religious institution and so exempt from the poor rate.[20]

The three streams in Sheffield's educational provisions for working people – the utilitarian, the religious and the humanitarian (or emancipatory) – had two characteristics in common: a revulsion from the street-and-tavern culture of booze and 'baccy', dominoes and dog-fighting; and a chronic frustration caused by the low levels of elementary education among their students.[21] However, efforts to bring about amalgamation so that they could pool their resources were unsuccessful.

In 1847 the mechanics' institute, under pressure from the Workers' Educational Institute (a new Ironside venture soon to be retitled the Hallamshire Mechanics' Institute) was persuaded to throw in its lot with the newly-founded Athenaeum, a recreational club for the well-to-do. A new building for both institutions was opened in 1849, mainly paid for out of funds initially intended for the mechanics' institute. There were vain hopes that the Sheffield School of Design and the

Sheffield Literary and Philosophical Society would share the new accommodation. However, middle-class members of the Athenaeum took the lion's share of the premises. In 1851 the two institutions separated.[22]

Two years later the committee of the mechanics' institute tried to persuade the Church of England Instruction Society to share the burden of providing science instruction. The secretary of the latter body replied to their request[23]

> We do not think it would be expedient for us to unite our own classes with those of the Mechanics' Institute in the subjects and on the terms proposed. . . . While I think the amount of *patent* vice here less than in any town of its size I know, I am perfectly conscious that there exists a festering mass of iniquity among our population, the baneful effects of which can be scarcely overrated. . . . [My] own conviction is that that the only mode of meeting this evil is the training of our juvenile population in an education which is based *distinctively* on the word of God, and the leavening with that word (coupled with periodicals of a distinctively Christian character), of the adult population of our land

The Hall of Science closed its doors in 1848 and the mechanics' library did the same in 1861. Although People's College, the mechanics' institute and the Church of England Instruction Society all survived beyond 1870, only the last achieved a modest prosperity. By 1860 a new building had been opened for the society which had been renamed the Church of England Educational Institute.[24] During the subsequent decade elocution classes were 'most popular', suggesting that the tone was lower middle-class. Evidently, as in the sphere of elementary education, the Anglican clergy were demonstrating considerable resource and staying power. In 1862 seventeen of their number were teaching there along with men of science, and members of the liberal professions'. Not least of the Church of England Educational Institute's advantages was its capacity to call upon the services of clergymen and the staff of the national schools as teachers. In 1866, for example, classes in mathematics and geography were being conducted by headmasters of church day schools. Among the honorary members in the 1860s were 'many leading Churchmen of that day', indicating the great resources of prestige which a national bureaucracy such as the established church could deploy if it chose.[25]

The success of the Church of England Educational Institute was matched by the school of design which, despite its unpromising beginnings, had carried off prize medals at the Great Exhibition of 1851 and moved into grander premises in 1857. Like the Church of England Educational Institute and Wesley College, the school of design had the backing of a national bureaucracy, in the school's case the government itself which provided over half the running costs.[26] The school's relative success is shown by the fact that in 1849 it drew over 550 class pupils while the equivalent institution in Birmingham could claim only 480 the previous year. Ironically, when a select committee of the House of Commons looked into the provincial schools of design in 1864, 'it was then stated that the only town which had reported contrary to the generally-held opinion that such schools could not be self-supporting was Sheffield.'[27]

In Birmingham adult education did not, as in Sheffield, consist of a set of fragmented reactions to the monster Demos haunting the streets and taverns. Instead, its progress was one aspect of: first, the growing confidence of urban radicalism and Dissent; second, the weaving of political ties between middle-class establishments and artisans, clerks and shop assistants in the later 1840s; and third, the political equipoise between older Tory and newer Liberal establishments which was coming into being at about the middle of the century.

On the face of it, the array of educational institutions for youths and adults at Birmingham in the mid-1840s looked very similar to the scene in Sheffield. There was a school of design as well as a 'Lit. and Phil.' (by then known as the Philosophical Institution) and also a polytechnic institution. The Philosophical Institution, which had been in existence since 1800, concentrated upon scientific topics and provided a lecture theatre, museum, laboratory and newsroom for a clientele whose middle-class social composition is suggested by the terms 'select', 'elegant' and 'brilliant' which occur in a description of the institution and its supporters published in 1825.[28] The Birmingham Polytechnic Institution, established in 1843, was the immediate successor of the mechanics' institute which had ceased to exist the same year.[29]

There were also, as in Sheffield, two other kinds of institution: instruction societies run by the denominations; and Owenite or Chartist ventures in popular education. A letter to *The Times* in 1848 claimed that in Birmingham[30]

> we have a literary and scientific society in connection with every large place of worship. There is St George's Instruction Society, St Mary's, St Luke's and other instruction societies, and various other church institutions, in which lectures are delivered *regularly* once, and frequently twice a week on different branches of science, by clergymen and others. The average attendance at each lecture room is two or three hundred. Attached to these institutions is likewise reading rooms and classes. Several dissenting congregations have also scientific institutions, in which lectures are *regularly* delivered. . . . [There] are also a number of general scientific associations . . . the result is that if any

particular evening in the week be fixed upon, say Tuesday, a person acquainted with the town, can reckon up about thirty or forty instructive and elevating meetings.

The author of the letter was a science lecturer. Against his evident enthusiasm should be weighed the consideration that the above institutions left few records and were mainly shortlived.[31] The same is true of schemes such as the People's Hall of Science, opened in 1846 to promote the 'instruction and amusement of the people and the improvement of their understanding, morals and health. . .'.[32] At about the same time the Athenic Institute was founded by a group of Christian Chartists to provide a similar mixture of instructional and recreational facilities. William Scholefield opened the People's Hall of Science and Lord John Manners became president of the Athenic Institute. Despite this patronage, the former venture collapsed in 1849 and the latter in 1852.[33] Neither had the staying power of People's College in Sheffield or the strong connection with a powerful local political movement which made Ironside's educational ventures significant.

In Sheffield the Hall of Science was the educational expression of a major local radical movement. In Birmingham this part was played by the Mechanics' Institute which was founded by men who were shortly afterwards to be active in the Birmingham Political Union and the disputes surrounding the town council: Richard Spooner, Thomas Attwood, Joseph Parkes and William Redfern.[34] As in Sheffield the Mechanics' Institute was intended to provide instruction in science and the industrial arts. However, the political philosophies of the two institutes were very different. At Sheffield in 1836 the physician Charles Favell had commended the local establishment on the grounds that education would produce gratitude and humility in the workforce; instruction 'should not make them impertinent'.[35] The previous year a leading official of the mechanics' institute in Birmingham had asserted quite the reverse:[36]

Men have not their due, and they are, and ought to be, discontented. The prevalent discontent, in truth, properly considered, is one of the most favourable signs of the times. . . . The workman has more knowledge, more mind – he *wants* more. He believes that more is to be had, and eventually he will have it. Very silly it is to lecture him out of his craving. It is nature's provision for the progress of society.

The waning of the Birmingham Mechanics' Institute coincided with the resurgence of local Conservatism in the mid-1840s.[37] Its immediate successor, the Birmingham Polytechnic Institution found survival difficult and, like the mechanics' institute in Sheffield at about the same time, began looking around for partners. This quest, however, was ultimately more successful than it had been in Sheffield. The clerks and assistants, who had recently founded a Mercantile and Literary Institute, were allowed in 1846 to share the premises of the polytechnic institution. One of the clerks' honorary secretaries was J. R. Allen, an ally of George Dawson in the early closing campaign. The same year the polytechnic institution proposed that all the literary institutions of the town – the philosophical, the polytechnic, the society of arts, the news rooms and 'other similar institutions' – should 'build a suite of rooms sufficient for the purpose of all these societies, and that the management should be consolidated, and thus rendered more efficient and less expensive'. In 1848 the plan was revived when the polytechnic received notice to quit from its premises in Steelhouse Lane. Intimations of mortality were presumably also experienced when in 1849 the Philosophical Institution ended its career as a consequence of a mounting debt and lack of public support.[38]

The movement for consolidation was spurred on partly by hopes that 'understanding' between social classes would be thus improved and partly by the promise of economies of scale.[39] W. P. Marshall, secretary of the Institution of Mechanical Engineers, was honorary secretary of a local committee which asked the government to allow town councils to support literary and scientific institutions in 1849. Three years later, Birmingham's Society of Artists invited Charles Dickens to attend a meeting at which the latter gave support to the project for 'an Institution where the words "exclusion" and "exclusivism" should be quite unknown; where all classes and creeds might assemble in common faith, trust and confidence.' The decisive resolution, proposed by Lord Lyttelton at a town meeting early in 1853 called for[40]

> a Scientific and Literary Institution upon a comprehensive plan, having for its object the diffusion and advancement of science, literature and the arts in this important community.

A committee was appointed and a circular then distributed which stated:[41]

> The Institute will consist of two departments; the first being to carry on similar objects to those of the late Philosophical Institution upon a more comprehensive and extended scale, with the addition of a public gallery of Fine Arts. The other department to be an Industrial Institute, or in other words, a School of Science applied to the arts, for artisans, the members of which will participate in the more essential advantages of the first department, in addition to various class instruction, and weekly progressive lectures on the different branches of science, with

special reference to the requirements of the town and neighbourhood.

Over £7,000 was subscribed. Several meetings of artisans were held in various parts of the town which received deputations from the committee, on which Sydney Gedge and Arthur Ryland were prominent. An act passed through parliament giving the town council permission to grant a block of land to the projected Birmingham and Midland Institute which duly began its work in 1854.[42] The annual report for 1858 recorded that the school of design had been given rent-free accommodation in the institute's building on Paradise Street.

In 1855 the industrial department ran three classes, in physics, chemistry and physiology. By 1868 the industrial department was running fourteen classes; chemistry, experimental physics, botany, practical mechanics, geology, physical geography, algebra and geometry, French, German, Latin, history, literature, grammar and writing. There were also special 'penny classes' in arithmetic and singing as well as 'penny lectures'.[43] By the early 1860s almost all the teachers were being paid for their work and at the end of the decade there were over 1,000 subscribers in the general department and about 1,500 students in the industrial department.[44] The cost of teaching in the industrial department was heavily subsidised by subscriptions to the middle-class general department. By 1882 over £20,000 had been transferred in this way between the departments making a sharp contrast to the sad experience of the Sheffield Mechanics' Institute when it amalgamated with the Athenaeum.[45]

Two aspects of the institute's work distinguish it from adult education establishments in Sheffield. The first is the broad range of its students and courses. In 1857, about 39 per cent of the students were recorded as 'artisans', a proportion which had risen to about 45 per cent ten years later. At the later date about 29 per cent of students were shopmen and clerks and about 17 per cent were simply recorded as 'females'. Students were evidently drawn to classes which would help advance their job prospects. In 1860 the committee of the industrial department was 'urgently requested' to establish a new writing class. Arithmetic was in such demand that by 1865 the teacher was complaining about the 'crowded state of the room'.[46] The chemistry class was in 1856 attracting 'chiefly young men engaged as assistants to chemists and druggists'. By 1859 the Institute Chemical Society was in existence whose members, many of them artisans, read papers 'on the scientific principles involved in the operation of their own trades'. Following the 1870 Pharmacy Act which established qualifying examinations, the chemistry teacher expressed his hope that[47] the Midland Institute may be to the chemists and druggists of Birmingham what the institution at Bedford Square is to the chemists and druggists of London.

In 1868 the botany teacher acknowledged that his class was composed 'for the most part of adults holding more or less responsible positions in life and having various aims. Some members of the class have passed their examinations as apothecaries, some as pharmaceutists, and some as certified teachers.' Presumably the pursuit of certificates was one reason for the 'numerously-signed requisition' received in 1866 asking for the formation of a Latin class.[48]

The second distinctive characteristic of the institute was its wholesale commitment to providing channels of social advancement for all its students. In contrast to the Church of England Educational Institute in Sheffield, the Birmingham establishment saw itself as the 'proud mother' rather than the 'stern father' of its progeny. Courses of instruction were deliberately arranged as graduated steps to greater accomplishment. For example, the penny lectures in a wide range of subjects were intended to create an interest amongst 'hard-working artizans' which could be satisfied through more systematic instruction in elementary and advanced classes at rather higher fees. Students in the chemistry classes under C. J. Woodward were put in touch with industrial processes and conditions, for example through visits to gas works, iron works and glass works, and recent advances in research practice.[49] Ex-students whose instruction had paid financial dividends in business were proudly reported. Some found employment at the institute itself.[50] A pamphlet issued in 1865 stated that a register was kept of students who had been taught at the institute 'who are desirous of obtaining situations, and to which register employers have access'.[51] The principal means of regulating the progress of students was the formal examination. The annual report for 1858 announced that each teacher would examine his students at the end of the spring term and award 'teachers' certificates' to those who had made satisfactory progress. 'Council certificates' based on examination by outsiders appointed by the council would be awarded to those who performed well on the basis of two-years' work. The examinations of the Society of Arts were also entered that year and those of the Department of Science and Art three years later.[52]

Looking back from 1882, John Henry Chamberlain recalled the institute's early development:[53]

> In the early days of the Institute the Council found, by experience, that artisans could not use the classes, because they were destitute of the elementary knowledge that was necessary even to enable them to understand the ordinary scientific phraseology of the teacher. So that from the beginning, the Institute has always given

elementary instruction in science subjects. It has, however, never . . . confined itself to elementary teaching only. It was not established for any such purpose. Its end and its aim have, at all times, been to take its students step by step into the higher branches of whatever subject they wished to study, and that the Institute felt itself in a position to teach. Throughout the whole range of our work, from the most elementary to the highest stage to which it can be carried, we test it by the only authoritative test by which such work can be tested, viz, by examinations conducted by qualified examiners. . . . Our range of subjects is so great that we cannot find any one national examination that will include them all, but in all cases we appeal to the highest tribunal that is open to us.

These confident tones were not peculiar to the 1880s. Twenty years previously, the council of the institute had expressed a hope that it might be the 'centre around which all the educational institutions which addressed themselves to the public at large might cluster'.[54]

The council's wish, expressed in 1861, had a similar ring to that espoused by the headmaster of the grammar school two years later when he foresaw the school adopting 'the position of a university, fostering and improving all the educational establishments of this neighbourhood'.[55] The hegemonic impulse, couched in terms of offering a comprehensive service in harmony with other central civic institutions, was common to school and institute. In 1849, for example, an industrial school had been built at Gem Street on land donated by King Edward VI Foundation. Training was to be provided for 'children of destitute parents, of all denominations, free of charge, in general accordance with the system of the Elementary Schools belonging to King Edward the Sixth's Foundation. . .'. One of the grammar school's governors, John Cale Miller of St Martin's suggested in 1857 that the foundation's elementary schools should be opened for free instruction on four evenings a week. He evidently envisaged such evening classes as being complementary to the evening classes for adults which 'will now be opened to the artisans of Birmingham in our MIDLAND INSTITUTE'. When a board of teachers was formed at the institute to help in running the industrial department, its chairman was Rev. E. H. Gifford of the grammar school. Three years later, classes in this department were being made available at reduced fees to pupils at elementary schools run by the various religious denominations.[56]

The school and the institute were complemented by a third institution: Queen's College, known before 1843 as the Birmingham Medical School. In 1830, its founder William Sands Cox had called for the cooperation of other local institutions in his ventures including the practitioners at the general hospital:[57]

I appeal to the Medical Officers to aid the system, to afford clinical instruction to the student, to lay open the book of nature, and not to allow the exertions of several distinguished individuals to remain unseconded. I would appeal to the governors of the school founded by King Edward VI, at some future period on the increase of their funds, to include in their scheme of education medical science, and to afford to the medical student the same advantages which are offered to the clerical scholar; and lastly, I trust the committee of the Botanical Gardens, which originated with the School of Medicine, will open with liberal hands its valuable stores to promote this grand object.

In 1839 he was writing to James Thomas Law, chancellor of the Diocese of Lichfield, about the need for a new clinical hospital which, 'would give to the parent the means of educating his son for a physician or surgeon beneath his eye; and in connection with the Grammar School, by drawing to the town families for the purpose of professional education, it would indirectly promote our prosperity.' By the early 1850s Queen's College included not only a medical department but also a theological department housed in an opulent building which 'might fairly be considered an imitation' of the grammar school, departments of engineering and law, and an arts department for junior students aged 16 years and over which provided instruction in a wide range of subjects (including languages, mathematics and science) leading to the examinations of the University of London.[58] In 1852 Sands Cox sought, without success, to extend the college even further by publishing a scheme for an evening institute attached to it.[59]

Sands Cox's scheme was published a few days after details of the planned Birmingham and Midland Institute were circulated. However, Chancellor Law, Sands Cox's influential patron, was also closely involved with the latter foundation. Queen's College had to be satisfied with the more limited objective of giving 'industrial instruction to those who belong to a higher class of society' than the clientele of the institute's industrial department. The warden of Queen's College (Chancellor Law) and the headmaster of the grammar school were both *ex officio* governors of the institute. Its establishment completed the formation of a trinity of prestigious educational institutions jointly seeking to provide a large proportion of the educational wants of Birmingham. These three institutions were widely felt to be jointly responsible for and representative of science, culture and education in Birmingham. For example, when in 1859 the British Association was pressed to return to Birmingham for its annual conference following a successful visit two years earlier, the invitation was sent by the mayor, the council of the Birmingham and Midland Institute, the governors of King Edward's School and the council of Queen's College.[60] Indeed, in the high summer of Birmingham's 'age of equipoise' men such as Law, Gifford and Miller could have been excused for nurturing the quiet hope that they were on a winning streak: that school, college and institute might become the pillars of a benevolent Anglican ascendancy in Birmingham's educational life, one which would ensure that the cultivation of the lower and middling orders would occur in ways which did not threaten the prestige and authority of the clergy and that part of the lay establishment of gentry, businessmen and professionals with which they were closely associated.

The sphere of adult education replicates the findings of chapter 4 which were that in Sheffield, unlike Birmingham, practices oriented towards industry, religion and politics were rigidly segregated in distinct institutional frameworks. There was a deep-seated inhibition within the social structure of Sheffield against making the transition from a social order whose primary foci of experience and identity were the encompassing and mutually reinforcing solidarities of the family, the tavern, the workshop and the parlour to a social order in which men, women and children could move happily between different institutional spheres and enter without a disabling sense of insecurity into a wide range of social relationships, some of them not quite consistent with each other and some with people outside the immediate circle of kin and friends. Birmingham's inhabitants were better equipped to adopt an attitude towards such institutional involvements which was mid-way between the absolute devotion to close and familiar circles and the outright hostility to commitments which threatened them which were the dominant responses of Sheffielders. In Birmingham a complex network of urban institutions gave inhabitants a feeling of manoeuvrability, a sense that they could find what they were looking for through crafty manipulation in association with chosen fellows. In Sheffield, such institutions were often perceived as alienating. They drew energies and resources away from the primary solidarities which formed the substance of local society. Such solidarities were means and ends in themselves.

The ready acceptance of formal examinations in Birmingham signalled the recognition by local people that these devices provided useful handholds in the scramble for advancement in an increasingly complex and bureaucratic society in which the family and work-group were, for many, inadequate sources of security by themselves. Henry Cole and Lyon Playfair found the Birmingham and Midland Institute thirsty for the schemes of the science and art department.[61] Likewise, Birmingham's middle-class families were eager to enter their children for the local examinations run by the ancient universities. Sheffield was more sluggish in its response.

MEDICAL EDUCATION

So far this analysis has focused upon adult education facilities directed at artisans and members of lower middle-class occupations. In the final part of this chapter some comments will be made upon the part played by establishments of learning in the competition for status and influence within professional establishments, paying particular attention to medical men. Professional men were the mainstay of polite culture in the arts and sciences. Three aspects of their involvement in this sphere must be distinguished. First, professional men from genteel families were part of the literary and 'philosophising' wing of the old order. Their breeding assured their status; their bookish vocations encouraged cultural pursuits. Membership of literary and scientific societies was one expression of these interests and the societies gained prestige by their participation. For example, the old Etonian Alfred Gatty, vicar of Ecclesfield, lectured frequently on topographical, historical and literary subjects at the 'Lit. and Phil.' and elsewhere. A leading litterateur and doyen of Birmingham debating societies was the lawyer Clement Ingleby whose family was well-established in law and medicine. He had been privately educated under masters at King Edward's school and later attended Trinity College, Cambridge. He helped to organise the Shakespeare tercentenary celebrations in 1864. In Sheffield, his counterparts were men like Herbert Bramley, son of the first town clerk and himself to be town clerk, and Bernard John Wake, a solicitor whose family had long-standing connections with the Norfolk interest. Bramley was 'a great lover of the fine arts' and had an impressive collection of books on logarithms in many languages while Wake was active in the Shakespeare Club and the 'Lit. and Phil.'. Another well-established legal family was represented on the Literary and Philosophical Society's committee by Michael Ellison, agent to the Duke of Norfolk.[62]

Amongst medical men Ferguson Branson and Corden Thompson at Sheffield and the Cox and Johnstone families at Birmingham were all well-established by the 1830s. Branson was an active supporter of the Sheffield School of Art and 'a painter of no mean order'. His father had entertained Princess Victoria to lunch in 1835. Thompson, president of the 'Lit. and Phil.' in 1832, boasted a lucrative practice and an extensive collection of paintings. The son of a cleric, the security of his social position is shown by the fact that when the Provincial Medical and Surgical Association met at Sheffield in 1845, Thompson was offered the presidency – and he refused it. The surgeon Edward Townsend Cox, a 'good old Tory' who also came from a clerical family was remembered for having challenged a physician at Birmingham General Hospital to a duel over some trouble connected with a book club. The social position of his son William Sands Cox is indicated by the fact that 'some days before the Queen's visit was made in 1858, it was to Mr Cox that application was made respecting the then mayor, upon whom there was some hesitation as to whether the honour of knighthood should be conferred.' The Johnstones were, however, the more distinguished medical family and when the council of the Birmingham Medical School was appointed in 1829 Edward Johnstone was made president and his younger brother John became vice-president.[63]

A second aspect of participation in scientific and literary societies was the pursuit of influence and acceptance by men who were 'marginal' by virtue of being newcomers or outsiders.[64] This included migrants into Birmingham or Sheffield without family connections there, Dissenters who felt excluded from patronage and privilege in the hands of the Anglican gentry, and medical and legal practitioners from non-genteel backgrounds. Immigrants to Sheffield such as the Nonconformist ministers Henry Hunt Piper and Peter Wright were both prominent in the Literary and Philosophical Society. The same institution served as a useful stepping stone in the rise to influence of George Calvert Holland. He was its president in 1833 and two years previously had held the same office in the mechanics' institute. The son of a Sheffield saw-maker, he became physician to the infirmary and an alderman. Robert Slater Bayley, founder of People's College, was an immigrant from Lichfield in 1836. He was a frequent lecturer on literary, historical and educational subjects. Arthur Ryland, promoter of the Birmingham and Midland Institute, was the Nonconformist son of a coach harness manufacturer. He specialised in opening up closed circles to new social influences. A prominent member of the Birmingham Law Society (as secretary, vice-president and finally president) Ryland was the first provincial solicitor to be elected to the council of the Incorporated Law Society. As has been seen, it was largely through his efforts that the act disqualifying practising solicitors from becoming county justices was amended.[65] This example introduces a third aspect of the cultural and educational activities of professional men which was the attempt by members of occupational groups such as architects, engineers, artists and doctors to raise their status and increase their capacity to regulate their own affairs. This movement was stronger in Birmingham than in Sheffield. The contrast between the two cities may be shown by examining the case of medical men.

The establishment of provincial medical schools was one aspect of a profound transformation in the conditions of medical practice during the three decades after 1830.[66] The divisions between the three 'estates' of physicians, surgeons and apothecaries – consisting respectively of 'gentlemen', 'craftsmen' and 'tradesmen' – were breaking down. By 1850 the modern division between consultants and general practitioners was becoming established and the Provincial Medical and Surgical Association had been created as an important representative body for the latter group. The development of hospital medicine applying new techniques of clinical-pathological research provided an increasingly large part of the subject matter of medical education after 1830. The systematisation and rationalisation of medical science contributed to a great improvement in the power position of the medical practitioner *vis-à-vis* his patients. As the cities grew in population the market for professional services widened considerably. Instead of having to solve problems defined by aristocratic sufferers who summoned doctors to their bedsides, medical men had the new security of large urban practices built up by charging graduated fees. With the backing of his educational qualifications the doctor could rely upon being of higher status than most of his patients. State legislation and professional associations such as the BMA (the successor of the Provisional Medical and Surgical Association) increasingly replaced aristocratic patrons as the arbiters of medical practice.

During the period 1830–70 Queen's College in Birmingham was one of the most ambitious and well-developed medical schools in the provinces. The Sheffield Medical School was much less enterprising and its very existence was frequently in jeopardy. During the late 1820s rival medical families in Sheffield sponsored two competing institutions. The Jacksons and Overends in alliance with Corden Thompson opened the Sheffield School of Anatomy and Medicine in October 1828. The Favells in association with Arnold Knight established the Sheffield Medical Institution in July 1829. Clannishness and political antipathy fed the rivalry. The Jacksons and the Favells both had a long-standing connection with the infirmary at Sheffield. However, their political dispositions were opposed. Charles Favell was relatively liberal and included among his connections G. C. Holland and Luke Palfreyman, both men with rather radical leanings. Favell and Arnold Knight were both active in connection with the mechanics' institute. The Jacksons had close kinship connections with the Overends, a Conservative Quaker family.[67] The antipathies between the two groups can only have been increased when in 1831 Corden Thompson, an ally of Overend, defeated Charles Favell in a contest to secure the appointment of physician to the infirmary.[68] The Overends' school was destroyed in 1835 by a mob protesting against the 'resurrection' of corpses for dissection, which evened up the balance between the two factions somewhat.[69] When Thompson refused the presidency of the Provincial Medical and Surgical Association in 1845 the position was awarded to Favell. Thompson gave as his reason for refusing the position 'that he was not in agreement with his medical brethren in the politics that were agitating the profession at that time'.[70]

By 1850 the rivalries had cooled and a single school, the Sheffield

Medical Institution was in existence with Wilson Overend as president. He was sufficiently liberal in politics to offer his benevolent support to People's College, though his lawyer brother William was a rampant Tory. Despite initial donations from Norfolk and Fitzwilliam and a loan from the town trustees the institution depended greatly upon student fees and subscriptions from the doctors themselves. In 1865 the school was unable to fill the chairs of anatomy, physiology, materia medica and botany. At a meeting of the council in March that year it was decided to close the school in the hope that it might later be reorganised on a sounder basis.[71]

A distinction must be made between, on the one hand, the weakness of 'the medical profession' in Sheffield – evidenced by rivalries amongst different families, and by the frailty of local 'collegiate' institutions – and, on the other hand, the signal success within Sheffield society of leading medical families.[72] The son of Charles Favell became archdeacon of Sheffield. Arnold Knight received a knighthood in 1841. Most striking was the upward mobility of the Overends. Hall Overend, the son of a clerk, had been apprenticed to a local apothecary. His eldest son Wilson became a magistrate and subsequently deputy lieutenant in both the West Riding and Derbyshire. Wilson's brother William took silk in 1851, stood as Conservative parliamentary candidate for Sheffield in 1857, and was chairman of the special commission on the Sheffield trade union outrages in 1867.[73] The rapid growth of the city and the paucity of active local gentry created a 'status vacuum' at the top of Sheffield society which avidly 'sucked in' professional men. Financial success, kinship ties and a willingness to undertake public work counted for more than the local strength of professional associations.[74]

By contrast, there was intense competition for positions of social leadership in Birmingham and the surrounding counties. Local doctors had among their ranks many men of long-established and unimpeachable gentility. This asset was exploited in the fight to establish a self-regulating medical profession with improved status and authority. The pretensions and privileges of lawyers and churchmen were deeply envied. When the Provincial Medical and Surgical Association was founded in 1833 its first president was Edward Johnstone, physician of Birmingham General Hospital. Its second president was his younger brother John, who held an MA degree from Merton College, Oxford, and was a friend of the Bishop of Lichfield. As has been seen, both brothers also had leading positions on the committee of the Birmingham Medical School. By 1843 the school had acquired a royal charter as the Queen's College. Three years previously, Queen's Hospital, the only provincial hospital in England expressly designed for teaching purposes, had also been opened in Birmingham.[75]

Two prominent features of the surging expansion of confidence amongst medical men in Birmingham were the ambitiousness of their vision and the ambiguous character of their relationship with the legal and clerical branches of the old order. William Sands Cox was not a modest man. His medical school was intended to become a central institution in not only Birmingham but the whole of the Midlands. He wanted the grammar school to 'afford to the medical student the same advantages which are offered to the clerical scholar' and was confident in 1830[76]

> that the School of Medicine will be fostered and supported, and that the day is not far distant when *Birmingham will become the seat of a grand scientific and commercial college.*

Nine years later he was eagerly anticipating the benefits which would accrue 'from the rapid communication in all directions with surrounding districts'. The new Queen's Hospital would draw professional families to the town and[77]

> we would thus be prepared to see eventually realised the
> prophetic and expanded views of our esteemed and venerated
> President, expressed at the anniversary dinner, June 4th 1831, that
> "Birmingham will become the seat of a Central University".

The charter of 1843 incorporating Cox's school as the Queen's College at Birmingham provided for departments of medicine and surgery, architecture, civil engineering, law, theology and – in a junior department – general literature and arts. Three years later the college was granted the right to issue certificates qualifying students to become candidates for the degrees of BA, MA, LLB, and LLD at the University of London. By 1851 the council of the college was extended to include representatives from the Institution of Mechanical Engineers, the Birmingham Architectural Society and the Birmingham Law Society.[78]

This expanding empire was, however, riven by a widely reverberating contest for status and authority among doctors, clerics and lawyers. The issues were presented in an extreme way in the early 1840s by Thomas Gutteridge, professor of anatomy at the Society of Arts. His views may well have been sharpened by the progress of a dispute within the latter establishment between the practising artists and 'non-professional committee members'. When the school of design was founded in 1842 the 'professional committee' of artists objected to their teaching arrangements being subject to the control of 'non-professionals'. They withdrew from the Society of Arts and set up their own Society of Artists.[79] Gutteridge was a skilled practitioner, 'a specialist and highly successful operator' who came from a tough breed. His sister once attacked the editor of the *Birmingham Daily Gazette* with an umbrella.[80] In 1843 Gutteridge was an unsuccessful candidate for a post at the general hospital. The position was awarded to a rival by a small clique of governors which included the successful applicant's father and father-in-law (an Anglican vicar) with the active connivance, alleged Gutteridge, of the solicitor John Welchman Whateley. The Whateleys, namely John Welchman and George, were between them not only governors of the hospital but also legal agents to the King Edward VI Foundation.[81]

Gutteridge did not take this lying down. Instead he wrote a pamphlet in which he complained that 'admission to the medical service was allowed or debarred mainly at the pleasure of active and meddlesome attornies' and that the Whateleys were operating 'in effect, *a register office for official appointments*, not only for the General Hospital, but also for various public institutions.'[82] Bitterly, Gutteridge continued:[83]

> The legal profession enjoys countless public advantages; –
> honours and riches, – peerages, judgeships, and offices of profit
> innumerable: the medical profession on the contrary has few of a
> public nature; its most distinguished posts are nearly all, as in this
> present instance, honorary yet not sinecures, and though
> laborious, not stipendiary. MEDICAL HONOURS ARE
> MEDICAL PROPERTY. The virtues and accomplishments of *Ash*,
> of *Withering*, of the *Johnstones*, and of *Booth* are the acquisition, and
> have become the inheritance, of the medical faculty. That
> inheritance shall not, without my loudest protest and sturdiest
> opposition, be seized by venal and unscrupulous attornies.

The Anglican church also came under his whip. There were fifty clergy amongst the hospital's governors and on its staff was the Rev. Peyton Blakiston whom Gutteridge accused of killing a patient with an overdose of Prussic acid. Blakiston was 'an interloper "amongst us" '.[84] The aggrieved Gutteridge declared:[85]

> *Medical rights, free from extra-professional encroachment*, is the cause I
> assert. . . . *Promotion by merit and not through lucre is* the maxim I
> have espoused, and *the upright distribution of honours to the worthy*,
> the principle by which I will stand or fall.

In the event Gutteridge fell. Despite the tentative support of two governors of the general hospital the allegations were dismissed after a discussion at the annual general meeting in 1844. During the meeting an effective speech against Gutteridge was made by Rev. Prince Lee, headmaster at the King Edward VI School.[86]

Indeed, as has been noticed, during the 1840s and 1850s Anglican interests extended their influence over Queen's College. The site for Queen's Hospital was purchased by the wealthy Samuel Warneford, rector of Bourton-on-the-Hill, whom Cox attended without fee for many years. Between 1838 and 1852 Warneford donated a total of £27,150 to the hospital and college. There were expectations, disastrously disappointed in 1855, of a large legacy on the occasion of his (no doubt eagerly anticipated) passage to celestial reward.[87] The price of Warneford's support was a commitment[88]

> to combine religious and scientific studies and pursuits; to make medical and surgical students good Christians as well as good practitioners . . . always and especially with a view to exemplifying the wisdom, power and goodness of God, as declared in Holy Writ.

The 1847 college charter insisted that the principal, vice-principal, treasurer, dean and the tutors in classics, mathematics and medicine should be Anglican. Effective control was given to a council stuffed full of Anglican clerics and the county gentry. Gradually day-to-day control narrowed even further, falling into the hands of the warden who was required to be a divine trained at one of the ancient universities. J. T. Law who held this office for many years, modelled the theological department on an Oxford college and hoped that in conjunction with the arts department it would become a 'flourishing College and nascent University, rising up with its appropriate chambers for students, lecture rooms, halls, courts and quadrangles'.[89] Law even began to speak (borrowing Johnstone's phrase) of 'our central University'.[90] However his vision assigned a distinctly subordinate place to the medical practitioners in Queen's Hospital.

The counter-attack of the medical men was not long in coming. In 1851 Sydenham College was opened by the staff of the general hospital. It was purely a medical school. There were no religious tests. It was governed by local doctors on a voluntary and unchartered basis. Fees were low. For seventeen years Sydenham College provided medical practitioners with an institutional base free from the interference of lawyers and divines.[91] Within Birmingham, the movement to improve the standing of the medical profession was led by impeccably genteel families, long-established locally, such as the Coxs and Johnstones. One of the Johnstones, a 'good Conservative Whig', even penetrated the ranks of the grammar school governors, as has been seen. However, while the resources of prestige and influence commanded by such families were an asset in asserting the authority of doctors *vis-à-vis* legal and clerical practitioners, these same resources did not prevent their medical colleagues from pursuing the object of collective self-regulation by the whole occupational group. The foundation of Sydenham College was one manifestation of this determined pursuit. Another was a demand in 1859 by the staff of Queen's College that the cantankerous Cox should retire from managing that institution's affairs. The charity commissioners were called in and a long process of legal wrangling ensued which issued in the act of 1867. As a result, the medical men of Queen's Hospital were freed from subjection to Queen's College, Sydenham College was amalgamated with the latter, and the Anglican bias built into Warneford's provisions was overthrown.[92]

One way of distinguishing the two cities is as follows. In Birmingham, relations among medical men were to a great extent governed by the existence of inter-professional rivalries amongst doctors, lawyers and clerics which took the form of disputes over the principles of management appropriate for established and newly-created institutions such as the general hospital, Queen's College, Queen's Hospital and Sydenham College. In Sheffield, relations were to a greater extent governed by intra-professional rivalries amongst medical families such as the Favells and Overends. These rivalries were superseded not by the establishment of strong collegiate institutions but by the syphoning of the leading participant families into a social world whose command posts were the vicarage, the assize court and the country house. These processes were aided by the fact that even well-born medical men such as Corden Thompson, Martin de Bartolomé and Ferguson Branson were 'new men' in the city. They were new in the sense of being immigrants: Thompson from Nottinghamshire (via Paris, Berlin and Vienna) in the mid-1820s; Bartolomé from Castille (via Edinburgh) in the late 1830s; Branson from Doncaster (via Winchester and Cambridge) in the early 1840s. Of these three, Bartolomé was the most clearly 'foreign' and despite his *hidalgo* pedigree complete assimilation into the higher reaches of genteel society in the West Riding was presumably more difficult for him than for Branson and Thompson. It is striking therefore that Bartolomé played a part in the formation of the Provincial Medical and Surgical Association and was the mainstay of Sheffields Medical School for eighteen years after 1848. '[In] 1866 it was acknowledged that he had become quite the recognised leader of the profession in the town.'[93]

The politics of collective organisation, public debate and conflict over the management of civic institutions were not exclusive to Birmingham's professional men. They were deeply ingrained throughout the middle, lower-middle and artisan sections of Birmingham society, producing complex alliances within and amongst these classes. In Sheffield, by contrast, the urban elites of professionals and businessmen were integrated, loosely, through a web of private and semi-private ties rather than through participation in public and professional associations. There were two major exceptions. One was the Church of England which bore the brunt of elementary school management and ran the most successful adult education institution locally with an attendance which compared very favourably with the Birmingham and Midland Institute.[94] However, the range of subjects offered by the Church of England Educational Institute in the 1860s suggests that the establishment's appeal was heavily directed at the new lower middle class aspiring to a commercial training.[95] Its sponsors did not benefit from complex links with a wide range of industrial, clerical and 'minor professional' occupations, with wealthy subscribers to the general department and with other educational institutions such as were developed in the Birmingham and Midland Institute. The other major exception was the Sheffield trade societies. As the *Sheffield Independent* declared in June 1867[96]

> The workmen of each trade thoroughly believe that they have a
> right to enclose for their own use their particular field of
> industry. . . . When arguments are addressed to them founded
> on the principle of the right of every man to use his industry and
> skill freely according to his own judgement, they quote the
> regulations of the bar and legal profession.

CHAPTER 7

'OLD FASHIONED IDEAS AND CUSTOMS'

THE ATTACK ON CLOSED CORPORATIONS IN BIRMINGHAM AND SHEFFIELD 1864–70

When Matthew Arnold, writing in the late 1860s, wanted an example of the threat of 'anarchy' produced by contemporary developments in the middle and working classes he repeatedly referred to the 'no-popery' rioting at Birmingham in 1867.[1] When he sought to typify 'the notion of defect in the essential quality of a working class' he cited the 'Needy Knife-Grinder', that central figure in Sheffield's economy.[2] Nonconformist manufacturers hooked on biblical texts and obsessed with the power bestowed by their new machinery; ignorant workers combining their physical force to wreak havoc in the name of 'liberty': these were Arnold's bogeys. The state of relations between social classes had been dramatised during the late 1860s by a series of events such as the investigations of the Schools Inquiry Commission, the Royal Commission on Trade Unions and the extension of the franchise to many skilled workers. However, in *Culture and Anarchy*, Arnold is not presenting a general plea on behalf of 'the upper class' but rather appealing for principles of social order, enforced by the state, which would give special recognition and a privileged position to styles of learning and forms of understanding embedded in the values and routines of Oxford.[3]

The development of large-scale industrial capitalism and gigantic manufacturing cities encouraged the growth of public bureaucracies to share the task of regulating the novel processes and solidarities coming into existence. However, the politics of the middle decades of the nineteenth century consisted to a great extent of attempts to employ the power of the local and central state either to strengthen or to weaken the defences surrounding institutions and social groups embedded in the old social order. Ironically, despite Arnold's hostility towards the 'Needy Knife-Grinder', Sheffield's trade societies were as much threatened by 'machinery' as were Oxford colleges and like Arnold they sought the protection of the state for their special interests. Accused during the Sheffield Outrages Inquiry of organising rattening and 'outrages', William Broadhead argued that such measures were necessary in order to enforce the rules of the trade societies which were under serious threat:[1]

> Is it your opinion that in all trades whether at Sheffield or otherwise they will, from not having means of enforcing the payment of contributions or the means of enforcing their rules, resort to rattening of some sort or another? – Yes sir, and I believe that if the law would give them some power, if there was a law created to give them some power to recover contributions without having recourse to such measures there would be no more heard of them.

In effect, like Arnold, Broadhead wished to call upon the resources of the state to buttress a declining interest, though in the latter case the challengers were based in Attercliffe and Brightside rather than South Kensington. Broadhead was reiterating a demand which had been made by the Sheffield Organised Trades five years before and which was often heard in that city during the 1860s.[5]

During the late 1860s the authority of the central state apparatus was brought into the local political equation at Birmingham and Sheffield through the investigations of two royal commissions whose outcome in each case was to help shift the balance of local forces to the disadvantage of social interests resisting 'modernisation'. In the years 1865 and 1866 the Schools Inquiry Commission paid special attention to the affairs of the King Edward VI Foundation in Birmingham. They heard evidence from the major participants in an intensely fought dispute over the control and management of the schools run by the foundation and also received a special report on the schools from the assistant commissioner, T. H. Green. The following year, 1867, the special commission of inquiry sat at the council hall, Sheffield to hear evidence on the 'Sheffield Outrages'. This evidence was the basis of a subsequent report to the Trades Union Commission. Each governmental inquiry was investigating a local conflict in which one of the main contenders was an entrenched vested interest dominating a vital local resource. In each case the vested interest being investigated recruited its membership largely through private connections and its affairs were exempt from any substantial degree of public scrutiny. In Birmingham this vested interest was the governing body of the King Edward VI Foundation. In Sheffield it consisted of the artisan societies in the light trades. In both towns there was local opposition to these 'irresponsible' bodies. In Birmingham it was organised and articulated by the Free Grammar School Association and the town council. In Sheffield opposition had no parallel organisational form but was pungently expressed by W. C. Leng of the *Sheffield Telegraph*.[6]

In this chapter the investigations of the two royal commissions will be located within a narrative account of related events in the political, industrial and educational spheres between 1864 and 1870. The object will be to argue that these events illustrate decisive shifts within the framework of social differentiation of which the class structures and institutional orders of Birmingham and Sheffield were aspects. In the wake of the decade of 'equipoise' between about 1854 and 1864, the social and political initiative in Birmingham moved definitely towards public institutions closely identified with the municipality, and away from voluntaristic associations and semi-private organisations subject to strong influences emanating from the county. In Sheffield the initiative moved irrevocably out of the hands of the neighbourhood-based institutions of the petty bourgeoisie and skilled working class towards the new large-scale industrial enterprises.

Sheffield's leading manufacturers were very new arrivals, their enterprises had expanded very rapidly, were operated on an unprecedented scale, and commanded (with few effective competitors nationally and internationally) a powerful strategic resource. The steelmen had no local manufacturing rivals, drew substantial amounts of capital and labour from outside Sheffield, and their leaders were wooed by the county and metropolitan establishments. Their principal concern was the management of the working class in the new residential areas of Attercliffe and Brightside. In other words, they had a special interest in some aspects of Sheffield life in so far as they affected a framework of operations which was national and international rather than municipal. These points may be expanded in comparison with Birmingham.

A high proportion of Birmingham's manufacture was oriented to the production of finished articles for export and local consumption.[7] The division of labour in production was largely encompassed within the boundaries of the city, strengthening bonds of interdependence between producers with complementary skills. These bonds were made more complex still by the symbiotic relationship between the gun and jewellery quarters and firms employing female and child labour, as was seen previously. Sheffield's light trades also produced finished articles but within a much narrower range of goods. Competition, secrecy and the rigid demarcation of occupational boundaries were more prominent aspects of relations between producers within the city. Unlike Birmingham, the labour for the new heavy industry was not drawn from artisan families in the old-established trades (at least before the 1880s). Whereas before about 1850 the pattern of

industrial differentiation in Sheffield had tended to strengthen neighbourhood commitments at the expense of municipal solidarity, after
that date the steel industry created strong links between production in
one sharply defined quarter of Sheffield and production in other cities,
with an equally detrimental effect on municipal solidarity. Although
steel firms produced some finished goods, for example, tools, and
although a railway carriage works had been erected near John Brown's
Atlas Works by the 1860s, a high proportion of steel products were sent
out of the city for final processing and assembly.[8] Among the new
products being manufactured by the 1860s were[9]

> Cast steel locomotive double crank axles, and tender and carriage
> axles; single crank and other marine shafts; cannon blocks,
> jackets, tubes and hoops for ordnance and hydraulics, forged out
> of solid ingots of cast steel; solid castings in steel, not forged or
> rolled, for railway wheels (with tyres in one solid piece), railway
> crossings, hornblocks or cheek plates, and a variety of other
> castings and forgings in steel for railway rolling stock, permanent
> way, machinery, ordnance, &c., &c.

In subsequent decades, the high costs of transport into and out of
Sheffield were to engender even greater specialisation in high-quality
steel, encouraging close collaboration with manufacturers and
customers elsewhere whose precise specifications had to be determined and met.[10] As will be seen, the principal aspect of local public
work which drew the attention of some steel manufacturers at least
was the provision of efficient education for their future workers.

A final point to be made before looking in more detail at the two cities
between 1864 and 1870 is that although the pivotal point of each
analysis is a conflict between rising and declining interests, the composition of the social groups concerned and the strength of their
members' commitment underwent important changes during the
period. It will be possible in some instances to notice the subtle re-
definitions of interest and shifts in allegiance which occurred as new
issues arose and as the increased importance of public municipal
institutions (in Birmingham) and heavy industry (in Sheffield)
imposed new systemic constraints upon social action.

SHEFFIELD

When the Dale Dyke Dam burst on 11 March 1864 it cost 240 lives in
Sheffield and destroyed nearly 800 dwellings.[11] Indirectly, the rushing
waters also helped to undermine the old Liberal establishment in that
city. This establishment was, in effect, led by Thomas Dunn and
Robert Leader at that time. One of their colleagues was Frederick

Mappin, managing director of Thomas Turton and Sons, file manufacturers.[12] Mappin was also a director of the water company which owned the dam as was Robert Hadfield, Liberal MP for Sheffield. The other Liberal MP, J. A. Roebuck was publicly sympathetic to the plight of the water company. One of Turton's other directors, W. A. Matthews, was a long-serving alderman on the town council.[13] This latter body failed to act effectively against the water company in spite of demands that it should be 'municipalised'. Facts of this kind gave Leng of the *Telegraph* ample ammunition to direct at Sheffield's leading Liberals. He implied that they had culpably failed to act against the water company in spite of its gross neglect.[14] However, despite Leng's hostility Roebuck, who was very popular amongst the Sheffield artisans, was successfully returned at the 1865 General Election.[15] Nevertheless, the political weakening of the old Liberal establishment and its supersession by an increasingly Conservative establishment headed by the new steel men was hastened by the events of the subsequent four years during which the participants in the water company drama were drawn into very different alignments. In particular, skilled craftsmen and important file manufacturers such as Mappin, who had been loosely associated through their support of Liberal candidates, were thrown into radical confrontation at the workplace.

During the 1860s two models of industrial regulation were available to members of the Sheffield trade societies. The first was an elaborated version of the unions' traditional insistence upon their responsibility to govern the practices of their trades, especially through their control over the labour supply. In 1859 the Sheffield Association of Organised Trades was founded. Its executive included William Broadhead of the saw grinders, William Dronfield, a printer, and Robert Applegarth, a carpenter. The association was dominated by skilled craftsmen, many of whom identified not with the masters or with the men but with 'the trade'. The principal goal of the association was to mediate in disputes within the local trades. Giving aid to workers against their masters was a secondary objective should the former fail. Indeed, the association insisted that it would aid masters in the case of unauthorised strikes. Its ultimate ambition was the deeply conservative one of restoring a 'gild-like corporate organisation of industry with legal powers of enforcement in which masters and men should be equally represented'.[16]

Arbitration was also a crucial feature of the second form of industrial regulation on offer, one which was associated with the name of A. J. Mundella, the Nottingham hosiery manufacturer.[17] Under the aegis of the Nottingham Chamber of Commerce, Mundella was the principal founder in 1860 of a board of arbitration and conciliation which was to fix piecework rates and the price of labour in the hosiery trade.

Mundella presided over this body during its first eleven years in the course of which the board's authority was successfully established. Its decisions did not have the force of law.[18] In this and in other ways Mundella's scheme differed from the association's model. The board in Nottingham had been established at the initiative of manufacturers and within an industry in which the division between employers and employees was much clearer than in the Sheffield light trades. Mundella's rationale was that masters and men, both of whom had the right to organise, should agree on matters of mutual interest. Conciliation was to take place within a framework which recognised the constraints of market forces and the importance of mechanisation.[19] By contrast, the Sheffield unions retained the ambition of manipulating the market through apprenticeship regulations and by putting men 'on the box' (i.e. paying them from union funds in times of slack trade). They were also, of course, hostile to mechanisation. In contrast to the strong and central emphasis in Sheffield upon preserving the rights and customs of the local trades, Mundella's scheme belonged to a broader political strategy of reform. This strategy encompassed working for the extension of the franchise (through the Reform League), for greater regulation of licensing hours (a cause dear to sabbatarians and campaigners for teetotalism), and for the rapid extension of educational facilities.[20] Such a strategy involved a more positive role for the state than the mere protection of local vested trade interests, a more wide-ranging cooperation between masters and men than submission to the dictates of local arbitration bodies, and a willingness to lend local energies to a national movement whose leadership tended to gravitate to the metropolis where constant pressure could be exerted upon Whitehall and Westminster.

During the mid-1860s the viability of the association's model of industrial regulation was severely tested and found wanting. Divisions within the local artisan population were made public at the Social Science Congress at Sheffield in October 1865 when John Wilson, a penknife grinder, read a paper condemning the practice of arbitration and the effects of trade unions upon the free working of the market: 'being a believer in free competition, I detest interference with any man's labour.' He also argued that 'invariably the most powerful combinations of operatives have failed when met by combined capitalists.' William Dronfield read a defence of the unions, declaring that they benefited not just workers but also the community at large. In the proceedings of the conference, Wilson's paper was published *in extenso*. Dronfield's was omitted.[21]

Wilson's prognostications were confirmed by the file strike of 1866. The file trade was a prominent part of a sector of Sheffield industry in which several firms combined steel production with the fashioning of tools. A large number of skilled craftsmen were employed by these

165

manufacturers, both on and off the premises. Such firms as Turtons, J. Kenyon and Co. (file makers), Spear and Jackson, Eadon and Sons (saw manufacturers) and Ibbotson Brothers (edge-tool makers) were at the centre of the conflict between craft traditions and large-scale mechanised industry. In February 1866 nearly 4,000 filesmiths, file grinders and allied workers struck over a wage claim and faced a lockout by the employers who were organised in a File Manufacturers' Association.[22] Frederick Mappin was prominent among them. Several of the employers promptly ordered file-cutting machines of a kind which had recently been successfully introduced in Manchester. Such machinery had been forbidden by the unions. A Machine File Grinding Company was established. In response, the file unions organised a cooperative society to undertake file-cutting by hand. They also joined the Association of Organised Trades.[23] For more than fifteen weeks the unions paid out well over £1,000 per week to their members. The association's attempt to arbitrate during March, which included a public debate between both sides at the public house owned by Broadhead, failed when the employers insisted upon the unions' unconditional acceptance of the new machines. By early June the file unions, popularly regarded as the strongest in town, were forced to send their men back to work on the new machines without a wage increase. The most that could be won, after further strikes in 1866 and 1867, was an agreement that employers should only employ skilled men on the machines.[24]

The strike was a crucial test of the power relative to each other of two forms of capitalist order. Probably nothing less could have stimulated the call for national support which went out from the association in spite of its members' strong parochial orientations. A conference of delegates met in Sheffield during July 1866, by which time the strike was over. There were delegates from the large national trade unions, county miners' associations (including the Yorkshire miners), local unions, trades councils (including Glasgow) and the International. Although the London Trades' Council and the amalgamated societies were cautious in their support, George Odger described the conference as 'one of the largest ever held in the cause of labour'. The conference proposed mutual support against lockouts, shorter hours, councils of arbitration and conciliation, schemes for cooperation, and amendment of the Master and Servant Law. A United Kingdom Alliance of Organised Trades was formed with its headquarters in Sheffield and its officials drawn lock, stock and barrel from the Sheffield association.[25]

For a brief moment the national initiative in trade union affairs lay with the Sheffield societies, local unions very deeply embedded in the old social order which were facing a direct challenge from the institutions of modern capitalism. However, despite their apparent organisational triumph, the Sheffield unions rapidly became isolated both locally and nationally. The ignominious defeat of the file unions in 1866 was soon followed by the 'Hereford Street outrage'. A can of gunpowder exploded at the house of a saw grinder who had disagreed with his union. The saw grinders operated in firms such as Eadon's which, like Turton's, were highly dependent upon skilled labour. The affair was a gift to leader writers. The Sheffield Chamber of Commerce seized the opportunity to call for an inquiry and was backed by the town council, the Cutlers' Company, the Manufacturers' Protection Society and, prudently, the Sheffield Association of Organised Trades. On this issue, the association acted in concert with the London Trades Council to whom the initiative in national trade union affairs now shifted. The London trades were not only very anxious to disassociate themselves from the odium which attached to Sheffield but were also strategically well-placed to campaign within the metropolis for a reversal of a recent court decision which denied the legality of trade unions. The ensuing royal commission on the trade unions, whose membership included J. A. Roebuck, resulted in an improvement of the legal status of trade unions, but a sharp condemnation of the Sheffield outrages. It confirmed the leadership of the metropolis, centre of the great amalgamated unions, within the national labour movement.[26]

The special commission of inquiry discovered that most cases of rattening and acts of violence against person and property occurred in the grinding trades. William Broadhead, the secretary of the Saw Grinders' Union and (until the inquiry) treasurer of the United Kingdom Alliance of Organised Trades was found to be a major instigator of the outrages. In the course of the examination of witnesses, Broadhead was established as 'a very bad man' who had 'imposed upon the public' while Dronfield, speaking on behalf of the organised trades both nationally and in Sheffield, was allowed to emerge as a 'respectable man'. The Sheffield Alliance's address to Lord Palmerston in 1863 condemning the outrages was praised as 'a respectable thing'.[27] Dronfield was told[28]

> If every society had so respectable a secretary as you, I do not doubt that they would be very much better off than they are.

The strategic advantage obtained by the larger employers as a consequence of not only the file strike but also the widespread condemnation of 'outrages' is shown in the evidence of William Bragge, managing director of John Brown and Company Ltd.[29] Browns had made a 10 per cent cut in wages earlier that year and faced a strike of the Ironworkers Union. A lockout had been successfully carried out using non-union labour from outside Sheffield.[30,31]

Are the men whom you now employ unionists or non-unionists? –

> They are non-unionists. Have you made it a rule that you will employ non-unionist only? – We have abstained from employing unionists. On what grounds? – On the ground of the coercion exercised by them when we employ them.

> Is it your custom, when a man comes into your employment, to send to the place from which he had come to ascertain what is his character? – It is our custom.
> Whether he is a union man or not? – Whether he is a union man or not.
> If he is a union man is it your practice to engage him or not? – We should not do so now, though formerly we did.

The publicity surrounding the inquiry gave Sheffield workers a bad name among readers of the national press and made it more difficult to advocate the defensive strategy of craft protection of which the 'outrages' were an extreme manifestation.[32] However, the behaviour of Broadhead and the grinders was not deviant in the eyes of their peers but rather showed extreme commitment to values held by a very large proportion of Sheffield's workforce. Although only twelve out of the sixty unions were directly implicated by the inquiry, the midnight work of the ratteners was an expression of strong occupational solidarities to be found within several Sheffield trades.[33]

Dronfield pointed out that rattening was most prevalent amongst grinders because the stealing of bands was relatively easy to carry out. However, the offence being punished might have occurred in a related trade, for example amongst forgers, whose work would be equally disrupted by a cessation of grinding. Rattening the grinders could be a means of indirectly enforcing contributions or restricting numbers of apprentices in a wide range of trades. A complex system of cooperation and compensation had developed amongst the unions.[34,35]

> Is it necessary that they (i.e. other unions) should be amalgamated with the grinders in order to cause them to ratten for them or not? – So far as I know of those amalgamations (and I am speaking now of the trades amalgamated amongst themselves, and not of the general amalgamation), the saw trade, the scythe, sickle and hook trade, the scissors grinders, and forgers, and I believe the sickle grinders and scythe forgers are in amalgamation among themselves. – And if anything happens to one branch they call upon the others to assist them in enforcing the rules? – This is what I understand to be the case.

Devilish union officials could not be blamed for all such practices since '[we] have cases where secretaries themselves have been rattened, and had their bands taken'.[36] Another witness sketched a typical scene:[37]

> We will suppose three men. Supposing three men were in a
> beer-house, and began to talk of trade matters, and in
> conversation it is found that one of the three owes money to the
> society, trades' unionists as a rule would not be surprised to hear
> of that man's tools being taken without the interference of any
> official or any one further than the three.

As Sydney Pollard has shown, the saw grinders' society was attempting to maintain a high level of wages by rigidly controlling entry into
the trade and maintaining idle saw grinders out of union funds. The
victims of the outrages instigated by Broadhead were maverick saw
grinders who were outside the union. They produced inferior goods at
low prices and took on several apprentices. The latter received an
inadequate training and subsequently had to be taken on the 'box' lest
they flood the market.[38] The victims of Broadhead had few friends in
Sheffield. Even the *Sheffield Telegraph* was forced to admit[39]

> that outside the immediate circle of roughs proper there are
> hundreds, and we very much fear, thousands who extenuate and
> palliate the dark deeds disclosed, and who secretly, if not openly,
> sympathise with Broadhead.

Nevertheless, the model of industrial regulation associated with the
reform strategy of advanced Liberalism became increasingly attractive
to Sheffield's union leaders after the traumatic experiences of 1865–7.
William Dronfield on behalf of the Organised Trades and the Reform
League, invited A. J. Mundella to come to Sheffield in 1867 as a
possible parliamentary candidate. The old Liberal establishment of the
city followed this lead by the artisans and at a subsequent mass
meeting Mundella was adopted as the candidate instead of J. A.
Roebuck. The latter had lost favour on a number of counts, including
his hostility to union witnesses during his service on the royal commission and his ambivalent attitude towards Gladstone's Reform Bill in
1867.[40] The political campaign during the 1868 General Election
showed that a considerable realignment of social forces had occurred
in Sheffield during the mid-1860s.

Early in 1868 Roebuck gave a lecture in Sheffield on capital and
labour which largely consisted of a rehearsal of the latter's faults. The
vote of thanks proposed after the meeting was defeated.[41] However,
Roebuck had the support of Leng's *Sheffield Telegraph*, his strident
opponent three years previously, and was also backed by several
substantial employers. He was invited to address employees at several
large works, including Turtons. Paradoxically, Roebuck had the
sympathy not only of large employers who wished to see the long-
established might of the local trade societies broken but also men who
saw Mundella as the leading edge of an alien movement, directed from

outside Sheffield, which was a threat to other local vested interests. Veterans of the old Democratic party came out for old 'Tear 'em', as did several wine and beer sellers including Broadhead who was a former landlord as well as a former union secretary. The latter told a meeting of working men that he feared that Mundella would represent the London trades rather than those of Sheffield.[42]

In his first major speech to his potential supporters Mundella declared himself to be in favour of the extension of the suffrage, the secret ballot, disestablishment of the church, financial and administrative reform in government, compulsory education, cooperation, and support for trade societies whose bargaining rights should be recognised and whose funds should be 'protected against the thief as effectually as the funds of the Bank of England or any other Joint Stock Company'. This programme had no appeal for larger employers such as William Bragge who felt they could run their businesses very well without trade unions. Mundella's middle-class supporters included Nonconformists such as W. J. Clegg, J. H. Barber, Robert Stainton and J. C. Calvert who supported a programme of sabbatarianism and teetotalism. Mundella also won favour with a number of the larger shopkeepers who, it may be surmised, because of their dealings with a wide cross-section of local working-class people as customers were more sensitive than the larger manufacturers to the aspirations of the Sheffield population.[43] The experience of 1865–7 had shown that the pursuit of self-respect and a comfortable standard of living by standing firm on the traditional rights of long-established crafts now carried severe political and even legal penalties. At this moment of uncertainty, with their old champion Roebuck as discredited in the eyes of artisans as was Broadhead before 'respectable' society, Sheffield's working-class population were receptive to the alternative which they were offered. As Broadhead foresaw, Mundella had the full backing of the London-based Reform League. George Howell, the league's secretary, claimed responsibility for doing 'what the local agents could not do, viz, unite the numerous trades into one committee for electoral purposes'.[44]

The 1868 General Election had a dual character in Sheffield. On the one hand, dyed-in-the-wool protagonists of the old politics of the tavern and vestry were in opposition to advocates of national reform movements seeking to influence and extend the use of the central state's power. On the other hand, the election marked the transposition into the party political arena of a class conflict being fought within industry. The larger employers were heavily in favour of Roebuck while the union leadership was predominantly behind Mundella. Four candidates stood at the poll, including George Hadfield who took little active part in the contest, and Edwin Price, who campaigned as a Conservative. The voting was as follows:[45]

Hadfield	14,797
Mundella	12,212
Roebuck	9,571
Price	5,272

Hadfield and Mundella were duly elected, with the help of heavy voting in their favour in the working-class districts of Nether Hallam, the Park, Attercliffe and Brightside.[46]

The victory of Mundella did not signify the capture of Sheffield by advanced Liberalism. A population in which 25 per cent of the voters were artisans even before 1867 could drum up little local enthusiasm for the Reform League amongst either the trade unions or the middle classes.[47] A city in which drink was considered a necessary companion to labour in both the light and heavy trades was relatively immune to the blandishments of the United Kingdom Alliance. The cause of educational reform certainly did not excite popular support. Subscriptions to the National Education League were meagre in Sheffield.[48] Significantly, the league whose leadership in Birmingham was firmly in the hands of the Liberal Party, was introduced to Sheffield under the aegis of both Liberals and Conservatives. A resolution in favour of the league was proposed in January 1870 by Robert Leader and seconded by his arch-rival W. C. Leng. The president of the Sheffield executive was William Bragge, whose anti-union sentiments have been noted, but its members included William Dronfield. The league's effective influence in Sheffield lasted only about a year since the local executive refused to act as mere fund-raisers for Birmingham.[49]

When responsibility for ensuring adequate elementary education in Sheffield passed to the school board in 1870, the results of the first election revealed the outlines of the coalition of establishments through which the city's affairs would be managed during the next quarter of a century. Of the fifteen candidates who were elected, the majority belonged to conservatively-inclined congregations of Anglicans (four), Wesleyans (three) and Roman Catholics (one) while only three (an Independent, a Unitarian and a Free Churchman) were sponsored by the National Education League. At the top of the poll, drawing the 'plumped' votes of Sheffield's Roman Catholics was Michael Ellison, the Duke of Norfolk's agent in the city. Eight of his colleagues were manufacturers, five of them in the steel industry: Robert Eadon, Charles Wardlow, Charles Doncaster, Mark Firth and Sir John Brown. The latter was to be chairman of the school board until 1879 when he was succeeded by Mark Firth.[50]

Of the five members of the school board also serving on the town council in 1870, only one (Sir John Brown) was a steel manufacturer. In fact, the decade after 1863 had seen a diminution of the proportion of council members who belonged to the steel industry with some slight recovery between 1868 and 1873 (see Table 23). A similar pattern is displayed with respect to council members classified as 'merchants and manufacturers' or otherwise identifiable as being fairly substantial employers both inside and outside the steel industry. Medical men and solicitors also lost ground although the latter recovered wonderfully well, an augury of their future significance in the council chamber.[51]

TABLE 23   *Membership of Sheffield Town Council 1863–73*

	1863	1868	1873
Steel manufacturers	12	7	9
All merchants and manufacturers	28	22	25
Medical men	2	1	1
Solicitors	4	2	5
Total number of council members	56	56	64

Sources: J. M. Furness (1893) and directories.

During the 1860s Sheffield Town Council suffered a very serious decline in its reputation which had barely recovered from Ironside's career. Even in the wake of the Dale Dyke disaster the council had not had the political will to take over the water company and so it remained heavily dependent upon the rates squeezed out of the local population. Trade unionists as well as employers were deeply disgruntled with the council. William Dronfield claimed in 1867 that six years earlier the Association of Organised Trades had been unable to carry out its own investigations into the local 'outrages'. A public meeting had been held and a committee formed 'but owing to the then mayor and the leading men of the town refusing to cooperate with them, the committee was dissolved without having gained any information on the subject.'[52] Such revelations gave plausibility to the *Saturday Review*'s suggestion that[53]

> there is a peculiar local and moral disease which we may venture to call Sheffieldism – a malaria and pestilential fog which saps the energies of Hallamshire in particular, and which infects the particular trade of cutlery and steel goods, or the employers in that particular trade, with an indigenous cretinism and a paralysis of the moral functions that secrete the function of responsibility.

In fact, as has been argued, the tide of social development which overwhelmed the traditional strongholds of the tavern and vestry also left the town council stranded, a relatively minor institution in the shadow of the steel manufacturers and the great landowners. Aldermanic robes had no special charm for most of them but a well-trained and compliant labour force was a necessary adjunct to their industrial investments. The town council could languish but the school board had to be a success.

BIRMINGHAM

The experience of Birmingham was very different. In 1865, William Harris, a prominent member of George Dawson's Church of the Saviour, joined the town council. E. P. Hennock writes:[54]

> In 1865 Harris's accession was an isolated case but from the perspective of a few years later he was a significant precursor. After 1867 we find a number of able recruits to municipal politics, 'belonging indeed to precisely the class of burgesses most desirable to the Council', to quote the words used of Joseph Chamberlain, who seem to have been brought there by their interest in the extension of popular education. Their accession was crucial. Having entered under what proved to have been a misapprehension, they stayed on, dealing with the pressing tasks with which the Corporation was faced at the time, and thereby raising considerably the ability and general tone of the Council.

The 'misapprehension' was that responsibility for ensuring adequate elementary education would eventually be given to the town councils, a belief which, in Hennock's view, helps account for the election of, for example, John Lowe (1863), George Dixon (1864), William Harris (1865), Jesse Collings (1868) and Joseph Chamberlain (1869). They were early participants in a movement which in the twenty years after 1862 increased the proportion of large businessmen on the town council from under 8 per cent of all seats to over 23 per cent while the proportion of small businessmen decreased from over 32 per cent to under 18 per cent.[55]

Hennock argues that Dawson's preaching played an important part in providing 'a new vision of the function and nature of the corporation'. This vision was responsible for 'the recruitment to the Town Council of the social and economic elite of the town whose abilities made the actual administrative improvements possible'.[56] The vision of local government which developed in Birmingham subsequently became widespread throughout the nation, argues Hennock, but it was first expressed in that city because 'the town was the stronghold of the National Education League, the body that stood for no compromise on the issue of public responsibility for education.' A further reason was that in the league and in the municipal reform movement 'the pacemakers were . . . the Unitarians, quasi-Unitarians and Quakers' who by comparison with other large towns 'formed an exceptionally high proportion of the religious spectrum in Birmingham'.[37] Certain questions arise, however. Why did Dawson's vision of municipal responsibility find such a sympathetic audience in Birmingham? Why were Birmingham's Unitarians, quasi-Unitarians and Quakers so much more active in municipal public service from the mid-1860s than their equivalents in Sheffield? Why did the National Education League, a provincial movement seeking to impose a national policy of universal, free, compulsory and unsectarian elementary education upon the central state, find its headquarters in Birmingham?[58]

The answers to these questions are suggested by the preceding chapters. Birmingham was a city characterised by a high degree of dynamic density and complex intermeshing between its institutional orders and classes. A strong sense of local identity focused upon the city itself had been developing since the late eighteenth century in the course of conflicts with county interests (for example, during the early years of the town council) and with central government (for example, during the period of Chartist disturbances). By the middle 1860s the social tendencies which during the 1830s and 1840s stimulated the aggressive campaign of Nonconformists against church rates and which swept the Birmingham Political Union onto the town council had progressed to the extent that the balance of political advantage between county and city was swinging strongly towards the latter. At the same time, the scale of the tasks of social management was growing beyond the capacity of voluntary associations and private endeavours to cope with them.

In these new conditions the political agenda was transformed. First, institutions in Birmingham tainted with the 'jobbery' and 'corruption' of pre-1832 styles of government came under renewed attack from opponents whose confidence had greatly increased. Second, control of public institutions financed through local taxation became a more important objective for all groups seeking to influence the city's affairs. Third, as central government increasingly took cognisance of the developing shape of institutional orders such as education and industry (for example through the royal commissions of the 1860s) and as the major political parties began to accept that the state could be used to implement major social reforms, so political leaders in Birmingham, as elsewhere, worked to construct organisational means of influencing these processes.[59] Just as Ironside was able to exploit the remarkably solidary neighbourhood structure of Sheffield society in his attempt to monitor and control the activities of Sheffield Town Council, so, at a higher level of integration, men like William Harris and Joseph Chamberlain were able to exploit the strong bonds of the Liberal establishment with the local working-class and lower middle-class population. Birmingham was experiencing steady industrial growth and differentiation and a relatively modest population growth.

Free from the sharp divisions which set masters against men in Sheffield, Birmingham was a secure base for launching a provincial movement to influence national politics.

Another consequence of the relative freedom from fears of lower-class unrest in Birmingham was that when divisions within and between the city's middle-class establishments became more pronounced in the mid- and late 1860s there were few inhibitions against bringing the conflicts into the sphere of public political debate. As has been seen, in Sheffield during this period the artisan population faced a choice between two modes of controlling industrial practices and managing relationships with larger employers. In Birmingham, members of the big bourgeoisie faced a similar choice, in this case between two ways of controlling civic institutions and managing relationships with the working population. The first model insisted upon the privileged position of the Church of England and the genteel and exclusive lay circles closely associated with it. The local labouring population was to be cared for through the charitable endeavours of a patrician establishment which cultivated its connections with the county and metropolis. The competing model denied that Anglican persuasion, genteel birth or knowing the right people should give special power or privilege within the public realm. Care for all members of the community was a primary function of public institutions rather than private charity, and these institutions should express the wishes of an enlightened citizenry, including the intelligent working class. In practice, of course, the wealthier citizens would exercise a disproportionate share of responsibility and influence in civic affairs just as in Mundella's arbitration scheme the employers retained many strategic advantages in industrial bargaining.

Dawson's preaching was a powerful expression of the latter approach. It had an obvious appeal not only to Dissenters but also to warehouse clerks and artisans of various faiths or none, to public servants, and to professionals and businessmen who felt excluded from the influence which they felt their achievements merited, both in their occupational spheres and in public life. Too much emphasis should not be laid upon the special charisma of Dawson. He was active in Birmingham affairs from the late 1840s but, as R. W. Dale recalled, his insistence upon 'the vital importance of securing for municipal office the wisest, the most upright, and the most able men in the town' was 'for some time without much effect'.[60] It emerged as a powerful ideology of an establishment settling into power during the decade following the 'age of equipoise' when a stage of social development had been reached which made its realisation a plausible objective. By the late 1860s, as will be seen, some of its echoes could be heard in the words of an Anglican who would soon be leading the opposition to Chamberlain on the school board.

In the early 1860s, dissatisfaction with the extent of educational provision was not rife amongst Birmingham's leading Liberals if the words of John Skirrow Wright in 1862 to the Social Science Association at London are any guide:[61]

> As regards education, the facilities for obtaining it are so great that no child or young person need be without the elements at least; in fact, there appears to be rather a want of scholars than schools. The free grammar school gives a gratuitous first-class education to several hundred boys, and its advantages are used by the principal inhabitants of the town, without respect to creed or sect. There are in connexion with this truly noble charity (its income is about 12,0001 per annum) several elementary schools, at which the sons and daughters of artisans can obtain, without cost, a good, sound, and most useful education; also attached to every church, and to several chapels, are day schools, where good elementary (and in some cases more advanced) education can be obtained at from 2d to 6d per week.

However, two years later, Wright was one of the two honorary secretaries of the Free Grammar School Association, a body set up in 1864 to campaign for fundamental reforms in the management of that 'truly noble charity'.[62] This remarkable change of temper was an indication of the growing confidence and aggression of a rising establishment which had first cut its political teeth in the late 1840s and early 1850s.

Education was an obvious sphere within which to attack the clerical establishment and its lay associates who had built up such a strong position in Queen's College and the grammar school. The issue was not simply the need to extend educational provision but also the wish to displace the old establishment from its privileged position of influence in the city's affairs and over the working population. In Birmingham, unlike Sheffield, formal education was by no means the only major institutional sphere connecting the upper and lower orders outside the workplace. As responsibility for the health and welfare of the population drifted increasingly into the public domain, the Liberal Party's political organisation in Birmingham was strengthened. By 1867, ward committees were established on a permanent basis.[63] Although the Birmingham Liberal Association, founded two years earlier, was initially intended to secure Liberal parliamentary representation, its machinery was also a means of capturing control of the town council.[64] Possession of this base offered a means of attacking the old establishment on a wide front.

As in Sheffield, the setting up of a royal commission offered an excellent opportunity of pouring opprobrium upon an institution which could be presented as thoroughly retrograde. The Free Grammar School Association, which rightly claimed support from 'leading gentlemen of the town, of all shades of political and religious opinions' criticised the secret and closed nature of the school's management and the fact that 'old fashioned ideas and customs were . . . perpetuated and such changes as were called for by the advancing spirit of the age were too long delayed'.[65] Before the commissioners, some members called for the foundation's funds to be partly devoted to improving preparatory schooling and girls' education, with a special eye to the needs of the 'middle middle class'.[66] W. L. Sargant, an Anglican and the association's first president, wanted an improvement in the teaching of mathematics and a more active involvement in the 'locals', the middle-class examinations which he had helped to sponsor.[67] Others, both Dissenting and Anglican, placed more emphasis upon educating the poor. John Skirrow Wright thought free schools for the poor should be established with foundation funds.[68] George Dixon, who succeeded Sargant as president, argued that children of poorer working-class families were largely excluded from the foundation's elementary schools.[69] He proposed that the schools in which such children were presently educated[70]

> should have either some possible or positive connexion with this foundation . . . whereby the poorest boy in Birmingham might have the opportunity, if he were qualified by his industry and talents of availing himself of that opportunity, that he should have the opportunity of rising from those lowest schools up to the highest.

The concept of an educational ladder to be scaled by virtue of talent was also implicit in the association's suggestion that a large share of places in the grammar school should be filled by competitive examination rather than by the nominations of individual governors.[71] It was also insisted that the share of resources devoted to boarders should be diminished[72]

> on the grounds that the whole of the powers of the masters should be devoted to the education of Birmingham boys, and that no part of it should be given to the instruction of boys coming from a distance.

The priority of the town's interests was also insisted upon in the selection of governors. T. H. Green emphasised the opposition of local opinion 'to the introduction of crown nominees or magnates of the neighbouring counties upon the board'.[73] However, the keenest-felt grievances were against the practice of excluding Dissenters and members of the town council from the governing body of the foundation. R. W. Dale, Congregationalist minister at Carrs Lane said that the people of Birmingham, a 'heartily liberal town' in which about half the population and very many public figures were Nonconformists, objected to 'using the social influence and prestige connected with the administration of a great public trust in the interests of a particular political and ecclesiastical party'. He coupled this complaint with an assertion that 'the great majority of the governors . . . ought to live in the town, or the immediate neighbourhood of it'. This is further evidence of the popular identification of the old Anglican establishment with county interests. Dale did not want Nonconformists to be placed on the governing body by virtue of their faith since 'the law should not recognise in any privileges or duties of citizenship a man's religious creed'.[74] George Dixon took this principle further by objecting to the requirements that the headmaster and second master should be selected from among the clergy.[75] This objection was a strong echo of the battle also being fought over the administration of Queen's College during these same years.[76]

The association's solution to the problem of placing capable and illustrious citizens, including Dissenters, on the governing body was to permit the magistrates and the town council to share in the appointment of governors. The mayor, Edwin Yates, and Arthur Ryland both pointed out that the town council already helped to manage a number of educational and cultural institutions, including the Birmingham and Midland Institute upon whose council representatives of the municipal corporation had served since 1854.[77] Here was the nub of the issue. As in the 1830s and 1840s it was a question of the relationship between two civic strongholds. One was closely identified with the old county-oriented Anglican establishment, and the other was becoming a major expression of the strong links between the Liberal establishment and its local constituency among lower middle-class and working-class interests within the city. In 1864, C. E. Matthews, writing a pamphlet in support of the association's case, had stressed that 'there are men enough in the present Council quite worthy to take their place by the side of the existing Governors.'[78] However, the relative fitness and 'respectability' of the two bodies was at the heart of this dispute, as it was in the case of Broadhead's saw grinders compared to Dronfield's Alliance of Organised Trades.

T. D. Acland, one of the commissioners, identified the problem as being 'the removal of social jealousies between two important and highly respectable bodies in the town of Birmingham'.[79] That judgement was unsatisfactory to John Cale Miller, rector of St Martin's and an ex-school governor. While he had 'the profoundest respect for the intelligence of the town council in their proper department' he doubted their being 'the best managers of a great educational establishment'. Miller recalled that the governors had preferred to keep nominations in their own hands because 'it was thought that we should secure to ourselves more respectable colleagues. . . .' They had feared that 'there might be little cabals and cliques in the council, which would not so readily secure the election of suitable men'.[80] Grantham Yorke, whose revulsion from Birmingham's 'barbaric' workshops has already been noticed, went further. As a governor for over twenty years, he believed that 'a large portion of the intelligent inhabitants of Birmingham' were well-satisfied with the current system of appointing the governing body and with the school's classical curriculum. He was determined to uphold that 'the school is a church school and is intended to remain a church school'. On all these points he cited the example of the 'great public schools'.[81]

The headmaster of the grammar school went furthest of all. Rev. Charles Evans wanted to take more boarders, make fee-paying general, extend the teaching of Latin into the elementary schools and generally free himself from 'local pressure which may often be unwisely exerted'. He eschewed the indignity of entering the 'locals' and proudly claimed that 'in the classical school the routine of the education is very much the same as that adopted in the great public schools.'[82] He proposed to the commissioners that King Edward VI Grammar School should stand alongside Eton, Harrow and Rugby in a category of great central endowed schools, eighteen in all, ministering to the educational needs of nine educational districts which would cover the whole of England.[83] It is not too fanciful to compare these grandiose aims with the attempt by the Sheffield trade societies to establish themselves as an important part of the leadership of a national trade union movement. However, the realisation of such aims was denied because the grammar school, like the Sheffield craft unions, continued to be primarily identified with and oriented towards a local clientele.[84]

T. H. Green was clear that the grammar school could never emulate Eton or Winchester.[85]

> Any head master would see that a school, situate in a noisy street in the middle of a smoky town, can never hope to draw largely on the 'genteel' classes. His chance of working it with distinction depends (speaking generally) on his success in getting the cream of the boys whose parents, as a class, want a mercantile education for them, and in stimulating them to seek the 'higher culture'. To do this he must take, as his test of promise, proficiency in the recognised elements of a mercantile education.

Here, *in nuce*, was a possible strategy for preserving and extending the practice of 'high reason and . . . fine culture' whose threatened disappearance troubled Green's contemporaries at the ancient universities. At issue was not simply the relative value of different kinds of knowledge but also the relative influence to be exercised by different sections of the middle class whose various ways of life and competing claims upon the deference of others were intimately related to the importance placed upon these forms of knowledge within the schools.

In the course of a masterly analysis of the grammar school and the disputes surrounding it, Green suggested a scheme which cleverly incorporated many of the association's proposals while throwing his intellectual weight behind the academic prejudices of Charles Evans, the headmaster. Green did not want to see the provision of education determined either by the blinkered market considerations of tradesmen or the equally narrow-minded snobbishness which caused the masters in the classical department to resist closer association with their less 'genteel' colleagues in the English department. He was, however, prepared to exploit snobbery and competitiveness, particularly among the petty bourgeoisie, in support of his objective of creating, through the education system, a channel which would carry traffic in two directions: the lower middle class and even those below this level would be impregnated with 'general culture' administered from above; potentially high-minded children from these social ranks would be promoted to positions of influence at the universities and elsewhere. Above all, there could be 'no better employment of educational endowments than as a balance in the interest of learning, to the attractions of money-making'.[86]

Green suggested that more elementary schools should be built by the foundation in the suburbs of Birmingham where the 'class of small shopkeepers is very strong'. Such schools would be of a higher academic and social standard than the national schools and would take a similar clientele to commercial academies. These new elementary schools would be financed by introducing fee-paying into the grammar school. The income from fees would also subsidise a large number of scholarships from the elementary schools to the grammar school. The latter would be reorganised into a preparatory department for the younger boys and English and classical departments for those senior boys who were able to pass an entrance examination. This examination would also be available to pupils from other schools. It would be possible for a bright boy to win scholarships taking him from an elementary school all the way to Oxford or Cambridge.[87]

Like the Free Grammar School Association, Green believed in an educational ladder. However, he differed from the association in two ways. First, his test of the foundation was not whether it satisfied the existing 'legitimate' demands of Birmingham's population but whether it did enough 'to tempt its pupils to seek a higher education than they seek at present'. He believed that in Birmingham 'the supply of education must precede and create the demand.'[88] In practice Green was conducting an excellent piece of market research on behalf of that constituency of educational practitioners which looked to Oxford and Cambridge for their guidance, the same constituency which the latter, hoped to cultivate through the 'locals'. Green found that Birmingham's businessmen preferred to have their sons trained through practical experience 'under the father's eye'. To them 'the Universities . . . are unknown ground.' A commercial career for their offspring from the age of 16 years was 'the natural course of things at Birmingham with the commercial, and to a large extent with the professional class'. Green's greatest expectations were directed at the old lower middle class in contrast to the greater pre-occupation of the Free Grammar School Association with the poor. Green had special hopes of small tradesmen such as the 'small baker or publican' who were not thriving in business and who commonly had 'a considerable but not very discriminating appreciation of intellectual decorations'.[89],[90]

> Such persons are easily encouraged by the appearance of a taste for books in their sons to seek for them a scholastic career, and the temptation of exhibitions and scholarships can be set before them with great effect. As a rule, it is not among the rich that the grammar school must seek for a large supply of boys to train for the University. Among them a University career will always be looked upon as a speculation, and as comparatively not a good one. To men with a less advantageous alternative before them, if a way is opened to it by exhibitions, it will offer much higher attractions. This is not the place to remark on the limitation of these attractions to churchmen, by the exclusion of dissenters from the ultimate prizes on which they depend, the fellowships and the masterships in grammar schools.

Green also hoped that by keeping fees in the English and classical departments at the same level parents could be induced through 'bribery' (his term) to 'prefer the "classical" to the "English" education for their sons by offering them the more costly educational article at the same price as the less'. Ideally, suitable boys should be in the classical department by the age of 13 years and the success of his plan depended upon 'the skill of the masters in picking out promising talent among the little boys'. Evidently, the system of 'sponsored mobility' which was later to become an important characteristic of English secondary schooling already had an influential advocate in T. H. Green. The sponsorship of talent through formal examinations would be aided by the exclusion of social undesirables through the introduction of fee-paying. Only the elementary schools would take responsibility for 'the rougher element now found in the English, and the lower region of the classical, school'.[91] As will be seen, the mode of thinking which lay behind Green's plan had considerable effect on the development of secondary education in Birmingham over the subsequent two decades.[92]

In Birmingham as in Sheffield, the late 1860s witnessed a process of realignment as new issues arose. In Sheffield, opposition to 'Broadheadism' was not the same as support for Mundella. In Birmingham, opposition to the foundation's governing body was not the same as support for the Liberal clique, increasingly strengthened by the active adherence of men of substance, which was securing its grip on the town council, organising its forces to capture Birmingham's parliamentary seats in the wake of the 1867 Reform Act, and subsequently hoping to win a majority on the new school board. The process of realignment may be traced from 1864 onwards.

The governors of the foundation and the committee of the Free Grammar School Association were both drawn from a similar range of occupations. Among the governors were to be found Anglican clergy (including Grantham Yorke and Isaac Spooner), doctors (including James Johnstone), legal practitioners (such as T. C. Snyd-Kynnersley, the stipendiary magistrate), and manufacturers (amongst whom were J. D. Goodman and J. T. Chance). The association's committee comprised eighteen manufacturers, five merchants, two well-to-do tradesmen, nine members of the legal profession, five other professional or semi-professional men and ten men of the cloth (of whom three were Anglican). Of the town council members on the committee, twelve were businessmen and three were professional men. The town clerk, a solicitor, was also on the committee.[93]

The professionals and businessmen in the association were anxious to diminish the extent to which the exploitation of their wealth and expertise was hindered by the persistence of bodies constituted like the school governors. Among the professional members of the committee were men such as William Harris who helped to found the Birmingham Architectural Society and served as honorary secretary of the Birmingham Liberal Association from 1867–70. He was an innovator in a number of fields. For example, he had been the first quantity surveyor in the Birmingham area to have an architect's training and also became known as the 'father of the caucus'. His colleagues included Walter Foster who was one of the association's two honorary secretaries. Foster was prominent in the British Medical Association, and a strong advocate of involvement by doctors in public work. Prominent among the businessmen were self-made men such as Arthur Albright, who developed the safety match, and the paper manufacturer James Baldwin. The committee was not confined to Liberals. J. B. Hebbert, who had helped to adapt Conservative Party organisation to new social and political conditions during the 1830s, and William Gover, a persistent clerical campaigner for improved elementary education, were both members.[94]

Gover's widely-publicised researches into the state of local schools for the poor in 1867 stimulated a last ardent attempt to improve school attendance by the old means of organised private charity.[95] The Birmingham Education Aid Society drew into temporary cooperation men on both sides of the recent dispute over the grammar school. The society's committee included George Dixon (as president), Jesse Collings, George Dawson and Joseph Chamberlain alongside T. C. Snyd-Kynnersley. The vice-presidents were R. W. Dale and Grantham Yorke. However, already sensitivity about the special interests of the Church of England made it necessary to have separate funds for the support of children attending denominational and un-denominational schools.[96] A large number of the children offered free education by the society did not remain at school and by 1868 it was clear that this voluntary exercise by the city's leading citizens was completely inadequate. This realisation coincided with the brilliant success of the Birmingham Liberal Association in capturing all three seats in the 1868 General Election.[97]

Earlier that year, Jesse Collings had reached the conclusion that elementary education throughout the nation would have to be 'secular (or unsectarian) . . ., compulsory as to rating and attendance and under local management'. He wanted to see created a national society which would uncompromisingly work for this end. Such a society 'would gather to its support the men of literature and science; powerful sections of Nonconformists, and the whole body of the people. It would effectually prevent the passing of any half measure. . . .'[98] The expression of such sentiments carried the message that an increase in the involvement of the state, both centrally and locally, in elementary education implied a growth also in the influence of the radical and Dissenting wing of the Liberal Party and hence a threat to the position of the Church of England.[99]

George Dixon, an Anglican who had served on the town council since 1864 and entered parliament in 1868 was ready to draw the merely practical conclusion that effective measures for schooling the poor could not be provided by voluntary action and therefore he accepted the necessity of the scheme for state action supported by Collings, Chamberlain, J. T. Bunce, and Harris. Although Dixon, whose initiative led to the foundation early in 1869 of the National Education League, preferred the term 'unsectarian' to 'secular', the alarm bells were already ringing loud in the camp of the Conservative Anglican establishment which controlled the national schools. Gover, who had joined with Dixon in the work of the Birmingham Education Aid Society, held aloof from the National Education League. Sargant also 'declined to join a movement which appeared extravagant in its object'.[100]

By the end of the year a Birmingham Education Union had been established under the presidency of a local aristocrat, the Earl of Harrowby, with the object of 'promoting the extension of the present system' and opposing 'the plan of free, rate-supported, secular schools'.[101] Apart from heavy clerical support in the city and county, the union had the adherence of Snyd-Kynnersley (as committee chairman), J. D. Goodman (vice-chairman) and, among its vice-presidents, foundation governors such as Grantham Yorke, and J. O. Bacchus. Its inaugural meeting was attended by Charles Evans, the grammar school's headmaster and the school governors, C. R. Cope and W. Matthews. However, other supporters included men who had earlier joined the committee of the Free Grammar School Association such as W. H. Blews and Sebastian Evans.[102] They were now on the opposite side of the fence to previous colleagues on that committee such as George Dawson, William Middlemore, Henry Manton, C. E. Matthews and Samuel Timmins who all flocked to the standard of the National Education League.

The league itself was divided on several issues such as the extent to which 'unsectarian' implied 'secular', whether free schooling should be confined to the poorest pupils, what share of the cost of education would be borne by the rates, and how rigorously compulsion was to be enforced. For example, A. J. Mundella was a fierce advocate of the need for compulsion but at odds with the league on other issues. When the government's education bill was introduced its provision for rate-aid to be given to voluntary schools run by the denominations divided moderates such as Dixon from radical Dissenters within the league who were determined to deny aid to the Church of England. A Central Nonconformist Committee was set up to fight the relevant clauses. Chamberlain became an influential member of this committee, serving with J. S. Wright, William Harris, and Jesse Collings. William Middlemore was its chairman with R. W. Dale and H. W. Crosskey as joint secretaries.[103]

By 1870 political groupings which six years previously had been polarised for and against the governors of the grammar school were realigned for and against the radical Nonconformist clique within the National Education League. Of the fifteen Liberal candidates for the school board, ten were members of the Central Nonconformist Committee.[104] Their eight opponents included several supporters of the Birmingham Education Union.[105] Through a failure of electoral management only seven of the fifteen successful candidates belonged to the Liberal group while the church party captured the other eight seats.[106] The deeply ironical consequence was that William Lucas Sargant and George Dixon, successive presidents of the Free Grammar School Association and both Anglicans inclined to moderation, found themselves at the head of two bitterly-opposed factions on the first Birmingham School Board.

To summarise: the importance attached to service on public municipal bodies in Birmingham increased as they acquired functions whose management had serious implications for relations between competing civic establishments and the relations between these establishments and the bulk of the population. The acquisition of particular functions and the way they were exercised did not occur automatically or as a necessary realisation of inexorable 'social tendencies' but were bitterly fought over as has been seen. The main axis of conflict in Birmingham divided a big bourgeoisie whose social networks were coordinated at the municipal level of integration. Alliances were formed by elements within this divided big bourgeoisie with members of social classes whose solidarities were traditionally focused upon the neighbourhood and the county. In Sheffield, the main axis of conflict set against each other members of social formations rooted in tight neighbourhood-based solidarities and others increasingly oriented to regional and national levels of integration. The town council was of relatively small strategic importance to either side.

In Birmingham, the conflict had ramifications in the political, religious and educational spheres in complex interaction with each other while the industrial sphere remained relatively undisturbed. By contrast, in Sheffield a direct clash between adherents of two modes of capitalist production in the industrial sphere imposed a new alignment of forces in the political sphere as evidenced during the 1868 General Election. Meanwhile the increasing scale of steel production presented the steel manufacturers with the task of managing a growing semi- and unskilled labour force. The provision of education was a responsibility which some leading steel manufacturers were prepared to share through the school board, coming to the aid of a clerical establishment which was not under serious attack locally but which was unable to cope with a rapidly growing population of school age.

J. P. GLEDSTONE AND W. L. SARGANT

Finally, it should be emphasised that George Dawson's message did not go unproclaimed at Sheffield. One of its advocates was J. P. Gledstone who served from 1862 to 1872 as minister at Queen Street Congregationalist Chapel which, ironically, was the place attended by Ironside in his youth.[107] Nor were civic pride and a belief in the virtue of public work on popularly-elected municipal bodies a monopoly of Birmingham's leading Dissenters. W. L. Sargant, a prolific writer whose participation in the disputes of the 1860s was at least as central as Dawson's, provides an example here.[108] A brief comparison of the writings of Sargant and Gledstone gives some insight into the state of 'civic morale' in Birmingham and Sheffield in the aftermath of the two royal commissions.

Sargant's *Essays of a Birmingham Manufacturer* were published between 1869 and 1871. Of particular interest are two essays entitled 'Characteristics of Manufacturers' and 'Limited Democracy'.[109] Sargant recalls the disturbances of the 1830s, especially before the 1832 Reform Act: 'I remember, not without trembling, the tumults of those days. I can testify to the truth of the assertion, that we were not far from bloodshed. Excitement was at its highest in Birmingham. . . .' He is in retrospect proud that '[in] passing the reform bill it was not London but Birmingham which took the lead (so that) . . . the example of rapid and energetic combination was set to the whole country.' The animosities of that period were part of 'the severe struggle by which the great towns set themselves free from the humiliating predominance of the country gentlemen'.[110]

Compared to other towns 'judged by their actions during the last generation, the manufacturing towns have a triumphant pre-eminence.' He is scornful of London with its notoriously bad water supply, wretched street lighting and 'absence of public spirit . . . in all classes'. He notes that 'not one of its great Parliamentary boroughs has obtained municipal powers.' In the trading city of Liverpool he could not find 'any proofs of superior intelligence' nor any newspaper which 'combines such a large circulation with sober and thoughtful writing as the three manufacturing journals, the *Manchester Guardian*, the *Leeds Mercury*, and the *Birmingham Daily Post*'. Considering the virtues of the manufacturing towns, Sargant finds that '[what] is true of the textile districts is still more true of the hardware towns.'[111] Compared to the more highly-mechanised northern towns, in a hardware town like Birmingham[112]

> the proportion of skilled and unskilled labourers is . . . reversed; the skilled labourers, the ingenious and trained mechanics, outnumber the mere drudges. As the class of employers is largely recruited from the cleverest of such workmen, there will be found great ingenuity and skill among the master class.

The view from Birmingham in 1869 gives Sargant ample grounds for optimism:[113]

> Many improvements have taken place under the writer's eyes: among the middle classes, a growth of public spirit, a submission to heavy local taxation for public buildings and sanitary improvements, an increased desire for education; among the working classes, a reduction of drunkenness, a greater sympathy with the richer classes, a desire for enlarged means of education, a more civilised deportment, and an augmented decency and propriety easily visible to those whose experience enables them to compare one period with another.

Sympathy amongst classes and a capacity for self-government were expressed *par excellence* in the manufacturing towns:[114]

> Go into any of the towns I have mentioned, and ask about the public buildings: you will find them nearly all the work of a generation. True those towns thirty years ago were only half as populous as they are now; but even then they had attained a surprising magnitude. . . . The growth of Town Halls and Courts, of Gaols and Lunatic Asylums, of Schools and Colleges, indicates a public spirit among the citizens: the Town Councils indeed, who have mainly erected them, are not in good odour with fashionable people, who feel towards them as toward democratic America; but the Town Councils, backed by the ratepayers, have shown a liberality in their outlay, which was impossible for self-elected Commissioners or close corporations, and which is not practised by the administrators of county rates. Among the town middle classes, public spirit has grown with the spread of democratic institutions.

Such happy thoughts were denied to J. P. Gledstone who published in 1867 a 'letter to the manufacturers, merchants and principal trades-men of the town of Sheffield' under the title *Public Opinion and Public Spirit in Sheffield*. It was written shortly after the inquiry into the Sheffield outrages. Unlike Sargant, he presented not a panegyric but an indictment. Gledstone found that among Sheffield's inhabitants there was an 'absence of the higher spirit of an educated community' which showed itself as utter 'helplessness under pressure of public work'.[115,116]

> We possess the elements of astonishing influence, but they are not consolidated. . . . Private life will show any one who cares to look into it, that very decided opinions are held upon questions affecting our social life. . . . Not less surely will it show that our opinions are disfigured by many prejudices and savour of a strong provincialism, that they are held in a significant number of cases with much warmth and intolerance of opposite views, and, above all, that we distinctly disapprove of public demonstrations for the sake of an idea. Opinion is a thing for the parlour and the club, not for the town; hence of opinion we have a full share, but of public opinion we have none, or next to none. We are an aggregate of men; we are not a community; we are thousands of Englishmen, but we are not united in our social life. Business and pleasure – which are of a personal nature – get, I fear, more than their due attention, while things which require self-denial and some amount of enterprise and generosity are grievously neglected.

Recalling the recent enquiry, Gledstone commented[117]

I leave it to others to trace . . . the share in stifling all honest expression of thought which must be given to our sixty trade unions – all of which are *secret* societies, avoiding publicity and a fair discussion within themselves and with spectators of their trade affairs; and many of which have resorted to the foulest and most cowardly methods of carrying out their policy, so gagging that part of the community which generally carries, by weight of numbers, any question which may be submitted to it for decision. The presence of a crowd of secret societies (numbering thousands of men, and standing in intimate relation to a large proportion of the monied classes of the town) and an absence of public opinion! how ominously suggestive!

We may, continued Gledstone, excuse ourselves but 'the rest of England is not so well satisfied. We would fain hope, for the honour of our country, that no other British town would, under such severe pressure and urgent duty, have failed to act with promptitude and vigour.'[118]

There were numerous other instances. The general infirmary was starved of funds. The distribution of prizes for the Cambridge Local Examinations had been delayed by the 'miserable difficulty' of failure to find a 'suitable gentleman . . . to take the chair'. When the Social Science Congress came to Sheffield 'we had to open the work of the Congress in a private music hall: well – call it by its right name – a singing saloon, and then we shall understand how sad was our plight.'[119] In fact,[120]

we are without public buildings of any size or worth . . . In respect of public buildings, we are far behind Leeds, Bradford, Manchester, Birmingham and Liverpool, each of which has buildings of a noble order, a plain evidence that these towns have no small devotion to public work.

The only cure was 'that our men of wealth and education accept the burden of living for others, as well as for themselves'. This entailed not merely service on the town council and gifts to charity but also 'a spirited fulfilment of obligations'. Newspapers were no substitute for the lack of 'public assembly' by citizens. 'A newspaper government is quite as hateful as any other, when not tempered and modified by thought and action coming from other sources.'[121]

Gledstone viewed the future with pessimism:[122]

Gentlemen, I fail to recognise any young men who are giving promise that they will be active, intelligent, disinterested friends of Sheffield beyond the trade relationships which they may sustain to it. There may be scores who are developing into quick merchants and enterprising manufacturers; but we have a right to look for more from them. Property and station bring their responsibilities. It is not enough that a man be successful in business; his increased wealth, his wider influence, his deep experience, are public property; and he fails in a serious respect if he simply settles down amongst his riches and lets the town struggle on. . . . The maiden speech of one of our junior merchants, or of any young gentleman holding a similar position, would be as sweet as May-blossom; and I earnestly beg of you, gentlemen, for the sake of our social advancement and honour, to prompt and aid all young men of your class to a speedy entrance upon public work.

Two comments will be made on these contrasting portrayals of civic life. First, they suggest that Arnold's view of the state of class feeling in the industrial provinces, with which this chapter began, is rather over-simplified. In Arnold's version, Nonconformity, love of machinery, hostility to established political and cultural authority, middle-class assertiveness and artisan aggression are different heads upon a single monster. However, while Sargant's Birmingham appears to justify Arnold's fear of a provincial middle-class challenge to London and Oxford, the scholar-manufacturer is proud of the 'decency and propriety' of the local working class. In Sheffield the threat of working-class violence is felt by Gledstone but he berates the local middle class for its lack of political ambition on either the local or national stage. Contrary to Arnold's stereotype, Sargant is an Anglican manufacturer proud of his city's relative freedom from machinery while Gledstone is an active Dissenting ideologue who is ashamed of losing face before the examiners of Cambridge University.

Second, the representation of class structures and relations between levels of integration implicit in the writings just examined coincide with the main lines of the preceding analysis, although Gledstone's gloom and the self-satisfaction of Sargant heighten the contrast between Sheffield and Birmingham. Sargant stresses the strong co-operative bonds between masters and men, the victory of the town councils over closed, self-elected bodies, the failing power of the county aristocracy, the superiority of his city to the metropolis, and Birmingham's national pre-eminence. By contrast, Gledstone finds that Sheffield's middle class lack public spirit and are excluded from influence over artisan institutions which are closed and undemocratic. Levels of integration above and below the municipality take precedence. From below, domestic affairs, the calls of the family business and trade union machinations draw energies away from municipal affairs; from above, the city of Sheffield has become exposed to enormous pressure from national opinion. While Sargant recalls times when 'Birmingham took the lead', Gledstone is ashamed of Sheffield's

189

'strong provincialism'. Through Birmingham an 'example was set to the whole country' but Sheffield has to be told that 'the rest of England is not so well satisfied.'

CHAPTER 8

MASTERING OUR EDUCATORS

TOWARDS A NATIONAL EDUCATION SYSTEM 1830–95

It is convenient at this juncture to pause in the analysis of processes in Birmingham and Sheffield in order to locate these two particular sequences of social development within the national context. This will be done by focusing upon education. In chapters 5 and 6 formal education in Birmingham and Sheffield was treated as a very convenient index of contrasting patterns of persistence and transformation in the class structures and other aspects of social differentiation in these cities. However, more emphasis will now be placed upon the specific part played by formal education within such configurations at both the national and local levels.[1] The distinctive contribution of education was the bestowal of legitimacy. In the course of the nineteenth century this institutional sphere gradually superseded organised religion as the major public arena within which the moral grounds of authority and status were instilled in the young. It provided a means by which the leadership of the old agrarian order could recoup some of the losses sustained as industrial development and the growth of the state increased the power of urban businessmen, officials and experts.

In the course of its slow decline the national bureaucracy of the Anglican church provided the cutting edge which enabled the gentry to secure a strong position in the educational sphere. The Church of England was deeply impregnated with the values of the threatened rural social order. According to W. F. Hook, who served in Birmingham during the early stages of a brilliantly successful career as a city parson, the rural parish exemplified the close personal relationship between the laity and their spiritual shepherd which should remain the clergyman's ideal. He recommended a probationary period

191

of service in the shires to all keen young clerics.[2] The Anglican clergy held powerful positions not only at the ancient universities but also as heads and masters of public and grammar schools and principals of teacher training establishments. The National Society, offspring of the church, was the leading provider of public elementary day schooling.[3] Anglican advances in Birmingham, through the King Edward VI Foundation, Queen's College and so on, were local variants on a broader pattern. The failure to match this success in Sheffield had its sequel in the intervention, from the national level where the ancient universities and the church held greater sway, of governmental agencies which pushed secondary and higher education in that city in an 'acceptable' direction. The work of the treasury committee responsible for distributing grants to the university colleges was complemented by the efforts of the Board of Education and the advice of Michael Sadler.[4] As a consequence, by the early twentieth century, secondary and higher education in Sheffield provided secure enclaves for 'liberal culture', the inheritor of the classical tradition which was so closely linked to the authority of the gentry and aristocracy.

Formal education has acquired a special significance in English society for two reasons. First, many businessmen and landowners resisted a strengthening of the repressive capacity of the central state apparatus along 'Prussian' lines. A major concern of these groups was the eliciting of popular acquiescence in the disposition of rewards and use of social resources in England. The classroom and lecture hall were important means of carrying this out.[5] Second, unlike the United States, France or those European societies which had experienced the Napoleonic imprint, England had no commonly-recognised charter of public rights and responsibilities expressed in terms of a few memorable principles and sanctifying the regime of a ruling class. The attempt of the Chartists to force such a set of principles into the constitution was a failure. The Bill of Rights was the property of a Whig aristocracy rather than nineteenth-century urban industrialists. Furthermore, English society witnessed no relatively clean break between an old aristocratic order and a new bureaucratic state, no capitalist 'putsch', no workers' revolution, no overwhelming defeat in war followed by the clean sweep of an occupying foreign power. This society acquired a hybrid ruling class made up of local and national establishments whose values and commitments were in many respects at odds with each other. Its governing principles were not easily stated. They could only be instilled through socialisation of the young into the inhibitions and routines which permitted its compromises to be maintained. The schools and colleges 'blooded' each new generation, introducing them to the governing irrationalities of English life. The function just described was not deliberately sought or introduced by any particular establishment. Rather, it was an unintended outcome of the conflicts between establishments within the educational sphere. Furthermore, members of the old rural order were at least as much aware of the potential harm that formal education could do to their interests as they were of the help it could provide.

In this chapter, four themes are developed. First, the ambiguous impact of the growth of science and the spread of examining bureaucracies is discussed. Second, two influential prescriptions for the use of education in mediating the transition between the old society and the new are compared with each other. Third, some of the implications for educational provision of tendencies within the working class and lower middle class are examined. Finally, some of the consequences of the expansion of education for relations within the middle class are analysed.

SCIENTISTS AND EXAMINERS

Education was a political minefield for three reasons. First, the bureaucratic machinery necessary to administer a national education system threatened to present a direct challenge to the localised, paternalistic control exercised by the aristocracy, gentry, clergy and businessmen.[6] Second, the questions of who were to be educated? how?, by whom? and at whose expense? would immediately open up latent conflicts within existing establishments, for example, between Dissenters and Anglicans. Third, an expanded network of educational institutions would bring into being new groups with influence and skills which would enable them to challenge the authority and privileges of these establishments.

If any single institutional practice may be said to have offered a direct and comprehensive challenge, in ideological terms at least, to 'old corruption' it was the external examination.[7] The slight chill in the air induced by the India Act of 1853, which opened up appointments in the Indian Civil Service to competition, had become a howling gale by 1870. In between these dates there had developed a number of large examining bureaucracies, not only in the Civil Service but also in all the major sectors of education. The College of Preceptors, which began examining in 1850, had been joined by Oxford and Cambridge Universities, the University of London, the Society of Arts, the Science and Arts Department at South Kensington and the Education Department at Whitehall. By the 1860s 'there were few parts of public life or educational effort upon which the examiner had not left his hand.'[8]

In a rapidly expanding society the external examination provided a medium by which a new and powerful hierarchy of educated experts might emerge.[9] The increasing influence of 'specialists' in the educational sphere may be shown by comparing two royal commissions: the first presided over by Lord Newcastle, a great territorial magnate, the second under the direction of James Bryce, a constitutional lawyer. [10]

When the Newcastle Commission investigated the state of popular education between 1858 and 1861, ten assistant commissioners were sent into the regions. They were instructed to make 'detailed inquiry amongst persons of intelligence of either sex conversant with the locality'. In particular they were to speak to '[the] employers of labour, the clergy of different denominations, the governors and chaplains of gaols, inspectors of police and other officers of justice, and the shop-keepers whose customers are labourers'. This information was supplemented by written evidence from clergymen and also lay persons such as Sir Arthur Hallam Elton (benefactor of a national school in Somerset), W. Ellis (a London merchant), Lord Lyttelton of Hagley (member of the Diocesan Board of Education), the Countess of Macclesfield (a local benefactor and philanthropist), J. G. Marshall (a Leeds mill-owner and school manager) and Colonel Stobart (a Darlington coal-owner and magistrate). In drawing up his evidence for the commissioners, Rev. James Fraser found himself citing (from Herefordshire) 'a gentleman of extensive local knowledge and long experience'. The commissioners received statistical returns from several bodies active in the provision of education, such as the National Society and the British and Foreign School Society. They also heard evidence from a score of 'educationalists'. However, they placed considerable weight upon the views of 'persons of all shades of opinion practically conversant with popular education in particular districts rather than those who had taken a prominent part in the public discussions of the subject'. The instructions to the assistant commissioners betray the aristocracy's suspicion of 'experts' and a clear assumption that the oversight of education for the poor, was properly in the hands of the 'natural' leaders of provincial society. [11] By contrast, in the early 1890s the Bryce commissioners who were investigating secondary education listened to the arguments of some eighty-five witnesses only a handful of whom did not derive their income from institutions mainly devoted to the management of formal education. These included spokesmen for the major educational departments of central government, the school boards and county councils, the universities and university college, teacher training establishments and several teachers' organisations. [12]

The introduction of new forms of knowledge, especially scientific knowledge, into the schoolroom presented a challenge to Oxford and Cambridge which combined the functions of Anglican seminary and finishing school for the genteel rich. In 1850 the Duke of Wellington, chancellor of Oxford University, announced that Oxford has no intention of introducing German methods of education. The election of Prince Albert to the chancellorship of Cambridge University, by a narrow margin, dramatised the degree of influence which had been achieved by advocates of modernisation.[13] The probing inquiries of royal commissions into the ancient universities were paralleled by the growth of a complex of scientific institutions in South Kensington, notably the Imperial College of Science and Technology. This latter development had the enthusiastic support of Prince Albert. He was president of the commissioners for the exhibition of 1851. The success of the Great Exhibition provided much of the money for the South Kensington complex. Imperial College was intended as the summit of a national system as described in the second report of the commissioners. With 'the active cooperation of the State, as well as of the public at large' a large scientific institution in the metropolis would be 'rendered capable, by means of scholarships and by other means, of affiliating local establishments over this country, in India, and Her Majesty's colonial possessions, whereby the results of its labours might be disseminated as widely as possible'. Britain was 'the only country which has neither supplied (in any practical or systematic shape) scientific nor artistic instruction to its industrial population; nor provided for men of Science and Art, a centre of action, and of exchange of the results of their labours.' If these needs were not speedily supplied Britain would 'run serious risk of losing that position which is now its strength and pride'. These comments implied a harsh criticism of the ancient universities.[14]

The leading member of the commission after Prince Albert was Lyon Playfair who had served as professor of chemistry at the Royal Manchester Institution during the early 1840s. Born in India, educated in Glasgow and Germany, employed as a young man in a Clitheroe textile firm, Playfair was an important representative of a powerful provincial scientific culture which was almost completely divorced from Oxford and Cambridge.[15] Arnold Thackray has argued that during the half-century after 1780 the pursuit of science offered many rewards to provincial urban elites, including Dissenting manufacturers, whose new wealth and local importance contrasted markedly with the marginality of their social status and their exclusion from established centres of political power:[16]

> The reasons for the choice of science were its possibilities as polite knowledge, as rational entertainment, as theological instruction, as professional occupation, as technological agent, as value-transcendent pursuit, and as intellectual ratifier of a new world order.

In his study of science in Victorian Manchester, Richard Kargon has identified a 'scientific-cultural network' which by 1840 included members of not only the Manchester Literary and Philosophical Society but also the Manchester Natural History Society (founded

1821), the Royal Manchester Institution (1823), the Manchester Mechanics' Institute (1824) and the Manchester Geological Society (1838).

By mid-century the contribution of Manchester's scientific institutions as a focus of civic integration linking religious, manufacturing and professional elites as well as (to a lesser degree) artisans had diminished. Two aspects of this change were: the increasing domination of science by self-taught 'devotees' and, later still, institutionally-trained 'experts' who formed their own national networks of communication and criticism; and the gradual re-orientation of the urban business elites towards national issues and institutions in which they sought to participate.[17] Thackray comments:[18]

> Manchester's aristocracy of manufacturers, by now legitimated and secure, abandoned both science and advanced religion as appropriate cultural symbols. The great manufacturing families found social issues, practical politics, and the reform of Oxbridge to be matters more congenial to third-generation taste.

As has been seen, in respect of both chronology and structure Birmingham and Sheffield presented patterns of development in their scientific institutions which differed from Manchester in important respects. However, evidence from the former cities does not contradict the generalisation that by the 1850s many manufacturers were peacefully sharing with the aristocracy and gentry the tasks of managing English society. Science and the external examination cannot be regarded as tools by which insurgent industrialists sought to displace the old landed class. In fact, such institutions were quite capable of being exploited with a conservative intention as may be seen in the work of two major polemicists concerned with popular education during the 1860s. Each spoke for social interests which wanted a particular amalgam of the old and new orders to be encouraged within the developing society. Their two prescriptions were, however, deeply at odds with one another.

MATTHEW ARNOLD AND HERBERT SPENCER

Herbert Spencer was an ardent advocate of science education. Matthew Arnold was deeply involved in the administration of the revised code, one of the principal engines of external examination after 1862.[19] Arnold and Spencer had each spent their early careers and formed their values in close association with men and institutions belonging to the old order. Their attachments were to opposing sides of the division between the Nonconformist petty bourgeoisie and the Anglican landed establishment. Both men had also experienced some

of the transforming potential of institutions oriented to a larger industrial society increasingly organised on a nation-wide basis.

Arnold had read classical 'Greats' at Oxford, served as private secretary to Lord Lansdowne when he was Lord President of Council and
for ten years held the position of professor of poetry at his Alma Mater.
However, he was also the son of the pioneering headmaster of a new
kind of public school at Rugby and became one of Her Majesty's
Inspectors of Schools. By contrast, Spencer was the son of a Dissenting
minister at Derby and familiar with the petty bourgeois radical circles
in the Midlands which George Eliot described in *Felix Holt*. As a young
man he had trained as a railway engineer, working mainly in the
Birmingham area where he met Joseph Sturge. Spencer became local
secretary in Derby for the Complete Suffrage Union, a body founded
by Sturge in 1842. While working in the Midlands, Spencer had
written articles for the *Nonconformist*, a journal edited by the Leicester
Congregationalist, Edward Miall, who was selected for attack in
Arnold's *Culture and Anarchy*.[20] Spencer was also for a short while
sub-editor of a radical paper produced in Birmingham called the *Pilot*.
This journal, founded by Sturge, conducted a campaign against
oligarchy and maladministration in local government.[21]

Spencer's book, *Education: Intellectual, Moral and Physical* (1861) and
Arnold's *Culture and Anarchy* (1869) were published in a decade when
the social fact of a mass education system was becoming accepted as an
inevitability. Spencer and Arnold each wished formal education to be
used in two ways: as a means of contradicting an abhorred feature
stemming from the old society and as a way of containing a repellent
possibility pregnant in the new order.

Central to the argument of *Culture and Anarchy* is a critique of *laissez-
faire* utilitarianism for its failure to curb the excesses of working-class
militancy. Arnold attacked middle-class 'shibboleths' such as individualism, love of machinery, and the belief in material wealth, population growth and untrammelled freedom. Throughout his argument
the 'middle class' is closely identified with the old tradition of
Protestant Dissent. Despite their industriousness and assertion of
negative freedoms the Dissenters are condemned for their lack of 'high
reason and . . . fine culture'. The threat of 'anarchy', Arnold believed,
could be removed by the pursuit of 'culture', that is by a continual
striving for harmony and perfection in self and society. Classical art
and poetry offered the basis for a model of 'sweetness and light'.
However, educational reforms were to be coupled with a determination to 'encourage and uphold the occupants of the executive power,
whoever they may be, in firmly prohibiting . . . whatever brings risk
of tumult and disorder'.[22]

Eight years before *Culture and Anarchy* appeared, Herbert Spencer
had written:[23]

If we inquire what is the real motive for giving boys a classical education, we find it to be simply conformity to public opinion. Men dress their children's minds as they dress their bodies, in the prevailing fashion. As the Orinoco Indian puts on paint before leaving his hut, not with a view to any direct benefit, but because he would be ashamed to be seen without it; so a boy's drilling in Latin and Greek is insisted on, not because of their intrinsic value, but that he may not be disgraced by being found ignorant of them – that he may have 'the education of a gentleman' – the badge marking a certain social position and bringing a consequent respect.

In place of the defunct tradition of classical education he recommended a 'rational curriculum' which did not 'neglect the plant for the sake of the flower':[24]

What knowledge is of most worth? – the uniform reply is – Science. This is the verdict on all counts. For direct self-preservation, or the maintenance of life and health, the all important knowledge is – Science. For the due discharge of parental functions, the proper guidance is to be found only in – Science. For the interpretation of national life, past and present, without which the citizen cannot rightly regulate his conduct, the indispensable key is – Science. Alike for the most perfect production and present enjoyment of art in all its forms, the needful preparation is still – Science, and for the purposes of discipline – intellectual, moral, religious – the most efficient study is, once more – Science.

Four years after the publication of *Culture and Anarchy*, Spencer devoted over twenty pages of his book *The Study of Sociology* to a critique of Arnold's opinions. He deprecated Arnold's 'longing for more administrative and controlling agencies':[25]

'Force till right is ready', is one of the sayings he emphatically repeats: apparently in the belief that there can be a sudden transition from a coercive system to a non-coercive one.

Spencer vigorously defended the provincial Dissenting tradition in which he had been bred, praising its 'originality' and 'independence'.[26]

Both men had visions of the perfectibility of men and women through education and believed that there were social forces favouring and opposing the realisation of their visions. In Spencer's view, the beneficent influence of industrialism was opposed by the threat of militarism and state power. Arnold, by contrast, identified industrialism with the rise of a middle class moving between the 'two cardinal points' of self-satisfied mediocrity and fanatical Dissent. His own best hopes, a strengthening of the state and 'the public establishment of schools for the middle class', were anathemas to Spencer. For the latter, all that was good in society, including its system of education, would grow within the complex bonds of private exchange and private association. Progress towards perfection was hindered, not advanced, by agents of state interference such as Arnold, the school inspector.[27]

In the event, external examinations were a device which enabled Arnold's successors at the ancient universities to combat the influence of both science and the state. In so far as institutional reforms and the emergence of new social classes were accepted as inevitable, examinations had many features which were attractive. They could be used to influence curricula and criteria of recruitment to schools and occupations. In this way they acted simultaneously upon the relationship between parents and schools, amongst students, between pupils and teachers, and finally, between educational establishments and the occupational structure. This influence was exercised with an ideological stress on universalism and 'fairness' combined with voluntarism and individualism. The onus of 'failure' was borne by the individual and was not to be seen as the consequence of inequalities built into the social structure. Examinations also had a standardising effect whose extent was ultimately national. In a rapidly changing social order they were a means of institutionalising competition within a vast section of the population through sets of bureaucratic rules which were subject to control 'from above'. Conflict about the content of these rules was increasingly confined within the upper reaches of society: for example, in South Kensington, Whitehall and the ancient universities. Not least, examinations provided an engine of influence amongst the growing middle classes which was outside the immediate aegis of the state.[28]

Examinations played a key role in J. L. Brereton's plan for the reform of middle-class education. He suggested that within each county a number of schools should be established for boys and girls between the ages of 12 and 15 years. Above them would be a school for boys aged between 15 and 17 years. These establishments were to be financed by a combination of fees and the labour of pupils on farms attached to the schools. Each year a county examination would be held under the patronage of the county aristocracy. Young men aged between 18 and 24 years whose parents were in 'respectable and independent circumstances' would compete for a 'County Degree' and 'County Honours'. The system was to be crowned with a 'County College' at Cambridge University. Brereton's proposal is a nice indication of the state of balance between the municipality and the county as foci of social life. It was quite widely discussed and the County College (later known as Cavendish College) was actually opened at Cambridge in 1873.[29]

However, the ground was rapidly occupied by the Local Examinations sponsored by Oxford and (soon afterwards) Cambridge. This movement was the product of cooperation between educationists in the large towns and reformers at Oxford who accepted Frederick Temple's view expressed in a letter to allies in Birmingham:[30]

> The education of the Middle Classes in England appears to me to suffer from two causes: the schoolmasters have no guide to direct them what subjects they should teach, or how they should teach those subjects; the parents no guide to direct them what schools they should prefer. . . . These difficulties would at once disappear if some Body capable of commanding the confidence both of teachers and parents were to undertake the task of guiding and testing the work done in these schools. I think that the University of Oxford might do this, and do it well.

In the same letter Temple warned against the 'plausible appearance and skilful puffing' to which schoolmasters were prone and offered instead a diet of 'solid knowledge and real cultivation'.[31] These were surprisingly confident remarks considering the very sharp criticism made by the commissioners who had investigated Oxford and Cambridge earlier in the same decade.[32] They indicate the deep reserves upon which the ancient universities could draw in the craving of important provincial establishments for their benediction. Some evidence of the battle being fought may be gleaned from William Lucas Sargant's comments at an education conference in 1857:[33]

> An appeal has been made to the public against Mr Temple's Scheme, on behalf of the College of Preceptors and of the Society of Arts. The ground, it is said, is already occupied by these institutions, and the present proposal is a poaching on their manor.

Sargant argued that the College of Preceptors could not 'claim the whole educational field on the ground of prior discovery' and considered that the Royal Society of Arts should confine itself to adult education in mechanics' institutes and people's colleges.[34]

The sponsorship of 'locals' was part of a strategy still being pursued by Oxford and Cambridge twenty years later when the university extension movement began (at Cambridge in 1873, in Oxford five years later). Benjamin Jowett of Balliol argued strongly that the ancient universities should take an active interest in the new local science colleges that were springing up. It was of the greatest importance that the education offered in such places should be truly liberal and not narrowly vocational or technical: 'we ought not to allow a great movement to slip out of our hands, and become what I may call a mechanics' institute movement, instead of a real extension of such an education as the university would wish to see given.'[35]

A THREAT FROM BELOW?

At issue was the question: how would the labouring population and lower middle class within the cities use their growing strength? Both of these social categories were divided internally, each containing groups whose origins lay in the old particularistic small-town order alongside others being brought into being by the universalising, nationalising tendencies expressed in increasingly complex market and bureaucratic networks. The lower middle class contained two groups both of which performed vital functions as intermediaries at the lower levels of systems of production and distribution. They were the petty bourgeoisie (or 'old' lower middle class) and the 'new' lower middle class.

Members of the new lower middle class occupational groups had three characteristics in common. First, educational qualifications – increasingly taking the form of certificates achieved in competitive examinations – were the basis of their claim to employment and income. Second, there was a rapidly expanding demand for their services. This demand created a dilemma. Elementary school teachers, postmen, policemen and railway clerks were widely recruited from the ranks of, for example, small tradesmen, farm labourers, domestic servants and artisans. To take on uneducated recruits was to court administrative inefficiency; to educate them above their fellows was to risk giving them a sense of their own importance which might make them difficult to control. In spite of this dilemma, their numbers grew rapidly. For example in 1846 the government established a system whereby elementary school teachers could gain augmentation grants and pension rights by passing an examination supported by training college courses and 'Queen's Scholarships'. By the time of the Newcastle Commission there were more than 7,000 certified teachers.[36] In 1862 Robert Lowe warned of 'the vested interests of those engaged in education':[37]

> If Parliament does not set a limit to the evil, such a state of thing will arise that the control of the educational system will pass out of the hands of the Privy Council and out of the House of Commons into the hands of the persons working the educational system.

The teachers were a highly visible element in a quickly growing sector of society. The number of white-collared clerks was also increasing. Their ranks doubled during the 1860s. This startling rate of growth was maintained in the following decade.[38]

The third and most unsettling characteristic of this new lower middle class was its cultural plasticity, the uncertainty of its socio-political allegiances. Its existence brought indirect benefits to the rich and powerful. As the chains of interdependence intervening between capitalist and producer and between producer and consumer grew longer, conflicts of interest amongst capitalist, producer and consumer became less clearly visible. The appearance of a new lower middle class which manned these intervening institutional orders also made the distinctions between rich and poor, powerful and weak less sharp. However, the unformed nature of this strategically important sector of society made it the object of great concern. In 1858, Frederick Temple commented: '[the] one thing the middle classes want and which they cannot get without help, is organisation.'[39] Despite tendencies towards organisation at the national level (for example through bodies such as the National Union of Elementary Teachers), the problem of how these social groups were to be incorporated within the urban industrial order was initially confronted at the municipal level of integration. As has been seen, there were significant differences between Birmingham and Sheffield in the proportion of the population engaged in such occupations and their rates of growth after mid-century.

There were also differences in the character of the manual labour force in the two cities. These differences, which increased after the 1840s, were local manifestations of a shift in the national economy. The proportion of the labour force engaged in manufacturing reached a peak of 32.7 per cent in 1851 and thereafter began gradually to decline. It had fallen to 30.7 per cent in 1881. However, within this section of the population the proportion of textile workers was reduced while that of metal workers increased from 15 per cent in 1851 to 23 per cent in 1881. The shift of emphasis away from textiles and towards iron, steel, engineering and mining was associated with two parallel but contrary tendencies. On the one hand, technological advances in steel-making and coal-mining encouraged very large concentrations of capital and semi- or unskilled labour. On the other hand, the 1850s and 1860s were decades of rising prosperity for artisan metal workers and allied tradesmen in both Birmingham and Sheffield as they were in many places for skilled craftsmen in the building and printing trades. In spite of the general trend towards increasing plant size a powerful fillip was given to small-scale workshop production of a kind which allowed artisan organisations a great deal of control over their craft and considerable bargaining power with those to whom they sold their skilled labour. Differentials in pay between skilled and unskilled workers steadily increased between the 1850s and 1880s. However, the other side of this coin was that the advance of mechanisation and the growth in size of the semi- and unskilled workforce threatened to undermine the basis of craft privilege. Perhaps such fears underlay the 'no-popery' riots of 1867 in Birmingham directed against the immigrant Irish. In cases where a strongly entrenched artisan class confronted this challenge at close hand resistance was bitter, as was seen when looking at Sheffield.[40]

It is important not to exaggerate the extent to which the success of the artisan elite and the increasing size of the unskilled labour force (especially marked in the 1860s) generated alarm higher in the social order. Highly organised craftsmen could bargain effectively with their masters but in return the latter could deal with recognised spokesmen and expect that agreements reached would be backed up by the moral authority of the craft union. Furthermore, many craft unions or trade societies had been formed in the late eighteenth and early nineteenth centuries before large factories were common or governmental bureaucracy a sizeable menace to their members. Their political attitudes had many similarities to those of the old lower middle class. Like small-town shopkeepers and manufacturers in the first half of the century artisans had veered between Painite Radicalism and parochial Conservatism.[41] They were, above all, a known quantity. At Sheffield in 1865, one year before the great strike by the Sheffield file unions and two years before the Sheffield Outrages Inquiry, the Dean of Chichester referred to the nation's artisans in almost affectionate terms:[42]

> Then comes the great body of men, advancing every day in importance and power, who have proudly assumed the title of the working classes. Hard-working men in other classes have reluctantly conceded the title, as claimed unjustly when claimed as an exclusive designation; but there it is, like all aristocracies, exciting an occasional growl, which the members of the favoured class consider as a compliment. This class can at once be described as consisting of the skilled artisans.

Furthermore, from the point of view of the middle class, the migration of unskilled labour to the towns helped to supply a growing demand for domestic servants. Between 1851 and 1881 the number of people in domestic service rose from just over 1 million to 1.8 million, or one in seven of the general working population. Women and young girls predominated. A powerful instrument was thus forged for instilling deferential attitudes amongst the lower classes. Its effects must have been strongly felt in the households set up by servants and ex-servants when they married.[43]

It has been seen that the distinction between skilled artisans and semi- and unskilled labourers was not the only significant form of differentiation within the urban labouring population. There were differences between cities with respect to the relative importance of female and child labour as opposed to adult male labour and in the significance of the division between 'respectable' and 'rough' working-class families (not the same as the division between high and low wage-earners). These differences were related to variations in working-class industrial bargaining strategies and responses to formal education. On the first-mentioned of these issues witness the Prince Consort at a conference on early school-leaving in 1857:

> The root of the evil will, I suspect, also be found to extend into that field on which the political economist exercises his activity – I mean the labour market – demand and supply. [This issue will] cut into the very quick of the working man's conditions . . . [for his children] constitute part of his productive power, and work with him for the staff of life. The daughters especially are the hand-maids of the house, the assistants of the mother, the nurses of the younger children, the aged and the sick. To deprive the labouring family of their help would be almost to paralyse its domestic existence.

Mixed motives apart (compare the words of Sydney Gedge in chapter 5), a concern for social order and material prosperity did not necessarily entail an unquestioning insistence on the value of formal education on the part of either clients or sponsors.[44]

DIVISIONS WITHIN THE BOURGEOISIE

The foci of debates on elementary education in the 1850s and 1860s suggest that the spectre of popular disturbance was receding. There was a reluctant recognition that the extent of elementary education would have to be increased, that established institutions were inadequate to cope with this task, and that new forms of provision were likely to alter the balance of power within the middle orders of English society. In particular, the Church of England was under threat. The *1851 Census* showed that one in three children of school age were neither at school nor in employment. However, it also showed that of all churchgoers only half were attending Anglican places of worship. Among the issues debated by pressure groups such as the National Public School Association, the Royal Society of Arts and the United Association of Schoolmasters were: the extent and manner of state involvement in education provision, the degree to which school management should reflect Anglican interests as opposed to those of ratepayers, the status of elementary school teachers, and the academic content of the elementary school curriculum. That such issues could be debated for so long without producing a mandate for legislative action suggests, first, that there was a lack of widespread fears concerning the political temper of the working class, and second, that there existed serious conflicts within the middle class.[45]

By 1846, W. F. Hook was prepared to admit that the purely voluntary system of educational provision had broken down.[46] However, nearly a decade later very little had been done to replace it. In 1854 an enthusiast for the voluntary system commented:[47]

> Such are the diversities of opinion which exist among educational philanthropists themselves, and the small degree of progress made in settling the primary elements of the problem, that upon no one point could thirteen men, picked out for the purpose from the whole House of Commons, find their way to an agreement. So much for the possibilities of education legislation in England.

In fact five education bills failed in the House of Commons during the following year. In 1858 the question was passed to members of the Newcastle Commission whose instructions were 'to consider and report what measures, *if any*, are required for the extension of sound and cheap elementary instruction to all classes of the people.'[48]

The sequence of royal commissions on education through the 1850s and 1860s – on Oxford and Cambridge, (1850–3), on the education of the poor (1858–61), on the top nine public schools (1860–4) and on the endowed schools (1864–8) – produced reports which strengthened the case for a 'national education system'. However, they also exposed a strong capacity to resist central government on the part of school managers, boards of trustees, headmasters and college fellows.[49] The opposition aroused by the Endowed School Commission, set up in 1869, and the functions given to the school boards in the following year were a sign that for the foreseeable future the particular shape of educational provision at the elementary and secondary levels would be primarily determined by the specific balance of political forces in particular local areas.[50] Before a 'national education system' could be created there would have to emerge a 'national' clientele oriented to a labour market and occupational structure whose determinants were national rather than local.

During the 1850s and 1860s the most powerful tendencies in this direction in the educational sphere were the growth of the public schools and the proliferation of formal examinations. These institutional developments have been the subject of valuable studies. Analyses of the public schools have tended to show the part they have played in facilitating the relatively smooth interpenetration of business, professional and aristocratic elites during the late nineteenth century. By contrast, investigation of examining agencies has tended to reveal considerable conflict and contradiction in their mutual relations.[51] Such a state of affairs was part of the overall confusion in the administration of education which was revealed by the Bryce Commission in 1895.[52] By that date education was managed through a Byzantine network of local and metropolitan agencies. The Education Department at Whitehall, the Science and Art Department at Southampton, the Charity Commissioners and the two older universities all cast their influence over the schools and colleges. The bodies named were relatively autonomous with respect to each other and co-existed with a host of *ad hoc* local bodies, over some of which they exercised control. These institutions included school boards, school attendance committees, voluntary aid associations, technical instruction committees and the governing bodies of grammar schools. As the Bryce Commission reported:[53]

> Each one of the agencies . . . was called into being, not merely independently of the others, but with little or no regard to their existence. Each has remained in its working isolated and unconnected with the rest. The problems which Secondary Education present have been approached from different sides, at different times, and with different views and aims. The Charity Commissioners have little to do with the Education Department and still less with the Science and Art Department. Even the borough councils have, to a large extent, acted independently of the school boards, and have, in some instances, made their technical instruction grants with too little regard to the parallel grants which were being made by the Science and Art Department. Endowments which, because applied to elementary education, were exempted from the operation of the Endowed Schools Acts, have been left still exempt; though the public provision of elementary education in 1870 and the grant of universal free elementary education in 1891 have wholly altered their position. The University Colleges, though their growth is one of the most striking and hopeful features of the last 30 years, remain without any regular organic relation either to elementary or to Secondary Education, either to school boards or to county councils.

These apparently paradoxical developments, a successful integration of potentially hostile establishments through the public schools and the appearance of serious contradictions within the administrative sphere of formal education, require investigation which must take into account the changing relations between old and new establishments and between the national, county, municipal and neighbourhood levels of integration. Alongside the relatively smooth reception of the most successful business families into more elevated circles must be seen the fierce confrontations which continued to occur in some of the manufacturing cities they left behind. Alongside the careful adjustments to an expanded clientele made by the great public schools run by prestigious headmasters must be seen the bitter conflicts by competing municipal elites for control over the management and curricula of local secondary schools.[54] In the preceding chapters the development of Birmingham and Sheffield between 1830 and 1870 was analysed in those terms. In the final part the analysis will be extended to the period after 1870.

CHAPTER 9

'A NOISY STREET
IN THE MIDDLE
OF A SMOKY TOWN'

ELEMENTARY, SECONDARY AND
HIGHER EDUCATION IN
BIRMINGHAM AND SHEFFIELD
1870–95

As a continuation of the theme of the preceding chapter, in chapter 9
the analysis commences by focusing narrowly upon differences in
patterns of formal education in Birmingham and Sheffield between the
establishment of the school boards and the publication of the Bryce
Report. However, the argument subsequently broadens. In the course
of chapter 10 and chapter 11 specific features of the evolving class
structures and institutional orders of the two cities are located in the
wider context of the development of the national society during the
late nineteenth and twentieth centuries. This chapter opens with a
comparative analysis of the development of elementary, secondary
and higher education in the two cities during the late nineteenth
century. It is argued that the policies of the school boards in the sphere
of elementary education reflected the contrasting processes of political
conflict and industrial growth whose early stages were noticed in
previous chapters. In the spheres of secondary and higher education
an apparently paradoxical pattern took shape. A classical or 'liberal'
curriculum held pride of place in Birmingham's secondary schools and
Sheffield's university college whereas a science-based curriculum was
dominant in Sheffield's secondary schools and Birmingham's university college. An explanation for this pattern is suggested in terms of
three aspects of local social structure: the relationships between the
middle class and local secondary schools in the two cities inherited
from the previous period; the orientations towards the local colleges of
industrialists in Birmingham and Sheffield; and the capacity of
municipal establishments in the two cities to institutionalise forms of

higher education contrary to metropolitan definitions which were subject to the influence of Oxford and Cambridge.

DIVERGING PATTERNS OF EDUCATIONAL DEVELOPMENT

In July 1880, at a great meeting to celebrate the opening of the Sheffield Central School, the Archbishop of York declared that in Sheffield 'the whole phenomenon of the establishment of the School Board had been a very remarkable thing indeed. The Board in Sheffield had scarcely ever been divided in its opinions during the nine years' chairmanship of Sir John Brown.' Election times had provided what little excitement there was, largely due to the efforts of H. J. Wilson and other Nonconformists hostile to public money being spent upon voluntary schools. During the first six years 'voluntarists' were in a majority on the board. In 1873 Mark Firth's nomination failed to arrive before the deadline and no election took place. In 1879 there were only sixteen candidates for the fifteen seats. Three years previously in 1876, the composition of the board had shifted in favour of moderate Liberal Nonconformists but Brown, Anglican and Conservative, had remained as chairman with Mark Firth, a New Connexion Methodist with more liberal leanings, as vice-chairman. As will be seen, the school board got on with its agreed task of building schools and filling them with an efficiency which was almost Kremlinesque. This epithet is also conjured up by the prevailing attitude on the board towards public opinion in the city which was indicated by the defeat in 1879 of a proposal to supply the local libraries, newspapers and the Athenaeum Club with copies of its minutes and 'such other information as may from time to time be printed and published by the Board'.[1] The public stance of the school board was, in effect: 'Trust us for we know best.' As Brown wrote to the local press in 1882[2]

> Choose for the School Board men of known intelligence, integrity, business ability, and strict justice. Let them be men of wise economy, but let them be educationists first, then send them to the work unfettered and ready to form an impartial judgement on actual experience.

He added that the school board had received 'the cordial support of such men as Mr Henry Wilson, Mr Thomas Moore and Mr Mark Firth, as well as others now living who hold utterly divergent views on both religion and politics.'[3]

The turbulence of school board politics in Birmingham made Sheffield's tranquil progress seem torpid by comparison. During the early years the fortnightly debates at Paradise Street were packed with the public and 'on a field day the Board Room was not unlike the Black Hole of Calcutta.'[4] The town council was dominated by Liberals and Nonconformists under the leadership of Chamberlain who became mayor in 1873. When the council failed that year to obtain an assurance from the board that money from the rates would not be spent on denominational schools, the council withheld payment. In a blaze of publicity the case went before Queen's Bench in London. Meanwhile the school board election fell due. It was proclaimed from an Anglican pulpit that the very angels in heaven were awaiting the result and that a Liberal victory would be followed by an inferno which would consume the town hall. In the event, torches were indeed lit and fireworks ignited but only to illuminate and glorify the progress of Liberal working men marching in celebration. Chamberlain and his clique now ruled both board and council. The issue of whether the Bible should be taught in schools run by the board was deeply contentious until 1879 when a workable compromise was reached and the sacred text admitted onto the curriculum. During the intervening years (until 1877) the National Education League had conducted a strident country-wide campaign one effect of which had been to help split the national Liberal Party and contribute to its defeat in the 1874 General Election.[5] If school board affairs in Sheffield may be described as being somewhat Kremlinesque, then the politics of education in Birmingham occasionally took on a little of the fervour lately summoned up by other hallowed writings in the People's Republic of China!

These differences between the school boards are what the previous analysis would lead us to expect. The battles in Birmingham were a continuation of the phase of municipal conflict which began in the mid-1860s. The greater single-mindedness of the Sheffield board may be understood as a response both to the heightening of class conflict in the industrial and political spheres during the mid- and late 1860s and to the increasingly evident failure of voluntary initiative, especially by the Anglican clergy, to keep up with the increase of population, which, as has been seen, had been occurring at a much more rapid rate in Sheffield than in Birmingham during the 1850s and 1860s.[6] The greater severity of the 'problem' in Sheffield compared to Birmingham led to a more vigorous programme of building schools and enforcing compulsory attendance in the former city, especially in the early 1870s. By the end of 1874 the Sheffield board had built fourteen schools to accommodate about 9,000 children and rented a further seven schools which made approximately another 1,500 places available. By contrast, the Birmingham board had built only seven schools with about 7,000 places and was renting a further four to accommodate about 1,300 pupils.[7] When Chamberlain took over the chairmanship in 1873 the pace speeded up. By 1876 a total of thirteen schools had been built (accommodating over 13,000 pupils) and fourteen more schools (for about 11,000 pupils) were on the drawing board.[8] By that time, however, the board in Sheffield was already planning its Central School which was to provide advanced training for older children. These schools opened four years before the equivalent institution in Birmingham commenced operation in 1884.[9]

By 1872 both school boards had established a staff of 'visitors' or school attendance officers. Although Birmingham had thirty-five men so engaged in 1880 and Sheffield only nineteen by 1887, the latter were evidently backed up much more effectively by the magistrates' bench than their colleagues in the Midlands. In Sheffield there were 774 summonses in 1874 to enforce the bye-laws with respect to compulsory attendance. Of these, 644 defendants were fined the maximum of 5 shillings and only seven escaped with a 1 shilling fine. By contrast, although the Birmingham board brought 3,150 prosecutions in 1876, only 454 cases resulted in a 5 shilling fine whereas the majority of those who were convicted suffered only a 1 shilling penalty. This was a small cost to parents for retaining the labour of their children. As late as 1887 the *Birmingham Daily Gazette* criticised the reluctance of Birmingham's magistrates to enforce compulsory attendance. Matters only began to improve significantly two years later when all such prosecutions were placed before the stipendiary magistrate.[10]

During the 1880s and 1890s differences between the emerging systems of municipal education were most clearly expressed in the realms of secondary and higher education. In 1872 the collegiate school in Sheffield was rescued from financial collapse by the efforts of a small group of Anglican gentlemen including Henry Wilson, Bernard Wake and Henry Pawson. There were ambitions to make it a 'good classical school' with some boarding provision.[11] However, the opening of the Sheffield Central School by the school board, in close cooperation with South Kensington, caused considerable anxiety at the collegiate. At the opening ceremony Earl Spencer had praised the 'association of education and the technicalities of trade' represented by the Central School. He stressed that 'in England, attention should be turned at once and very fully to the soundest and best possible system of technical education, because of the certainty of increasing rivalry in trade concerns' with the continent.[12] By 1883 S. O. Addy, an ex-student and teacher at the collegiate was bitterly complaining about this 'educational palace' built 'illegally' with rate-payers' money. The new establishment, he feared, 'was intended to monopolise the whole of the middle-class education of the town'. When it was opened the collegiate headmaster 'took fright' and fled to a public school in Jersey 'where he now flourishes with probably ten-fold the income and the reputation he had acquired in Sheffield.'[13] Addy's rather comical distress and confusion is nicely conveyed in the anecdote with which he ends his pamphlet:[14]

A poor boy applied for admission to the Grammar School. The Head Master thought that the applicant was more fitted for a Board School than a Grammar School, and recommended him to apply to the Central School. 'Oh!' said the boy, 'I have applied there and they won't take me'. 'Why?' inquired the Head Master. 'Because I am not clever enough.' And this to an old Cambridge scholar and able head of an ancient school which was founded to teach, and for centuries has taught, the Greek and Latin Literature and all polite learning, a foundation which has existed nearly 280 years and never drawn a penny from the State! *O rem impudicam &c*! Well, we live in strange times and there are plenty of people ready to rush in where angels fear to tread. What may be the end we may not wholly foresee.

In the event the collegiate had become part of Wesley College by 1885, a consolidation which did not halt a progressive decline in support. By the years 1898–9 there were more vacancies than candidates for admission to Wesley College and the grammar school. Finally, in 1905 both these schools amalgamated and fell under the control of the school board's successor, the Sheffield Education Committee.[15]

When Birmingham School Board's Seventh Standard School was opened in 1884 (followed by a sister institution in Waverley Street eight years later) the chairman of the board's education committee was Rev. E. F. M. MacCarthy, not only an Anglican cleric but also the head-master of a local endowed school. Waverley Road School was something of a showpiece, containing workshops and a scientific labora-tory, and providing teaching in mechanics, chemistry, machine drawing, geometry, and wood and metal work.[16] In contrast to Sheffield, these events were not accompanied by a decline in support for the local endowed schools. Before the Bryce commissioners in 1894, MacCarthy felt able to urge not only the building of more 'board secondary schools' with a technical bias but also a loosening of their dependence on South Kensington. MacCarthy was headmaster at one of the nine endowed secondary schools which the King Edward VI Foundation managed by the mid-1890s, and was secure in the know-ledge that these schools were not only supreme in the local status hierarchy but also catering for approximately 2,500 boys and girls. Following the dispute over the foundation in the mid-1860s, various schemes had been proposed for its management, all being opposed by the town council. By 1894, an agreed scheme had been in operation for a decade. This final compromise allowed the town council to nominate eight of twenty-one governors. The elementary schools were replaced by seven grammar schools, three for boys and four for girls, taking pupils up to the age of sixteen. Two high schools, one for boys and one for girls, provided courses up to the age of 19. The schools all became mainly fee-paying.[17]

When the Bryce commissioners asked MacCarthy in 1894 whether the higher grade schools at Bridge Street and Waverley Street might 'expunge the endowed secondary school' he replied that they met 'different educational needs' and that there was 'no competition between the two'.[18] Earlier he had insisted that the board's higher grade schools would in fact relieve the endowed grammar schools of 'scholars with whom they could not adequately deal'. The endowed schools were more literary, the board schools more technical. Of the former, said MacCarthy, the high schools led to Oxford and Cambridge, the grammar schools to the local Mason College (opened in 1880) or directly into commerce and the professions. The higher grade schools, on the other hand, qualified their pupils for 'the better classes of employment with respect to the manufactures, and on the commercial side for the smaller commercial posts'.[19] MacCarthy believed that those board school children who sought entry to the endowed secondary schools should only be admitted at the age of 11 or thereabouts. A child transferring later would have 'a mental equipment much narrower in range than the pupils among whom he finds himself of corresponding age'. Such children would have to be chosen by formal examination, however fallible that system: 'The difficulty is that you have to satisfy the public.'[20] Rev. A. R. Vardy, the headmaster of the Birmingham Boys' High School was asked whether the passage of ex-board schools into his establishment had produced 'difficulties . . . of what are called a social nature'. He replied,[21]

> No, not at all. But I think this is an important point, and one which ought to be made clear to the Commission. I am bound to say that most of those who have been previously in public elementary schools are to some extent picked boys. Many of them, for instance, are the sons of public elementary schoolmasters; others, one or two, the sons of men who are connected with public elementary education, sub-inspectors or assistant examiners. There are a few who are the sons of artizans, but I think most of them come from homes where education is more thought of.

Evidently a formal examination at the age of 11 would tend to perform the task, whose desirability was noted by T. H. Green thirty years earlier, of excluding 'the rougher element' from the upper reaches of the endowed schools in Birmingham.[22]

By the mid-1890s, a form of tripartite organisation of secondary education was thus developing in Birmingham. It depended upon a high degree of cooperation among local practitioners. Vardy stressed the integrated character of the Birmingham education system:[23]

First of all, the city is not too large for those engaged in public work to know one another; secondly, a good many educational institutions are connected by having on their governing bodies members of other governing bodies. For instance, on the governing body of King Edward's Foundation there are five or six who are also governors of the Mason College. Thirdly, in Birmingham happily very intimate relations have for many years existed among teachers of all grades of schools. We have been in the habit of seeing a great deal of each other.

When A. P. Laurie visited Sheffield in the mid-1890s as an assistant commissioner he found a pattern of educational organisation and management very different from Birmingham's. His highest praise was reserved for the Sheffield High School for Girls which had been founded in 1878 by the Girls' Public Day School Trust. Wesley College, by now largely dependent upon recruits from local private preparatory schools, passed muster but the grammar school made 'a disappointing impression'. Its headmaster complained of competition from the technical school which had been founded in 1888 and stated that the best boys from the elementary schools did not compete for his entrance scholarships. They preferred the higher grade (that is, the Central) school. A new extension was being built at the latter institution. Laurie commented that 'any University college that could get possession of [it] . . . for their science department would think themselves very fortunate.' The grammar school's other competitor, the technical school, had originally been part of Firth College, founded by Mark Firth in 1879, but had passed under the control of the town council in 1890. It was Laurie's view that 'both have suffered from the separation'. The technical school had fallen away from 'university standards' and Firth College had lost the 'close association between university and technical work' appropriate to a 'great manufacturing district'. In fact, in its overall appearance Firth College was 'more suited to the mechanics' institute of a small town than to the University College of Sheffield'.[24] Laurie's overall conclusion was that there was[25]

> no attempt at any organisation of the higher education of the town. The higher grade school, while engaged in work of immense value for the great mass of the townspeople, is making no use of the greater facilities for teaching languages and preparing special boys for the university possessed by the grammar school and Wesley College. While these institutions again seem to be hardly aware of the existence of Firth College, which struggles on without the support it should have from the secondary schools. The girls' high school, again, is quite isolated from the work which the higher grade school is doing for girls. . . . Then the technical school, instead of arranging with the

214

other secondary schools in the town for a slightly modified
training of boys who wish to enter its senior department, must
needs start a boys' school of its own without proper class-rooms,
playground, or adequate school organisation, and compete with
the schools in which these things are provided.

In the two cities there were very different biases with respect to two
kinds of school: on the one hand, secondary schools with a classical
tradition and hopes (however much dimmed) to send their best pupils
to Oxford and Cambridge and, on the other hand, higher grade
schools controlled by the local school board and placing a greater
emphasis upon technical teaching. In Birmingham the King Edward VI
Foundation's secondary schools catered for about 2,500 students by
the mid-1890s while Waverley Street and Bridge Street between them
had an attendance of only about 1,100 pupils.[26] By contrast, Sheffield's
higher grade or Central School boasted over 1,000 young people compared to the mere 600 or so taught in the Sheffield Grammar School,
Wesley College and the High School for Girls taken together. As
Laurie pointed out, these latter institutions were isolated from the
board schools in Sheffield not only organisationally but also geograph-
ically. High up in the residential suburb of Broomhill, away from the
pall of smoke which polluted the valley, they 'monopolised all clean-
liness, fresh air and sunshine'.[27] By contrast, the King Edward VI
schools in Birmingham were neither isolated from nor threatened by
the local board schools. In return for keeping its headquarters 'in a
noisy street in the middle of a smoky town' the foundation had reaped
a massive reward in local influence and prestige.

At the university college level there were equally striking differences
between developments in the two cities. In 1897 Firth College amalgamated with the technical school and the medical school to become
Sheffield University College. The expanded institution applied to join
Victoria University which was a federation of colleges in Manchester,
Liverpool and Leeds. Its application was met with a blunt refusal. In
1902 the Victoria University broke up and the college at Leeds was
encouraged by the Privy Council to apply for incorporation as the
Yorkshire University. Confronted with the threat of Leeds becoming
the only university city in the county, Sheffield made a late and
desperate bid for a charter which was granted in 1905. However, for
the first seven years of its life Sheffield University was required to
submit all its statutes and ordinances to the three northern universities
for their approval.[28]

A different trajectory was followed in Birmingham. Professor T. H.
Huxley opened Mason College in 1880. After a decade of gradually
increasing cooperation, the medical faculty of Queen's College became
part of Mason College in 1892. By 1898 this establishment had become

Mason University College, control passing from the hands of the college trustees appointed by Josiah Mason and becoming vested in a court of governors drawn from throughout the Midlands but dominated by Joseph Chamberlain. The latter was already committed to the creation of a massively-endowed University of Birmingham, a civic university inspired by the examples of Edinburgh and Glasgow. Birmingham University was established in 1900, the first civic university in England, providing a model which was different from the federal pattern in the north, the sprawling examination arrangements of London University and the collegiate system of Oxford and Cambridge. Within two years of the university's inauguration, a new 25 acre site was being prepared at Edgbaston, this development being aided by a massive donation from Andrew Carnegie in the United States.[29] In 1903, while Sheffield University College was still desperately striving for some kind of higher recognition, Chamberlain was twitting R. B. Haldane, soon to be chairman of the treasury committee supervising the distribution of government money to the provincial colleges. Inspired by a visit to the Technische Hochschule at Charlottenburg in Germany, Haldane had been campaigning since 1902 to raise the status of the scientific institutions in South Kensington. He proposed to Chamberlain that following London's example there could be 'a second start for the Centre of England, to be localised in Birmingham University'. Chamberlain's public reply was to declare that Haldane was 'by no means first in the field, but still welcome, however late'.[30]

Apart from this large disparity in the power of the drive towards university status in Birmingham and Sheffield there were also important differences in the balance of social forces active within and upon the local colleges and in the curricular emphases which predominated. In both cities the leading part was played by professional men. As has been seen, the project of creating a 'grand scientific and commercial college' or a 'Central University' had been mooted by Birmingham's medical men in the early 1830s, although Anglican clerics at Queen's College were carrying this banner by the late 1840s.[31] A reaction to the domination of the Church of England and county interests upon Queen's College probably contributed to Josiah Mason's insistence in 1870 that no religious creed or dogma should be taught in his projected college, that its courses of instruction should develop a sound practical knowledge of scientific subjects 'excluding mere literary education', and that its doors should be open to all in the town and district. Although Mason had made his fortune in pen-nibs, his closest advisers were a lawyer and a doctor.[32] In the succeeding decades the combined influence of medical and scientific practitioners within Mason College was to be paramount. In Sheffield it was to be otherwise.

The initial stimulus in Sheffield came from the University of Cambridge and the Church of England. During the winter of 1874–5 the learning of the ancient university was brought to Sheffield by way of university extension lectures. Their most prominent local advocate, Rev. Samuel Earnshaw, had made a small fortune at Cambridge as a private tutor before coming back north. By 1877, Earnshaw was heard to say that the Cambridge lectures had produced 'a most marvellous effect' on the conversation and reading of 'the upper middle class'. When Firth College was founded two years later, the 'literary education' abhorred by Mason in Birmingham was well established within it. The executive committee identified 'the cultivation of that higher learning' as its 'primary object' although it hoped 'that a time may come when . . . technical education may be included in the curriculum.' Such a time would be 'whenever the needful resources for this shall be available'. They were very slow in arriving. A proposal in the early 1880s to establish a technical school in connection with the college drew a meagre response from local businessmen. Nearly a third of the small sum subscribed came from the Duke of Norfolk. The most prominent business sponsor was Frederick (soon to be Sir Frederick) Mappin who was subsequently to behave sometimes 'as if the Technical School – and later the University – was a branch of his own works'.[33] The technical school remained an inferior element within the college. In 1890 it fell under the control of the town council (following the provisions of the Technical Instruction Act) and a junior department was opened whose studies were developed in cooperation with the local school board. Although by 1905 the technical school had been back in the university fold for eight years it was tucked away on a separate site apart from the main buildings at Western Bank.[34] It was all reminiscent of the aversion felt by the Church of England Instruction Society towards the Sheffield Mechanics' Institute half a century before.

In Birmingham the Technical Instruction Act led to the science teaching of the Birmingham and Midland Institute being taken over by the municipal authority. This was a blow to the institute's ambition, which may be read between the lines of its annual reports, of fusing with or even competing with Mason College. Although the institute was cooperating with the school board through its branch classes by 1873, eleven years later it had raised its sights and proudly claimed to be 'an Industrial College' offering all the social and intellectual benefits of 'University life'. It was able to 'satisfy any acknowledged want in the educational work of the town', was capable of 'developing and satisfying the higher intellectual needs of the town', and was 'in some degree realising for the many the best attributes of a college career'. However, when the city council took over the institute reluctantly acknowledged that 'the change, even if it had not been desirable, was

217

inevitable'. By 1900 the institute had appointed Granville Bantock as the principal of its school of music and its annual report for that year asserted that the new University of Birmingham would need a faculty of music which 'should find its home in the Institute'.[35] This evident passion for entry into the 'university stakes' was in marked contrast to the hiving off of 'contaminating' elements in Sheffield.

Although in both cities the medical schools were cautious about associating closely with the new colleges, academic cooperation began half a decade earlier in Birmingham than in Sheffield. Once installed, the medical men of both cities yielded to none in their ambition to obtain academic autonomy and degree-awarding powers. However, the alliances and strategies in which they participated were very different. In Sheffield they had by 1885 successfully bargained for a specially-privileged position in the appointment of their own staff.[36] In Birmingham they shared in a strong movement within the science faculty.

Birmingham's University College was dominated by men such as the professors of mathematics, physics and anatomy.[37] The arts faculty, including E. A. Sonnenschein (classics), MacNeile Dixon (English) and J. H. Muirhead (philosophy) was only weakly represented on the charter subcommittee which planned the shape of the new university. Sonnenschein complained in 1898 that 'comparing Birmingham with other colleges . . . in no other place was so much as *twice* the amount spent on science than was spent on Arts.' Whereas Birmingham had only four arts professors to seven science professors equivalent ratios were 13:9 in Edinburgh, 8:8 in Glasgow, 8:9 in Manchester, 8:6 in Liverpool and 52:34 in Leipzig. The arts faculty redressed the balance a little through appeals to Chamberlain. Nevertheless, the latter continued to insist that the university would give 'exceptional attention . . . to the teaching of Science in connection with its application to our local industries and manufactures'. The new site at Edgbaston was dominated by buildings equipped for the study of engineering, mining and metallurgy. It was Oliver Lodge's impression during the 1900s that 'the arts professors were only admitted on suffrance' in Birmingham University.[38]

Apart from a few local men such as the industrialist Sir George Kenrick and the lawyer C. G. Beale, 'a graduate of Cambridge . . . [who] understood these things better than some of the others', the main allies of the arts faculty in Birmingham were the members of the treasury committee responsible for distributing government grants to the university colleges, a body whose successor was the university grants committee. The treasury committee strongly pressed the claims of arts subjects. In view of the preceding analysis it is not surprising to find that one of the two leading figures in the campaign which led to this committee being established in 1889 was William Hicks, principal of Firth College. The tradition of appealing for external help and guidance, already expressed by Sheffield's eager participation in the university extension movement, was thus continued.[39]

TOWARDS AN EXPLANATION

It is not the intention to follow all the twists and turns of the politics and management of education in the late nineteenth century. The following generalisations may be made which summarise, and slightly extend, the above remarks. During the period of intensive building of elementary schools during the 1870s, the Sheffield School Board was united, businesslike, determined and secretive while the Birmingham School Board's highly-publicised divisions were the stuff of popular politics. It may be added that during its subsequent career the Birmingham board acquired a reputation for high spending on its building and staff while, as R. W. Dale delicately expressed it, the Sheffield board was 'pointed to in many parts of the country as an example of extremely economical expenditure'. In the 1930s it was recalled that the 'School Board had been a very economical body' which underpaid its schoolteachers.[40] As Vardy's remarks to the Bryce Commission suggest, by the mid-1890s a much higher degree of consensus had been achieved amongst educationists and politicians in Birmingham. This was shown, for example, in the widespread support for the opening of a municipal technical school by the technical school committee which would complement the work of the higher grade schools on the one hand and Mason College on the other. In effect, while the school board trained the artisans, the technical school committee would educate their supervisors.[41]

Despite the promising start of the 1870s by the 1890s Sheffield had a disorganised array of educational institutions, many of them operating on a shoestring and often directly competing with each other. By their side, the Birmingham schools and colleges were a model of integration offering a systematically-organised pattern of routes leading to different occupational levels. Within this system, literary education leading to university entrance and entry into the higher reaches of the professions held pride of place. It is noteworthy that Vardy and MacCarthy of the King Edward VI schools played a major part in developing a local system of teacher training for the elementary schools.[42] The values of the high school permeated the Birmingham schools, making more 'tolerable' to its supporters the great extension of advanced technical education. No such counter-balancing process occurred within the advanced schools developed by the Sheffield board. At the higher level, paradoxically enough, the pattern was reversed. The arts faculty remained weak compared to the science faculty in Mason College but in Sheffield it was the technical school which had a marginal existence on the fringes of Firth College. When the latter institution first advertised its courses, mathematics and classics were prominently displayed (perhaps in unconscious mimicry of the traditional Cambridge curriculum) followed by ancient and modern history. Physics and chemistry were there as well, although the latter was hived off into the technical school as were subsequent developments in metallurgy and engineering. When the new government grant became available in 1889 one of the first items on the shopping list of William Hicks was a professor of English literature.[43]

Three reasons can be suggested for this pattern of curricular emphases. The first refers to the long-standing connection between the foundation schools and the professional and mercantile members of Birmingham society. A comparison of census data in 1851 and 1891 gives an indication of changes in the relative importance of these occupations in the two cities (see Table 24).[44] The rate of increase in both categories was more pronounced in Sheffield than Birmingham

TABLE 24 *Professional, mercantile and related occupations: Birmingham and Sheffield 1851, 1891*

Number employed per 1,000 population at Birmingham and Sheffield in 1851 and 1891		
	1851	1891
1 Professional, literary, educational, scientific, artistic occupations		
Birmingham	23.2	28.8
Sheffield	12.8	23.2
2 Mercantile occupations		
Birmingham	9.1	25.5
Sheffield	6.3	19.2

Sources: 1851 Census, 1891 Census.

although both groups remained proportionately larger (and much larger in absolute terms) in the latter city.[45] The foundation was peddling prestigious wares in a well-established and expanding market. Its reputation was bolstered by the fact that at the opening of the twentieth century the mayor and four of the city's parliamentary members had attended schools belonging to the foundation as well as fifteen of the forty-nine gentry and magistrates listed in Pike's *Contemporary Biographies*.[46] At the lower end their work was supplemented by the Birmingham and Midland Institute which registered sixty-one students for a new book-keeping class in 1876 and from 1885 was teaching commercial French as a service to what the instructor called Birmingham's 'army of commercial workers'.[47]

By contrast, the equivalent schools in Sheffield had a dismal reputation. It is likely that a substantial proportion of the members of professional and allied occupations who were active in Sheffield by the 1890s were either upwardly mobile or immigrants to the city in view of their rate of increase over the preceding decades. Lacking sentimental family attachments to the Sheffield secondary schools up on the hill such people evidently preferred not to use the facilities on offer. The following exchange during evidence to the Bryce commissioners by J. F. Moss, the secretary of the school board, suggests that they went either 'up market' and patronised boarding schools or 'down market' to the benefit of the board schools:[48]

> What becomes of the boys of the middle and wealthier classes in Sheffield who do not go to the grammar school or to the public and other boarding schools at a distance? – Of course only a small proportion can be received in the grammar school, and some of our city councillors and others have sent their boys to the central higher school

Although the King Edward VI Foundation's capacity to serve a thriving Birmingham clientele bolstered up literary or 'arts' studies at the level of secondary education the natural continuation for those students from professional families who wished to pursue the highest prizes was not entry to Mason College but to Oxford and Cambridge which were by the 1890s at the height of their renewed prestige. A provincial degree would mean less and lead to less. As a consequence, Mason College was in thrall to the promoters of academic specialisms which could demonstrate their relevance to the business life of the city. This consideration introduces the second suggested reason for the differences between the curricular tendencies in Birmingham and Sheffield: the orientations towards the local colleges of the cities' businessmen.

In 1884 Charles Lapworth claimed that the male population of Mason College was predominantly drawn from the sons of local manufacturers. A survey of all entrants in 1893 demonstrates the tendency to recruit from industrial and commercial families, especially from the higher reaches of the middle classes. Stanley Baldwin and Neville Chamberlain both studied at the college. The profits generated by Birmingham business in the late 1890s made a large contribution towards the endowment of some half-a-million pounds which Chamberlain succeeded in raising for the university.[49] However, the support of business was not spontaneously given, but had to be actively sought by the university. Thus, although the creation of a faculty of commerce (a great rarity amongst universities and university colleges in the late 1890s) was initially suggested by the Birmingham Chamber of Commerce, its first head, Professor William Ashley, was confronted with much local scepticism. He deliberately cultivated close relations with Birmingham businessmen. For example, he drew upon the advice of the Birmingham and Midland Society of Chartered Accountants when devising a pioneering course in accountancy. By the early twentieth century he was providing some firms with 'almost tailor-made mixes of economics and technology for their needs; for example, metallurgy and commerce for the son of a Wolverhampton brewer'. A special course devised for the jewellery trade, combining trade work with commercial training, marked a point of contact between this outward-looking movement of the academics and another movement developing within businesses which had become very sensitive to foreign competition during the years of depression in the late 1870s and mid-1880s.[50]

A specialised school for jewellers was established in 1888 to improve standards of workmanship in the almost complete absence of any apprenticeship schemes. Similar ambitions lay behind the support of the Birmingham Trades Council for the higher grade schools. In the brass trade, employers such as R. H. Best and trade unionists such as W. J. Davis supported the establishment of trade continuation schools.[51] It is important not to exaggerate the willingness of the majority of employers and workers to work towards these ends but three structural aspects of Birmingham's industry which distinguish it from industry in Sheffield may have stimulated interest. They are the long-standing tradition of innovation in most sectors of business, the weakness of apprenticeship (which would have provided an alternative pattern of training), and the existence of a large number of businesses of middling size which would jointly benefit from 'external' agencies providing services in the spheres of manpower training and research.[52]

In Sheffield, in spite of the establishment of some relatively large firms in the light trades by the 1890s, 'the small firm and "outwork" system survived and were still, in many ways, typical for the industry.'[53] Despite the radical weakening of their position in the aftermath of the confrontations which occurred in the 1860s, the trade societies clung to old attitudes. 'In the early nineties, of 40 societies examined, 32 limited apprentices to members' sons only, and only two . . . would permit an apprenticeship of less than seven years. Most societies had further numerical restrictions. . . . Virtually every one of these rules was ignored.' Nevertheless, as late as 1905 the Britannia-metal smiths were attempting to restrict the teaching of their trades in the city's schools as being detrimental to their apprenticeship regulations. By contrast, in the heavy trade, firms which were already large by the 1870s grew much larger through expansion and amalgamation. Brown's and Firths amalgamated in 1903. Jessops became the world's largest crucible-steel producers in the early twentieth century. In the decade before 1914 at least eight of the firms in this sector were employing over 2,000 workers with a further six firms employing over 1,000 people. The majority of steel workers were outside unions before the 1890s.[54]

The very large steel firms, such as Vickers who had over 60 acres of land in use in the early 1900s, devoted a substantial part of their budgets to research and development. Through their adoption of the Siemens regenerative furnace and entry into ordnance work Vickers had responded to the challenge of trade depression in the late 1870s and 1880s by virtually creating 'a new business'. By the early 1900s they were supporting a design staff of 300–400 people. Such firms were less interested in boosting the prestige of civic educational institutions than exploiting the talents of particular individuals doing relevant work. J. O. Arnold, head of the technical school from 1889, provided a number of steel firms with the results of his metallurgical researches. Commercial rivalries imposed a demand for secrecy which, as an academic, he found irksome. In his relations with local businessmen he had a much lower degree of freedom and initiative than Ashley at Birmingham. By 1909 Arnold was complaining on behalf of the university of an 'attempt by a limited number of manufacturers to dictate to its professors'.[55]

Sir Frederick Mappin, who was the Sheffield industrialist most completely devoted to the progress of the technical school as an institution, had been a leading figure on the side of the manufacturers during the file strike of 1866. As the dominant personality in Sheffield's file trade, Mappin had a greater interest than many in the development of a system of training in engineering and metallurgy which would wrest control over the formation of the attitudes and practices of the skilled labour force away from the trade societies.[56] A similar strategy may be seen operating in the very rapid progress made by the Sheffield School Board in providing technical instruction. Evening science classes were started by the board as early as 1874. The severity of the battle to make new industrial techniques acceptable to the local artisan population and its leaders is shown by the fact that as late as 1893 the Sheffield Federated Trades Council (successor body to the Association of Organised Trades) was demanding that 'machine-cut' files should be so labelled in recognition of their supposed inferiority. Many employers were equally resistant to advanced formal training. In 1883 it was stated that 'most of the best men that have been educated in the Sheffield school [of art] have been taken up by other towns in consequence of not having received enough encouragement in the town.'[57] Breaking down the unions' residual resistance to new techniques and increased managerial control probably had a higher priority than providing future managers with university training. In 1904 a local steel manufacturer told the Sheffield Society of Engineers that[58]

> there was . . . a feeling that a young man having an engineering or a science degree was an indication that too much time had been spent in theory for him to have the necessary workshop experience, and it might stand in the way of his securing the position he applied for.

These attitudes were deeply ingrained. Compare the following:[59]

> nobody believed in graduates. There was a grudging acknowledgement of their existence, but an outright rejection of the notion that they might be helpful. . . . I was taught nothing, not because I already knew enough, but because I was adjudged industrially ineducable.

The writer was a graduate trainee in a small Sheffield steel mill in the 1950s.

The third reason to be suggested for differences in curricular emphases between the two cities is of special relevance at the university college level. It is the much smaller capacity of Firth College, which lacked strong support from the local professional and business classes and which was much more dependent than Mason College on central government funding, to mount any effective resistance to metropolitan definitions of the character of higher education. This part of the argument opens up for consideration the relationships between, on the one hand, the municipal and provincial social networks to which the businessmen, professionals and administrators of Sheffield and Birmingham respectively belonged and, on the other hand, the social configurations focused upon London, Oxford, Cambridge and the leading public schools. The development of the relationships just indicated was conditioned by and in turn conditioned the transformations which occurred in the class structures of Birmingham and Sheffield during the last third of the nineteenth century and the years leading up to the First World War. An exploration of some aspects of the variations between the two cities in these respects may help to account in some degree for differences between them not only in their educational arrangements but also in their local patterns of industrial relations and public administration.

CHAPTER 10

COALESCENCE, CONFLICT AND COMPROMISE

INDUSTRY, EDUCATION AND LOCAL GOVERNMENT IN BIRMINGHAM AND SHEFFIELD 1870–1914

In both Birmingham and Sheffield a coalescence between the leader-ships of the old rurally-oriented order and urban industrial society was well under way by the end of the century. However, this process occurred half a generation earlier in South Yorkshire than in the West Midlands. Furthermore, in Sheffield it was focused upon regional and national social networks while in Birmingham it occurred at the municipal level of integration. Finally, in Birmingham this process of osmosis was complemented by a subtle mingling of old and new values and practices in key institutional orders, facilitating a complex intermeshing of social groups within the middle, lower middle and working classes in that city. By contrast, the growing intimacy between leading Sheffield industrialists and the occupants of country houses and metropolitan corridors of power was accompanied by a rigidifica-tion and further institutionalisation of the social barriers between classes and status groups within Sheffield itself. In the longer term the refusal of the masters of Sheffield's heavy industry to share authority in the workplace left them open to a drastic and direct industrial challenge during the First World War. Indeed, representatives of their employees sought, with eventual success, to achieve total control in the sphere of local government. By contrast, in Birmingham education, industry and local government were managed in a way which fostered compromise between traditional and modern practices and dispersed conflict between social classes. In Sheffield these three institutional orders were arenas of bitter conflict between the advocates of old and new ways and their management perpetuated class hostilities.

This argument will be developed initially through an analysis of the part played by Birmingham Liberalism in mediating the transition between the old order and the new in that city. The political strategies adopted by Chamberlain in the 1870s and 1880s will be compared with those of Ironside thirty years previously. Subsequently, the part played by municipal institutions and the white-collar occupations in processes of class formation in the two cities will be briefly considered. Finally, the analysis of education carried out in the last chapter will be broadened out to include more detailed examination of the processes through which distinctive political and industrial institutions took shape. The emphasis throughout will be upon the joint contribution of the three institutional orders to the development of class structures and, equally important, their common subjection to constraints and pressures inherent in class structures.

JOSEPH CHAMBERLAIN AND BIRMINGHAM LIBERALISM

Birmingham in the late nineteenth century is stamped with the name of Joseph Chamberlain.[1] He was the city's mayor between 1873 and 1876 and its leading parliamentary representative from 1876. He dominated Liberal councils in Birmingham and much of the surrounding area through the National Liberal Federation (founded as the National Education League's successor in 1877) and the 'caucus' system of ward representation.[2] Following the split in the Liberal Party over Home Rule in 1886 which separated him from Gladstone, Chamberlain was the undisputed boss of the Liberal Unionists in the West Midlands.[3] His monocle, swept-back hair and bristling eyebrows were the stock-in-trade of local and national political cartoonists. As mayor, Chamberlain's municipalisation of the local gas companies was a brilliant financial success drawing heavily upon his experience as a businessman used to the accounting side of large-scale enterprises. At a stroke he provided the town with a valuable source of income apart from the rates. This success, and the favourable trade conditions of the period, prepared local opinion for the takeover of the water works company which followed. Finally, the Artizans' and Labourers' Dwellings Act of 1875 gave Chamberlain the opportunity to push through a massive improvement scheme in the city centre. The slums around Bull Street and New Street were swept away and a start was made on laying out Corporation Street, planned on the pattern of a grand Parisian boulevard.[4]

In the 1870s and 1880s Chamberlain gave municipal corporations the importance and respectability, almost the glamour, which Ironside had tried to bestow upon vestry meetings three decades previously. Chamberlain declared in 1874[5]

I am inclined to increase the duties and responsibilities of the local
authority, in whom I have myself so great a confidence, and I will
do everything in my power to constitute these local authorities
real local Parliaments, supreme in their special jurisdiction.

By 'local authority' Chamberlain meant town council. Substitute
'ward-mote' for 'town council' and the speaker could easily be Isaac
Ironside. Both men were flamboyant radicals who established novel
organisations in an attempt to capture political strongholds and put
new ideas into practice. Their political methods drew similar
criticisms. In 1853 the editor of the *Sheffield Independent* wrote of
Ironside's Democratic Party[6]

It has aimed to set up a dictatorship, armed with a set of organised
cliques called 'central democratic associations' and 'ward motes';
it has endeavoured to engross all local offices in the hands of
subservient nominees of the moving power.

Over thirty years later, the *Dart* carried the following comment on a
recent election in the Birmingham 'caucus' which was made up of
Liberal representatives from the various Birmingham wards:[7]

To be faultlessly exact it ought to be said that a few gentlemen met
in the various wards and appointed themselves, and a number of
others not present, to form the 'Caucus' for the year. Probably not
more than two per centum of the Electors of Birmingham took any
part whatsoever in the business. Yet this fraction of the public will
coolly take upon itself to dictate a policy to the other ninety-eight
per cent of the voters, and will consider that man guilty of a sort of
high treason who shall dare to question its authority. The
members of the Town Council, the members and the *policy* of the
School Board, and practically, the whole Government of the town
will be fixed for us by this august body of two per cent, not two per
cent of the *population*, bear in mind, but of the registered voters.

The *Sheffield Independent* was helping to bury a failed enterprise. The
Dart was protesting about the behaviour of a municipal elite which had
wielded power effectively for well over a decade. Ironside's political
venture was directed at the level of the neighbourhood during a period
when the increasing density and interdependence of urban industrial
life was throwing up problems which could only be tackled effectively
at a higher level of integration. Chamberlain, however, could point to
the progress already made towards expanding the functions of the
municipal authority in other towns such as Manchester.[8] By comparison, Birmingham was backward in the early 1870s. Birmingham's
Liberals also benefited from the strong tradition of civic responsibility,
albeit focused upon voluntary associations, which had become well-

established in the middle decades of the century, for example in the educational sphere.

Birmingham made Chamberlain at least as much as Chamberlain made Birmingham. The city provided a secure base from which the politician could launch his national campaigns and it proved to be a safe retreat even in 1886. As member for Sheffield (a distinction which Chamberlain himself had unsuccessfully sought in 1874) A. J. Mundella had far less natural sympathy with his constituents and had to rely heavily upon Robert Leader to keep him in touch with local feeling.[9] Mundella found little scope within Sheffield for his own reforming zeal. His passion for education, more practical and sustained than that of Chamberlain, found its sphere of exercise at the national level, in the Education Department at Whitehall.[10]

Chamberlain and Ironside both attempted to use a political base at one level of integration as a launching pad from which to secure reforms at a higher level. As has been seen, Ironside failed to link up with parallel movements in the religious and industrial spheres and was unable to adapt his political strategy to the constraints and opportunities of the municipal sphere.[11] By contrast, Chamberlain benefited from a tradition of municipal politics well-established in Birmingham by the 1870s, in which every subtle nuance could be understood and exploited within a densely-textured network of family, business and religious ties. In this respect he followed in the wake of G. F. Muntz and Charles Geach. The latter, who had been mayor in 1847, was an international banker who had greatly improved the town council's financial management and was very active in movements such as the Anti-Corn Law League.[12] Within Birmingham Geach's influence was far-reaching and exercised with ease. 'He had singularly agreeable manners. His grasp of the hand was firm and cordial. . . . In his appearance there was evidence of power and influence that rendered any assumption superfluous'; the accomplished politician, in fact. However, as a member of parliament for nearby Coventry, Geach 'was not a fluent speaker, indeed he was hesitating, and sometimes his sentences were much involved'. He only spoke upon those financial topics with which he was perfectly familiar. Muntz, whose impressive command of a Birmingham audience has been noticed, was also singularly awkward amongst the gentlemen at Westminster.[13] Chamberlain had no such problems. Self-confident and businesslike, he was perfectly happy moving from the details of the Land Clauses Act to the first principles of political philosophy and back again to some other specific point of practice. Thus, for example, as president of the Board of Trade giving evidence to the Royal Commission on the Housing of the Working Classes in 1884, he paused in the midst of a commanding lecture on the Artizans' Dwellings Act to inform Lord Salisbury that 'everything in the shape of natural or artificial monopoly should if possible be undertaken by the community.' When his questioner rather dolefully suggested that expenditure by public bodies was likely to be 'unduly pressed by the influence of experts and . . . permanent officers' Chamberlain was quick to claim that this was less likely in local government than in Whitehall: 'The control of public opinion and of public interest is very much more direct in the one case than in the other.' His Lordship quickly retreated into the details of compulsory purchase with Chamberlain in hot pursuit.[14]

As he moved from the municipal level to the national level and subsequently in 1895 to the international level as colonial secretary in Salisbury's Conservative government, Chamberlain was capable of adapting the rhetoric of Birmingham politics to the challenge of mobilising influence within successively more complex structures. By 1885 he was advocating the extension throughout Britain, including its rural areas, of a system of popularly-elected local authorities with powers of compulsory purchase, to be capped by a central board, also democratically-elected. Eighteen years later he was visualising the Empire as 'a voluntary organisation based on community of interests and community of sacrifices, to which all should bring their contribution to the common good'. The Empire was 'so wide, its products are so various; its climates so different that there is absolutely nothing which is necessary to our existence, hardly anything which is desirable as a luxury which cannot be produced within the boundaries of the Empire itself.'[15] Apart from the reference to the climate, he could have been talking about Birmingham.

There is a double irony in the career of Birmingham Liberalism during this period. The first is that despite the association of Chamberlain's name with the implementation of 'modern' techniques in public administration and political organisation the well of popular feeling upon which he drew was essentially pre-industrial. Although an American visitor, impressed with the application of business methods to municipal affairs, labelled Birmingham 'the best-governed city in the world' and in spite of the fact that Chamberlain's political machine was dubbed the 'caucus' in the style of big-city Democratic politics in the United States, the driving animus of Birmingham Liberalism was very English and very traditional.[16] It was fed by the long-standing hostility of small traders and artisans, particularly the Nonconformist element, to county society, the aristocracy and the Church of England. Evidence for this can be found in the pages of a book published by a Yardley solicitor in 1882, justifying the work of the National Education League.[17]

According to Francis Adams, the secretary of the league, the fundamental division in English society was between supporters of an aristocratic and Anglican tyranny based in the counties and at the metropolis and the advocates of local public bodies enacting the freely-expressed will of the community. The conflict between the education unions of Birmingham and Manchester and the National Education League was described in such terms:[18]

> The new programmes [of the two unions] were put forth under the sanction of a long array of Archbishops, and Bishops, Dukes, Earls and Tory Members of Parliament. While the League could hardly boast a Coronet, the 'Unions' had very little else to boast of. Their lists were wholly uncontaminated by any association with popular institutions or their representatives. They were Conservative organisations, as much as the League was a Liberal and Democratic organisation.

Later he writes,[19]

> Instead of relying on sectarian jealousy and rivalry, on denominational patronage and private charity, the members of the League appealed to public spirit, to local Government, and National resources, and to the cooperation of the parents and people.

Adams proudly points out the league's debt to the struggles of the Dissenters since Reformation times:[20]

> They had a noble history, which gave them a title to be heard as a part of the people, on questions affecting welfare, which it would have been ignominious to surrender. They had by immense sacrifice, exertion, and courage, defeated the design of the ecclesiastical leaders of the Reformation, that our Church government should be made to embrace the whole body of the people. From a despised and persecuted minority they had grown into a power. They had been especially the missionaries of religious and political instruction to the poor, and had defended the rights of minorities. They had obtained a paramount influence over the middle classes, and had shaken to its foundation the traditional authority which the church claimed over the lower orders.

In Adam's view, the league's campaign belonged to the most recent phase of a process of development, which had already lasted for centuries, whereby public opinion and social institutions were to a steadily increasing extent embodying the highest moral principles. Nonconformity was part of this movement although 'in its entirety and comprehensive character it was neither wholly religious nor philanthropic. It was social, industrial and political and was in fact the forecoming of the great wave of advancement which later times have witnessed.'[21]

In the first chapter of Adam's book there are eleven references to

Herbert Spencer's *Descriptive Sociology*.[22] It will be recalled that Spencer came from a petty-bourgeois Nonconformist background. Adams accepts the sociologist's view, most clearly set out in *Social Statics*, that the course of social change tends to be away from a state of internecine strife and towards one of heterogenous interdependence amongst spontaneously cooperating individuals. Altruism would increasingly be expressed in social institutions.[23] Adams, however, moved beyond Spencer and many Dissenters in welcoming the part played by the state, especially popular local government, in providing services such as elementary education for the people.[24]

Birmingham Liberalism in the 1870s and 1880s may be seen in the historical context of the earlier part of the nineteenth century when advocates of *laissez-faire*, utilitarianism and radical Dissent entered into a practical alliance with each other. A number of basic principles and political implications were left unresolved by the parties to this alliance. They united on the basis of their common hostility to an 'obstructive' or 'tyrannical' government which was vested in aristocratic, clerical and Tory interests at every level from parliament to the parish vestry. However, as the political significance of collective organisations (such as the trade unions) and public bureaucracies increased, the practical alliance which had been established underwent a severe crisis with respect to philosophy and strategy. Radically contrasting solutions were sought by different men. Edward Miall for example, gave himself to the Liberationist cause. Herbert Spencer provided *laissez-faire* with a new intellectual framework. John Stuart Mill began to see great virtues in 'collectivism' and even 'socialism'. The league's secretary expressed another view, one which drew upon the diverging orientations of militant Nonconformity, statism and Spencerian analysis, refocusing them upon the ideal of popular Liberal local government. Despite the mutual antipathy of Spencer and the leader of Birmingham's Liberals, the influence of the intellectual synthesis is clear in the political programmes of Chamberlain.[25]

In practice, in Birmingham the great Liberal mission of the 1870s and 1880s was to displace the old Anglican and Tory establishment from its institutional strongholds or to outflank them by expanding the town council's functions at the expense of 'denominational patronage and private charity'. By 1878 there was only one Conservative member of the council. Four years later Satchell Hopkins, a local Conservative leader, claimed that none of his party could win admittance to the board of guardians and that the 'caucus' had taken control of the board of governors of the King Edward VI Foundation and the council of the Birmingham and Midland Institute.[26]

There is a second, and deeper, irony in the progress of Birmingham Liberalism under the leadership of Chamberlain. A party with an anti-aristocratic ideology, feeding on the prejudices of the Nonconformist petty bourgeoisie and with the proclaimed objective of promoting the welfare of the general population was led, by a politician whose fortune had been made in big business, into close alliance with the party of Anglicanism and the landed interest. Furthermore, according to an analysis of voting trends in the late 1870s and early 1880s the decisive political shift occurred at a time when working-class hostility to the 'caucus' had reached a level which threatened to break the Liberal Party's monopoly of parliamentary seats in Birmingham.[27] By the mid-1870s the ruling Liberals were adopting the same smug and superior attitude towards their Conservative opponents that the foundation's governors, when they were a 'Tory trust', had taken towards the town council. The editor of the *Birmingham Daily Mail* had declared in 1874[28]

> The Conservative element is quite out of place in municipal matters. What is it that the 'Conservative Party' are going to conserve? Is it the mud, or the smallpox?

By the end of that decade, however, the Conservatives were winning an increased proportion of votes at municipal elections in the poorest working-class areas near the city centre and also in the richest middle-class areas in the business centre and at Edgbaston. The Liberal Party's management of municipal institutions stimulated this protest from wealthier ratepayers, disgusted with the cost of the improvement scheme which had been stigmatised as a 'bubble company', and from members of working-class communities who had seen their houses being torn down to make way for law courts. Despite plans to build new houses for the displaced families, few were constructed by the council. In fact, many of the old residents 'followed the factories to other parts' so increasing the tendency towards increased residential segregation by class. The council was also attacked as a bad employer which underpaid its workers.[29]

By the late 1880s at least four political organisations were active in municipal politics: Liberal Unionists, Conservatives, Gladstonian Liberals and the Social Democratic Federation. Working-class origins and antipathy to Chamberlain were increasingly valuable assets for candidates, particularly in less well-off districts such as Bordesley. However, the SDF, which represented the nascent political wing of the Labour movement, failed to reap a rich harvest of votes. Instead, an increasingly sophisticated Conservative organisation which was prepared, unlike Chamberlain's party, to put up candidates with artisan and petty bourgeois backgrounds won support through skilful populist propaganda.[30] The better-off working men in the outlying parts of the city, less badly hit by unemployment during the late 1870s and 1880s, retained their loyalty to Gladstonian Liberalism. In 1889 the Gladstonian Sir Walter Foster was confident of electoral support in the eastern, and possibly the northern suburbs: 'The working classes here have all the pluck.'[31]

By the mid-1890s, Chamberlain had entered a cabinet headed by the leader of the Conservative Party. In Birmingham the Conservative and Liberal Unionist Parties were slowly but steadily moving towards closer cooperation. By 1900 the Bishop of Coventry had become chairman of the Birmingham School Board. Five years later, Satchell Hopkins' hopes for the creation of a Bishopric of Birmingham became a reality.[32] These changes were expressions of a major realignment within the city's bourgeoisie and its relationship to the local labouring population. During the last two decades of the century, business and professional establishments whose predecessors had been radically divided in the 1830s and 1840s, followed by a softening of animosities during the 1850s and early 1860s and a further period of serious division from the late 1860s to the 1880s, began to knit together socially, politically and economically.

One index of gradual coalescence in the realm of opinion is provided by the reports and editorials of the *Birmingham Daily Post* and the *Birmingham Daily Gazette*. The *Post* was edited by J. T. Bunce, a close political colleague of Chamberlain, between 1862 and 1898.[33] The Conservative *Gazette*, which in 1876 was warning that the spread of elementary education would tend to lead to an increase in white-collar crime, was by the late 1890s campaigning hard alongside the *Post* in favour of Chamberlain's efforts to obtain a university charter for Birmingham. This is just one instance of the trend towards consensus between the 1870s and 1890s.[34]

ASPECTS OF CLASS FORMATION: PRELIMINARY COMMENTS

By the end of the century Birmingham and Sheffield were both participating in the gravitation of all forms of wealth in town and countryside into the Conservative Party. The movement had become strong in Birmingham about two decades later than in Sheffield. Crucially, the process of social and political fusion was focused at the level of the municipality in Birmingham whereas in Sheffield the national level was strategic. It is impossible to isolate this difference between the two cities from three other differences between them: the relative lateness of the development of large-scale heavy industry in Birmingham (compared to Sheffield); the great increase in the complexity and prestige of civic institutions since mid-century in Birmingham (compared to Sheffield)[35]; and the long tradition and influential presence of professional, mercantile and white-collar occupations in Birmingham (compared to Sheffield).[36] These dissimilarities are also closely associated

233

with differences between the two cities in the extent to which the growth of large-scale heavy industry was associated with tendencies towards class division. The above points will now be expanded.

The use of joint-stock methods of finance, which was associated with the growth of very large steel firms in Sheffield during the 1860s, was a comparative rarity in Birmingham before 1880. However, during the last two decades of the century this practice became more common as Birmingham's industry underwent a period of considerable innovation and diversification, continuing up to the First World War. Electrical engineering and chemicals were leading sectors. The Austin Motor Company, still in its infancy, employed 700 people by 1907. By 1914 the General Electric Company at Witton had 2,000 on the payroll, Dunlop Rubber had engaged 4,000 hands and Cadbury's at Bournville were employing 6,000 people. Such firms were at the head of a movement which involved the exploitation of new materials and techniques and the steady replacement of skilled labour by machine minders. This movement was not new in Birmingham's industry but the scale on which it was occurring within the city was unprecedented.[37]

As has been seen, Birmingham's professional and lower middle-class inhabitants were integrated through a host of literary, recreational and educational enterprises into a thriving municipal culture. By contrast, Sheffield's lower middle-class citizens are likely to have experienced a higher degree of anomie within a city which had no thriving or well-defined civic life.[38] Apart from differences in the structural position of the white-collar occupational groups within the two cities, the greater relative and absolute size of this contingent in Birmingham arguably had two effects: it strengthened the body of opinion which recognised the importance of formal education as a means of social advancement, an orientation which tended to stress individual effort as opposed to the exercise of collective strength; and the presence of such people within businesses and in distinct residential districts is likely to have weakened the consciousness of a starkly dichotomous class structure fostered by workplace experiences in large-scale industrial enterprises.

The social tendencies indicated above were strengthened by the strong identification of many of Birmingham's leading employers and their close associates with the city to which their workpeople belonged.[39] This contrasts sharply with Sheffield and introduces a further stage in the argument. There were important differences between the two cities with respect to the level of integration at which coalescence primarily occurred between old and new establishments, the former oriented towards rural society and the latter rooted in the business life of the city. In the case of Birmingham it occurred through their mutual occupation of a complex and sophisticated network of institutions at the municipal level. In the case of Sheffield it occurred through the entry of the leading industrialists into a world of business, politics, and socialising centred not upon the municipality but upon Whitehall, the City of London and the Carlton Club to which the leading landowners already belonged. This was most evident in the case of the great Sheffield steel firms which entered the armaments business, initially in the 1850s and 1860s, very heavily during the late 1880s.[40] The progress of Vickers, for example, was intimately tied up with decisions made in central government. By the end of the First World War Vincent Caillard of Vickers was writing privately of 'the special relations we have with the War Office and the Admiralty.'[41] Tom Vickers, chairman between 1873 and 1915 'disliked publicity; he disliked speech-making, and the ornamental side of his position; politics did not interest him; local affairs were a duty, not a pleasure.'[42]

When Conservative candidates were needed for parliamentary elections they could not be found among substantial local citizens. They were taken from the county (as in the case of Stuart Wortley of the Wharncliffe dynasty) and drafted in from Scotland Yard or Oxford University. When the Sheffield Liberals wanted somebody to fight Attercliffe in 1885 they called in the son of the Lord Chief Justice. They were not able to drum up a well-established local celebrity of the same stamp as George Dixon, William Kenrick and Joseph Chamberlain who all stood in Birmingham at this period.[43] It is unlikely that Sir Frederick Mappin, one of the few leading industrialists to maintain a public identification with the Liberals, would have been popular in such a thoroughly working-class constituency.

The above remarks do not ignore the fact that Birmingham politicians and businessmen acquired great influence in the surrounding counties and in the metropolis, nor that steel manufacturers and landed magnates sat in the mayoral chair at Sheffield. For example, the Duke of Norfolk served as Sheffield's mayor for two years from 1895.[44] However, while the latter may be seen as falling within the sphere of 'noblesse oblige' the former was a manifestation of the power of a strong regional political influence centred on a civic bourgeoisie which was developing a high degree of social integration by the 1890s.[45] There is some evidence for this last point in the reminiscences of E. A. Knox, who served as vicar of Aston from 1891 to 1895 and as Suffragan Bishop of Coventry based at St Philip's rectory in Birmingham from 1895 to 1904.[46] Despite some bitter battles with Nonconformists on the school board he remembered Birmingham as being 'an intensely hospitable city' with 'a civic consciousness stronger, perhaps, than any other English city'.[47] It is possible that the strengthened Anglican hierarchy in Birmingham may have played an important part in healing up the wounds left by the split between local Liberals in the mid-1880s. On the one hand, Knox and Bishop Gore had links through Conservatism to Joseph Chamberlain; on the other hand, good working relations were established with notable union leaders such as W. J. Davis, who like many trade unionists remained a Gladstonian, and prominent employers such as the Cadburys who did not desert the Liberal Party in 1886.[48] Knox praised the 'receptive friendliness' of the Society of Friends. At Richard Cadbury's funeral, Knox was invited to read the Benediction. Furthermore,[49]

> The conditions of Birmingham town-planning were exceptionally favourable to the existence of a kind of brotherhood or family of prominent citizens, living together in delightful homes at Edgbaston, within easy reach of the city, and taking an active part in its municipal and church life.

During his years at St Philip's rectory Knox found that[50]

> I was within five minutes' walk of the Town Hall, the Council House, the Midland Institute, the Art Gallery and the Free Library. No civic meeting or function of any importance could occur that was not almost at my door. All the chief business offices were practically within sight of my windows, and so were the chief clubs and hotels. The termini of the trams, which radiated to the parishes in this direction and that, were within my parish. . . . The Bank of England was my neighbour. . . . St Philip's Rectory stood almost at the door of the two main lines. . . . Fast trains took me directly to all our chief towns.

Compare this description of Sheffield in the mid-1890s:[51]

> On entering Sheffield from the railway station, we find ourselves in a valley crowded with steel works and with the surrounding population. We are in the centre of the working portion of Sheffield, and in the midst of a large population of artisans. We must climb uphill for about three miles to reach the residential part of Sheffield. We then find ourselves in the suburb of Broomhill, planted high above the smoke and dirt, with the moorland country beginning just behind it, and beautifully green with trees and gardens. I know of no manufacturing town where the contrast between the dwelling places of the rich and the poor are so strongly marked, or the separation between them so complete.

In both Birmingham and Sheffield the huge factories and monotonous workplace routines of large-scale industrial capitalism were a gigantic social fact by the end of the century. However, as has been seen, the two cities had followed very different trajectories of industrial development since 1830. One aspect of this was that professional and mercantile activity had been much more strongly established in Birmingham at the beginning of the period and this lead was maintained. The relative importance of the neighbourhood, the county, the municipality and national networks as foci of social solidarity and bases for mobilising influence had undergone transformation, but in very dissimilar ways in the two cities. More specifically, Birmingham and Sheffield had manifested very different patterns of development in the achievement of social integration between the old genteel social hierarchies and the new urban industrial order. Not least, the more gradual shift in the balance of power between establishments and social classes in Birmingham had instilled a deeply-ingrained habit of compromise which was far less evident in Sheffield. These differences combined to produce a considerable dissimilarity between the cities in the organisation of formal education, industrial relations and local government administration in the years around the turn of the century.

BIRMINGHAM: FUSION AND COMPROMISE

At Birmingham in each of these three organisational spheres tendencies towards social fission and conflict were counteracted by institutional arrangements which embodied complex compromises between the practices of a rural and small-town social order and those of modern urban industrial bureaucracies. During the late 1880s the King Edward VI Foundation was still under attack for its social exclusivity and literary bias.[52] However, even so strong an advocate of technical education as Rev. H. W. Crosskey, and one so conscious of the desirability of 'a thoroughly well-organised system', conceded that 'the old classical training has its own charms, its own power, and its own glory.'[53] In 1884 Crosskey reviewed the disorganised pattern of educational institutions in the large towns:[54]

> Their number and character have been determined by the intensity with which particular individuals may have felt desirous of supplying local wants; the special tastes and idiosyncracies of rich people willing to give 'of their substance' to promote education; the character and extent of ancient endowments available in any district, and the personal dispositions of the members of the boards charged with their administration; the resources of particular Churches and the educational zeal of their members; *the degree to which class distinctions are recognised and respected.*

While Crosskey was anxious to see a local technical college established and indirectly criticised the lack of 'high scientific training' in the high school, the hidden principle of the 'system' he proposed was that facilities should be expanded so that the effective demand from all local clients could be met with minimum disruption of existing vested interests.[55] 'Class distinctions' would be disguised and preserved by an emphasis upon the age at which students left school:[56]

> A well graded system of schools does not . . . mean a system under which the scholar passes from one kind of school to another, but a system under which schools exist which give as good an education as possible to each set of scholars in a community according to the time which they can devote to their education. . . . Were there enough Board Schools, and were these schools well scattered throughout the town so as to be found amongst our larger as well as our smaller houses, I am convinced that in a few years 'class' difficulties would disappear. It would soon be understood that the age at which the scholars are expected to leave, and not social distinctions, affected their management.

In fact, by 1895 the system of elementary and secondary education which was developing in Birmingham was a complex amalgam of the schemes of T. H. Green (the advocate of liberal culture) and Crosskey (the disciple of technical education). It also included some provision for promotion from the board elementary schools: a lure to higher scholarship according to Green's vision, a necessary though inadequate redistribution of local resources according to the critique of the trades council.

In the industrial sphere there was a similar tendency to adapt established practices to rapidly changing structural conditions. As had been seen, throughout the period 1830–70 two widespread features of Birmingham's industry had been the use of cheap juvenile labour and the development of increasingly close institutional bonds between employers and craftsmen, ultimately through the medium of the trades council established in 1866.[57] These institutional links became especially strong in the period of Liberal dominance and by the 1880s trade union officials were widely represented on local public bodies such as the board of guardians. Artisan leaders and employers had a mutual interest in keeping unskilled labour cheap while maximising the selling price of goods: the employer and the craftsmen, the latter often acting as a sub-contractor, could then bargain over a 'reasonable' distribution of the profit. Unable to rely upon the strike as a weapon, union leaders 'carefully nurtured the approach of the honest, sincere, straightforward Englishman, appealing to the employer, as one reasonable, humanitarian gentleman to another'. The extent to which the trades council felt it belonged to the same social world as the masters is shown by its members' interest in the Patents Act and the Bankruptcy Act during the early 1880s.[58]

However, by the mid-1890s the spread of mass production in large factories, especially on the outskirts of Birmingham, had generated employment conditions which led to the decline of the craft unions and were soon to provide many recruits for general unions of semi- and unskilled labourers. By 1893 the trades council had many members who were pressing for an improvement in the wages and conditions of these workers.[59] Nevertheless, the determination to maintain established institutional links with employers, links which were themselves an attempted re-creation of the shared normative order of the early nineteenth century, may be seen in the career of the local brass-workers' leader.

W. J. Davis, a member of the parliamentary committee of the TUC and a very influential man in Birmingham, founded the National Society of Amalgamated Brassworkers in 1872. He was elected to the school board in 1876 and to the town council three years later. By the end of the century his union had members in all branches of the brass trade including many workers in the bicycle and motor car industries. During the 1890s the spread of mass production techniques in the brass industry was associated with a decline of sub-contracting, an increased number of craftsmen becoming wage-earners paid directly by firms, and new demands for improved basic wages for all hands.[60] Davis, who had begun his career when sub-contractors were dominant in the union and cheap unskilled labour a welcome commodity now found himself campaigning for a minimum wage and the abolition of 'sweated labour'. However, he continued to resist the use of the strike weapon.[61]

Davis believed that masters and men should be jointly responsible for, and proud of, their industry. Conciliation and arbitration were the correct way to resolve disputes. He told an official arbitrator in 1899[62]

> We represent a community of interests. The employers find the capital, business capacity and enterprise, and should have the lion's share of the profits. We find the technical skill and muscle which the product requires. The stomach must be fed; raiment and shelter is essential for the reproduction of mankind. Therefore you must apportion fairly the profits as between Capital and Labour.

This had been Davis's approach since his first successful appeal to arbitration in 1873. By 1891 he was successfully negotiating with the Brass Trade Manufacturers Council for permanent conciliation boards and later he gave full support to the alliances promoted in the metal trades by E. J. Smith, a craftsman turned employer. These schemes conceded 'closed shop' status and special bonuses to unions in return for their support in enforcing throughout the trade the selling prices fixed by boards on which masters and men were both represented. Davis found that the court of Birmingham opinion was as valuable a forum at the turn of the century as it had been in the 1840s. When the employers were reluctant to accept arbitration in 1897 he forced them to meet by threatening to expose the sweatshops. Twelve years later he was using the same strategy, this time calling in the Bishop of Birmingham to boost his case.[63]

The great mission of Davis's career was to institute a system of industrial training and promotion which would recreate in modern conditions the best features of apprenticeship. Such a plan entailed the hearty cooperation of employers with workmen and the systematic use of educational facilities. His ambition was to see established[64]

> a minimum standard which shall regulate trade custom and recognise skill, dexterity, or ingenuity at their trade value, and give the best mechanics an opportunity of earning wages in proportion, and as a reward for their extra zeal and accomplishments.

In 1910, after a lengthy campaign, a scheme was inaugurated whereby workers were classified by the union into seven grades with different rates of pay. By attendance at the Municipal Brass Trades School young workers could improve their grade. Disputes about the grade to which a worker should belong were to be resolved by an examination conducted by the managers of the school in conjunction with representatives from the employers and the union.[65] Evidence of this kind from the brass trade is significant not only because of Davis's great influence on industrial relations in Birmingham but also because the skilled brass workers had an intermediate position in local industry, being in everyday contact with small and large employers and experiencing the pressures of mechanisation upon a craft tradition. Their position was in these respects similar to the Sheffield file unions. However, the latter were fighting a long rearguard action to defend a system of apprenticeship that had been strong when the brass-workers were still without a union. As has been seen, Sheffield's technical school was sponsored by an employer deeply hostile to union involvement in the training and regulation of the workforce.

A third sphere where old and new forms were combined was in local government. The town council under Liberal control had improved the sanitary conditions of Birmingham, re-shaped its physical centre and acquired control of some basic amenities but it had done relatively little to offer direct help to poor working-class families. The benefits to business men of the improvement scheme and later, the extension of municipal boundaries in 1891, 1909 and 1911 to create a Greater Birmingham were fairly evident. White-collar workers and artisans were presumably a large proportion of the people who used the magnificent free libraries. However, provision of relief for the unemployed who refused to go the workhouse was left to voluntary agencies. The building of improved working-class housing, neglected under the improvement scheme, was left to paternalistic employers such as the Cadburys who laid out Bournville after 1895. A merging together of the long tradition of private charity with the new and expanding bureaucratic capacity of the local state occurred in the years around the turn of the century. It was encouraged by the increased influence of the Church of England under the aegis of E. A. Knox and Charles Gore, the Bishop of Birmingham, both of whom formed close links with the Society of Friends. Addressing the National Housing Reform Council in Birmingham in 1906, Gore stressed 'the debt we owe to Mr Cadbury'.[66] By 1889 the city council had passed plans for building working-class houses in Ryder Street which were completed the following year. When the project was proposed the council was pointedly reminded about the deficiencies of the improvement scheme: 'when it was accepted no one dreamed that we were going to destroy 855 dwellings without putting any artisans' houses in their place.' A more extensive project in Lawrence Street was sanctioned in 1891. By 1900 the council had also constructed four terraces of two-storey tenements in Milk Street. The housing committee, appointed the following year, presented the first scheme to be approved under the 1909 Housing and Planning Act.[67]

Another strand in this general development was the creation of the City of Birmingham Aid Society in 1906, coordinating the work for the poor of several charitable organisations. It acquired a semi-public character, working closely with the city council and the board of guardians.[68] In the period between 1905 and 1914 when the provision of labour exchanges and national insurance schemes was being widely discussed 'the most consistent and active proponents of social legis-lation were the members of the Birmingham Chamber of Commerce'. Significantly, the most striking contribution to this debate of the Sheffield Chamber of Commerce was to recommend its own city's system of technical education and the introduction of compulsory military training.[69]

SHEFFIELD: FISSION AND CONFLICT

Charitable donations, many of them channelled through the Church of England, were the preferred form of benevolence amongst Sheffield's industrialists: a park here, a hospital or a church there.[70] The town council did little to supplement their efforts before the last decade of the century. Control of basic services fell belatedly into its hands, beginning with the acquisition of the local water works company in 1888. A serious attack on insanitary conditions did not get underway until 1903 with the substitution of ashpits for ashbins. Between 1871 and 1915 Sheffield 'had the worst library system in any town of impor-tance in the country'. Until 1897 the administration of local government was dispersed over at least four sites 'in the meaner streets of the town'. In 1888, Alderman W. J. Clegg, a leading Liberal, informed the Select Committee on Town Holdings that Sheffield had not put the Artizans' Dwellings Act into force even though a great proportion of the Duke of Norfolk's property in the Park was 'in a most deplorable state and not fit to live in'. A local solicitor gave evidence of rack-renting by the Duke who had 'not adopted the principle that the lessee, at the termination of the lease, has any moral claim upon him'. Slum clearance on any scale in Sheffield did not begin until 1903. Subsequent plans to erect houses for working-class occupiers ran into considerable political opposition. However, when unemployment became a serious problem in 1903 there was more determined action by the city council which employed out-of-work labourers on municipal projects.[71]

The stirring into life which began in the early part of the new century was a response to increasing pressure from below. The Sheffield Labour Representation Committee, founded in 1903, placed slum clearance, corporation housing development and the direct employment of labour by the city council high on its list of demands.[72] In local government as in education the decisive pressures emanated from the development of class conflicts in the industrial sphere. In 1884, Robert Leader had recognised the priority of this sphere when giving evidence in Sheffield to the Royal Commission on Technical Instruction. Discussing the possible development of Firth College as a school of technology he commented[73]

> But the life of the thing will not be in the public bodies of the town; it must be in the manufacturers and workmen of the town. If the great manufacturers who feel the inefficiency of their men from want of scientific and artistic training, take the matter in hand there will be a great success, but if they hold aloof, as one is led to fear they will from the scanty attendance of manufacturers this morning; if they show indifference, I do not think the proposal can be supported by other agencies. Therefore, the real appeal must be to those who conduct our great manufactures, and upon whom the prosperity of the town depends.

Class relations in Sheffield during the late nineteenth century were governed by a dialectic of indifference and fear. Indifference was sustained by the great social distance between managers and workers in large industrial enterprises combined with the virtual absence of civic life and the daily retreat after work into neighbourhoods and suburbs whose geographical location reinforced a sense of separateness. When the city council tried to build some working-class houses at High Storrs in 1899, there were dangers of the *cordon sanitaire* being broken. Councillor Muir Wilson of Whiteley Wood Hall, half a mile away, was very insistent that the site was unsuitable. The scheme was abandoned and later a much more 'acceptable' tenant, a local authority grammar school, was found.[74] The High Storrs episode typifies the other element of the dialectic, the fear that a group's 'proper' sphere will be invaded and alien rules and assumptions imposed. Such a response tended to generate a determination to resist to the last and not compromise willingly. This was the response of the trade societies to the introduction of machinery in the 1860s and it was also the response of the large steel manufacturers, relatively untroubled by unions before the 1890s, to the development of labour organisation in their plants. It is not surprising that the major successes of the Sheffield Labour movement have been in the sphere of local government where they could capture a citadel that was very weakly defended by the Sheffield bourgeoisie. Once in power, the Labour Party showed itself equally uncompromising. However, that is to anticipate the argument.

The parliamentary election of 1868 which was examined in chapter 7 occurred at an early point in a long process of social development which was to leave employers in a dominant position within Sheffield's heavy industry while the political wing of the local Labour movement acquired a commanding position on the city council. Three subsequent parliamentary elections, those held in 1874, 1885 and 1894, illustrate this process. In 1874 George Hadfield retired as one of Sheffield's two MPs. Joseph Chamberlain accepted an invitation from H. J. Wilson, one of his most devoted followers in Sheffield, to fight the constituency.[75] Chamberlain received the support of the Sheffield Trades Council and Wilson's radical Sheffield Reform Association.[76] However, Robert Leader and the more moderate Liberals preferred another candidate as Mundella's running mate. In the event, Mundella's companion in parliament after the 1874 General Election was neither Chamberlain nor his moderate Liberal rival but Roebuck. As in 1868, Roebuck was supported by the large employers. The extent of their alienation from Liberal causes is shown by the rejection of the arbitration principle by the management at Browns' and Vickers' membership of the new National Federation of Associated Employers of Labour.[77] The General Election of 1885 revealed the extent to which patterns of residence were reinforcing political hostilities and preferences. Hallam and Ecclesall, middle-class suburbs, were strongly Conservative but Brightside and Attercliffe were markedly Radical. According to a student of nineteenth-century poll books this was 'the first clear case of political division following from class housing patterns'.[78]

The radicalism of Sheffield's working-class inhabitants should not be exaggerated. Pelling points out that in the period 1885–1910 only Attercliffe was continuously Liberal or Labour. In 1900 the Conservatives won Brightside 'and probably could have won Attercliffe if they had contested it'. A major factor was the dependence of the steel industry upon military expenditure, a form of spending for which the Liberal Party was not enthusiastic. Both the steel industry and the cutlery trades were increasingly attracted by protectionist ideas which found a stronghold in the Conservative Party. Sir Howard Vincent, member for Sheffield Central was a pioneer in this cause. It is, incidentally, an ironic fact that although Chamberlain was rejected by Sheffield in 1874 both of his *causes célèbres*, education for the working classes and trade protection for their employers, found their strongest advocates amongst Sheffield's parliamentary representatives: Mundella and Vincent.[79]

A further bastion of Conservatism was the Church of England which worked hard to win hearts and minds in poor areas like St Simon's parish. The vicar had as early as 1857 acquired a Baptist church, its former congregation 'desiring to move to the suburbs'. In 1877 William Odom moved to this living with its gasometer, breweries and cutlery works. 'There was not a tree nor a foot of garden within the parish, nor did it contain a Nonconformist place of worship.' He rapidly created a network of recreational and welfare organisations for his parishioners following a strategy similar to that of Knox in Aston a little while later.[80] The attitude to its flock adopted by the hierarchy is nicely conveyed by the words of Bishop Godwin to a meeting of Sheffield working men in 1878:[81]

> You would scarcely believe it, but I think of Sheffield every day of my life. You don't know why? I will tell you. I shave every morning. I have a box which contains seven Sheffield razors – one for every day of the week. . . . They were good Englishmen who made those razors and they did not skimp their work. . . . The man who throws his whole heart and soul into the making of a razor, or into the management of a diocese, that is the man who is worthy of being called a man, and who shall stand erect before GOD in the great day of account.

This line of approach may have been different from that of the lady from the Visiting and Bettering Society who in the 1840s urged the Church of England in Sheffield to press on with the task of 'training up . . . well-educated, sober, loyal and obedient subjects'; but the message was effectively the same.[82]

The retreat of Sheffield's middle-class voters to the western suburbs produced the contradictory result that although union leaders were making very little headway in bargaining with employers the representatives of labour were beginning to find their way relatively easily onto the town council and other related bodies. Giving evidence before the Royal Commission on Labour in the early 1890s, several members

of the Sheffield Federated Trades Council complained of the un-
willingness of Sheffield employers to participate in setting up
machinery for conciliation and arbitration. W. F. Wardley reported
that repeated appeals to the Cutlers' Company and the Sheffield
Chamber of Commerce concerning the establishment of a joint board
of arbitration had been ignored. He commented, with a touch of
sarcasm[83]

> I think a good many employers of labour would not risk being
> subjected to examination by this board. I think they would rather
> do what is honest and fair than bring every detail before a board
> composed of practical, sensible, rational men. That is my opinion.
> In many cases it is a question of might over right; I think the thing
> would come to an end.

In 1893 the town council attempted to set up a chamber of arbitration in
cooperation with the chamber of commerce, the Sheffield Federated
Trades Council and the Cutlers' Company. Although arbitrators were
appointed in 1894 and 1895 no appointments were made in 1896. The
scheme was 'still-born'.[84]

Wardley had, however, been elected to the town council in 1890 as a
Liberal. Three other working men from the trades council had preceded him. Two more followed in 1895 and 1897. Charles Hobson of
the Brittania-metal smiths was also elected to the school board and
Guardians of the Poor in 1894. Although during the 1890s such men
were elected for the central wards containing the old cutlery trades, by
the turn of the century the centre of working-class municipal politics
was shifting to Attercliffe and Brightside.[85]

The Attercliffe by-election in 1894, caused by the elevation of the
sitting member to the peerage, revealed the continuing strength of
resistance to working-class candidates within the Liberal Party. When
the trades council asked Charles Hobson to stand 'in the Labour
interest', his candidature was vetoed by the president of the Sheffield
United Liberal Association. The man who exercised this veto was Sir
Frederick Mappin. He was expressing the deep reservations felt by
local employers concerning the safety of allowing working-class representatives to exercise political power.[86]

Between 1891 and 1911 the heavy trades overtook the light trades in
terms of numbers employed within Sheffield. This shift was associated
with radical alterations in the industrial and political strategies of
organised labour. As in Birmingham, the years around the turn of the
century saw the emergence of strong rivals to the old craft unions.
Jonathan Taylor was actively expanding the membership of the Gas
Workers and General Labourers Union in the early 1890s. The railway-
men and tramwaymen were also acquiring organisation. Although the
steelworkers were very poorly organised the number of engineers in

the ASE increased from 884 in 1893 to 3,117 by 1914. The leadership within these new unions was (in contrast to Birmingham) badly represented on the trades council but it rapidly acquired a dominant influence within the Labour Representation Committee which was set up in 1903. In Birmingham at that time, men like Davis could point to three decades of reasonably successful manipulation of arbitration machinery and privileged access to the ears of employers and politicians. In Sheffield there was no such check upon a new movement which discarded the strategy of arbitration and turned towards a full-blooded socialist programme. By 1906 the LRC, in close association with the Independent Labour Party, had won three seats on the city council. Two years later its members created the Trades and Labour Council to represent a membership and set of policies which were virtually excluded from the Sheffield Federated Trades Council, the latter still dominated by the old craft unions in the light trades. Thus by 1908 Sheffield had two trades councils. The following year it acquired its first Labour MP, fifteen years before Birmingham.[87]

The philosophy of the Sheffield Trades and Labour Council was given extreme expression in the course of the shop stewards movement during the First World War. It was, as J. T. Murphy of the Sheffield Workers' Committee pointed out 'an engineers' war', one which gave unprecedented importance to production workers in the munitions industry of which Sheffield was a major centre. Conflicts on the shopfloor over the use of unskilled labour led to widespread strikes and the setting up of unofficial workshop committees by men dissatisfied with the national leadership, especially within the ASE. In his pamphlet *The Workers' Committee: an outline of its principles and structure*, J. T. Murphy envisaged the creation of a new structure of worker representation, reaching up to the national level but solidly based upon local committees, each of which would be the deliberative body and the voice of all workers of whatever union or skill level in a particular workshop. On this basis, ascending through a hierarchy of local industrial committees, plant committees, national industrial committees, local workers' committees (uniting different industries) and at the summit, a national workers' committee, Murphy envisaged the creation of 'the great Industrial Union of the Working class'.[88] His basic message is summarised in the following passage:[89]

> increasingly insistent has been the progress towards *government by officials*. . . . It allows small groups who are . . . remote from actual workshop experience to govern the mass and involve the mass into working under conditions which they have had no opportunity of considering prior to their inception. The need of the hour is a drastic revision of this constitutional practice which demands that the function of the rank and file shall be simply that

of obedience. . . . Real democratic practice demands that every member of an organisation shall participate actively in the conduct of the business of the society. We need, therefore to reverse the present situation, and instead of leaders and officials being in the forefront of our thoughts the questions of the day which have to be answered should occupy that position. . . . We desire the mass of men and women to think for themselves, and until they do this no real progress is made, democracy becomes a farce, and the future of the race becomes a story of race deterioration.

Thought is revolutionary: it breaks down barriers, transforms institutions, and leads onward to a larger life. To be afraid of thought is to be afraid of life, and to become an instrument of darkness and oppression.

The year is 1917 but the message is that of Isaac Ironside.

CHAPTER 11

'A SERIOUS DANGER TO THE UPPER CLASSES'

SUMMARY AND CONCLUSION

Before the themes of this book are drawn together a brief visit will be made to a fictional morning-room in Half-Moon Street, London. The year is 1895. A young man is being interviewed by his prospective mother-in-law:[1]

> *Lady Bracknell*: . . . I have always been of the opinion that a man who desired to get married should know either everything or nothing. Which do you know?
> *Jack* (after some hesitation): I know nothing, Lady Bracknell.
> *Lady Bracknell*: I am pleased to hear it. I do not approve of anything that tampers with natural ignorance. Ignorance is like a delicate exotic fruit; touch it and the bloom is gone. The whole theory of modern education is radically unsound. Fortunately in England, at any rate, education produces no effect whatsoever. If it did, it would prove a serious danger to the upper classes, and probably lead to acts of violence in Grosvenor Square.

Lady Bracknell was the outraged and outrageous spokeswoman of a class for whom 'land had ceased to be either a profit or a pleasure' and whose matrons and dowagers were being forced to place even higher upon their lists of 'eligible young men' the offspring of persons 'born in what the Radical papers call the purple of commerce'.[2] Oscar Wilde, with all the advantages of Irish descent, was a brilliant commentator upon the peculiarities of the English at this period. The plot of *The Importance of Being Earnest* revolves around the subtleties of role-playing by the gentry in town and countryside. Dr Chasuble, the ridiculous Hertfordshire canon, epitomises the waning authority of

the rural clergy while Lane, the sardonic London man-servant, illustrates the dependence of genteel town society upon a working class
whose ways remained mysterious to their masters.[3]

In Jack's words, Lady Bracknell was 'a Gorgon. . . . She is a monster
without being a myth, which is rather unfair.' Unfair, perhaps, but
useful since her attitudes are an extreme but vivid version of the state
of feeling in an important section of London Society. Agricultural
depression and death duties were conspiring to produce the effect that
'land gives one position, and prevents one from keeping it up. That's
all that can be said about land.' Investments were a different matter.
Jack's 'a hundred and thirty thousand pounds in the Funds' were a
great point in his favour. He was a Liberal Unionist but 'they count as
Tories. They dine with us. Or come in the evening at any rate.'[4] Such a
concession was one aspect of an increasing alignment between genteel
families and commerce in the latter part of the century.

However, urban life had its dangers not least of which was the
growing pressure for 'social legislation'. It gave Lady Bracknell great
pleasure to imagine that her nephew's fictitious friend Bunberry had
been blown up as a consequence of dabbling in such dangerous
matters: 'he is well punished for his morbidity.' Social currents nearer
at hand were unsettling also, not least the wave of German idealism
which was running through the ancient universities and public
schools, encouraging their alumni to take seriously their civic responsibilities towards the whole community. This ideology had acquired
one form of expression in Birmingham through the preaching of
George Dawson but made its full impact upon metropolitan society
rather later, especially through the influence of T. H. Green and his
disciples. Lady Bracknell's niece proclaimed that '[we] live in an age of
ideals' but her aunt would merely concede that 'German sounds a
thoroughly respectable language.'[5]

From her point of view, Lady Bracknell was right about education. It
did pose a potential threat to the tissue of assumptions and practices
which bolstered the middle ranks of the aristocracy. Her gunboat
marital diplomacy depended upon a widespread supposition that
being 'well-connected' was infinitely preferable to being 'well-
educated' and an indispensable complement to a substantial income.
Bradshaw's Railway Guide was no substitute for Burke's Peerage nor a
handbag for an unblotted escutcheon. In the event, cunning and a
chance discovery in the Army Lists did more for Jack than he could
have achieved by taking a degree at the London School of Economics
and Political Science.

This last institution was founded by the illustrious Fabians, Sidney
and Beatrice Webb, in the same year that Wilde's play was published.
The final three words in the school's title indicate the threatening
aspect of education in the Bracknell view. LSE was established with

money bequeathed for the 'propaganda and other purposes of the (Fabian) Society and its Socialism'. Inspired by the example of the Ecole des Sciences Politiques the Webbs hoped to train cadres of Socialist administrators and specialists who would move into the corridors of power in central and local government. It offered the prospect of an alliance between technologists and bureaucrats on the one hand and organised labour upon the other, a union of 'producers by hand and by brain' such as was envisaged in the new constitution of the Labour Party whose programme 'Labour and the New Social Order', was drawn up by Sidney Webb in 1918. However, as the national level of integration increased in importance in the years around the turn of the century the Conservative bastions of landed society and commerce, both with London bases of great ancestry, had the considerable strategic advantage of being well-established in metropolitan networks of influence. It was easier for them to move into closer association than it was for the Labour Party to coordinate its disparate provincial networks. The subsequent progress of the LSE was an indication of the balance of influence within the capital. Despite the Webbs' ambitions, it soon settled down into being a business college whose special aim was to study 'the concrete facts of industrial life'. The Commercial Education Committee of the London Chamber of Commerce lent the institution some lecture rooms 'with a view to encouraging an interest in the City on commercial questions by young men engaged in business during the day'. Jack Worthing would perhaps have been pleased to note that this committee especially recommended railway economics as an appropriate focus of study within the school.[6]

EDUCATION AND CONTRADICTION

In 1895 the prognosis was not so clear. The Science and Arts Department at South Kensington had built a large empire based upon the award of grants for 'technical instruction', a term whose interpretation was treated generously.[7] Rivalry between South Kensington, Whitehall, and the universities at Oxford, Cambridge and London acted in conjunction with the variegated growth patterns of municipal educational institutions to produce a 'system' which, when viewed from a national perspective, was lacking in order. More precisely, it embodied several principles of order none of which was fully realised.

A dilemma which was to inform educational politics for at least half a century, and which indeed still remains unresolved had been indicated in the Taunton Report. Its authors noted that many 'tradesmen and others just above the manual labourers' were unwilling to allow their offspring to mix with 'the class beneath them' and eschewed the good accommodation and competent teaching of the public elementary schools in favour of inferior and more expensive private schools. Higher up the social scale, secondary school teachers with good classical backgrounds were worried about the possible influx of 'roughs'. One possible strategy for placating such valuable supporters of traditional establishments would have been to syphon off all instruction for the industrial classes into a separate hierarchy of schools. The higher grade schools with their strong technical bias, the science colleges in the provinces and the South Kensington institutions together provided by the 1890s a well-developed framework for such a solution. Indeed in 1884 the Samuelson Committee had called for 'specialist institutions of high rank' to train captains of industry. However such a course offered, at the very least, the possibility of two divided and potentially hostile elites coming into existence, the one legitimised by a cultural tradition reaching back to Richard Hooker and transmitted in Oxbridge and the public schools, the other grounded in a Baconian tradition of equal ancestry and recruited through open channels of meritocratic promotion by bright boys from the higher grade schools.[8] The 'brigadiers' and 'generals' of the latter regime might be susceptible to metropolitan wining and dining but what of the NCO's in Sheffield? Did the facilities for such subtle seduction exist throughout the manufacturing provinces?

The legislation of 1899 and 1902 was not simply a response to the educational disarray criticised by the Cross and Bryce Commissions. It was also part of a larger pattern of arrangements which tended to inhibit the development of a powerful and separate scientific-bureaucratic network of establishments such as had appeared in Germany, Britain's strongest European competitor. The acts of 1899 and 1902 unified the administrative machinery of South Kensington, the Charity Commission and the Education Department at Whitehall, and replaced the school boards by local education authorities with powers to regulate both elementary and secondary education. During the five years after 1902 the regulations and administrative decisions of the new board of education, created by the 1899 Act, had the effect of imposing in many areas a clear distinction between elementary schools, whose official object was to prepare the mass of children during 'the school years available . . . for the work of life', and secondary schools within which a literary curriculum had an assured place. The higher grade schools which had been developed by local school boards, often with financial help from South Kensington, came under strong pressure either to restrict their activities within a less ambitious 'higher elementary' framework or to introduce a greater element of literary instruction and become 'secondary' schools.[9]

The confidence with which these changes were driven through, despite the opposition of some school boards (including Birmingham) and the hostility of some elementary school teachers, owed much to their compatibility with ideological tendencies in the university and public schools.[10] These were furnishing a new set of justifications for the authority of the ruling establishments in national life. J. H. Muirhead, who became professor of philosophy and political economy at Birmingham in 1897, was a typical exponent of the new philosophy. Muirhead's teachers at Balliol in the 1870s had included T. H. Green, R. L. Nettleship and A. C. Bradley. Among his fellow students were Charles Gore, Viriamu Jones, Robert Baden-Powell and Alfred Milner.[11] A central tenet of Muirhead's beliefs was[12]

> the doctrine of the existence and effective operation in the life of every normal uncorrupted man . . . of a reference in all he feels and does to a good wider than that which occupies him in the pursuit of his own particular interests or that of his own particular group.

In effect, the social and spiritual mission of the Evangelical parson was to be inherited by lay professional men whose lives would thereby re-acquire the sense of legitimacy and purpose which had been endangered by crises of religious faith and the steady weakening of the ecclesiastical order. In Muirhead's case this entailed not only bicycling around the poorer districts of Birmingham but also manoeuvring hard 'as a traveller in Oxford goods' to maximise the influence of a liberal curriculum in educational institutions. More generally, the new credo gave its disciples a contempt for money-making as a goal and a hostility to narrow academic specialisation, especially in the applied sciences. In its most diluted form it gave a sense of moral superiority in being 'an all-round chap'. A subtle elision occurred between the concept of the 'gentleman' and the concept of the 'professional'.[13]

Through the public schools this set of attitudes which sanctified the games field and glorified the Raj spread through the professions and the ranks of the well-born.[14] It was to be found among city gents and Fabians alike. The sentiments it fostered provided a *lingua franca* within networks of 'old boys' who in their adult lives held leading positions in establishments which in other ways were deeply at odds with each other. As the institutional complexity of urban industrial society increased at the national level the public boarding schools performed a major function in providing a degree of social integration among establishments. In view of the incompatibility between important aspects of the cultures and practices of these establishments—for example, between the strong residual particularism of county hierarchies, the market concerns of the City and the bureaucratic impulse of civil servants—collaboration was well served by an ethos which stressed close bonds between people formed before entry into specific occupational groups, which emphasised individual character rather than group qualities, and which laid great emphasis upon mutual tolerance. These requirements were fulfilled by 'the public school spirit'. Through the local authority grammar schools aspects of this culture were pressed upon the lower middle classes in the provinces. Many grammar school teachers received their training in day training colleges which were attached to the provincial colleges after 1890. The influence of men like Muirhead was deeply felt within such institutions, taking the place which the Anglican clergy had filled in a previous generation.[15]

Despite the dominance of science and technology in Birmingham University, which persisted into the twentieth century, the purveyors of 'Oxford goods' were in general well protected by the strong departmental boundaries which typically developed in the provincial universities. The strength of particular departmental 'cultures' encouraged a high degree of 'subject loyalty' amongst secondary school teachers, themselves the mentors of future pedagogues in the elementary schools. In this way horizontal links at each level of the education system were weakened and vertical bonds strengthened. The ethos of liberal culture and the values of Oxbridge and the public schools were thus transmitted downwards.[16]

The strategy which was being pursued, consciously or not, by the turn of the century was to accept the claims of scientific knowledge as a legitimate arena of advanced learning but to resist the development of either completely separate high-level scientific teaching institutions or educational institutions in which scientific learning was completely integrated with the arts. In 1904 R. B. Haldane declared: 'You cannot, without danger of partial starvation separate science from literature or philosophy. Each grows best in the presence of the other.'[17] A sentiment apparently so unexceptional was in fact ridden with social and political implications. The 'collection' curricular mode permitted the admittance of potentially threatening areas of knowledge into association, but not too close association, with liberal culture. The latter was recognised as the superior form. This pattern was repeated through the incorporation of the Science and Arts Department into Sir Robert Morant's fold in Whitehall. A similar approach was expressed in the regulations for secondary schools in 1904 which insisted on Latin and limited the hours available for science teaching. The school certificate regulations of 1914 imposed a 'group' system. Pupils had to collect examination passes in three groups: English subjects; foreign languages; science and mathematics.[18]

The educational settlement of the early twentieth century inhibited the development of links between education, industry and the state of the kind which Prince Albert and Lyon Playfair had envisaged in the 1850s.[19] In the conclusion of a comparative study of the iron and steel industries in Britain and Germany P. W. Musgrave points out this contrast:[20]

> The comparison that immediately stands out is between the organised German system and the haphazard British system. In Germany from about 1812 there has been a plan. In Britain nothing substantial was done on a national scale till the establishing of the elementary system in 1870, and this was repeatedly allowed to probe forward in an uncontrolled way into the field of secondary education. Even the 1944 Act did not really fit technical or further education into the three-stage system that it created. . . . The organisation of the German system ensured that the links between the various stages and institutions within the system were good. The curriculum was perhaps prescribed, but at least each stage fitted into the next. Above all the link from the schools to the universities was established early in the nineteenth century, thereby establishing high standards, perhaps at the cost of rigidity. Examinations were also controlled by the grant of privileges. The levels of examinations were linked first with the civil service, and after the industrial revolution industry had to accept the same standards to compete in recruiting labour. The links of the German system are possibly best seen in the case of apprenticeship, where the industry and trade unions cooperate to lay down the *Berufsbild*, the theoretical part of which is translated into educational terms in the *Berufsschule*. In Britain such links were very slow to come.

The burden of Musgrave's argument is that in England there have been persistent inconsistencies between the 'products' of education and the 'needs of industry and that the involvement of the state has done little to reduce these 'system contradictions'. However, the failure to develop along the German pattern brought definite social and political benefits to establishments in government, the professions and rural society whose predecessors had been relatively unchallenged at mid-century and who wished to minimise the losses sustained as England became more centralised, more bureaucratic, more urban and more industrial.

The success of this approach owed much to the inherited advantages of an early lead in industrial development and the receipts flowing in from the network of international trade and finance centred upon London. A relatively high degree of 'irrationality' could be permitted in the mutual relations of institutional orders so long as the City was reaping a satisfactory profit, the status norms of county society were left relatively unchallenged, the legal, medical and other professions allowed to build up their relatively autonomous empires, Oxbridge colleges and public school headmasters permitted to glory in a sense of tradition, and the municipal corporations allowed to pursue their varying policies of civic development. However, the other side of the coin was a denial, whether implicit or stridently expressed, of the worth and respectability of the social classes most deeply involved in manufacturing production. Furthermore, Britain had an electoral franchise which was one of the narrowest in Europe at the time of the First World War.[21] This war and the years immediately preceding and following it were a crucial watershed in English social development which witnessed a profound transformation of the conditions which gave plausibility to the arrangements described above. These processes lie outside the scope of this present work but the following brief quotation from a recent book by Keith Middlemas conveys their significance:[22]

> By 1922 it had become clear that a sufficient number of union and employers' leaders had accepted the need of formal collaboration with the state. TUC and employers' organisations crossed a threshold which had not even existed before the war, and behaved thereafter in some degree as estates of the realm, to the detriment of more ancient, obsolete estates, the municipalities, the churches, the 'colleges' of professional men, and the panoply of voluntary bodies, so important in the political system of the nineteenth century.

In conclusion, the contrasting trajectories followed by Birmingham and Sheffield since 1830 will be summarised.

SUMMARY

It has been argued that variations between Birmingham and Sheffield during the period after 1830 in the internal organisation and mutual relations of education, industry and local government were aspects of very different processes of class formation in the two cities. Three strategic determinants of these differences were identified. The first was the mode of social differentiation within each city. Industry in Birmingham produced a very wide range of goods and had a very complex division of labour. Manufacture was balanced by well-developed commercial and service occupations, including the 'old professions'. By contrast, Sheffield supported a much narrower range of industrial production, albeit subject to an intense local sub-division of labour, and occupied a much more highly specialised position within the national division of labour. Furthermore, commercial and service occupations were less well developed than in Birmingham. Second, there was a very pronounced difference between the scale of social organisation within Sheffield as opposed to the surrounding county society, especially in the early part of the period. No such great disparity existed between Birmingham and its rural hinterland. The balance of power between town and countryside was skewed much more strongly in favour of the latter in South Yorkshire than it was in the West Midlands. Third, Birmingham was at the centre of a very active network of communications not only within its region but also nationally. By contrast Sheffield was much more isolated both regionally and nationally.

The distinctive class structures of the two cities were profoundly affected by these three conditions. In the early part of the period Sheffield's skilled working class and petty bourgeoisie were bound into dense neighbourhood solidarities. These not only supported a host of taverns and Sunday schools but also sustained the authority of several trade societies able to enforce a high degree of control over industrial production and labour recruitment. Larger employers and professional men, both relatively sparse, accepted the social and political leadership of the county. They were unable to establish strong collective associations amongst themselves or develop effective institutional means of either influencing or transforming the behaviour of the workforce. In Birmingham the habit of participating in formal associations, both for the pursuit of reform and for the protection of aspects of the *status quo* was much more highly developed. A complex web of institutional bonds in the educational, political, religious and industrial spheres provided a framework for interaction which was more susceptible to subtle adjustments in power and opinion than the encompassing particularism of Sheffield. The commitment of members of working-class families in Birmingham to a plurality of occupational spheres weakened their capacity and will to resist innovations promoted by the larger employers. However, their involvement in political and welfare organisations alongside leading businessmen and professionals gave artisan inhabitants a sense of participation in the management of social reform. Birmingham's middle-class establishments were in a stronger position *vis-à-vis* both the urban labouring population and the environing county society than their counterparts in Sheffield.

The increase in the population size and productive capacity of both manufacturing cities which was underway by 1830 had manifestations in the development of three related aspects of the structures outlined above: the significance, relative to each other, of the neighbourhood, municipal, county and national levels of integration; the relationships between social classes; and the norms and practices expressed within the institutional orders of education, industrial relations and local government.

In the case of Sheffield an increased degree of initiative was at first acquired by solidarities focused upon the neighbourhood. This took

256

the form of movements to defend perceived political, spiritual and industrial rights which were felt to be under threat from tendencies towards centralisation. However, these movements among skilled labourers and the petty bourgeoisie had few significant institutional connections with each other. Their primary objective was not so much to displace existing establishments operating at a higher level as to re-assert rights in their own spheres which were felt to have been whittled away.

The processes of urban industrial growth in Sheffield had by the late 1860s produced a new manufacturing Leviathan whose demands ran directly counter to the norms and practices of important existing political and industrial establishments in 'old' Sheffield. At the same time a high degree of mutual dependence developed between Sheffield's new and largest employers and the occupants of regional and national networks of influence focused upon stock exchanges, country houses and Whitehall. Attercliffe and Brightside became the locale for a pattern of social and industrial life which had few resemblances with the routines of artisan communities oriented to the light trades. The fabric of habits, prejudices and social connections which had grown up around the old industries of Sheffield had little to offer the new. Given the fact that in north-east Sheffield they were virtually creating a new settlement, and given their strong links with regional and national rather than municipal and neighbourhood networks, the steel manufacturers could by-and-large ignore 'old' Sheffield.

However, a sharp confrontation did occur during the 1860s within the intermediate sector of Sheffield industry which combined heavy steel work with the production of tools. Firms within this sector experienced the effects of a contradiction between the manufacturing processes and forms of labour regulation dominant in the light trades on the one hand and the heavy trades upon the other. The rapid expansion of the heavy steel industry after mid-century altered the balance of power within Sheffield between these two sectors sufficiently for employers in the intermediate sector to adopt a more aggressive approach to the craft unions. Despite an almost unmitigated defeat in the ensuing conflict the trade societies made few efforts over the next four decades to adapt their defensive strategies. The division between religious, political and industrial organisations among the working class remained very marked, one instance being the hostility between the Labour Representation Committee and the Sheffield Federated Trades Council in the early twentieth century. The policy of the Sheffield Workers' Committee revealed the continuing strength in that city of Ironside's radical philosophy with its anarchist tendencies.

Education in Sheffield expressed in its development the dialectic of indifference and fear which governed class relations in that city. Before 1870 most participating groups in the working class and middle class preferred to look after their own narrow interests, excluding outsiders. The Sunday schools were in a relatively thriving state compared to public day schools supervised by clerical watch-dogs. Middle-class private schools offering commercial training survived in a healthier state than more pretentious secondary schools foisting classical learning upon their pupils. Middle-class residents were not willing to pay good money for second-rate liberal culture; more prosperous families preferred to send their children off to boarding school. Working-class inhabitants resisted clerical attempts to interfere with the training of their young. Trade union control over apprenticeship was perhaps at least as potent a means of socialising young Sheffielders as church day schools. However, the rapid growth of the heavy steel industry brought into being a vast new section of the working class subject to neither apprenticeship regulation nor the failing enterprise of the church. Through the school board the new manufacturing elite of Sheffield constructed a system of elementary and secondary schooling which reinforced their control over their semi- and unskilled workers and reduced the degree of control exercised by the trade societies over industrial training.

However, four characteristics of Sheffield education persisted after 1870. First, in spite of the involvement of some steel manufacturers in the school board, especially during the 1870s, and the participation of some other businessmen on this body, employers were generally unwilling to support educational enterprises beyond the 'basic' provision supplied by the elementary and higher grade schools.[23] The technical school, the school of design and Firth College were starved of local support. Second, members of professional and white-collar occupations were a much smaller proportion of the population in Sheffield compared to Birmingham after 1870 as before. This fact contributed to the relative weakness of classical secondary education in Sheffield. Third, both before and after 1870 educational institutions with an aura of 'refinement' derived from their connection with the ancient universities or the Anglican hierarchy were reluctant to associate closely with institutions devoting themselves solely to technical training. The aversion of the Church of England Instruction Society towards the Sheffield Mechanics' Institute anticipated the separation of the technical school from Firth College. Fourth, a strong ethos of self-sufficiency and self-government was expressed in the Nonconformist Sunday schools, People's College and even (despite its reliance upon government grants) the school of design. However, the more 'refined' section of Sheffield's educational order looked outside Sheffield for guidance and support. For example, the national Anglican establishment provided external support for the Church of England Educational Institute. Wesley College had similar backing from national Methodist organisation. Firth College was inspired by the university extension movement and subsequently received financial support from the treasury committee in whose origination its own principal had played a major part.

The growth of the heavy steel industry was accompanied by strong tendencies towards residential segregation by income and status. The steel workers were huddled around huge plants in Attercliffe and Brightside, the old light trades still clung to the centre of town, the Park district in the east was a warren of decaying slums, and the white-collar professional and managerial families lived up on the salubrious slopes to the west and south-west. The transference of social and political initiative from the neighbourhood level towards regional and national networks had left the town council with few functions, little income and a very modest respectability. Its functions, at least, began to grow after the turn of the century as the pressure from working-class political organisation increased. The capture of seats on the town council by political representatives of labour was encouraged by two circumstances: the strength and obduracy of the large employers which inhibited a purely industrial strategy; and the growth of clear working-class constituencies within large areas of the borough.[24]

In the case of Birmingham the increase in the population and wealth of the city which was underway by 1830 stimulated a challenge to county-oriented establishments from within the financial, manufacturing and professional bourgeoisie. The challenge was mounted at the municipal level over church rates, control of the new town council and the management of the King Edward VI Foundation. Although the challengers, many of them radical Nonconformists, drew upon the support of some artisans and petty traders, the rights vested in neighbourhood communities were not at issue as in Sheffield. Indeed, the customary privileges of Birmingham's artisans were being eroded in local industry. At issue were the conditions under which public authority within Birmingham should be exercised. In contrast to Sheffield, the shift in initiative was lateral, not downwards. Unlike in Sheffield, this initiative was exercised aggressively, not defensively. It was used to attack existing ecclesiastical privileges and to capture the new municipal corporation. Furthermore, in contrast to Sheffield, religious, political, industrial and educational institutions (such as the mechanics' institute) were all drawn upon in mobilising support. On the other side, the general hospital, the King Edward VI Foundation, the Loyal and Constitutional Society and the ecclesiastical hierarchy together belonged to a similar network of inter-related institutions. By the early 1850s the two opposing networks began to institutionalise the bargaining and conflict taking place between their memberships. This was expressed in joint ventures such as the Birmingham and Midland Institute and the merging of the street commissioners with the town council. Complex cross-allegiances developed as new issues arose such as the part to be played by the central and local state in social management. For half a generation influence was shared between the contesting parties of the 1830s and 1840s.

As has been seen, the new business leaders in Sheffield after the 1850s found some aspects of 'old' Sheffield redundant and other aspects obstructive. A vigorous attack was made on the latter, mainly through engaging in conflict with the craft unions. The former were largely ignored and by-passed. Although it was useful to have a few steel manufacturers in the municipal corporation and the Cutlers' Company was a convenient talking shop, there was not a great deal in 'old' Sheffield that 'new' Sheffield could use. A very different pattern emerged in Birmingham. During the late 1860s and early 1870s a new establishment captured the town council and proceeded to magnify its status and extend its functions. This establishment did not attempt to sweep away the complex infrastructure of civic life which had been developing since the 1830s, not least in the educational sphere. Rather, its members fought to extend their grasp over existing institutions and were sharply resisted. Not until the 1880s did the governors of the King Edward VI Foundation cease to oppose schemes suggested by the town council for their reform. Meanwhile, employees of the foundation such as MacCarthy and Vardy were worming their way into positions of great influence over the public system of elementary and secondary education. However, these political conflicts and bureaucratic manoeuvres were fought over an institutional terrain which while continually being adapted was neither ignored nor dismantled. In fact, this infrastructure served to bind together social groups whose skills and resources were thoroughly interdependent, especially so in a city with such a complex division of labour. There was no clear dichotomy between an 'old' Birmingham and a 'new' Birmingham such as existed in Sheffield.

However, four changes did occur in Birmingham with the emergence of the new regime. First, the network of civic institutions was greatly expanded through the implementation of Chamberlain's so-called 'municipal socialism'. Second, men whose predecessors had for decades been protesting about the exclusivity of an Anglican lay and ecclesiastical hierarchy worked hard to make the town council and the school board their own political monopoly. Through intense propaganda they maximised the prestige and authority of the municipal corporation. From this base they moved out to acquire commanding positions for themselves in the leading voluntary associations such as the Birmingham and Midland Institute. Third, a new rhetoric of civic authority was broadcast. The relationship between the civic community and its municipal corporation was infused with the sense of moral purpose previously attached to the relationship between the Evangelical vicar and members of his flock. Emphasis was placed upon public works which would improve the living standards of whole neighbourhoods. Finally, Chamberlain's Liberals built up and very effectively managed an urban political constituency through an organisation which gave a sense of participation to the 'class of master-workmen' whose members John Macdonald observed at a 'caucus' meeting in 1886:[25]

> Some talked with gestures more or less emphatic to the men next to them; others skimmed over Dr Dale's pamphlet, or produced their newspaper extracts, made marginal notes, or scribbled something – the heads of their speeches perhaps.

However, local Conservatives gradually learned to imitate some of the techniques of popular persuasion pioneered by Chamberlain. Furthermore, members of the newly-dominant elite acquired some of the patrician habits of their rivals as they settled into power. Macdonald noted in 1886 the great value of[26]

> the parks, the gardens, the public institutions, the scholarships, the works of art, with which in the short space of twenty years the Masons, the Rylands, the Tangyes, the Nettlefolds, the Adderleys, the Calthorpes, the Middlemores, the Chamberlains, the Rattrays, and others have enriched and adorned their city.

In this list the old guard and the new stand side by side. During the subsequent quarter of a century a gradual social coalescence occurred. As has been seen, during the same period within the spheres of education, industrial relations and local government a subtle compromise was reached between the norms and practices of large-scale urban-industrial bureaucracies on the one hand and the old agrarian and parochial order on the other. In the educational sphere, a hierarchy of 'post-elementary' institutions offered a higher classical education, technical training and, between the two, preparation for white-collar occupations. Educationists in the city were arguing that recruitment into such schools should not take place after early adolescence. In the industrial sphere, collaboration between unions and employers was widespread. The city council was expanding its functions in the sphere of social welfare. Underpinning all was a strong awareness by civic leaders of the desirability of keeping in close contact with popular opinion.[27]

These processes were aided by the growing magnitude of Birmingham's professional and white-collar occupational sector. Their patronage of educational and cultural organisations in the city strengthened these integrative institutions. Lower middle-class inhabitants were more likely to develop attachments to such institutions than were semi- and unskilled labourers employed within very large mechanised plants, a sector of industry which acquired predominance in Birmingham at least twenty years after this occurred in Sheffield.

Birmingham's municipal establishments were far better placed to exercise a moderate degree of 'management' of developments in local industry than were their peers in Sheffield. The improvement scheme, the re-drawing of constituency boundaries in 1884 and the city extensions of 1891, 1909, and 1911 were all, in part, attempts to direct or exploit socio-economic change in ways which would maintain or increase the influence of the 'city fathers'.

The development of Birmingham from 1830 to 1914 manifested a gradual shift in the balance of influence between countryside and city towards the latter within a regional bloc which throughout the period grew in its sense of collective identity and national importance. Increasingly Birmingham was established as the regional capital. Whereas the craft unions and the church burgesses became ill-fitting archaic survivals in modern Sheffield, Birmingham provided a social order which was able not only to welcome the increasing part played by new-fangled machinery and examination boards but also to adapt aspects of its traditional inheritance such as the King Edward VI Foundation.[28]

> Birmingham and its surrounding area achieved the adaptation of traditional values to urban and industrial life, if not with theoretical perfection, then at least with appreciable practical success.

The above verdict comes at the end of a recent study of Birmingham and the West Midlands between 1760 and 1800.[29] There are strong reasons for applying it to Birmingham one hundred years later.

A final note is in order on the sociological approach adopted throughout this book. Although a recurrent concern has been the interplay between the institutional orders of education, industry and local government they have not been treated as internally consistent 'systems'. Rather, each has been seen as an arena within which members of establishments and social classes have engaged in conflict and compromise as aspects of their pursuit of advancement or survival in a developing society. However, the analysis has gone beyond a quasi-Weberian survey of the strategies of competing status groups engaging in contingent encounters. Transformations in the class structures and institutional orders of Birmingham and Sheffield have been interpreted as aspects of processes of social development in the course of which an urban industrial society has taken shape in the midst of a commercialised agrarian society. The strategic determination of processes of class formation and control over institutional orders has tended to move away from lower and towards higher levels of integration. At the same time more complex forms of social differentiation and more bureaucratic modes of integration within human configurations have developed. The capacities and dispositions of participants in the educational, political and industrial spheres have been explained in terms of their location within this developing class structure. Their conflicts and accommodations have produced patterns of management in these spheres which have in turn influenced the development of the class structure.

It has been seen that very different modes of articulation between old and new social orders developed in Birmingham and Sheffield. In spite of strong likenesses in urban and rural technology, institutions and social classes within the two cities were differentiated and integrated in very dissimilar ways. Thus, for example, in Sheffield before 1850 practices within elementary schooling tended to work against the prevailing structure of industrial regulation and there were few overlaps between educational involvements and activities in the political sphere. In Birmingham, by contrast, tendencies within all three spheres were much more complementary and the three institutional orders were much more closely interrelated.

There is, of course, a long-term tendency for education, industry and the political management of local government to develop a minimal consistency with each other which flows from the interdependence of the particular processes occurring within each sphere. However, one may not assume that a 'need' for the accumulation of industrial capital and the reproduction of capitalist relations of industrial production necessarily has priority within this nexus of institutional relations. The 'need' of genteel interests rooted in the rural order for the accumulation of cultural capital and the reproduction of social relations securing their own authority has imposed constraints just as powerful as those stemming from industrialists and the system of industrial production. Very different patterns in these respects were noticed in Birmingham and Sheffield after 1850. Also noticed was the successful promotion of liberal culture and denigration of industrial activity at the national level after the turn of the century. In this analysis the pursuit of generalisations about the relative determinacy of the educational as opposed to the industrial or political spheres is superseded by the assumption that the development of all three institutional spheres was an aspect of transformations within the broader framework of social differentiation. Within this broader framework the important distinctions are two: between the institutions and solidarities of the rural social order as opposed to those of the large manufacturing cities; and between dominant, intermediate and subordinate social classes whose composition and consciousness were a product of the complex intermeshing between the old society and the new.

NOTES

1 W. L. Sargant, 'The Characteristics of Manufacturers' in Sargant (1869), 3.

2 In the period 1880–99 there were 82 half-millionaires or millionaires in manufacturing occupations compared to 89 in commercial occupations. In the period 1900–14, the figures were 79 and 129 respectively. Rubinstein (1977a), 102; F. M. L. Thompson (1963), 28–9, 112–13; Bateman (1883), 515; Spring (1978), 3.

3 This approach differs from Rubinstein's argument that the increasing differentiation of commercial, manufacturing and landed elites led to their becoming 'more self-sufficient'. Rather, a more complex structure of interdependence developed on terms which were being continually fought over. Rubinstein (1977a), 120.

4 One pertinent example of this is Barrington Moore's analysis: 'After 1840 the landowning class found in the support of factory laws a convenient way of answering manufacturers' attacks on the Corn Laws . . .' Moore (1969), 35. Unfortunately, Moore's treatment of nineteenth-century England is one of the least convincing sections of an otherwise impressive book. One weakness, for example, is his encapsulation of commercial and manufacturing groups within one urban bourgeoisie which tends to be treated as a single social actor. B. Moore (1969), 35, 423. See also J. R. B. Johnson (1976a); D. Smith (1982) (forthcoming).

5 Guttsman (1951); Guttsmann (1954); Guttsman (1974); Perkin (1969), 427–37; F. M. L. Thompson (1963), 292–302; Pumphrey (1959); Hanham (1960); Bamford (1967); Wilkinson and Bishop (1967); Glennerster and Pryke (1964); Rubinstein (1977a), 123–5.

6 Lee (1963); Briggs (1963); F. M. L. Thompson (1963); Vincent (1967); Vincent (1972); Dyos (1968); Dyos and Wolff (1973); Hennock (1973);

J. Foster (1968); J. Foster (1974); Nossiter (1975); Laqueur (1976); Garrard (1976); Garrard (1977); Gadian (1978); Lees (1979); D. Fraser (1973); D. Fraser (1976a); D. Fraser (1979a); D. Fraser (1979b); Cannadine (1980).

7 D. Fraser (1979b), 36. It perhaps begs a question to describe British industrialisation as 'rapid'. Compared to what?

8 For example: Skocpol (1979); B. Moore (1969).

9 Britain has not experienced a modernising capitalist 'putsch' such as apparently occurred as a consequence of the Meiji Restoration. Beasley (1972); Kamatsu (1972).

10 B. Moore (1978), 379, 474; Briggs (1950); Stearns (1978).

11 See ch. 11, 27.

12 Vigier (1970); Meller (1976); Hennock (1973); R. G. Wilson (1971).

13 When the 1911 Census was published Sheffield's Master Cutler commented: 'Of course, I'm glad we've beaten Leeds.' Walton (1968), 240.

14 Mathias (1969), 413.

15 For further discussion of levels of integration see D. Smith (1977b), 96–8. See also Hopkins and Wallerstein (1957); D. Fraser (1976a); Elias (1978), 138–45.

16 Perkin (1969), 63–7.

17 D. C. Moore (1966); D. C. Moore (1971) (cf. Hennock (1971)); R. W. Davis (1976); Stevenson (1977); Codrington (1930); Teichman (1940); Philips (1975); Philips (1977); Zangerl (1971); Quinault (1975).

18 To some extent these bureaucracies were means of entry into the aristocracy. F. M. L. Thompson (1963), 45–75; Chadwick (1966); Donajgrodski (1977), 22–3; Harries-Jenkins (1977).

19 Younger sons frequently had to make their careers in the towns, thus strengthening the links between urban and rural society. F. M. L. Thompson (1963), 64–75.

20 F. M. L. Thompson (1963), 64–70, 82–5, 178–9; Jewson (1974).

21 E. P. Thompson (1974); E. P. Thompson (1978).

22 D. Fraser (1976a), pt 1; Webb (1906).

23 Peel (1971), 33–55.

24 Eliot (1866).

25 Checkland (1964), 33.

26 Bateman (1883), 130, 127, 365, 337, 168, 334, 72, 219. Based upon PP 1874, LXXII, pts I and II, Return of Owners of Land 1872–3 (England and Wales); PP 1874, LXXII pt III (Scotland); PP 1876, LXXX (Ireland).

27 Sargant (1869), 3–4.

28 Ibid., 5, 6, 10.

29 For example in 1878 it was calculated that 'personal property' in Britain had grown from £1,300 million in 1819 to £5,000 million in 1875, a growth which was relatively unaffected by changes in price level. From about mid-century the growth rate of domestic fixed capital was more rapid than the rate of population increase. Giffen (1878), 185; Giffen (1889), 59, 155; Pollard and Crossley (1968), 196–8.

30 Horace Mann calculated in 1851 that non-attendance at churches was most common in the large towns. The returns of the 1851 Religious Census suggested that nearly half of church accommodation in England and Wales belonged to Dissent. PP 1852–3, LXXXIX (henceforth 1851 Religious Census), 155, 181–2.

31 Skeats and Miall (n.d.); Adams (1882); Watts (1978).

32 See ch. 7.

33 Vincent (1972), 28–9.

34 J. F. C. Harrison (1961).

35 Checkland (1964), 82–5, 310–12; Pollard (1968).
36 Millerson (1964); Reader (1966).
37 E. Hughes (1952); E. Hughes (1965).
38 E.g. Dandeker (1977).
39 Cullen (1975). See also *Transactions of National Association for Promotion of Social Science* (henceforth *Trans. NAPSS*).
40 Ben-David (1962), 47–62, 68–76; Ringer (1979), 32–112, 206–59.
41 Donajgrodski (1977), 23–4.
42 Attempts to manage these task through a coordination of neighbourhood resources met opposition from establishments located at a higher level of integration. See ch. 4.
43 'Chief clerks are now the real rulers of England; they have already a power too despotic.' Lord Montague in 1870 quoted in P. Smith (1967), 43.
44 Jenks (1927); Erickson (1949); Clements (1955); Malchow (1976); Redford (1964).
45 The introduction of compulsory national service in 1916 was a climax of this process. A. J. P. Taylor (1965), 53–56.
46 See ch. 6.
47 Pollard (1959), 65–77; Corbett (1966); Mendelson *et al.* (n.d.); Hobsbawm (1964); Gray (1976); Moorhouse (1978); Roberts (1958); Malchow (1976).
48 Bechhofer and Elliott (1976), 78–81.
49 Bechhofer and Elliott (1976); Neale (1972); Hennock (1963); Nossiter (1975); Checkland (1964), 301–3; Mayer (1975).
50 Checkland (1964), 303; Hurt (1972), 110–46; Dalvi (1957).
51 D. Ward (1975); Cannadine (1977a).
52 *The Economist*, 20 June 1857, 669. Italics in original.
53 Ibid., 670.
54 Pelling (1967); P. F. Clarke (1972); Cornford (1963).
55 One issue which revealed some of these tensions was the introduction of the new Poor Law. For example Brundage (1978); D. Fraser (1976b).
56 Clegg *et al.* (1964).
57 Gutchen (1961); Lambert (1962); Gosden (1966), 43–56; R. H. Parsons (1947); McMenemey (1959).
58 Sir Walter Foster, a Birmingham physician who achieved national fame, summed up in 1883 a philosophy he had applied for twenty years: 'in town councils, local boards and boards of guardians there is plenty of work . . . to do, useful to the community and good for the profession. . . . I would gladly see medical men taking their due share in the important and responsible work of local government.' *Edgbastonia* (henceforth *Edg.*) (1884), 4, 98–9.
59 For the impact of migratory tendencies on working-class families see M. Anderson (1971).
60 Lee (1963), esp. ch. 2.
61 Vincent (1968), 41–3.
62 Spring (1951); F. M. L. Thompson (1963), 238–68; Cannadine (1977b).
63 Checkland (1964), 189–212.
64 G. Griffiths (1870), 380.
65 One instance is Tom Taylor's sharp criticism of Toulmin Smith's nostalgia for the ancient parochial system of government at the 1857 Social Science Congress in Birmingham. T. Taylor (1858).
66 D. Fraser (1965); J. T. Ward (1966); F. M. L. Thompson (1959); Spring (1951); Spring (1954); Mee (1972); Cannadine (1977b); Miall (1842), 3–6; Mole (1973), 822–9.
67 Roach (1959), 143.

CHAPTER 2
BETWEEN NEIGHBOURHOOD AND NATION: THE
FRAMEWORK OF SOCIAL DIFFERENTIATION IN
BIRMINGHAM AND SHEFFIELD 1830–70

1 Austen (1816) (1966 edn), 310.
2 Ibid., 309.
3 W. Burns (1961); R. Williams (1963), esp. ch. 5.
4 F. C. Williams (1903).
5 Stainton (1924), 328–9; Odom (1926), 47–8.
6 F. C. WIlliams (1903), 33.
7 Ibid., 42–3.
8 Cross-references were excluded.
9 Degree of complexity may not vary directly with degree of differentiation since interaction does not necessarily take place within all potential relationships between differentiated 'parts'.
10 PP 1852–3, LXXXVIII *et seq*. (hereafter *1851 Census*). The categories in Table 2 are constructed as follows: 1 = XI,7–11,XIV,7–14; 2 = XII,6,7,12; 3 = III,1–6,IV,1–4,XI,1–6; 4 = VII,1 ('merchants' to 'commercial travellers' inclusive); 5 = VIII,1–6; 6 = XII,1,XIII,1–2; 7 = VI,2 (excluding 'gardeners' and 'innservants'); 8 = XVI,1; 9 = XV,1; 10 = I,1–2.
11 PP 1865, XX, *Children's Employment Commission, Fourth Report* (henceforth *CEC Sheff. 1865*), rep. 2.
12 W. H. Smith (1831), 121. Italics in original.
13 W. B. Stephens (ed.), *The Victoria County History, vol. 7: The City of Birmingham* (henceforth *VCH*), 33; Mathias (1969), 111–12; Linton (1956), 165; Goodfellow (1942).
14 Kellett (1969), 10. Italics in original.
15 Ibid., 144–5.
16 G. B. Hill (1880).
17 Linton (1956), 165–7, 228–36; Hopkinson (1971); Hopkinson (1950).
18 Blackman (1962), 93–4.
19 Mee (1972); Mee (1975); Raybould (1968); Raybould (1973).
20 Eliot (1866) (1972 edn), 79.
21 *Warwickshire Directory 1850*; *Worcester Directory 1855*; *Birmingham and Black Country Directory 1855*.
22 *Sheffield Directory 1862* (henceforth *Sheff. Dir. 1862*); Clegg (1970), 31–2.
23 Sanford and Townsend (1865), vol. 1; Perkin (1969), 88; Bateman (1883), 334; *Sheff. Dir. 1841*, 148; *Sheff. Dir. 1852*, 102.
24 F. M. L. Thompson (1963), 47–8; J. M. Furness (1893), 3.
25 J. R. B. Johnson (1970), 97; Olsen (1973); Rowley (1975).
26 R. Waterhouse (1954), 183.
27 Bateman (1883), 72, 119, 140,168, 210, 212, 264, 270, 285, 334, 473, 490.
28 F. M. L. Thompson (1963), 30; Cannadine (1975), 729.
29 Bateman (1883); according to David Spring, Bateman provides 'with respect to acreages, especially where agricultural land was involved . . . a reasonably reliable guide to the structure of British landownership in the 1870s.' Introduction to 1971 edn., 19.
30 Where total landholdings of owners are recorded as below 3,000 acres or gross annual rent below £3,000 per annum, Bateman does not give details of distribution of acreage and rent between counties. In one case where land is held in more than one county but gross annual rent is over £3,000 per annum the relevant owner's estate is placed in the upper left quarter of Table 4. Bateman (1883), 28.

31 See Spring (1954); J. T. Ward (1966).
32 Tunsiri (1964), 66–83.
33 Verney (1924), 67; Tyack (1972), 8.
34 Wentworth House, the Fitzwilliam seat and Wortley Hall, home of the Wharncliffe dynasty were, respectively, about 8 miles north-east and north-west of Sheffield. *Sheff. Dir. 1862*, 526, 542–3.
35 Lloyd (1913), 182.
36 Holland (1843), 10.
37 Wickham (1957), 18.
38 R. N. R. Brown (1936), 182.
39 PP 1889, LXV, *Report on an epidemic of small-pox at Sheffield during 1887–88*, 286, quoted in Olsen (1973), 338.
40 Odom (1917), 48.
41 On the fourth and fifth Earls Fitzwilliam, see Mee (1972), esp. 1–35.
42 Holland (1843), 214, 259; Wickham (1957), 84–9.
43 Donnelly (1975a); Baxter (1976a); Baxter (1976b); Donnelly and Baxter (1975).
44 E. P. Thompson (1974).
45 A future mayor of Sheffield, the brewer, Thomas Moore, was nearly ruined financially when in 1853 the Duke of Norfolk attempted to eject him from the ducal land on which his brewery was built. This is just one illustration of the undercurrent of bad feeling. Stainton (1924), 250–1; J. M. Furness (1893), 4.
46 See ch. 4.
47 J. B. Stone (1904), 7; F. C. Williams (1903), 53–6.
48 Money (1977), 24–47, 158–84; J. M. Norris (1958).
49 Edwards (1877), 125–31, esp. 128–9.
50 *VCH*, 155–6.
51 Linton (1956), 168–71; Blackman (1962), 84.
52 Vincent (1972), 18–19.
53 Bunce (1858), 112–13; *Edg.* (1883), 3, 65–8.
54 Briggs (1949); Gammage (1972), ch. 2; D. Fraser (1962).
55 G. Griffiths (1870), vol. I, 91.
56 Durkheim (1949), 257–8.
57 *VCH*, 101–2: Best (1940), 7–20; Checkland (1948); A. Wilson (1974), 84–93.
58 Pollard (1959), 50–1; *VCH*, 110.
59 Allen (1929), 49–64, 112–41, 151–72; Pollard (1959), 54–9; Fox (1955), 58–62; Court (1938).
60 Parker (1830), 18; D. Fraser (1976a), 46.
61 Timmins (1866), 604–5.
62 *CEC Sheff. 1865*, evid. 126.
63 Vance (1967), 118–19.
64 Pollard (1959), 127–8. See ch. 7.
65 *VCH*, 118.
66 Behagg (1979), 459, 466.
67 Ibid., 461.
68 Ibid., 459, 470–8; D. A. Reid (1976); E. P. Thompson (1967), 72–6.
69 Corbett (1966), 37.
70 Tholfsen (1954).
71 *VCH*, 126–8.
72 See ch. 4.
73 London Trades' Council (1861), 13–14, 84–7, 104.
74 *VCH*, 122; *Sheffield Independent* (henceforth *SI*), 15 April 1854.
75 Pawson and Brailsford (1862), 150.

76 *VCH*, 123, PP 1843, XIV *Children's Employment Commission, Second Report*, evid. E10. This report contains a section devoted to Sheffield (henceforth *CEC Sheff. 1843*) and a section devoted to Birmingham (henceforth *CEC Birm. 1843*).

77 *CEC Sheff. 1865*, rep. 2.

78 *CEC Sheff. 1843*, rep. E1–2.

79 Ibid., rep. E3; *CEC Sheff. 1865*, rep. 3.

80 *CEC Birm. 1843*, rep. F17–18.

81 J. S. Wright (1858), 538.

82 PP 1864, XXII, *Children's Employment Commission, Third Report* (henceforth *CEC Birm. 1864*), rep. ix–x, 52–3; *CEC Birm. 1843*, rep. F18–19.

83 Sargant (1866), 102–3; PP 1873, LXXI pt 1 (henceforth *1871 Census*), Tables 17 and 19. Domestic servants are otherwise recorded. The figures for Bristol and Leeds are, respectively, 50.0 per cent and 61.7 per cent.

84 Welton (1858).

85 Ibid., 416.

86 *CEC Birm. 1843*, evid. f179.

87 *CEC Sheff. 1865*, rep. 2.

88 *Morning Chronicle*, 20 January 1851.

89 R. E. Leader (1905), 39–44; Armytage (1950); C. O. Reid (1976), 384–7.

90 Pollard (1959), 65–6; Behagg (1979), 469.

91 London Trades' Council (1861), 85–7; PP 1867, XXXII, *Sheffield Outrages Inquiry* (henceforth *Out. Inq. 1867*), 348.

92 Pollard (1959), 67–9.

93 *Out. Inq. 1867*, vii–xvi.

94 *SI*, 18 May 1867, quoted in Pollard (1959), 154.

95 The town hall was 'so constructed as to make enthusiasm infectious . . . the galleries and floor are so arranged that all the component parts of the whole meeting are in touch with one another.' Knox (1935), 187.

96 On G. F. Muntz, see Edwards (1877), 79–88; Flick (1975). On William Scholefield see *Edg.* (1891), 9, 100–105.

97 Edwards (1877), 79–81.

CHAPTER 3
'THEIR BRUTAL, BLOATED, MINDLESS FACES . . .':
CLASS STRUCTURES AND INSTITUTIONAL ORDERS IN BIRMINGHAM AND SHEFFIELD 1830–70

1 *Birmingham Journal* (henceforth *BJ*), 26 September 1855, quoted in D. A. Reid (1976), 77.

2 R. E. Leader (1905), 47.

3 Stainton (1924), 219.

4 Cannadine (1975), 732; D. A. Reid (1976), 83.

5 *CEC Birm. 1843*, evid. f173, f180.

6 *CEC Birm. 1864*, evid. 119.

7 *Sheff. Dir. 1841*, 9; C. O. Reid (1976), 218.

8 Quoted in D. A. Reid (1976), 89.

9 Ibid., 101.

10 Ibid., 97.

11 Ibid., 98.

12 Ibid., 97.

13 See chs 4 and 7.

14 Pollard (1959), 76.

15 D. A. Reid (1976), 78.
16 See ch. 7.
17 *VCH*, 280; Money (1977), 221–8.
18 R. E. Leader (1905), 60. On Wilkinson, see Odom (1926), 56–7.
19 Donnelly (1975b); Morrison (1926), 52, 65.
20 *CEC Birm. 1843*, evid. f170.
21 Ibid., f180.
22 Ibid., f172.
23 Ibid., f173.
24 Edwards (1877), 19–36; Baxter (1976b).
25 *CEC Sheff. 1843*, evid. e3.
26 Ibid., e7.
27 Ibid., e7.
28 Ibid., rep. E14.
29 Ibid., evid., 313. On Elliott, see Odom (1926), 3–5.
30 'To respectable Sheffield, Leeds could appear as a kind of Utopia!' Storch (1977), 46. In 1866 about a quarter of Sheffield's electors were artisans. *SI*, 9 January 1866; Pollard (1959), 121.
31 *CEC Sheff. 1843*, evid. e12.
32 On 'restricted codes' see Bernstein (1965).
33 *CEC Sheff. 1843*, rep. E16.
34 *1851 Census*.
35 The percentages were calculated from Horace Mann's data in the *1851 Religious Census* as follows. Morning and evening attendances only are taken into account except in the case of Quakers where afternoon meetings took the place of evening services. 55 per cent of the smaller figure is added to the total of the larger. Hennock (1973), 358.
36 Currie (1968), esp. pt 1.
37 In 1850 it was noted that 'Wesleyan Methodists form a numerous and influential body in Birmingham.' *Bir. Dir. 1850*, 11.
38 *Sheff. Dir. 1832*, 28.
39 *Bir. Dir. 1850*, 38.
40 Bunce (1865), 522.
41 *CEC Sheff. 1865*, evid. 44.
42 *Out. Inq. 1867*, 352, 415.
43 Bunce (1878), 139.
44 J. M. Furness (1893), 3, 83, 125, 153, 185, 186, 202, 244–5, 267.
45 Stainton (1924), 271; Fletcher (1972), 11.
46 Walton (1968), 173; J. M. Furness (1893), 89; see also D. Fraser (1976a), 78–85; Armytage (1948a), 146.
47 On the organisation of Hospital Saturday and Hospital Sunday see J. E. Jones (1913); J. E. Jones (1909), 27, 49–50.
48 Odom (1926), 22–6.
49 Holland (1843), 133–4, 135, 208. Italics in original.
50 Chapman and Bartlett (1971), esp. 240–1; Beggs (1853), 339–40; G. J. Johnson (1865); Langford (1873), vol. 2, 162; *Biograph and Review* (1880), 3, 251–6.
51 Gaskell (1971), 159; *SI*, 2 February 1850. G. F. Muntz and W. Scholefield were presidents of the Freehold Land Society in Birmingham.
52 For Joseph Parkes' role in this process see Finlayson (1973), 194–9.
53 On the Central Board of Health see Gutchen (1961).
54 Bunce (1878), 316–17; Gill (1948).
55 *Bir. Dir. 1850*, 61–9; Bunce (1878), 329–30.

56 *Sheff. Dir. 1852*, 25. The church burgesses also provided stipends for three ministers to assist the vicar of Sheffield. Their income in 1862 was a mere £2,200 per annum. Pawson and Brailsford (1862), 29–30.

57 Pawson and Brailsford (1862), 28–32; R. E. Leader (1906); J. D. Leader (1897).

58 *Sheff. Dir. 1852*, 27–30.

59 Hennock (1973), 25–7.

60 J. M. Furness (1893), 11, 12, 14, 17, 22; J. D. Leader (1897), 486. J. M. Furness lists occupations of council members, 63–73.

61 Bunce (1878), 96–141 esp. 138–9.

62 Hennock (1973), 22; Bunce (1878), 150–1; Buckley (1929); Finlayson (1973).

63 Bunce (1878), 184–220, 221–67, (esp. 223, 234, 235), 270–1, 281–2, 296–7, 332.

64 Ibid., 337, 342. Significantly, Joshua Toulmin Smith was counsel for the street commissioners in 1850. Ibid., 334. See below.

65 See chs 7 and 10.

66 J. M. Furness (1893), 4.

67 Ibid., 86, 87, 88, 90, 91, 92, 93.

68 Ibid., 98–9, 94, 127–8.

69 Pollard (1959), 66.

70 Walton (1968), 208; Hawson (1968), 7. The gas company finally passed into public ownership in 1949. Roberts (1979), 43.

71 See ch. 7.

72 See ch. 7.

73 Erickson (1959), 141–7; Pollard (1959), 159–64; J. D. Scott (1962); Willis (1926); A. J. Grant (1950).

74 Pawson and Brailsford (1862), 125–6.

75 Erickson (1959), 141–3.

76 Ibid., 143–5, 162–3; Pollard (1959), 162.

77 Pollard (1959), 331–3.

78 Ibid., 91–2; Cairncross (1949). See ch. 4 for discussion of sources of capital in Sheffield steel.

79 Lloyd (1913), 342–5; Pollard (1959), 164–75.

80 See above n. 37.

81 Pawson and Brailsford (1862), 150–2; Linton (1956), 234; *CEC Sheff. 1865*, evid. 30.

82 Linton (1956), 234–41; Olsen (1973), 342–5.

83 Holland (1843), 51.

84 *SI*, 4 July 1865, quoted in Gaskell (1974), 257.

85 Gaskell (1974), 257–8.

86 C. Parsons (1978), 3.

87 *VCH*, 125.

88 Duggan (1975).

89 Ibid., 463.

90 Wise (1950), 215; Timmins (1866), 390, 403, 454–6; Vance (1967), 113.

91 Timmins (1866), 443, 635; Vance (1967), 113, 116.

92 Timmins (1866), 608; Vance (1967), 119.

93 Vance (1967), 123.

94 *VCH*, 94–5, 129.

95 Ibid., 14.

96 Cannadine (1975).

97 Olsen (1973), 340–1.

98 Cannadine (1980), 81.

99 *1851 Census* categories constructed as in Table 2. 1871 categories as follows:
1 = 10, 6–10 and 15, 8–14; 2 = 3, 1–9; 3 = 6, 1; 4 = 7, 1–6; 5 = domestic
servant (general), coachman, groom, housekeeper, cook, housemaid,
nurse; 6 = general labourer, factory labourer, assistant shopman,
assistant shopwoman; 7 = 17, 1.

100 *VCH*, 10; Wise (1950), 216–20.

101 Linton (1956), 238; Blackman (1962), 85, 93; Pawson and Brailsford (1862),
63.

102 cf. J. Foster (1974), 161–4.

103 On Ironside see Salt (1960a); Salt (1960b); Salt (1967a); Salt (1968); Salt
(1971a); Salt (1971b); On Dawson see Hennock (1973), 63–79; R. W. Dale
(1877); W. W. Wilson (1905); J. M. G. Owen (1902), esp. ch. 3; Driver (1948),
52–3.

104 Salt (1971b), 183–4.

105 Ibid., 201.

106 Salt (1971a), 39–40, 45–6.

107 J. T. Smith (1851), 12, 198, 205, 207, 217.

108 Salt (1971a), 40–52.

109 R. W. Dale (1877), 47–8, 52–3; Hennock (1973), 66, 74, 76–9; Langford
(1873), 393–4, 402 ff.; J. M. G. Owen (1902), 23–5; A. W. W. Dale (1898), 131.

110 R. W. Dale (1877), 46.

111 Hennock (1973), 76–9.

112 A. W. W. Dale (1898), 101.

113 See above 246–7.

CHAPTER 4

FROM CONFLICT TO EQUIPOISE: POLITICAL, INDUSTRIAL AND
RELIGIOUS CONFLICT IN BIRMINGHAM AND SHEFFIELD
1830–64

1 Useful background material on the political development of early
nineteenth-century Sheffield may be found in: Fletcher (1972); Crawshaw
(1954); Walton (1968); Pollard (1959); Armytage (1951).

2 On the Rawson family see Stainton (1924), 343–4. On the Parker family see
Odom (1926), 232.

3 Wickham (1957), 104; Stainton (1924), 339; Wallis (1957), 61, 353–4, 356;
Fletcher (1972), 10; J. M. Furness (1893), 509.

4 *Sheff. Dir. 1841*, 8; Stainton (1924), 66–84. Borough magistrates were first
appointed in 1848. J. M. Furness (1893), 88.

5 *Sheff. Dir. 1852*, 13–18; *Bir. Dir. 1850*, 3–8; Wickham (1957), 71–2; Mole
(1961), 114–98; J. M. Furness (1893), 509–11. On J. A. Roebuck see Odom
(1926), 234; Stainton (1924), 46–50; R. E. Leader (1897).

6 On Ward see Jennett (1954); Inkster (1973), 109–10, 116; Odom (1926),
176–8; Stainton (1924), 234–5. On Holland see J. D. Leader and S. Snell
(1897), 102–3; Odom (1926), 121–3; Stainton (1924), 227–8; Cohen (1950).
On Montgomery see Odom (1926), 22–6; Holland and Everett (1854–6). On
Hodgson see Odom (1926), 87–8.

7 Walton (1968), 159.

8 Respectively: Edward Smith (R. E. Leader (1875), 322–5), J. W. Pye-Smith
(Stainton (1924), 301–2), Edward Bramley (Fletcher (1972), 49), William
Fisher (Odom (1926), 82–3); Henry Hoole (Stainton (1924), 296); Robert
Leader (Stainton (1924), 265–6; Odom (1926), 14–16) and Thomas Dunn
(Stainton (1924), 233–4).

9 Vincent (1972), 127; Stainton (1924), 81; Odom (1926), 146.

10 See above 44.

11 Currie (1968), 81.

12 Ibid., 43.

13 Wickham (1957), 67.

14 Ibid., 74, 88, italics in original; *Sheff. Dir. 1841*, 6.

15 Wickham (1957), 123, 128–9.

16 Ibid., 129.

17 Salt (1971b), 188–91; Crawshaw (1954), 98–122; Fletcher (1972), 7–10.

18 Respectively: T. E. Mycock, W. R. Harrison, W. Crowther, W. Harvey, T. Platts, I. Scholefield, W. Groves and C. Alcock. Fletcher (1972), esp. ch. 2; occupations given in J. M. Furness (1893).

19 Salt (1971a), 38.

20 *SI*, 23 October 1852.

21 Wickham (1957), 101; Pollard (1959), 46; Pollard (1957), 121.

22 Wickham (1957), 132, 133–4.

23 Salt (1971a), 43–52; Roberts (1979), 18, 21.

24 Fletcher (1972), 34, 38–41. On William Overend see Stainton (1924), 261–2; Odom (1926), 139–40.

25 Armytage (1955a), 480–1. On J. D. Ellis see Erickson (1959), 145; Odom (1926), 165–6; Stainton (1924), 333–5. On W. Bragge see Erickson (1959), 39, 40, 145, 168; Stainton (1924), 262. On John Brown see Erickson (1959), 31, 39, 41, 143–5, 161; Odom (1926), 161–4; Stainton (1924), 306–9.

26 J. M. Furness (1893), 17, *Sheff. Dir. 1849*; *Sheff. Dir. 1852*.

27 Apart from the above-mentioned, Benjamin Vickers and William Moulson were on the council in 1848, a total of twelve leading industrialists in the heavy trades. In 1853 the following appear to fall into that category: T. B. Turton, E. Vickers, W. A. Matthews, W. Groves, S. Jessops, J. Howarth, W. Moulson, C. Atkinson and T. Gatley. J. M. Furness (1893), 22; *Sheff. Dir. 1852*.

28 J. M. Furness (1893), 24–7, 30–2. In 1863 the aldermanic bench included the following large manufacturers in the heavy trades: T. Jessop (mayor), G. Beardshaw, W. A. Matthews, R. Jackson and J. Brown. Councillors included: A. Beckett, D. Ward, T. Jowitt, R. T. Eadon and J. Bramall. *Sheff. Dir. 1862*; Pawson and Brailsford (1862).

29 Pawson and Brailsford (1862), 124; Odom (1926), 171.

30 J. M. Furness (1893), 128; S. Harrison (1864). On the Dale Dyke disaster see below, 163–4.

31 On Mark Firth see Odom (1926), 79–82; Stainton (1924), 251–7.

32 1868: T. Jessop, J. Brown, R. Jackson, G. Barnsley, J. Nicholson, J. Bramall, R. Hadfield. 1873: T. Jessop, W. H. Brittain, J. Gamble, J. H. Andrew, E. Tozer, W. Bragge, J. Knott, J. Shipman, R. Hadfield. J. M. Furness (1893), 37, 42.

33 On Wostenholme see Odom (1926), 178–9; Stainton (1924), 246–7.

34 Doe (1976), 181–2.

35 Ibid., 181.

36 Ibid., 185.

37 Fletcher (1972), 55.

38 Odom (1926), 172.

39 *Sheff. Dir. 1852*, 476; Stainton (1924), 249. On Cammell see also Odom (1926), 164–5; Erickson (1959), 19, 32, 144–5, 161.

40 Doe (1976), 181, 183–4.

41 Payne (1967), 522; Erickson (1959), 145; Cottrell (1980), 113–25.

42 Mark Firth, Methodist and Liberal, was not typical of the large steel masters. By and large, the latter remain shadowy figures, preoccupied with their business affairs.

43 March (1966), e.g. 31–7, 39–47, 77.

44 Salt (1968); Salt (1960b), 168–87; Fletcher (1972), 37–8; Armytage (1955a), 474–8; Briggs (1972), 52–86.

45 Marx wrote to Engels: 'Money is the only interesting point for me in my intercourse with these Calibans.' Armytage (1955a), 475.

46 Pollard (1959), 170.

47 Ibid., 125, 163.

48 See ch. 7.

49 Burn (1964), 17.

50 Ibid., 15–16.

51 Ibid., 21–2, 74–5.

52 Perkin (1969), 208–17, 347–53; Vincent (1972), 72–6.

53 E.g. Griffiths (1870), *passim*.

54 See below, 101–3.

55 Dent (1880), 444.

56 In 1865 M. D. Hill, recorder of Birmingham, recollected a time when Dissenters had been a majority of the school governors. *Birmingham Daily Post* (henceforth *BDP*), 14 October 1865. The governor's strategy of seeking legal recognition of threatened customs was similar to that being pursued by local trade unions in the 1830s and 1840s.

57 Morrison (1926), 106–11; Dent (1894), 441; Mole (1961), 66.

58 Whateley was the son-in-law of Isaac Spooner, vicar of Edgbaston. *General Hospital, Birmingham: proceedings of Annual General Meeting*, 20 September 1844, (henceforth *Gen. Hos. 1844*).

59 Quoted in *Report of Proceedings of Town Council in relation to the Bill of Governors of the Free Grammar School 1842*, (henceforth *Town Council 1842*), 27.

60 *T. Gutteridge to Earl of Dartmouth on Election of Medical Officers at General Hospital, 1844* (henceforth *Gutteridge 1844*).

61 *Gen. Hos. 1844*; Mole (1961), 65–8; *Aris's Gazette*, (henceforth *AG*), 3 June 1839.

62 Flick (1978), 12–13.

63 Ibid., 22, 25. On George Edmonds see Edwards (1877), 140–54.

64 Flick (1978), chs 3–5, esp. 81, 101; cf. Ferguson (1960).

65 *Edg.* (1888), 8, 1–8.

66 D. Fraser (1976a), 43, 45; Mole (1961), 198.

67 Flick (1978), 116 ff., 128.

68 Ibid., 119; Bunce (1878), 105.

69 Flick (1978), 125 ff., esp. 113, 164; D. Fraser (1976a), 73.

70 Hennock (1973), 28, 30. On Hawkes see *Edg.* (1890), 10, 177–87. On Baldwin see *VCH*, 305–6; G. H. Osborne, *Birmingham Biography*, (henceforth Osborne), vol. 1, 33.

71 Langford (1873), vol. 1, 95, 100; D. Fraser (1976a), 144, 198–200; Tunsiri (1964), 214–28. See above 46–8.

72 Behagg (1979), 467; Edwards (1877), 108; Corbett (1966), 30; Showell (1885), 187. Italics in original.

73 Ram (1976), 31, 34–5, 37.

74 The influence of these closely-linked families on Birmingham's public life has often been noticed. See for example Bushrod (1954); Hennock (1956); Hennock (1973); Bailey (1952).

75 On Goodrick see *Edg.* (1886), 6, 17–21.

76 Tangye (1889), 101.
77 On Manton see *Edg.* (1903), 23, 193–9.
78 *Edg.* (1887), 7, 97–101 (W. Morgan); *Edg.* (1887), 7, 17–24 (W. Middlemore); Edwards (1880); *Biograph and Review* (1880), 3, 251–6 (J. S. Wright).
79 *Edg.* (1885), 4, 176; Vincent (1972), 30; Morrison (1926), 200.
80 Hennock (1973), 176.
81 Bunce (1899), quoted in Tunsiri (1964), 144. See also Kellett (1969), 125–34.
82 **On the Calthorpe family see Cannadine (1975).**
83 Cannadine (1980), 156; Hennock (1973), 107.
84 Hatherton Diary, 29 November 1839 and 22 December 1853, quoted in Tunsiri (1964), 67, 103.
85 Tyson (1960), 169–8.
86 Dent (1880), 533; Langford (1873), vol. 1, 100; *VCH*, 305–6; *Biograph and Review* (1880), 3, 251–2.
87 Langford (1873), vol. 1, 58, 102–3, 413–14.
88 *VCH*, 307.
89 Gill (1952), 415, 417–18, 419; Cannadine (1980), 156.
90 On Ryland see Bunce (1878), 340, *Edg.* (1882), 2, 76–9. On Law see Morrison (1926), 42; Langford (1873), vol. 1, 228–34.
91 Jaffray, a Liberal businessman who later helped found the *Birmingham Daily Post*, exemplified a tendency towards assimilation between urban and rural interests. In 1874 he stood as parliamentary candidate for East Staffordshire. His son married the daughter of Sir Francis Edward Scott. In 1880 it was written: 'With the characteristics of a cultivated town life Mr Jaffray combines the tastes of a country gentleman' *Edg.* (1885), 5, 161–6, esp. 165–6. On R. L. Chance see Langford (1873), vol. 1, 368–74; *VCH*, 98, 109, 137; Tunsiri (1964), 128–31. On George Dixon see *Edg.* (1886), 6, 1–6.
92 Waterhouse (1954), chs 1 and 2; Woodward (1928), 1–51.
93 Bunce (1899), 21; Mole (1961), ch. 6; Tunsiri (1964), 255–62. On J. C. Miller see Mole (1966). On J. A. James see Langford (1873), vol. 1, 466 ff. On Van Wart see Edwards (1877), 101–7.
94 On Pakington see J. N. Williams (1973), 51–60; Pakington (1858). On Adderley see Childe-Pemberton (1909), *Biograph and Review* (1879), 2, 528 ff.
95 J. N. Williams (1973), 23.
96 On M. D. Hill see R. and F. Davenport-Hill (1878); J. N. Williams (1973), 17–22. On the Hill family and education see Dobson (1959); Dobson (1960). George Lea is discussed in Mole (1961), ch. 6. For James on education see Langford (1873), vol. 1, 125.
97 Walter Showell recalled that Allday 'the "Stormy Petrel" of modern Birmingham' had been horsewhipped by G. F. Muntz on one occasion. Hennock (1973), 32 ff; Flick (1978), 198; Showell (1885), 173.
98 Edwards (1877), 70.
99 Hennock (1973), 33, 104; Avery (1866), esp. 86–7.
100 On Harris see *Edg.* (1911), 31, 61–70; Hennock (1973), 81.
101 *AG*, 3 March 1851, quoted in Mole (1976), 8. Italics in original.
102 Dawson Collection, XV, 29.
103 Dawson (1866), 23.
104 See ch. 10.
105 These comparative remarks require three qualifications with respect to Sheffield: political divisions within the middle class between supporters of the Liberal and Conservative Parties persisted; some of the former (e.g. Robert Leader of the *Sheffield Independent*) were less hostile to the trade unions than many of the latter (e.g. W. C. Leng of the *Sheffield Telegraph*);

and to a significant extent the new large-scale capitalists were able to ignore rather than try to destroy 'old' Sheffield.

CHAPTER 5
'THE TRAINING UP OF WELL-EDUCATED, SOBER, LOYAL AND OBEDIENT SERVANTS': ELEMENTARY AND SECONDARY EDUCATION IN BIRMINGHAM AND SHEFFIELD 1830–70

1 *Education Census 1851*, Table, P. Gosden (1966), 10–22. On the earlier 1846 Minutes see J. R. B. Johnson (1970), esp. 117.
2 In 1846 the percentage of marks made in signing marriage registers in Birmingham parish was 29 per cent (men); 47 per cent (women). The equivalent proportions in Sheffield were 34 per cent (men); 53 per cent (women). In 1864 the figures were for Birmingham parish 26 per cent (men); 35 per cent (women) and for Sheffield 27 per cent (men); 42 per cent (women). Sargant (1867a), 134–5.
3 *CEC Sheff. 1843*, evid. e11.
4 *CEC Birm. 1843*, evid. f195.
5 Dent (1894), 17; *Sheff. Dir. 1862*, 21; *BJ*, 30 February 1865; PP 1867–8, XXVIII, *Schools Inquiry Commission* (henceforth *SIC*), vol. 4, 565–6.
6 *SIC*, vol. 18, 250–5, esp. 251. On Sheffield Grammar School see also G. C. M. Smith (1937), J. R. Wigfall (1937).
7 C. E. Matthews (1864), 21.
8 *Town Council 1842*, iii.
9 Tyson (1960), 129; *VCH*, 552–3; G. Griffiths (1861), 473; PP 1867–8, XXVIII, Pt XII, Report of T. H. Green, assistant commissioner (henceforth *Green Report*), 104–5. On the King Edward VI Grammar School see also C. Foster (1940), 196–201; PP 1861, XXI, *Royal Commission on State of Popular Education in England and Wales* (henceforth *Newcastle*), vol. 1, 537–9; Science and Art Department, *Seventh Annual Report 1859*, 25–6; Gifford (1858); Bunce (1895), Hutton (1952).
10 *Town Council 1842*, viii; C. E. Matthews (1864), iii–iv, 12–20; G. Griffiths (1861), 562–4.
11 G. Griffiths (1861), 16–17; *Green Report*, 93; letter from W. L. Sargant, *BDP*, 13 December 1865. The Edgbaston Proprietary School was the successor to the Hills' ventures at Hill Top and Hazelwood where Sargant had been a pupil. Sargant (1870), 185–91; C. E. Matthews (1864), 13; Gill (1952), 384; Dent (1894), 439.
12 Letter from W. L. Sargant, *BDP*, 13 December 1865.
13 C. E. Matthews (1864), 16–18; *Green Report*, 105–6, 121–2, 144.
14 The *Gentleman's Magazine* (November 1855), 499.
15 Gifford (1858), 131–2, 134.
16 Sargant (1870), 200.
17 *Green Report*, 110–12.
18 Calculated from *Education Census 1851*, Table P, clvii, clxv.
19 Holland (1843), 220–1. Birmingham Statistical Society for the Improvement of Education; 'Report on the state of Education in Birmingham', *Journal of Statistical Society*, (1840), vol. 3 (henceforth *Birm. Stat. Soc. 1840*), 25–49. The figures for Birmingham in Table 14 are based upon the summary table presented in *Birm. Stat. Soc. 1840*, 49.
20 The *Sheffield Directory* of 1849 lists twenty-five 'Gents' and Ladies' Boarding and Day Schools'. *Sheff. Dir. 1849*, 237–9; *Bir. Dir. 1849*, 299–301; *Green Report*, 110; Holland (1843), 220.

21 *Green Report*, 119.
22 cf. Jewson (1974).
23 Private adventure schools in Sheffield are discussed in Board (1959), esp. 74–99.
24 *SI*, 19 January 1839; *SI*, 30 March 1839, cit. Board (1959), 84; Board (1959), 79–80, 91, 95, 122, 157; Austen (1957); Porter (1932), 83.
25 *Green Report*, 119.
26 Among the alumni of the Sheffield Grammar School were Robert Leader (Odom (1926), 15), Evangelical parson W. B. MacKenzie (ibid., 50), the surgeon Wilson Overend (129) and the lawyer William Overend (139), the solicitor Henry Vickers (144), the railway engineer Joseph Locke (155) and the ubiquitous T. A. Ward (177). The collegiate's ex-students included the churchman and historian E. L. Cutts (39), H. A. Favell, an archdeacon (45), the surgeons William Fisher Favell (120), Richard Favell (121) and Arthur Jackson (123), the solicitors Arthur Thomas (142) and Charles Macro Wilson (147), the architect J. B. Mitchell-Withers (156), the steel manufacturer W. H. Brittain (160), the gentleman-scientist H. C. Sorby (199) and the assayer A. T. Watson (203).
27 Stainton (1924), 313. The steel manufacturer Thomas Vickers was also educated in Germany. Odom (1926), 176.
28 *SIC*, vol. 9, 335.
29 Erickson (1959), 4, 32. The locally-educated included self-made men such as Mark Firth who went to a private day school and John Brown who attended 'a small school held in an attic'. Stainton (1924), 251; Odom (1926), 162.
30 See Ball (1971); Cotton (1949); Davy (1931); Wallis (1953); Easton (1900).
31 *SIC*, vol. 18, 243.
32 Ibid., 243, 663; *The establishment, principles, discipline and educational course of the Wesleyan Proprietary Grammar School, Sheffield 1839*.
33 *SIC*, vol. 18, 232–3, 667; Board (1959), 167–9; Atkinson (1861); *SI*, 16 December 1863; *Sheffield Telegraph* (henceforth *ST*), 11 January 1872.
34 Board (1959), 135; W. G. Matthews (1977), 282.
35 Quoted in Tyson (1960), 263.
36 *CEC Sheff. 1843*, evid. e8.
37 Ibid., evid. e25.
38 F. Adams (1882). See ch. 2.
39 Frost (1978), 83.
40 Laqueur (1976), 39, 46, 60–1, 92–3.
41 Rev. H. W. Bellairs, HMI for South Midland District, argued strongly that the clergy should make an improvement in the quality of paid schoolteachers a primary task. Committee of Council on Education, *Minutes 1847–8*, vol. 1, (1848), 106–7.
42 Hurt (1972), 88–91; Laqueur (1976), 65, 85–6, 92–3; C. O. Reid (1976), 175–6; *CEC Birm. 1843*, evid. f195, f197; rep. F35.
43 A distinction may, perhaps, be made between two notions of 'respectability': the first emphasises the distance between the norms of 'rough' and 'respectable' working class people; the second emphasises conformity to the norms of middle-class people as being desirable. Working-class people who were respectable in the first sense might well resist an appearance of deference or subordination to the dictates of middle-class groups. For two examples of the use of the concept of 'respectability' as a bargaining token in negotiations between working-class and middle-class establishments see ch. 7. For an alternative approach see C. O. Reid (1976).

44 *CEC Sheff. 1843*, rep. E27, E28; C. O. Reid (1976), 174.
45 *CEC Birm. 1864*, evid. 98.
46 A formulation in terms of this interplay between 'sponsor power' and 'client power' allows a more subtle representation of the expression of class relationships within formal education than one which lays undue stress on a single determining factor such as patterns of client demand or the control motivations of middle-class sponsors. Contributions to this debate include Laqueur (1976); J. R. B. Johnson (1976b); Frost (1978); West (1978).
47 According to J. Corrie, a local magistrate. Cullen (1975), 125.
48 *Birm. Stat. Soc. 1840*, 25, 26, 38; Frost (1978), 131. The agent was J. R. Wood.
49 Holland (1843), 220, 221; Cullen (1975), 131.
50 The following data probably tend to understate day school attendance in Birmingham and overstate day school attendance in Sheffield for the reasons given. Figures for public day school attendance in Birmingham are based upon *Birm. Stat. Soc. 1840*, 43, Table 10.
51 Ibid., 38; *CEC Sheff. 1843*, rep. E20, E21.
52 For estimates of attendance among working-class child population in Birmingham at Sunday and day schools see Frost (1978), 48, 51.
53 According to J. R. Wood, of the 16,757 enrolled Sunday scholars in Birmingham 4141 also attended day school. *Birm. Stat. Soc. 1840*, 38.
54 cf. Hopkins (1974); J. Rowley (1978).
55 *CEC Sheff. 1843*, evid. e11.
56 *CEC Birm. 1843*, evid. f192.
57 *Robson's Directory of Birmingham and Sheffield 1839*, 466, 803; Board (1959), 170–7; Leinster-Mackay (1974), 12.
58 *CEC Sheff. 1843*, evid. e5.
59 Money (1976).
60 *Birm. Stat. Soc. 1840*, 27; Holland (1843), 220.
61 PP 1870, LIV, *Return confined to the municipal boroughs of Birmingham, Leeds, Liverpool and Manchester, of all schools for the poorer classes of children* (henceforth *Fitch 1870*).
62 *Fitch 1870*, 44, 54.
63 *CEC Sheff. 1843*, evid. e11, e16; rep. E22, E23–4.
64 Ibid., evid. e30, e30, e31, e34, e34.
65 *Birm. Stat. Soc. 1840*, 38; Holland (1843), 220; *1851 Education Census*, Table 5.
66 See below.
67 *CEC Sheff. 1843*, evid. e31.
68 Ibid., evid. e33.
69 Ibid., evid. e20.
70 Ibid., evid. e2, e3.
71 Ibid., evid. e16.
72 Ibid., evid. e3.
73 Ibid., rep. E26.
74 *CEC Birm. 1843*, rep. F36.
75 Ibid., rep. 185–91; *Birm. Stat. Soc. 1840*, 39.
76 There had actually been a decrease in public day school provision in Birmingham in 1829 when the Charity Commission put a stop to an arrangement whereby the King Edward VI Foundation subscribed to the national school at Pinfold Street. During the previous four years the foundation had also closed down several small English schools, *VCH*, 551.
77 On Evangelicalism see Bradley (1976); Binfield (1977).
78 Mole (1961), ch. 3; Mole (1976), 6–9; Wickham (1957), 82.

79 Langford (1873), vol. 1, 468–9, 470–1; Ram (1976), 32–3, 35–6, 38; Mole (1973), 820. On Samuel Bache see *Dictionary of National Biography* (henceforth *DNB*), II, 318.
80 Mole (1973), 822; Mole (1961), ch. 3 esp. 65, 68–9, 88 ff.
81 Mole (1973), 826–8; Mole (1961), 61; Memoir of the Rev. John George Breay . . ., Birmingham (1841); The Faithful Pastor delineated . . ., Birmingham (1839); Langford (1873), vol. 1, 449–50; *Bir. Dir. 1850*, 16. For other examples of clerical enterprise in education see *CEC Birm. 1844*, evid. f191–f195.
82 Mole (1973), 828. It has been calculated that between 1828 and 1851 the average age of the local Anglican clergy fell from 54½ years to 42 years. Frost (1978), 272.
83 Wickham (1957), 82. On Thomas Sutton see Odom (1926), 55.
84 *CEC Sheff. 1843*, evid. e1, e2, e6.
85 Eltringham (1939), 147; C. O. Reid (1976), 257; Holland (1843), 220.
86 *CEC Sheff. 1843*, evid. e4, e6, e8, e9.
87 Ibid., e8.
88 *CEC Sheff. 1843*, rep. E31. Italics in original.
89 On Earnshaw see Odom (1926), 39–42; Stainton (1924), 278–9.
90 Earnshaw (1857), 73, 74. Earnshaw wrote as the representative of the Clerical Committee on Education in Sheffield.
91 Mole (1973), 831; Mole (1961), 65–8 and ch. 6. For Yorke's work see Langford (1873), vol. 1, 45–6, 56 and several other references therein. On Bull see *CEC Birm. 1843*, evid. f192–4. Miller's evangelical work is described in Mole (1966).
92 *Bir. Dir. 1850*, 16–17.
93 See Table 20.
94 *Bir. Dir. 1850*, 16.
95 Only seventeen charity and endowed schools (including three infant schools) were recorded by J. R. Wood as having been established before 1831 in Birmingham. *Birm. Stat. Soc. 1840*, 40.
96 In his study Frost concludes that the period from 1829 to 1851 witnessed a sustained expansion in 'provided' schooling (as opposed to 'private') schooling for working-class children in Birmingham. He lays considerable stress on the impetus provided to middle-class sponsors by the Chartist agitation and its aftermath in the 1830s and 1840s. This present argument puts more emphasis than does Frost upon conflict within the middle-class. The persisting radical tendencies which Frost found among some teachers, especially Dissenters, may have reflected a relative lack of fear that social disorder was imminent. Such an explanation may also apply to the political ideology of the Mechanics' Institute at Birmingham (see ch. 6). It is important to consider the various sectors of formal education in relation to each other in order to grasp their class implications. Frost (1978), 335–43, 376–8.
97 See Table 10.
98 *Fitch 1870*, esp. 19–21, 30, 44, 78; *SIC*, vol. 9, 335–6 (Fitch's Report – Appendix I). Fitch's statistics for Birmingham distinguish inspected schools, non-inspected schools (mainly denominational) and private (including ragged) schools. His Sheffield data distinguish 'superior' and 'lower' private schools (the latter only being recorded here), and in the public sphere, 'national and parochial' schools, 'other' public elementary schools, workhouses, reformatory and orphanage schools. As Fitch suggested, his Sheffield figures have been uniformly increased by 15 per cent to take account of a probable failure to identify some schools. Table 22

must be regarded as a very approximate guide to the distribution of students among types of school.

99 *Fitch 1870*, 51.

100 *SIC*, vol. 9, 335–6. It is noticeable that although the very rapid growth of Sheffield's population during the 1850s and 1860s is likely to have made the task of eliciting attendance a more pressing one in that city than in Birmingham the standard of existing accommodation seems to have been higher in Sheffield. In 1871 Sheffield's school board recorded that there already existed 'efficient' accommodation for 30,702 children out of an estimated total 'need' for 39,978 places. The same year Birmingham's school board recorded an estimated total 'need' of 54,958 places of which 38,405 were already in existence in schools supplying 'efficient' accommodation. In other words, Sheffield's educators had 'efficient' accommodation for about 77 per cent of their potential working-class clients while Birmingham could supply 'efficient' schooling for under 70 per cent of its putative pupil population. In fact, the Education Department at Whitehall conducted its own survey which suggested that Birmingham had 'efficient' accommodation for only about 63 per cent of the prevailing 'need'. The department argued that local officials had not only undercalculated the numbers of children not receiving education but also . had been too generous in their assessment of 'efficiency' in the case of several private schools, Bingham (1949), 292; A. F. Taylor (1955), 282; Birmingham School Board, *Report* 1870–3, esp. 9.

101 Earnshaw (1857), 76. Italics in original. Another local cleric, Rev. J. Lettis Short, recommended the virtues of instructing 'the wage-class' in the principles of political economy. Short (1866); cf. Goldstrom (1972); Gilmour (1967).

102 E.g. J. E. White's reports on Turtons, Joseph Peace & Co., Ward and Payne's, Sanderson Bros and Jessops. *CEC Sheff. 1865*, evid. 30–33. See also John Wilson's paper at Social Science Congress in 1865 and ensuing discussion. J. Wilson (1866a).

103 *Trans. NAPSS 1866*, Sheffield Meeting 1865, 371.

104 Stephenson (1856); Stephenson (1857); J. P. Norris (1857); Hopkins (1975).

105 Winfield (1857), 247.

106 Ibid., 247.

107 Bunce (1857), 278, 280. Italics in original.

108 Ibid., 287. Italics in original.

109 See ch. 7.

110 Gedge (1858).

111 Ibid., 164, 165.

112 Ibid., 167.

113 Ibid., 169–70.

114 Ibid., 171.

115 Langford (1873), vol. 1, 134–5.

116 Gover (1858); *CEC Birm. 1864*, evid. 154–63, esp. 156.

117 Gover (1858), 171–2.

118 Checkland (1964), 26–7, 37.

119 Corbett (1966), 22.

120 Langford (1873), vol. 1, 452.

121 *CEC Birm. 1864*, 152.

CHAPTER 6
MECHANICS AND MEDICAL MEN: ADULT EDUCATION AND
MEDICAL SCHOOLS IN BIRMINGHAM AND SHEFFIELD 1830–70

1 For examples of the latter see J. F. C. Harrison (1961), *passim*.
2 At the Literary and Philosophical Society's inaugural meeting,
   Montgomery recalled Byron's sneer at 'classic Sheffield'. Porter (1932), 13;
   Holland and Everett (1854–6), vol. 3, 338.
3 Porter (1932), 32–3.
4 W. White (1895), 12.
5 Ibid., 15, 18, 57. Some of the teachers, including two Cadburys, served on
   the town council. Hennock (1973), 146.
6 Yorke (1846); *VCH*, 225.
7 Langford (1873), vol. 1, 58, 123.
8 Pawson and Brailsford (1862), 80. Italics in original.
9 Committee members of the mechanics' institute are listed in the minute
   books. See esp. vols 1 and 2. For Literary and Philosophical Society
   committee members see Porter (1932), 83 ff.
10 J. Taylor (1938), 152–5; Board (1959), 121–3.
11 Eltringham (1939), 148; C. O. Reid (1976), 318–19, 340, 365; See also Salt
   (1966); Holland (1843), 232–8; J. Taylor (1938); Rodgers (1840); Inkster
   (1975); Inkster (1976a).
12 *Sheffield Mercury* (henceforth *SM*), 26 October 1839; Holland (1843), 238; C.
   O. Reid (1976), 208–9. This censorship was supported by relatively 'liberal'
   professional men such as Charles Favell and G. C. Holland, both medical
   practitioners.
13 Pawson and Brailsford (1862), 83.
14 Holland (1843), 231.
15 Stainton (1924), 327–8; Odom (1926), 77.
16 On R. S. Bayley see Odom (1926), 185–6.
17 On People's College see Stainton (1926), 128–9; G. C. M. Smith (1912).
18 *SI*, 6 August 1842; Board (1959), 129–30; G. C. M. Smith (1912), 13–41;
   C. O. Reid (1976), 322–3.
19 J. Wilson (1866b), 308.
20 G. P. Jones (1932), 11–19; Salt (1971b), 193–7; Salt (1960a), 135; Salt (1960b),
   76–8.
21 E.g. Holland (1843), 235.
22 Salt (1971b), 196; Board (1959), 125, 128; *ST*, 10 November 1849, 24
   November 1849, 1 November 1851; C. O. Reid (1976), 358.
23 'Ms relating to Sheffield Mechanics' Institute', no. 43, letter of 6 January
   1853, quoted in Inkster (1976a), 298. Italics in original.
24 Pawson and Brailsford (1862), 84.
25 Ibid., 85; Odom (1917), 11.
26 *Sheff. Dir. 1862*, 23.
27 Inkster (1975), 467; Langford (1873), vol. 1, 225; Stainton (1924), 132.
28 Langford (1873), vol. 1, 113–14, 116–18, 120–8; C. Foster (1940), 68; Drake
   (1825).
29 Joseph Sturge bought the library of the defunct mechanics' institute and
   promptly re-sold it to the polytechnic institution. Langford (1873), vol. 1,
   120–2.
30 *The Times*, 19 September 1848, quoted in Inkster (1975), 465. Italics in
   original.
31 Ibid.
32 *VCH*, 229.

33 *Bir. Dir. 1850*, 19; Langford (1873), vol. 1, 124; C. Foster (1940), 71.
34 *VCH*, 227–9.
35 Favell (1836), 7.
36 The *Analyst* (1835), ii, 280–2, quoted in *VCH*, 228. Italics in original.
37 See ch. 4.
38 Langford (1873), vol. 1, 56, 124, 128, 133.
39 Ibid., 254.
40 Ibid., 249–50, 252, 257.
41 Ibid., 258.
42 Ibid., 264, 266, 268, 290.
43 E. Smith (1869), 448.
44 Birmingham and Midland Institute Annual Report (henceforth *BMIAR*) 1869.
45 *BMIAR 1881*.
46 Langford (1873), vol. 1, 291; E. Smith (1869), 448; *BMIAR 1860*; *BMIAR 1865*.
47 *BMIAR 1856*; *BMIAR 1859*; *BMIAR 1871*.
48 *BMIAR 1866*; *BMIAR 1867*.
49 *BMIAR 1856*; *BMIAR 1864*; *BMIAR 1865*.
50 Ex-students teaching at the institute included C. J. Woodward (chemistry) and Albert Cresswell (practical mechanics); *BMIAR 1863*; *BMIAR 1864*.
51 *BMIAR 1865*.
52 *BMIAR 1858*; *BMIAR 1861*.
53 *BMIAR 1881*.
54 *BMIAR 1860*.
55 See above, 115.
56 Langford (1873), vol. 1, 131–2; Miller (1857); Miller (1858), 197; *BMIAR 1856*; *BMIAR 1859*.
57 Morrison (1926), 36–7.
58 Ibid., 80–1, 115–18.
59 Langford (1873), vol. 1, 258; Waterhouse (1954), 26.
60 Waterhouse (1954), 25, 156; Langford (1873), vol. 1, 267.
61 Langford (1873), vol. 1, 260, 262, 376, 378.
62 Odom (1926), 47–8; Stainton (1924), 328–30 (Gatty); *Edg.* (1883), 3, 65–8 (Ingleby); Stainton (1924), 296–7, 312–13 (Wake); ibid., 313–14 (Bramley); ibid., 315–16 (Ellison).
63 Leader and Snell (1897), 106 (Branson); ibid., 100–1; Odom (1926), 133–4 (Thompson); Morrison (1926), 3–4 (Edward Townsend Cox); Edwards (1877), 132–9; Morrison (1924), 198 (William Sands Cox); ibid., 33, 38–40, 205; Johnstone (1909) (Johnstone).
64 cf. Inkster (1977).
65 Board (1959), 91–3 (Hunt, Wright); Inkster (1977), 138–9; Leader and Snell (1897), 102–3 (Holland); Odom (1926), 185 (Bayley); *Edg.* (1882), 2, 76–9 (Ryland).
66 The following paragraphs draw upon Holloway (1964), esp. 304–5, 311, 316–19.
67 W. S. Porter (1928), 20–1, 74. See Leader and Snell (1897), 83–8, 116, 146; Odom (1926), 123–5 (Arthur and Henry Jackson); Odom (1926), 128–9, 139–40; W. S. Porter (1928), 15; Leader and Snell (1897), 114–16 (Overend family); Fletcher (1972), 7, 9 (Palfreyman).
68 W. S. Porter (1928), 17.
69 Donnelly (1975b).
70 Leader and Snell (1897), 101.

71 W. S. Porter (1928), 21, 39, 75; C. O. Reid (1978), 322–3; Chapman (1955), 113–15.
72 On Sheffield medical societies see Snell (1890). The 'Medical Society' founded in 1841, for instance, 'simply ebbed away'. Other attempts were subject to a 'process of atrophy and decadence', ibid., 20, 40, 48.
73 W. S. Porter (1928), 20, 22; Inkster (1977), 137–8; Leader and Snell (1897), 116; Stainton (1924), 261–2.
74 The Jackson family, for example were related both to the Overends and to the Wakes. Bernard Wake, Arthur Jackson's father-in-law, was a solicitor who 'held a position of very great influence in Sheffield'. A prominent Anglican, Wake made many substantial charitable donations. It is probable that his local standing owed more to his position in this network of kin and personal influence than his early presidency of the Sheffield Law Society. Stainton (1924), 296–7; Leader and Snell (1897), 86.
75 Morrison (1926), 31, 63–4, 80–4, 107–8.
76 Ibid., 36–7. Italics in original.
77 Ibid., 80–1.
78 Vincent and Hinton (1947), 50; Morrison (1926), 108–111. The award-granting powers mentioned were in addition to the existing powers to award MB and MD degrees.
79 Langford (1873), vol. 1, 208–17.
80 F. C. Williams (1903), 82.
81 *T. Gutteridge to James Taylor on the corrupt system of election of medical officers 1843* (henceforth *Gutteridge 1843*), esp. 3–5.
82 Ibid., 3, 4. Italics in original.
83 Ibid., 13. Italics in original.
84 *Gen. Hos. 1844*; *Gutteridge 1843*, 13.
85 *Gutteridge 1843*, 15. Italics in original.
86 A committee of inquiry was demanded by John Suckling and Richard Hasluck. It is interesting that Suckling was an associate of W. Sands Cox. *Gen. Hos. 1844*; *J. Suckling, The Queen's College, Birmingham Enquiry by Charity Commissioners. Reply for W. Sands Cox, 1859.*
87 Griffiths (1862), 361; Morrison (1926), 60–7; Thomas (1855).
88 Morrison (1926), 67.
89 Ibid., 108–11, 114.
90 Ibid., 117.
91 Vincent and Hinton (1947), 55, 58; Morrison (1926), 119–20.
92 Morrison (1926), 120–43.
93 Odom (1926), 133; Leader and Snell (1897), 57, 71–5, 100–1, 106, 155; Stainton (1924), 285.
94 In 1862 there were 512 students on the books at the Sheffield institution compared to 717 at the Birmingham and Midland Institute. Pawson and Brailsford (1862), 85; Waterhouse (1954), 37.
95 Odom (1917), 10–11.
96 *SI*, 8 June 67, quoted in Pollard (1957), 133.

CHAPTER 7
'OLD FASHIONED IDEAS AND CUSTOMS': THE ATTACK ON CLOSED CORPORATIONS IN BIRMINGHAM AND SHEFFIELD 1864–70

1 A meeting in Carrs Lane addressed by William Murphy, a 'notorious agitator', led to violence and the reading of the Riot Act. Arnold (1869), 187–8, 196, 209–10; *VCH*, 402.

2 Arnold (1869), 201. Arnold's father, Thomas, had used the *Sheffield Courant* as a platform for expressing his views on social questions in a series of thirteen letters from July 1831 onwards.
3 See McCarthy (1971); McCarthy (1964).
4 *Out. Inq. 1867*, 248 (q13241).
5 Pollard (1957), 131.
6 March (1966), 38–47.
7 See ch. 2.
8 Pawson and Brailsford (1862), 179.
9 Ibid., 119–20.
10 Warren (1964), esp. 142; Pollard (1959), 159–64.
11 S. Harrison (1864), 93, 157; B. Grant (1864).
12 On Mappin see Odom (1926), 91–5; Stainton (1924), 345–6.
13 March (1966), 31–3; *SI*, 10 June 1865; J. M. Furness (1893), 69; *Sheff. Dir. 1862*.
14 E.g. *ST*, 18 March 1864, 23 March 1864, 6 May 1864.
15 Stainton (1924), 46–50; J. M. Furness (1893), 510.
16 Mendelson (n.d.), 18–19.
17 On Mundella see Armytage (1951); Higginbotham (1941).
18 Higginbotham (1941), 10–15; Armytage (1951), 33 ff.
19 Mundella was an associate of Cobden whose Anglo-French free trade treaty was signed in 1860. Armytage (1951), 30–2.
20 A prominent local supporter of these causes was H. J. Wilson. See Fowler (1961a); Stainton (1924), 355–6.
21 J. Wilson (1866b), 480; Armytage (1948a), 146–7. On Dronfield see also Thornes (1976).
22 Lloyd (1913), 315.
23 J. Brown (1975), 53; Pawson and Brailsford (1862), 150; Pollard (1959), 140; Mendelson (n.d.), 26.
24 Mendelson (n.d.), 26–7; Pollard (1959), 140.
25 Mendelson (n.d.), 28; Armytage (1948a), 146.
26 Mendelson (n.d.), 29–30.
27 *Out. Inq. 1867*, evid. 293 (q15,403), 291 (q15,332), 292 (q15,369).
28 Ibid., evid. 292 (q15,370).
29 In the light of Bragge's evidence it is worth noting that he was a prominent supporter of technical education in Sheffield. His stance on this issue and on the employment of unionists are both consistent with a desire to minimise worker control over the manufacturing process. See ch. 9. Erickson (1959), 39, 40.
30 *Out. Inq. 1867*, evid. 444 (qq23,345–9).
31 Ibid., evid. 444 (qq23,359–61, 23,376–8).
32 Armytage (1948a), 147.
33 *Out. Inq. 1867*, rep. xvi.
34 Ibid., evid. 291 (qq15,323–56).
35 Ibid., evid. 291 (qq15,341–2).
36 Ibid., evid. 291 (q15,354).
37 Ibid., evid. 33 (q1,638). Evidence of J. Thompson.
38 Pollard (1957), esp. 128–9.
39 *ST*, 19 July 1867, quoted in Pollard (1957), 135.
40 Higginbotham (1943), 286–90.
41 Ibid., 288.
42 *ST*, 25 August 1868; *SI*, 25 August 1868. Roebuck's executive committee included W. C. Leng, Mark Firth, F. T. Mappin, Thomas Jessop and Robert Jackson. Apart from these members of the big bourgeoisie, W. Crowther,

an old supporter of Ironside, also sat on the committee. *ST*, 10 October 1868; Fletcher (1972), 85–6.

43 Fletcher (1972), 60, 84; Higginbotham (1943), 290–3; Odom (1926), 135–7 (W. J. Clegg), 63–4 (J. Calvert); Stainton (1924), 286–8 (R. Stainton).

44 R. Harrison (1972), 67. On Mundella's connection with the Reform League see Armytage (1951), 40 ff.

45 J. M. Furness (1893), 510.

46 *SI*, 27 November 1868; Fletcher (1972), 87.

47 Data on franchise based on returns made by the union clerks in Sheffield to central government in 1866.

48 *SI*, 5 March 1870.

49 *SI*, 18 January 1870, 4 April 1871; Fletcher (1972), 99–102.

50 *SI*, 11 November 1870; Bingham (1949), ch. 1 and app. 12; Fletcher (1972), app. C.

51 By 1883 there were eight solicitors on the council; by 1892 the figure had risen to eleven. J. M. Furness (1893), 52, 61, 63–74.

52 Quoted in Gledstone (1867), 6.

53 *Saturday Review*, 2 November 1867.

54 Hennock (1973), 82.

55 Ibid., 34.

56 Ibid., 172.

57 Ibid., 175, 176.

58 On National Education League see A. F. Taylor (1960); Adams (1882); Hamer (1977), ch. 7.

59 The processes just described interacted in complex ways with the development of a 'national' party system expressing some aspects of 'national' opinion. cf. Vincent (1972), 33.

60 R. W. Dale (1877), 46.

61 Quoted *CEC Birm. 1864*, evid. 152.

62 *SIC*, vol. 4, pt 1, 1001 (q.18,109). In association with George Baker, a leading Quaker, Wright had called the public meeting at which the association had been founded. Baker became the association's treasurer. *Edg*. (1907), 27, 483 ff.; *Biograph and Review* (1880), 3, 251–6.

63 Hennock (1973), 133.

64 *VCH*, 307.

65 *SIC*, vol. 4, pt 1, 1006, 1007.

66 Ibid., 984 (q18,021), 1005 (q18,122). Evidence of W. L. Sargant and J. S. Wright.

67 Ibid., 980–1 (q17,992), 982 (q17,996).

68 Ibid., 1003–4 (qq18,111–12).

69 Ibid., 980 (q17,990), 986 (qq18,035–7).

70 Ibid., 980 (q18,037).

71 Ibid., 1012.

72 Ibid., 988 (q18,049). Evidence of G. Dixon.

73 *Green Report*, 96.

74 *SIC*, vol. 4, pt 1, 965 (q17,927), 970 (q17,948), 967 (q17,929).

75 Ibid., 987 (qq18,039–45).

76 See above, 157–8.

77 *SIC*, vol. 4, pt 1, 1010–11, 957 (q17,892), 992 (q18,071). Evidence of Yates and Ryland.

78 C. E. Matthews (1864), 26.

79 *SIC*, vol. 4, pt 1, 1003 (q18,113). Evidence of Wright.

80 Ibid., 959–60 (q17,895), 961 (q17,902). Evidence of Miller.

81 Ibid., 993 (q18,074), 993–5 (q18,075), 997 (qq18,076–77). Evidence of Yorke.

82 Ibid., 542 (q5,631), 545 (q5,677), 547 (qq5,707–10), 548 (q5,719), 552 (qq5,786–7), 556 (q5,835), 558 (q5,860), 559 (qq5,871–4), 561 (q5,887). Evidence of Evans.

83 Ibid., 565–7.

84 Just as the London-based amalgamated societies, closer to central government than were the Sheffield unions, played a leading role in the Trades Union Congress (founded 1868), so the prestigious and well-connected headmasters of national public schools such as Eton, Winchester and Shrewsbury were essential to the success of the Headmasters' Conference (founded 1869) in becoming an effective influence on government policy. The latter organisation was founded by heads of grammar schools threatened by government legislation on endowed schools but within a year the leading public schools were showing interest. In 1879 the conference met at Eton. Simon (1974b), 103–8, esp. 107; Stansky (1962).

85 *Green Report*, 109.

86 Ibid., 118, 131, 140.

87 Ibid., 108–10, 115–16, 140–1.

88 Ibid., 134, 111.

89 Ibid., 134, 135.

90 Ibid., 135.

91 Ibid., 116–17, 137, 141. Turner (1960).

92 See ch. 9 and ch. 10.

93 *SIC*, vol. 4, pt 1, 1007, 1034. Three of the association's committee have not been identified. D. Smith (1976), 69–70, 75–6.

94 *Edg.* (1911), 31, 61–70; *Edg.* (1884), 4, 97–100; *Edg.* (1888), 8, 1–8; King (1901); *VCH*, 305; D. Smith (1976), 76. Gover was principal of Saltley Training College.

95 Gover (1867).

96 Birmingham Education Society, *Annual Report 1868*, esp. 7. Collings, a Unitarian, was a close political ally of Joseph Chamberlain. *Edg.* (1893), 13, 177–85.

97 Birmingham Education Society, *Annual Report 1869*, 10–13, 17.

98 Collings (1870), 16, 49.

99 cf. Reeder (1980), 2–3.

100 Adams (1882), 197; Marcham (1969), 308–9; Sargant (1872), 2.

101 Birmingham Education Union, *Report of Conference at Birmingham, December 9th 1869*, 4, 5.

102 Ibid., 3, 6, 8, 55. Evans, a barrister and litterateur, had been a close political associate of George Dawson. *DNB*, supp. II, vol. 1, 637; Hennock (1973), 77–8, 133–4; Gammage (1972), 80–1.

103 *Report of First General Meeting of National Education League . . . October 12th and 13th 1869*, Marcham (1969), 296–300, 585a; A. F. Taylor (1960), 137–9.

104 Joseph Chamberlain, R. W. Dale, Charles Vince, Jesse Collings, J. S. Wright, Henry Holland, H. W. Crosskey, William Middlemore, George Dawson and J. Cooper.

105 E.g. Sampson Lloyd, Rev. J. H. Burges, J. Gough and Rev. F. S. Dale.

106 Adams (1882), 251; Sargant (1872), 17–19.

107 Fletcher (1972), 47; Salt (1971b), 184.

108 Sargant (1856); Sargant (1857a); Sargant (1957b); Sargant (1866); Sargant (1867a); Sargant (1867b); Sargant (1874).

109 Sargant (1869), 1–61, 137–204.

110 Ibid., 15, 143–4, 197.

111 Ibid., 10–11, 12, 18, 20–3, 27.

112 Ibid., 13–14.
113 Ibid., 198–9.
114 Ibid., 156–7.
115 Gledstone (1867), 5.
116 Ibid., 4.
117 Ibid., 4–5. Italics in original.
118 Ibid., 5–6.
119 Ibid., 7–9.
120 Ibid., 9.
121 The last remark is evidently directed at W. C. Leng. Ibid., 11, 12–13.
122 Ibid., 13–15.

CHAPTER 8

MASTERING OUR EDUCATORS: TOWARDS A NATIONAL
EDUCATION SYSTEM 1830–95

1 The following discussion and, indeed, the whole book is a contribution to a process of empirical inquiry and theoretical discussion which must also take account of inter-societal comparisons. See, for example, Archer (1979), Ringer (1979), Smith (1982) (forthcoming). The need for local studies was clearly signalled a decade ago: 'the dynamics of local action remain obscure. What seems to be needed, though the programme is an ambitious one, is a combination of educational research, social-structural analysis and local economic histories in order to examine the functions of schools and the purposes of schools within well-defined communities and regional economies.' J. R. B. Johnson (1970), 99–100.
2 Mole (1973), 817. On Hook see W. R. W. Stephens (1878).
3 Burgess (1958); W. B. Stephens (1973), esp. 13–20.
4 See ch. 9 and ch. 11.
5 In the course of movement away from a predominantly rural and agrarian society force was frequently used locally and with the backing of law or custom in relations between retailers and customers, landlords and tenants, masters and men and so on. However, the issue here is what part should be played by physical repression directed by central government in managing a developing urban industrial society. E. P. Thompson (1966); B. Moore (1969).
6 This threat was a medium or long term one. During its early years the Education Department 'drew into its network of control the essentially voluntary but completely reliable agents of the local clergy, local elites, and denominational training colleges'. J. R. B. Johnson (1970), 117. On the development of educational administration under governmental auspices see esp. Gosden (1966); Bishop (1971); Archer (1979); J. R. B. Johnson (1968); J. R. B. Johnson (1972); Sutherland (1972b); Hurt (1972).
7 Roach (1970); Montgomery (1965).
8 Roach (1970), 4–5.
9 On 'experts' in education see J. R. B. Johnson (1977).
10 PP 1895. XLIII et seq., Report of Royal Commission on Secondary Education (henceforth Bryce).
11 Newcastle, vol. 1, 11, 157–71, 179–82, 276–89, 292–6, 314–17, 361–8, 461; vol. 2, 10, 19.
12 Bryce, vol. 1, 81–4. A similar pattern is revealed in the Cross Commission. PP 1888, XXXV, Final Report of Royal Commission appointed to Inquire into

Elementary Education Acts (England and Wales) (henceforth *Cross*), vol. 1, iii–v.

13 Crowther (1965), 190.
14 PP 1852–3, LIV, *Second Report of Royal Commission for Exhibition of 1851*, 10–11.
15 On Playfair see W. Reid (1899); Crowther (1965), 105–71.
16 Thackray (1974), 686. For an attempt to sketch the normative and cognitive order implicit in the curricula of mechanics' institutes see Shapin and Barnes (1977).
17 Kargon (1977), 27–33.
18 Thackray (1974), 696.
19 Arnold (1862).
20 Sutherland (1973a), 9; McCarthy (1971) *passim*; Peel (1971), 10–12, 43, 100; Duncan (1911), chs 1–5; Arnold (1869), 193–4.
21 Through the *Pilot*, Spencer probably had contact with other prominent Birmingham radicals such as Henry Hawkes, a lawyer who began his career in the office of Joseph Parkes and later became in turn coroner and mayor of Birmingham. *Edg.* (1890), 10, 117–18.
22 Arnold (1869), 166–70, 199, 219–41.
23 Spencer (1861), 2.
24 Ibid., 4.
25 Spencer (1873), 6.
26 Ibid., 7.
27 Arnold (1869), 193–6; Arnold (1864), 162; Spencer (1873), 238–9.
28 See also Rothblatt (1974).
29 Roach (1970), 52–3.
30 Quoted in Sargant (1857a), 336.
31 Ibid.
32 PP 1852, XXII, *Report of Royal Commission on the University of Oxford*; PP 1852–3, XLIV, *Report of Royal Commission on the University of Cambridge*; Montgomery (1965), 44–51.
33 Sargant (1857a), 342.
34 Ibid., 342–3.
35 PP 1881, LVI, *University of Oxford Commission*, pt 1, evid. 155, quoted in Roach (1959), 142; Draper (1923), chs 1, 2.
36 Hurt (1972), 86–147, esp. 96; J. R. B. Johnson (1970), 116–19.
37 *Hansard*, 13 February 1862, quoted in Tropp (1957), 87–8.
38 Checkland (1964), 218.
39 Quoted in Reeder (1980), 218.
40 Checkland (1964), 142, 164–5, 217–19, 230–2. On 1867 riots see Dent (1894), 560.
41 Bechhofer and Elliot (1976), 79–80; E. P. Thompson (1966).
42 Chichester (1866), 45.
43 Deane and Cole (1962), 143; Perkin (1969), 143; Checkland (1964), 216.
44 A. Hill (1857), 373.
45 *1851 Religious Census*, 181–2; *1851 Education Census*, 52; D. K. Jones (1977), 13–27; Hurt (1971), 186–222; Montgomery (1965), 76–8; Tropp (1957), 48–57.
46 Hook (1846).
47 Hinton (1854), 3, quoted in D. K. Jones (1977), 23.
48 D. K. Jones (1977), 24; *Newcastle*, vol. 1, 1. My italics.
49 E.g. through the establishment of the Headmasters' Conference.
50 See Stansky (1962) and ch. 9.

51 Bamford (1967); Mack (1938); Mack (1971); Wilkinson and Bishop (1967); Montgomery (1965), esp. xii.
52 Gosden (1966), 77–81.
53 *Bryce*, vol. 1, 17–18.
54 For several examples in the West Midlands see G. Griffiths (1870), *passim*.

CHAPTER 9
'A NOISY STREET IN THE MIDDLE OF A SMOKY TOWN':
ELEMENTARY, SECONDARY AND HIGHER EDUCATION IN
BIRMINGHAM AND SHEFFIELD 1870–95

1 Stainton (1924), 109: Fowler (1961a), esp. 36–42, 60–2; Bingham (1949), 15–18.
2 Bingham (1949), 18.
3 Ibid., 19. Henry Wilson, Anglican snuff manufacturer, is not to be confused with Henry Joseph Wilson, Nonconformist smelter. Odom (1926), 108–9.
4 A. W. W. Dale (1898), 476.
5 *BDP*, 19 November 1873; *BDP*, 21 November 1873; A. F. Taylor (1955), chs 2 and 3; A. F. Taylor (1960), esp. chs 9 and 10; Adams (1882), chs 6–9.
6 See above, 65–6, 131–2.
7 Bingham (1949), 34, 36, 37; A. F. Taylor (1955), 133, 135.
8 A. F. Taylor (1955), 120.
9 Bingham (1949), 39; *Birmingham School Board Report 1884*, 14–15.
10 A. F. Taylor (1955), 144; Bingham (1949), 60, 68; *Birmingham School Board Report 1870–1876*, 41; J. Chamberlain (1876), 17–18. See also Birmingham School Board, *Report on compulsion as applied to school attendance in Birmingham* (1878), Birmingham. *BDG*, 15 September 1887; *Birmingham School Board Report 1889*, 25; See also Gammage (1972), ch. 5, esp. 132–40.
11 *ST*, 11 January 1872. See also *ST*, 12 January 1872; *ST*, 13 January 1872; *ST*, 30 January 1872; *SI*, 27 January 1872.
12 Stainton (1924), 108.
13 Addy (1883), 11.
14 Ibid., 13–14.
15 Cotton (1949), 1–9; Hawson (1968), 75; Stainton (1924), 86.
16 *Birmingham School Board Report 1884*, 14–15; *Birmingham School Board Report 1892*, 35–6. On MacCarthy see *Edg.* (1882), 2, 49–59. The technical curriculum at Bridge Street School, the higher grade school opened in 1884, is described in Crosskey (1885a), 375–9.
17 *Bryce*, vol. 2, 178–9 (qq1,740, 1,748). Evidence of A. R. Vardy. Ibid., vol. 3, 45–6 (q6,394), 47–8 (qq6,401–8), 57 (q6,552). Evidence of MacCarthy. Bunce (1895), 21–3; Bunce (1885), 527–8; Muirhead (1911), 525–60. On A. R. Vardy, headmaster of the boys' high school in 1894, see *Edg.* (1900), 20, 148 ff.
18 *Bryce*, vol. 3, 60 (qq6,597–8).
19 Ibid., 46 (q6,394), 58 (qq6,564–8).
20 Ibid., 44 (q6,385), 45 (q6,388), 53–4 (q6,482).
21 *Bryce*, vol. 2, 196 (q1,934).
22 See above, 181.
23 *Bryce*, vol. 2, 202 (q1,996).
24 Walton (1968), 212, 231; *Bryce*, vol. 7, 166, 169, 172, 175. Laurie also noted the 'large private day school kept by Mr Newall' who was, ironically, an ex-employee of the Sheffield School Board. Ibid., 165; Bingham (1949), 98.

25 *Bryce*, vol. 7, 177.
26 *Bryce*, vol. 3, 43 (qq6,380–2).
27 *Bryce*, vol. 7, 165, 167, 168–9, 173.
28 Chapman (1955), chs 8–10 and 205–6.
29 Vincent and Hinton (1947), esp. 17–22, 25, 28, 82.
30 Quoted in Ashby and Anderson (1974), 72–3.
31 See ch. 7.
32 The lawyer was G. J. Johnson, the doctor J. G. Blake. Vincent and Hinton (1947), 61; Burstall and Burton (1930), 9.
33 Chapman (1955), 15–16, 17, 23, 24, 36, 39. Mappin was made a baronet in 1886. Odom (1926), 92. His central position in the file trade has already been noted.
34 Chapman (1955), 71, 78, 131, 173.
35 *BMIAR 1873; BMIAR 1884; BMIAR 1885; BMIAR 1888; BMIAR 1889; BMIAR 1890; BMIAR 1900.*
36 Vincent and Hinton (1947), 53; Chapman (1955), 120, 130.
37 Respectively R. S. Heath, J. F. Poynting and Bertram Windle.
38 Somerset (1934), 9–10; Vincent and Hinton (1947), 30, 34, 82; Burstall and Burton (1930), 33; Sanderson (1972), 104.
39 Sanderson (1972), 104–5; Vincent and Hinton (1947), 37; Chapman (1955), ch. 3, esp. 48, 51.
40 PP 1887, XXIX *Cross Commission, Second Report*, evid. 728 (q34,951); 'Current Topics', *Some Random Recollections: Forty Years of Education in Sheffield*, (1938), 1–25 (newspaper cuttings relating to Sheffield, vol. 44, Sheffield Local History Collection).
41 *BDG*, 12 March 1897; Gammage (1972), 239–52.
42 This statement is based on a survey of the annual reports of the Birmingham Higher Education Society and the Birmingham Teachers' Association. MacCarthy was an honorary secretary of the former and Vardy a founder of the latter. The role of Vardy is mentioned in J. H. Smith (1903). Sonnenschein was also active in this field. See, for example, Birmingham Teachers' Association, *Fifteenth Annual Report*, 1889. The genteel hegemony of Vardy and McCarthy no doubt provoked the candidature of W. Ansell, representing elementary school teachers, for the school board in 1894. Presumably he drew the 'plumped' votes of his colleagues. He came top of the poll. *BDP*, 13 November 1894; *BDP*, 14 November 1894; *BDP*, 19 November 1894. See also D. Smith (1976), 72–3.
43 Chapman (1955), 27, 81, 170 ff., 199, 207 ff., 229 ff., ch. 19.
44 The two categories in Table 24 are constituted as follows: with respect to 1891, 1 = 'Professional Occupations (with immediate subordinates)', 1–8 (excluding 'students') plus 'Books, Prints and Maps', 1–2 plus 'Houses, Furniture and Decorations', 3. 2 = 'Commercial Occupations', 1–3. PP 1893–4, CVI *et seq. Census, England and Wales* (henceforth *1891 Census*), vol. 3, Table 7. The categories for 1851 are constituted as in Table 2 (ch. 2). Note that 'scientific persons' are included in category 3 of Table 2 within 'professional, literary, artistic'. While the boundaries of the categories in Table 24 are unlikely to be strictly comparable between 1851 and 1891 they are comparable between the two cities at each date. The figures provide a rough indication of variations between Birmingham and Sheffield with respect to the rate and degree of expansion in the broadly-defined occupational areas identified.
45 Between 1851 and 1891 both cities experienced approximately the same degree of proportional population growth.

46 Three of the eight aldermen listed and a third of the eighteen councillors included in that volume were also foundation *alumni*. Pike (n.d.). These figures include ex-pupils of the Edgbaston Proprietary School which merged with the foundation in 1884. Shewell (1951), 198–200.

47 *BMIAR 1876; BMIAR 1885.*

48 *Bryce*, vol. 3, 89 (q6,956).

49 Lapworth (1884), 18; Burstall and Burton (1930), 57; Sanderson (1972), 69–70, 98–9.

50 Sanderson (1972), 195–6.

51 Gammage (1978), 28; *BDP*, 10 February 1888, quoted in Gammage (1972), 242; R. D. Best (1940), ch. 6; Dalley (1914), 377–85.

52 For example, in 1900 Birmingham's brewers established a school of malting and brewing at the university. Sanderson (1972), 85.

53 Pollard (1959), 206.

54 Ibid., 135–7, 171, 212, 226.

55 Scott (1962), 19, 48; PP 1886 XXI, *Royal Commission on Depression of Trade, Second Report*, 108 (q3,431); Trebilcock (1971), 4–5; Sanderson (1972), 88–9, 102–3; Sanderson (1978).

56 Mappin's character is suggested by the contemporary comment: 'in whatever he did, he was "boss".' 'Big and little guns', *South Yorkshire Notes* (1899), 1, 3, 215; quoted in J. Brown (1975), 53.

57 Pollard (1959), 115; Mendelson *et al.* (n.d.), 40; PP 1884, XXIX *et seq.*, *Second Report of Royal Commission on Technical Instruction* (henceforth *Samuelson*), vol. 3, 555–6 (q7,727). Evid. of J. B. Mitchell-Withers.

58 Stainton (1924), 142.

59 Hattersley (1976), 145.

CHAPTER 10
COALESCENCE, CONFLICT AND COMPROMISE: INDUSTRY, EDUCATION AND LOCAL GOVERNMENT IN BIRMINGHAM AND SHEFFIELD 1870–1914

1 On Joseph Chamberlain see Garvin and Amery (1934–69); Gulley (1926); Hurst (1962); P. Fraser (1966); Dolman (1895); Browne (1974); Howard (1950).

2 Watson (1907); Herrick (1945); McGill (1962); Tholfsen (1959); Chamberlain (1878).

3 For a valuable discussion see Hurst (1962).

4 Briggs (1952), 19, 69–80.

5 Quoted in Hennock (1973), 120.

6 *SI*, 9 April 1853.

7 *Dart*, 19 March 1886. Italics in original.

8 Briggs (1952), 70.

9 Higginbotham (1941), 68–9, 118–19.

10 Armytage (1948b).

11 See chs 3 and 4.

12 Langford (1873), vol. 1, 424.

13 Edwards (1877), 81, 130.

14 PP 1884–5, XXXI, *Royal Commission on Housing of Working Classes* (henceforth *Housing WC*), vol. 2, 454 (qq12,489–93).

15 Howard (1950), esp. 484–5; Garvin and Amery (1934–69), vol. 5, 45, 148; Briggs (1952), 87.

16 Ralph (1890).

17 Adams (1882).

18 Ibid., 207–8.

19 Ibid., 324.

20 Ibid., 104.

21 Ibid., 41.

22 Spencer was officially connected with the Birmingham Natural History and Microscopical Society when it established a sociological section in 1883. His published work was indexed by an Edgbaston devotee, F. Howard Collins. Another follower was W. R. Hughes, Birmingham's city treasurer from 1867 to 1898. Duncan (1911), 231; Briggs (1952), 125.

23 Spencer (1850).

24 D. Smith (1977a), 25.

25 Arnold's neglect of Spencer in *Culture and Anarchy* (in favour of Mill and Miall, both of whom suffer attack) has been a precedent followed by recent critical surveys of nineteenth century literature. Raymond Williams mentions Spencer only once in *Culture and Society*. Terry Eagleton ignores him in *Criticism and Ideology*. Considering the concern of both Williams and Eagleton with the use of the 'organic analogy' and the spirit of *laissez-faire* their neglect of a writer who combines both is interesting. The social critique of Spencer and Adams exemplifies the richness of the Dissenting tradition and its tendency to emphasise divisions between the old landed aristocracy and the towns rather than differences between masters and men within the city. R. Williams (1963), 166; Eagleton (1976), 102–3, 106; D. Smith (1977b), 20–1, 31–2; Vincent (1972), 183–94; G. L. Williams (1976); Richter (1966); Hamburger (1965); B. Webb (1926), 123.

26 Green (1973), 88; Briggs (1952), 170.

27 Green (1973), 89.

28 *Birmingham Daily Mail* (henceforth *BDM*), 30 October 1874 quoted in Green (1973), 89.

29 *Housing WC*, vol. 2, 447 (q12,398); Green (1973), 91, 93–4. For an assessment of the relationship between Birmingham's sanitary conditions and variables connected with mortality in the period 1870–1910, see Woods (1978). Woods argues that 'the degree of association between sanitary conditions and mortality variables is lower than one might expect if in fact an improvement in the former were capable of influencing the latter to a very marked degree.' Woods (1978), 56.

30 Green (1973), 95. The development of Birmingham Conservatism can be traced through the speeches and reminiscences of J. B. Stone who became M.P. for East Birmingham in 1895. See *Biograph and Review* (1880), 3, 65 ff.; Stone (1880); Stone (1904); Levy (1909).

31 Hurst (1962), 53. See also 23–4.

32 Ibid., 63.

33 On Bunce see *Edg.* (1892), 12, 34–8; *Edg.* (1899), 19, 129.

34 Gammage (1972), 64–89, 173, 271.

35 In this instance the term 'civic' refers initially to institutions such as the King Edward VI Foundation, Queen's College and the Birmingham and Midland Institute which acquired great prestige in the 1850s and which in that decade were closely identified with the town as a whole (see chs 6 and 7). Subsequently, the town council was deliberately built up as the centre of civic life.

36 See Table 24.

37 *VCH*, 127, 150–3, 167, 203–4.

38 J. P. Gledstone's pamphlet, discussed in ch. 8, has some remarkable Durkheimian overtones. On anomie see Durkheim (1970), 241–76, 288–9.

39 In a recent article G. M. Norris suggests that 'paternalist capitalism' is characterised, *inter alia*, by deference to a bourgeoisie which exercises a 'welfare' function. He argues that '[in] the final analysis . . . the maintenance of paternalist capitalism rests on the retention of local ownership by an identifiable group of individuals and families who have historical ties with the locality.' By contrast, 'capitalists whose economic power base is national or international are not in a position to promote a system of paternalist domination.' The latter point clearly applies to Sheffield. Birmingham's political and economic life retained the aura of paternalist capitalism to a remarkable degree. G. M. Norris (1978), esp. 477–9.

40 Pollard (1959), 161–2, 224; J. D. Scott (1962), 20–3.

41 Caillard to Albert Vickers, 9 March 1918, quoted in Trebilcock (1971), 16.

42 J. D. Scott (1962), 41.

43 Howard Vincent, MP for Sheffield Central from 1885, had been director of Criminal Investigations at Scotland Yard. Ellis Ashmead-Bartlett, MP for the Ecclesall Division from 1885, had been president of the Oxford Union. The son of the Lord Chief Justice was Hon. Bernard Coleridge, himself a lawyer. Stainton (1924), 52, 59; Fletcher (1972), 181. On the Kenricks see Church (1968).

44 Earl Fitzwilliam was Lord Mayor of Sheffield in 1909. Hawson (1968), 340.

45 See Cannadine (1978).

46 Knox (1935).

47 Ibid., 213.

48 Ibid.; Dalley (1914), 268–9, 308 ff.

49 Knox (1935), 214.

50 Ibid., 160.

51 *Bryce*, vol. 7, 165.

52 Gammage (1972), 208.

53 Crosskey (1885b), 284, 291.

54 Ibid., 283–4. My italics.

55 Ibid., 291.

56 Ibid., 286–7.

57 See ch. 2.

58 Fox (1955), 64–5; Corbett (1966), 46.

59 Fox (1955), 68; Corbett (1966), 49 ff.

60 Dalley (1914), esp. chs 5, 6, 9.

61 Fox (1955), 68–9. Davis led a strike just before his retirement in 1920, reportedly because he 'wanted to see what a strike was like'. R. D. Best (1940), 77.

62 Dalley (1914), 211.

63 Ibid., 36, 170–1, 183–4, 267; Fox (1955), 65–6; E. J. Smith (1895).

64 Dalley (1914), 272.

65 Ibid., 279.

66 E. O. Smith (1895), 332; Briggs (1952), 160.

67 Vince (1902), 356–7, 362; Briggs (1952), 162; Nettlefold (1914); Cadbury (1915).

68 The brass manufacturer R. H. Best was an active supporter of the aid society. R. D. Best (1940), ch. 4. Joseph Chamberlain's nephew, Norman Chamberlain, was very active in social work in the early twentieth century as well as being a city councillor. Hay (1977), 448.

69 Hay (1977), 441–3.

70 Canon Odom's *Hallamshire Worthies* contains many instances. See, for example, entries under John Brown (who built All Saints Church,

Brightside), Robert Hadfield (who 'in a quiet way . . . helped Mount Zion Chapel, Attercliffe'), A. J. Hobson (who 'took a special interest in the Royal Infirmary and other charitable institutions'), Thomas Jessop (who provided Jessop's Hospital), etc. Odom (1926), 163, 168, 169, 171.

71 Hawson (1968), xvii, xviii, 129; Walton (1968), 230, 239; PP 1888, CCII, *Select Committee on Town Holdings*, 42 (q964), 155 (q3,511), 161 (q3,672); evid. of G. T. Simpson and W. J. Clegg. On Clegg see Stainton (1924), 304–5; Odom (1926), 135–7.

72 Mathers (1979a).

73 PP 1884, XXIX *et seq.*, *Royal Commission on Technical Instruction, Second Report*, vol. 3, 557 (q7,732).

74 Hawson (1968), 107–8.

75 On the 1874 Election see Fowler (1963); Hurst (1972); D. G. Wright (1973).

76 The Sheffield Trades Council was founded in 1872, the Sheffield Reform Association in 1873. Mendelson *et al.* (n.d.), 36; Hurst (1972), 685.

77 Fowler (1963), 153; Hurst (1972), 686, 694–5.

78 Vincent (1972), 23. The more active and powerful town council in Birmingham was able to use its influence to disperse some of these tendencies, albeit for its own political advantage. By the mid-1880s a stronghold of Conservative votes was developing in five wards close to the city centre. The town council ensured that when the boundaries of the parliamentary constituencies were redrawn under the 1884 Redistribution Act each of the Conservative wards was swamped by one or more Liberal ones. Green (1973), 97.

79 Pelling (1967), 232 ff.; Stainton (1924), 52; Armytage (1948b).

80 Odom (1917), 37 ff.; Knox (1935), 134 ff.

81 Odom (1917), 21.

82 See above, 116.

83 PP 1893–4, XXXIV, *Royal Commission on Labour* (henceforth *Labour*), vol. 3, 537 (q19,351). See also ibid. 539–68. Evid. of W. F. Wardley, R. Holmshaw and S. Uttley. Holmshaw and Uttley gave similar evidence to Wardley.

84 Hawson (1968), 312.

85 Mendelson *et al.* (n.d.), 41, 45, 48; Pollard (1959), 145.

86 J. Brown (1975), 51, 53.

87 Pollard (1959), 234, 332–4; *Labour*, vol. 3, 79 ff. Evid. of J. Taylor; Mendelson *et al.* (n.d.), 49, 57; Stainton (1924), 44; *VCH*, 316.

88 Murphy (1917), 15.

89 Ibid., 4. Italics in original.

CHAPTER 11
'A SERIOUS DANGER TO THE UPPER CLASSES':
SUMMARY AND CONCLUSION

1 Wilde (1895), 151.

2 Ibid., 151–2.

3 Ibid., 142–3, 157–8, 160–3.

4 Ibid., 151, 152, 153, 159, 176.

5 Ibid., 149, 175.

6 Sanderson (1972), 191, 192; Nowat (1968), 18; PP 1898, XXIV, *Special Reports on Educational Subjects*, 86 quoted in Sanderson (1972), 192.

7 Gosden (1966), 55.

8 *SIC*, vol. 1, 297; Mack (1971), 31–2; *Samuelson*, vol. 1, 525; Cardwell (1972), 99–100; Kearney (1970); Webster (1975).

9 The strengthening of the 'grammar school' element in Sheffield's secondary education was abetted by Michael Sadler's report to the city's education committee in 1903 which recommended, *inter alia*, a considerable increase of secondary school education for girls. In later years a more left-wing local authority was to insist that King Edward VII School should lose its independent governors and disband its OTC. Sadler (1903); Hawson (1968), 75, 79; Armytage (1976), 269; Board of Education, *Elementary Code* (1904); Banks (1953), 22–123; Eaglesham (1956); Simon (1974a), 176–246; Sturt (1967), 404 ff.; Tropp (1957), 160–82.

10 Rev. E. F. M. MacCarthy, a strong influence on the Birmingham School Board, had argued in the mid-1890s for either an 'ideal' school board elected by the local ratepayers with powers over all forms of education below the university level or a new special school board for secondary schools. He refused to serve on the Birmingham Education Committee created after the 1902 Education Act. *Bryce*, vol. 3, 50–2 (qq6,425–66); A. F. Taylor (1955), 260; Sturt (1967), 407–8; Richter (1964); Rothblatt (1968); Roach (1959), esp. 147 ff.; Fowler (1961b); Richter (1966).

11 Muirhead (1942), 38–51.

12 Ibid., 88.

13 Richter (1964), 9 ff.; Muirhead (1942), 90, 91, 108, 110–11, 128; Somerset (1934); Rothblatt (1968), 91, 249 ff., 266–7, 272.

14 Mack (1971), 123–30.

15 Armytage (1955b), 255 ff.; Muirhead (1942), 162–3; De Montmorency (1909), esp. 610–11, 618.

16 In this way, the 'collection curriculum' in English secondary schools performed a significant political function. D. Smith (1976), esp. 5–6; Bernstein (1973b).

17 Quoted in Armytage (1955b), 247–8.

18 Banks (1953), 174–7; Extracts from the elementary code and the regulations for secondary schools of 1904 may be conveniently found in Maclure (1979), 155–9. Maclure notes Eaglesham's suggestion that the introduction to the Elementary Code may have been written by a man who had been professor of poetry at Oxford University. If this is the case it is a striking indication of the power of the Arnoldian tradition! Ibid., 154.

19 See above, 194–5.

20 Musgrave (1967), 264. For a local attempt to introduce aspects of the German system see above, 240.

21 H. C. G. Matthew *et al.* (1976), 724–5; Moorhouse (1973), 352.

22 Middlemas (1979), 20–1.

23 Bingham (1949), 310–13.

24 During the mid-1920s Sheffield became the first large English borough in which the Labour Party achieved a majority on the city council. Ironically, like Birmingham eight decades previously, Sheffield came into confrontation with central government over the proper extent of municipal power. Sheffield's city council repeatedly came into conflict with the Treasury and the Ministry of Health, departments dominated by Neville Chamberlain. Rowett (1979), 13; Hawson (1968), 25–6; Mowat (1968), 471–3; Middlemas (1979), 230–3; F. Miller (1979).

25 Macdonald (1886), 250.

26 Ibid., 245.

27 It is, to say the least, interesting that for much of the period between 1923 and 1940 the Conservative Party and the national government were dominated by two ex-students of Mason College, Birmingham: Stanley Baldwin and Neville Chamberlain (the latter being Joseph's son). Baldwin

owed his wealth to the family iron works near Birmingham. The Baldwin-Chamberlain years witnessed, at the national level the slow but cumulative growth of institutionalised consultation between management, unions and government; a large programme of social legislation in housing, pensions and related areas; the gradual implementation of a tripartite system of 'post-elementary' education dominated by the grammar schools and legitimised by the 'eleven-plus' examination; and an increase in the amount of attention being paid by politicians and civil servants to means of assessing and influencing public opinion. Middlemas (1979), 214–65, 337–70; Mowat (1968), 338 ff.; A. J. P. Taylor (1965), 236–7; Simon (1974b), 116–48.

28 Hawson (1968), 307–9.
29 Money (1977), 282.

BIBLIOGRAPHY

I   *Sources mainly referring to*:

    (a) Sheffield
    (b) Birmingham
    (c) General background

II   *Other sources*:

    (a) Unpublished theses and dissertations
    (b) Official publications
    (c) Newspapers, directories, annual reports, etc.
    (d) Other source material from:
        (i)   Birmingham collection
        (ii) Sheffield local history collection

Abbreviations

Trans. NAPSS   *Transactions of the National Association for the Promotion of Social Science*
      THAS   *Transactions of the Hunter Archeological Society*

I(a) SHEFFIELD

Addy, S. O. (1883) *Middle-class Education in Sheffield*, Sheffield.
Armytage, W. H. G. (1948a) 'William Dronfield and the good name of the Sheffield workman in the 1860's', *Notes and Queries*, 193, 145–8.
Armytage, W. H. G. (1950) 'Joseph Mather – Poet of the filesmiths', *Notes and Queries*, 195, 320–2.

Armytage, W. H. G. (1955a) 'Sheffield and the Crimean War: politics and industry 1852–1857', *History Today*, 5, 7, 473–82.

Armytage, W. H. G. (1976) 'South Yorkshire: the emergent concept in the system of education', in Pollard and Holmes (1976), 262–74.

Arnold, T. (1832) *Thirteen Letters addressed to the Editor of the Sheffield Courant on our Social Conditions*, London.

Atkinson, G. B. (1861) *On the Establishment of a School of Practical Science*, Sheffield.

Austen, J. (1943) 'A Sheffield chemist's jottings in the thirties', *THAS*, 5, 21–6.

Austen, J. (1957) 'Notes on Milk St. Academy and its founder', *THAS*, 7, 202–5.

Barraclough, K. C. (1976) *Historic Industrial Scenes: Sheffield Steel*, Moorland Publishing, Hartington.

Baxter, J. L. (1976b) 'Early Chartism and Labour class struggle: South Yorkshire 1837–1840', in Pollard and Holmes (1976), 135–58.

Bellamy, J. M. (1970) *Yorkshire Business Histories*, Bradford University Press.

Bingham, J. H. (1949) *The Period of the Sheffield School Board*, J. W. Northend, Sheffield.

Blackman, J. (1962) 'The food supply of an industrial town: a study of Sheffield's public markets 1780–1900', *Business History*, 5, 1, 83–97.

Bramley, E. (1957) *A Record of the Burgery of Sheffield Commonly called the Town Trust from 1848 to 1955*, J. W. Northend, Sheffield.

British Association (1910) *Handbook and Guide to Sheffield*, Sheffield.

Brown, J. (1975) 'Attercliffe 1894: how one local Liberal Party failed to meet the challenge of Labour', *Journal of British Studies*, 14, 2, 48–77.

Brown, R. N. R. (1936) 'Sheffield: its rise and growth', *Geography*, 21, 175–84.

Chapman, A. W. (1955) *The Story of a Modern University: A history of the University of Sheffield*, Oxford University Press.

Cole, S. (1882) *Statement on the Work of the (School) Board*, Sheffield School Board, Sheffield.

Cotton, E. L. (1949) *Notes for the History of High Storrs School*, Manuscript in Sheffield Local History Collection, annotated by Mary Walton, (1953).

'Criticus' (1869–1874) 'The Churches and Chapels of Sheffield: Their Ministers and Congregations' Sheffield Local History Collection.

'Current Topics' (1938) *Some Random Recollections: Forty Years of Education in Sheffield*, manuscript in Sheffield Local History Collection.

Davey, A. S. (1931) *The Collegiate School, Sheffield: list of names of pupils and masters 1866–1874*, manuscript in Sheffield Local History Collection.

Doe, V. (1976) 'Some developments in middle class housing in Sheffield 1830–1875', in Pollard and Holmes (1976), 174–86.

Donnelly, F. K. (1975b) 'The destruction of the Sheffield School of Anatomy in 1835: a popular response to class legislation', *THAS*, 10, 167–72.

Donnelly, F. K. and Baxter, J. L. (1975) 'Sheffield and the English revolutionary tradition, 1791–1820', *International Review of Social History*, 20, 398–423.

Earnshaw, S. (1857) 'Upon the state of education among the working classes of the Parish of Sheffield', in A. Hill (1857), 71–6.

Earnshaw, S. (1861) *The Church and the Artisan*, London.

Easton, A. P. (1900) 'Wesley College, Sheffield', *The Temple Magazine*, 558–61.

Eltringham, G. J. (1939) 'The Lancasterian Schools in Sheffield', *THAS*, 5, 147–52.

Favell, C. (1836) *The Value and Importance of Mechanics Institutions*, Sheffield.

Flinn, M. W. and Birch, A. (1954) 'The English Steel Industry before 1856: with special reference to the development of the Yorkshire steel industry', *Yorkshire Bulletin of Economic and Social Research*, 6, 2, 163–77.

Fowler, W. S. (1961a) *A Study in Radicalism and Dissent. The Life and Times of Henry Joseph Wilson 1833–1914*, The Epworth Press, London.

Fowler, W. S. (1963) 'Why Chamberlain fought and lost in Sheffield', *THAS*, 8, 152–6.

Furness, J. M. (1893) *Record of Municipal Affairs in Sheffield, 1843–1893*, Sheffield.

Furness, H. S. (1931) *Memories of Sixty Years*, Methuen, London.

Gaskell, S. M. (1971) 'Yorkshire estate development and the freehold land societies in the nineteenth century', *Yorkshire Archeological Journal*, 43, 158–65.

Gledstone, J. P. (1867) *Public Opinion and Public Spirit in Sheffield*, Sheffield.

Goodfellow, A. W. (1942) 'Sheffield's waterway to the sea', *THAS*, 5, 246–53.

Grant, A. J. (1950) *Steel and Ships, the History of John Brown's*, Michael Joseph, London.

Grant, B. (1864) *The Sheffield Flood and its Lessons*, London.

Hall, A. J. (1937) 'The coming of a University: Dawn 1822–1879', *Sheffield University Magazine*, December, 9–12.

Hall, A. J. (1938) 'The coming of a University: Break of Day 1879–1905', *Sheffield University Magazine*, June, 77–83.

Hall, T. W. (1937) 'The Late Sidney Oldall Addy M.A.' *THAS*, 4, 221–5.

Harrison, S. (1864) *A Complete History of the Great Flood at Sheffield*, Sheffield and London.

Hattersley, R. (1976) *Goodbye to Yorkshire*, Gollancz, London.

Hawson, H. K. (1968) *Sheffield: the Growth of a City*, J. W. Northend, Sheffield.

Helps, A. (1845) *The Claims of Labour*, Sheffield.

Hicks, W. M. (1886) *Local Colleges and Higher Education for the People*, Sheffield.

Higginbotham, M. (1943) 'A. J. Mundella and the Sheffield election of 1868', *THAS*, 5, 285–93.

Hill, F. H. (1860) 'An account of some trade combinations in Sheffield', *NAPSS*.

Holland, G. C. (1843) *The Vital Statistics of Sheffield*, Sheffield.

Holland, J. and Everett, J. (1854–1856) *Memoirs of the life and writings of James Montgomery*, 7 vols, Sheffield.

Hopkinson, G. C. (1950) 'The development of inland navigation in South Yorkshire and North Derbyshire, 1697–1850', *THAS*, 7, 229–51.

Hopkinson, G. C. (1971) 'Road development in South Yorkshire and North Derbyshire 1700–1850', *THAS*, 10, 14–30.

Hurst, M. (1972) 'Liberal versus Liberal: the General Election of 1874 in Bradford and Sheffield', *Historical Journal*, 15, 4, 669–713.

Hurst, M. (1974a) 'Liberal versus Liberal 1874: a rebuttal', *Historical Journal*, 17, 1, 162–4.

Hurst, M. (1976) 'Liberal versus Liberal 1874: a surrebuttal', *Historical Journal*, 19, 4, 1001–4.

Inkster, I. (1972) 'A note on itinerant science lecturers 1790–1850', *Annals of Science*, 3, 235–6.

Inkster, I. (1973a) 'The development of a scientific community in Sheffield, 1790–1850: a network of people and interests', *THAS*, 10, 99–131.

Inkster, I. (1973b) 'Science instruction for youth in the industrial revolution – the informal network in Sheffield', *Vocational Aspect*, 25, 91–8.

Inkster, I. (1975) 'Science and Mechanics' Institutes 1820–50: the case of Sheffield', *Annals of Science*, 32, 5, 451–74.

Inkster, I. (1976a) 'The social context of an educational movement: a revisionist approach to the English Mechanics' Institutes', *Oxford Review of Education*, 2, 3, 277–307.

Inkster, I. (1976b) 'Culture, institutions and urbanity: the itinerant science lecturer in Sheffield 1790–1850', in Pollard and Holmes (1976), 218–32.

Inkster, I. (1977) 'Marginal men: aspects of the social role of the medical community in Sheffield 1790–1850', in Woodward and Richards (1977), 128–63.

Jones, G. P. (1932) *The Development of Adult Education in Sheffield*.

Jones, G. P. (1937) 'The Political Reform Movement in Sheffield', *THAS*, 4, 57–68.

Jones, K. V. (1915) *The Life of John Viriamu Jones*, Smith, Elder, London.

Leader, J. D. (1897) *The Records of the Burgery of Sheffield Commonly called the Town Trust*, Sheffield.

Leader, J. D. and Snell, S. (1897) *Sheffield General Infirmary 1797–1897*, Sheffield.

Leader, R. E. (1875) *Reminiscences of Old Sheffield*, Sheffield.

Leader, R. E. (1897) *Life and Letters of John Arthur Roebuck*, Sheffield.

Leader, R. E. (1905) *Sheffield in the Eighteenth Century*, Sheffield.

Leader, R. E. (1906) *History of the Company of Cutlers in Hallamshire*, 2 vols, Sheffield.

Linton, D. L. (ed.) (1956) *Sheffield and its Region: a Scientific and Historical Survey*, British Association, Sheffield.

Livesey, J. (1840) *Mechanics Churches: a letter to Sir Robert Peel on church extension in the populous towns and manufacturing districts*, London.

Lloyd, G. I. H. (1913) *The Cutlery Trades*, London.

Mackerness, E. D. (1976) 'Early history of Sheffield School of Art' in Pollard and Holmes (1976), 247–61.

Mathers, H. (1979a) 'Preparation for power: the Sheffield Labour Party from 1890 to 1926', *Bulletin of the Society for the Study of Labour History*, 39, 12.

Matthews, W. G. (1977) 'The Free Writing School, Sheffield and its Masters', *THAS*, 10, 280–5.

Mee, L. G. (1975) *Aristocratic Enterprise: the Fitzwilliam Undertakings 1795–1857*, Blackie, London.

Mendelson, J. *et al.* (n.d.) *The Sheffield Trades and Labour Council 1858–1958*. Sheffield Trades and Labour Council, Sheffield.

Murphy, J. T. (1917) *The Workers' Committee: an outline of its principles and structures*, Sheffield Workers' Committee, Sheffield.

Odom, W. (1917) *Fifty Years of Sheffield Church Life 1866–1916*, J. W. Northend, Sheffield.

Odom, W. (1926) *Hallamshire Worthies*, J. W. Northend, Sheffield.

Olsen, D. J. (1973) 'House upon house: estate development in London and Sheffield', in Dyos and Wolff (1973), 333–57.

Osborn, F. M. (1952) *The Story of the Mushets*, Nelson, London.

Parker, J. (1830) *A Statement of the Population etc. etc., of the Town of Sheffield*, Sheffield.

Parsons, C. (1978) *Schools in an Urban Community: A Study of Carbrook 1870–1965*, Routledge & Kegan Paul, London.

Pawson and Brailsford (1862) *Illustrated Guide to Sheffield and Neighbourhood*, Sheffield.

Pollard, S. (1954) *Three Centuries of Sheffield Steel: the story of a family business*, Marsh Bros, Sheffield.

Pollard, S. (1957) 'The ethics of the Sheffield outrages', *THAS*, 7, 118–39.

Pollard, S. (1959) *A History of Labour in Sheffield*, Liverpool University Press.

Pollard, S. and Holmes, C. (eds) (1976) *Essays in the Economic and Social History of South Yorkshire*, South Yorkshire County Council Recreation, Culture and Health Department, Barnsley.

Porter, W. S. (1928) *The Medical School in Sheffield 1828–1928*, J. W. Northend, Sheffield.

Porter, W. S. (1932) *Sheffield Literary and Philosophical Society 1822–1832*, J. W. Northend, Sheffield.

Roberts, D. E. (1979) *The Sheffield Gas Undertaking*, East Midland Gas, Leicester.

Rodgers, P. (1840) *A lecture on the origin, progress and results of Sheffield Mechanics' Institute*, Sheffield.

Rowbotham, S. (1976) 'Anarchism in Sheffield in the 1890's', in Pollard and Holmes (1976), 159–72.

Rowett, J. (1979) 'Sheffield under Labour control', *Bulletin of the Study of Labour History*, 39, 12–13.

Rowley, G. (1975) 'Landownership in the spatial growth of towns: A Sheffield example', *East Midland Geographer*, 6, 4, 200–13.

Sadler, M. E. (1903) *Report on Secondary and Higher Education*, Sheffield Local History Collection.

Salt, J. (1960a) 'The Sheffield Hall of Science', *Vocational Aspect*, 12, 25.

Salt, J. (1966) 'The creation of the Sheffield Mechanics' Institute: social pressures and educational advance in an industrial town', *Vocational Aspect*, 18, 143–9.

Salt, J. (1967a) *Chartism in South Yorkshire*, University of Sheffield Local History Publications.

Salt, J. (1967b) 'Early Sheffield Sunday Schools and their educational importance', *THAS*, 9, 179–84.

Salt, J. (1968) 'Local manifestations of the Urquhartite movement', *International Review of Social History*, 13, 350–63.

Salt, J. (1971a) 'Experiments in anarchism 1850–4', *THAS*, 10, 37–53.

Salt, J. (1971b) 'Isaac Ironside 1808–1870: The motives of a radical educationalist', *British Journal of Educational Studies*, 19, 183–201.

Sanderson, M. (1978) 'The Professor as Consultant: Oliver Arnold and the British Steel Industry 1900–1914', *Economic History Review*, 31, 4, 585–60.

Scott, J. D. (1962) *Vickers, a History*, Weidenfeld & Nicolson, London.

Seed, T. A. (1907) *Norfolk Street Wesleyan Chapel, Sheffield*, Sheffield.

Seed, T. A. (1952) *Pioneers for a Century 1852–1952*, S. Osborn, Sheffield.

Short, J. L. (1866) 'The politico-economic value of a sound elementary education of the wage-class', *Trans. NAPSS*, Sheffield Meeting 1865, 347–56.

Skinner, E. F. (1932) *A Short History of the Sheffield Royal Hospital 1832–1932*, Greenup & Thompson, Sheffield.

Smith, E. A. (1975) *Whig Principles and Party Politics*, Manchester University Press.

Smith, G. C. M. (1912) *The Story of the People's College 1842–78*, Sheffield.

Smith, G. C. M. (1937) 'Sheffield Grammar School', *THAS*, 4, 145–60.

Snell, S. (1890) *History of the Medical Societies of Sheffield*, Sheffield.

Stainton, J. H. (1924) *The Making of Sheffield 1865–1914*, E. Weston, Sheffield.

Taylor, J. (1938) 'A nineteenth-century experiment in adult education: The Sheffield Mechanics' Library and Sheffield Mechanics' Institute', *Adult Education*, 2, 151–60.

Thornes, V. (1976) *William Dronfield 1826–1894*, Sheffield City Libraries, Sheffield.

Trebilcock, C. (1971) *The Vickers Brothers: Armaments and Enterprise 1854–1916*, Europa Publications, London.

Vickers, J. E. (1972) *Old Sheffield Town: A Historical Miscellany*, E. P. Publishing, Wakefield.

Wallis, P. J. (1950) 'King Edward VII School Sheffield', in *Yorkshire Illustrated*, 13–15.

Wallis, P. J. (1953) *Sheffield Collegiate School 1836–1885: a biographical register*, Sheffield Local History Collection.

Wallis, P. J. (1957) 'Sheffield Church Burgesses: a biographical register', *THAS*, 7, 51–62, 144–57, 194–9, 344–58.

Walton, M. (1968) *Sheffield: its story and achievements*, S. R. Publishers and Sheffield Corporation, Sheffield.

Warren, K. (1964) 'The Sheffield rail trade, 1861–1930: an episode in the locational history of the British steel industry', *Transactions of Institute of British Geographers*, 34, 131–57.

Wickham, E. R. (1957) *Church and People in an Industrial City*, Lutterworth Press, London.

Wigfall, J. R. (1937) 'Sheffield Grammar School', *THAS*, 4, 283–300.

Willis, T. W. (1926) '150 Years of Progress, 1776–1926', *House of Saben*, 12, 12, 24–36.

Wilson, J. (1866a) 'The extension of the Factory Acts to other industrial occupations', *Trans. NAPSS*, Sheffield Meeting 1865, 302–8.

Wilson, J. (1866b) 'What are the best means of establishing a system of authoritative arbitration between employers and employed in cases of strikes and lock-out', *Trans. NAPSS*, Sheffield Meeting 1865, 476–80.

Wright, D. G. (1973) 'Liberal versus Liberal 1874: Some comments', *Historical Journal*, 16, 3, 697–703.

I(b) BIRMINGHAM

Allen, G. C. (1929) *The Industrial Development of Birmingham and the Black Country*, Allen & Unwin, London.

Avery, T. (1866) 'On the municipal expenditure of the Borough of Birmingham', *Journal of Statistical Society*, 29, 78–91.

Badham, C. (1864) *Thoughts on classical and commercial education*, Birmingham.

Barnsby, G. J. (1977) *The Working-class Movement in the Black Country 1750–1867*, Integrated Publishing Services, Wolverhampton.

Beggs, T. (1853) 'Freehold Land Societies', *Journal of Statistical Society*, 16, 338–46.

Behagg, C. (1979) 'Custom, class and change: the trade societies of Birmingham', *Social History*, 4, 3, 455–80.

Best, R. D. (1940) *Brass Chandelier*, Allen & Unwin, London.

Best, R. H. *et al.* (1905) *The Brass Workers of Berlin and Birmingham: A Comparison*, Birmingham.

Best, R. H. (1907) *The City of Birmingham and Society: its future aims*, Birmingham.

Birmingham Statistical Society (1840) 'Report on the state of education in Birmingham' *Journal of the Statistical Society*, 3, 25–49.

Briggs, A. (1948) 'Thomas Attwood and the economic background of the Birmingham Political Union', *Cambridge Historical Journal*, 9, 2, 190–216.

Briggs, A. (1949) 'Press, public and early nineteenth century Birmingham', *Dugdale Society Occasional Papers*, 8.

Briggs, A. (1950) 'Social structure and politics in Birmingham and Lyons', *British Journal of Sociology*, 1, 1, 67–80.

Briggs, A. (1952) *History of Birmingham Volume 2: Borough and City 1865–1938*, Oxford University Press.

British Association (1913) *Handbook for Birmingham*, Birmingham.

Browne, H. (1974) *Joseph Chamberlain, Radical and Imperialist*, Longman, London.

Bryman, A. (ed.) (1976) *Religion in the Birmingham Area: Essays in the Sociology of Religion*, University of Birmingham, Institute for the Study of Worship and Religious Architecture, Birmingham.

Buckley, J. K. (1929) *Joseph Parkes of Birmingham*, Methuen, London.

Bunce, J. T. (1857) 'On feeding and evening schools, the former as a means of prolonging, the latter as a means of resuming education', in A. Hill (1857), 277–87.

Bunce, J. T. (1858) *The Birmingham General Hospital and Triennial Musical Festivals*, Birmingham.

Bunce, J. T. (1865) 'On the statistics of crime in Birmingham as compared with other large towns', *Journal of Statistical Society*, 28, 518–26.

Bunce, J. T. (1878) *History of the Corporation of Birmingham*, vol. 1, Birmingham.

Bunce, J. T. (1885) *History of the Corporation of Birmingham*, vol. 2, Birmingham.

Bunce, J. T. (1895) *The History of King Edward's Foundation in Birmingham*, Birmingham.

Bunce, J. T. (1899) 'Birmingham life sixty years ago', *Birmingham Weekly Poster*, 13 May.

Burstall, F. W. and Burton, C. G. (1930) *Souvenir History of the Foundation and Development of the Mason Science College and the University of Birmingham*, University of Birmingham.

Cadbury, G. (1915) *Town Planning, with special reference to the Birmingham Schemes*, Longmans Green, London.

Cannadine, D. N. (1975) 'The Calthorpe Family and Birmingham, 1810–1910: a "conservative interest" examined', *Historical Journal*, 18, 4, 725–60.

Cannadine, D. N. (1977c) 'Politics, propaganda and art: the case of two "Worcestershire lads" ', *Midland History*, 4, 2, 97–122.

Chamberlain, J. (1876) *Six Years of Educational Work in Birmingham*, Birmingham School Board, Birmingham.

Chamberlain, J. (1878) 'The Caucus', *Fortnightly Review*, 24, 721–41.

Chapman, S. D. and Bartlett, J. N. (1971) 'The contribution of building clubs and freehold land society to working-class housing in Birmingham', in Chapman (1971), 221–45.

Checkland, S. G. (1948) 'The Birmingham Economists', *Economic History Review*, 1, 1, 1–19.

Childe-Pemberton, W. S. (1909) *Life of Lord Norton 1814–1905*, John Murray, London.

Church, R. A. (1968) *Kenricks in Hardware 1791–1966*, David & Charles, Newton Abbot.

Collings, J. (1870) *An outline of the American School System with Remarks on the Establishment of Common Schools in England*, Birmingham.

Corbett, J. (1966) *The Birmingham Trades Council*, Lawrence & Wishart, London.

Court, W. H. B. (1938) *The Rise of Midland Industries 1600–1838*, Oxford University Press.

Crosskey, H. W. (1885a) 'Report of committee to inquire into provisions for technical instruction now existing in Birmingham', *Proceedings of Birmingham Philosophical Society, 1884*, 4, 2, 326–85.

Crosskey, H. W. (1885b) 'The organisation of education institutions in large manufacturing towns, with special reference to the provision required for technical instruction', *Proceedings of Birmingham Philosophical Society 1884*, 4, 2, 283–302.

Crosskey, H. W. (1886) 'A plea for a Midland University', *Proceedings of Birmingham Philosophical Society 1885*, 5, 2, 231–55.

Dale, A. W. W. (1898) *The Life of R. W. Dale*, London.

Dale, R. W. (1877) 'George Dawson: politician, lecturer and preacher', *Nineteenth Century*, 2, 44–61.

Dalley, W. A. (1914) *The Life Story of W. J. Davis, J.P.*, Birmingham.

Davenport-Hill, R. & F. (1878) *The Recorder of Birmingham, A Memoir of Matthew Hill*, London.

303

Davis, G. B. (1884) 'On the training of teachers for public elementary schools', in Cowper (1884), vol. 4, 14–34.

Dawson, G. (1866) *Inaugural Address at the Opening of the Free Reference Library*, 26 October 1866, Birmingham.

Dent, R. K. (1880) *Old and New Birmingham*, Birmingham.

Dent, R. K. (1894) *The Making of Birmingham*, Birmingham.

Dobson, J. L. (1959) 'The Hill family and educational change in the early nineteenth century. 1. Thomas Wright Hill and the school at Hill Top, Birmingham', *Durham Research Review*, 10, 261–71.

Dobson, J. L. (1960) 'The Hill family and educational change in the early nineteenth century. II. Hazelwood School: the achievement of Rowland Hill and his brothers', *Durham Research Review*, 11, 1–11.

Dolman, F. (1895) 'Joseph Chamberlain's Municipal career', *Fortnightly Review*, 57, 904–12.

Drake, J. (1825) *The Picture of Birmingham*, Birmingham.

Driver, A. H. (1948) *Carr's Lane 1748–1948*, Carr's Lane Church, Birmingham.

Duggan, E. P. (1975) 'Industrialization and the development of urban business communities: research problems, sources and techniques', *Local History*, 2, 457–96.

Edwards, E. (1877) *Personal Recollections of Birmingham and Birmingham Men*, Birmingham.

Edwards, E. (1879) *The Old Taverns of Birmingham*, Birmingham.

Edwards, E. (1880) *John Skirrow Wright: A Memorial Tribute*, Birmingham.

Elkington, F. (1854) 'The present state of the medical profession compared to its state prior to the Apothecaries Act, 1815', introductory address at Sydenham College, Birmingham.

Ferguson, H. (1960) 'The Birmingham Political Union and the Government 1831–2', *Victorian Studies*, 3, 3, 261–76.

Finlayson, G. B. A. M. (1973) 'Joseph Parkes of Birmingham 1796–1865: a study in philosophical radicalism', *Bulletin of Institute of Historical Research*, 46, 186–201.

Flick, C. (1975) 'Muntz metal and ships' bottoms', *Transactions of the Birmingham and Warwickshire Archeological Society*, 87, 70–88.

Flick, C. (1978) *The Birmingham Political Union and the Movement for Reform in Britain 1830–1839*, Archon Books, Connecticut.

Fox, A. (1955) 'Industrial relations in nineteenth-century Birmingham', *Oxford Economic Papers*, 7, 57–70.

Fraser, D. (1965) 'Birmingham and the Corn Laws', *Transactions of Birmingham Archeological Society*, 82, 1–20.

Fraser, P. (1966) *Joseph Chamberlain*, Cassell, London.

Gammage, M. T. (1978) 'Art and industry: the origins of the Birmingham School for Jewellers and Silversmiths', *Journal of Educational Administration and History*, 10, 1, 27–35.

Garvin, J. L. and Amery, J. (1934–1969) *Life of Joseph Chamberlain*, 6 vols, Macmillan, London.

Gedge, S. (1858) 'The school and the manufactury—both sides of the question', *Trans. NAPSS*, Birmingham Meeting 1857, 164–71.

Gifford, E. H. (1858) 'Statistics of King Edward's Grammar School, Birmingham', *Trans. NAPSS*, Birmingham Meeting 1857, 130–4.

Gill, C. (1948) 'Birmingham under the Street Commissioners', *University of Birmingham Historical Journal*, 1, 255–87.

Gill, C. (1952) *History of Birmingham: Manor and Borough to 1865*, vol. 1, Oxford University Press.

Gover, W. (1858) 'Our work; or, remarks upon the results of an inquiry into the state of education of the working classes in Birmingham, as affected by the demand for labour, and by other causes', *Trans. NAPSS*, Birmingham Meeting 1857, 171–3.

Gover, W. (1867) *Day School Education in the Borough of Birmingham: a letter to G. Dixon, Mayor*, Birmingham.

Green, C. (1973) 'Birmingham's politics, 1873–1891: the local basis of change', *Midland History*, 2, 2, 84–98.

Greenslade, M. W. (1976) *A History of the County of Stafford (Victoria County History)*, Oxford University Press.

Griffiths, G. (1861) *History of the Free Schools, Colleges, Hospitals and Asylums of Birmingham*, London.

Griffiths, G. (1870) *Going to Markets and Grammar Schools*, 2 vols, London.

Griffiths, P. G. (1976) 'The Caucus and the Liberal Party 1886', *History*, 61, 202, 183–97.

Gulley, E. C. (1926) *Joseph Chamberlain and English Social Politics*, Columbia University Press, New York.

Hastings, R. P. (1979) 'The Birmingham Labour Movement 1918–1945', *Midland History*, 5, 78–92.

Hay, R. (1977) 'Employers and Social Policy in Britain: the evolution of welfare legislation, 1905–1914', *Social History*, 2, 4, 435–55.

Heward, C. (1978) 'The Department of Science and Art: examinations for the masses', unpublished paper, University of Warwick.

Hibbs, C. (1869) 'Trades Unions: are they consistent with the laws of political economy?', Birmingham.

Hill, G. B. (1880) *The Life of Sir Rowland Hill; and the History of Penny Postage*, 2 vols, London.

Hopkins, E. (1974) 'Working-class attitudes to education in the Black Country, in the mid-nineteenth century', *Bulletin of History of Education Society*, 14, 41–6.

Hopkins, E. (1975) 'Tremenheere's Prize Schemes in the mining districts', *Bulletin of History of Education Society*, 15, 34–7.

Howard, C. H. D. (1950) 'Joseph Chamberlain and the Unauthorised Programme', *English Historical Review*, 65, 477–91.

Hughes, A. (1904) *Report on the Secondary and Higher Education of the City*, Birmingham.

Hurst, M. C. (1962) *Joseph Chamberlain and West Midland Politics 1886–1895*, Dugdale Society Occasional Paper no. 15, Oxford.

Hutton, T. W. (1952) *King Edward's School, Birmingham 1552–1952*, Basil Blackwell, Oxford.

Johnson, G. J. (1865) 'On the benefit building societies and freehold land societies of Birmingham', *Journal of Statistical Society*, 28, 506–17.

Johnstone, C. J. (1909) *History of the Johnstones 1191–1909*, Edinburgh.

Jones, J. E. (1909) *A History of the Hospitals and Other Charities of Birmingham*, Birmingham.

Jones, J. E. (1913) 'The voluntary hospitals and Hospital "Saturday" and "Sunday" Funds', in British Association (1913), 292–5.

King, W. (1901) *Arthur Albright, Notes on His Life*, printed for private circulation, Birmingham.

Langford, J. A. (1858) 'Parks and public recreations for the people', *Trans. NAPSS*, Birmingham Meeting 1857, 447–9.

Langford, J. A. (1873) *Modern Birmingham and its Institutions*, 2 vols, Birmingham.

Lapworth, C. (1884) *The Mason College and Technical Education*, Birmingham.

Leinster-Mackay, D. P. (1974) 'Private schools in nineteenth century Warwickshire: part 1', *Warwickshire History*, 2, 5, 3–23.

Levy, E. L. (1909) *The Midland Conservative Club (1883 and after)*, Birmingham.

Macdonald, J. (1886) 'Birmingham: a study from the life', *Nineteenth Century*, 20, 234–54.

McGill, B. (1962) 'Francis Schnadhorst and Liberal Pary Organisation', *Journal of Modern History*, 34, 1, 19–39.

Marcham, A. J. (1976) 'The Birmingham Education Society and the 1870 Education Act', *Journal of Educational Administration and History*, 8, 11–16.

Matthews, C. E. ('Historicus') (1864) *The Grammar School of King Edward the Sixth in Birmingham; its history and suggestions for its improvement*, Birmingham.

Miller, J. C. (1857) Letter to Rev. E. H. Gifford, Head Master of the Grammar School of King Edward VI, Birmingham, on evening schools for the working classes in connection with that foundation, Birmingham.

Miller, J. C. (1858) 'Adult Evening Schools', *Trans NAPSS*, Birmingham Meeting 1857, 194–9.

Mole, D. E. H. (1966) 'John Cale Miller: a Victorian rector of Birmingham', *Journal of Ecclesiastical History*, 17, 1, 95–103.

Mole, D. E. H. (1973) 'Challenge to the Church: Birmingham, 1815–36', in Dyos and Wolf (1973), 815–36.

Mole, D. E. H. (1976) 'Attitudes of churchmen towards society in early Victorian Birmingham', in Bryman (1976), 3–11.

Money, J. (1976) 'The schoolmasters of Birmingham and the West Midlands', *Social History*, 10, 1, 129–53.

Money, J. (1977) *Experience and Identity: Birmingham and the West Midlands 1760–1800*, Manchester University Press.

Morrison, J. T. J. (1926) *William Sands Cox and the Birmingham Medical School*, Cornish Bros. Birmingham.

Moss, D. J. (1978) 'A study in failure: Thomas Attwood, MP for Birmingham 1832–9', *Historical Journal*, 21, 3, 545–70.

Muirhead, J. H. (1911) *Birmingham Institutions*, Cornish Bros, Birmingham.

Musgrove, A. (1918) *A Short History of the Birmingham Law Society 1818–1918*, Birmingham.

Nelson, G. K. (1976) 'Religious groups in a changing social environment', in Bryman (1976), 45–59.

Nettleford, J. S. (1914) *Practical Town Planning*, St Catherine's Press, Birmingham.

Norris, J. P. (1857) 'On the working of the Staffordshire Certificate and Registration scheme and on the best method for its extension to all schools', in A. Hill (1857), 204–15.

Owen, J. M. G. (1902) *The Chronicles of Our Church*, Birmingham.

Pakington, J. S. (1858) 'Address on education', in *Trans. NAPSS*, Birmingham Meeting 1857, 36–43.

Peacock, R. (1976) 'The 1892 Birmingham religious census', in Bryman (1976), 12–27.

Philips, D. (1976) 'The Black Country magistracy 1835–60', *Midland History*, 3, 3, 161–90.

Pike, W. T. (n.d.) *Birmingham at the opening of the Twentieth Century: Contemporary Biographies*, Brighton.

Ralph, J. (1890) 'The best governed city in the world', *Harper's Monthly Magazine*, 81, 99–110.

Ram, R. W. (1976) 'Influences on the patterns of belief and social action among Birmingham Dissenters between 1750 and 1850', in Bryman (1976), 29–43.

Raybould, T. J. (1968) 'Systems of management and administration on the Dudley estates, 1774–1833', *Business History*, 10, 1–11.

Raybould, T. J. (1973) *The Economic Emergence of the Black Country: A Study of the Dudley Estates*, David & Charles, Newton Abbot.

Reeder, D. (1970) 'The making of a garden suburb: Edgbaston in the 19th century', Unpublished paper, Urban History Group.

Rowley, J. (1978) 'Education and the working classes in the Black Country in the mid-nineteenth century: a further dimension', *History of Education Society Bulletin*, 21, 18–24.

Sargant, W. L. (1856) *The Science of Social Opulence*, London.

Sargant, W. L. (1857a) 'On the proposed middle class examinations as a means of stimulating the education of the lower classes', in A. Hill (1857), 334–45.

Sargant, W. L. (1857b) *Economy of the Labouring Classes*, London.

Sargant, W. L. (1866) 'On the vital statistics of Birmingham and seven other large towns', *Journal of Statistical Society*, 29, 92–111.

Sargant, W. L. (1867a) 'On the progress of elementary education', *Journal of Statistical Society*, 30, 80–135.

Sargant, W. L. (1867b) *Recent Political Economy*, London.

Sargant, W. L. (1869) *Essays of a Birmingham Manufacturer*, vol. 1, London and Birmingham.

Sargant, W. L. (1870) *Essays of a Birmingham Manufacturer*, vol. 2, London and Birmingham.

Sargant, W. L. (1871) *Essays of a Birmingham Manufacturer*, vol. 3, London and Birmingham.

Sargant, W. L. (1872) *Essays of a Birmingham Manufacturer*, vol. 4, London and Birmingham.

Sargant, W. L. (1874) *Taxation, past, present and future*, London.

Showell, W. (1885) *Dictionary of Birmingham*, Birmingham republished with an introduction by Asa Briggs (1969), S.R. Publishers.

Simon, A. (1973) 'Joseph Chamberlain and free education in the election of 1885', *History of Education*, 2, 1, 56–78.

Smirke, R. S. (1913–1916) *Reports on Birmingham Trades prepared for use in connection with the Juvenile Employment Exchange*, HMSO, London.

Smith, D. (1976) 'The urban genesis of school bureaucracy: a transatlantic comparison', in Dale *et al.* (1976), 66–77.

Smith, E. (1869) 'The education work of the Birmingham and Midland Institute', *Trans. NAPSS*, Birmingham Meeting 1868, 447–8.

Smith, E. J. (1895) *The New Trades Combination Movement: its principles and methods*, Birmingham.

Smith, E. O. (1895) 'Municipal finance, or local taxation and local expenditure as illustrated by the case of the City of Birmingham', *Journal of Royal Statistical Society*, 58, 327–58.

Smith, J. H. (1903) 'Story of the first teachers' association', in Association of Church School Managers *Conference Guide*, Birmingham.

Smith, W. H. (attrib.) (1831) *The Picture of Birmingham*, Birmingham.

Somerset, E. J. (1934) *The Birth of a University: a Passage in the Life of E. A. Sonnenschein*, Basil Blackwell, Oxford.

Somerville, A. (1848) *The Autobiography of a Working Man*, London.

Stephens, W. B. (ed.) (1964) *Victoria County History*, vol. 7: *The City of Birmingham*, Oxford University Press.

Stephenson, N. (1856) *Birmingham: its educational condition and requirements*, Birmingham.

Stephenson, N. (1857) 'On the nature and administrative machinery of prize schemes', in A. Hill (1857), 125–60.

Stone, J. B. (1880) 'Mr J. B. Stone on the Radical government of the town', Birmingham Conservative Association, Birmingham.

Stone, J. B. (1904) *Annals of the Bean Club*, Birmingham.

Tangye, R. (1889) *'One for All': An Autobiography*, London.

Tholfsen, T. R. (1954) 'The artisan and the culture of early Victorian Birmingham', *Historical Journal*, 4, 2, 146–66.

Tholfsen, T. R. (1959) 'The origins of the Birmingham caucus', *Historical Journal*, 2, 2, 161–84.

Thomas, V. (1855) *Christian Philanthropy exemplified in a memoir of Rev. S. W. Warneford*, Oxford.

Timmins, S. (ed.) (1866) *Birmingham and the Midland Hardware District*, London.

Vance, J. E. (1967) 'Housing the worker: determinative and contingent ties in nineteenth century Birmingham', *Economic Geography*, 43, 2, 95–127.

Vince, C. A. (1902) *History of the Corporation of Birmingham*, vol. 3, Birmingham.

Vincent, E. W. and Hinton, P. (1947) *The University of Birmingham: its history and significance*, Cornish Bros, Birmingham.

Ward, L. O. (1973) 'Joseph Chamberlain and the denominational schools question', *Journal of Educational and Administrative History*, 5, 2, 21–4.

Waterhouse, R. (1954) *The Birmingham and Midland Institute 1854–1954*, published by the institute, Birmingham.

Watson, R. S. (1907) *The National Liberal Federation*, London.

Whitcut, J. (1976) *Edgbaston High School 1876–1976*, published by the governing body, Birmingham.

White, W. (1895) *The Story of Severn Street and Priory First-Day Adult Schools*, Birmingham.

Williams, W. M. (1858) 'On the teaching of social economy', *Trans. NAPSS*, Birmingham Meeting 1857, 509–17.

Wilson, W. W. (1905) *The Life of George Dawson*, Birmingham.

Winfield, J. F. (1857) 'On factory schools', in A. Hill (1857), 140–9.

Wise, M. J. (ed.) (1950) *Birmingham and its Regional Setting: A Scientific Survey*, British Association, Birmingham.

Woods, R. (1978) 'Mortality and sanitary conditions in the "Best governed city in the World" – Birmingham 1870–1910', *Journal of Historical Geography*, 4, 1, 35–56.

Woodward, C. J. (1928) *Short History of the Birmingham and Midland Institute*, unpublished manuscript in Birmingham Reference Collection.

Wright, J. S. (1858) 'On the employment of women in factories in Birmingham', in *Trans. NAPSS*, Birmingham Meeting 1857, 538–44.

Yorke, G. M. (1846) A few words on 'self-improvement' delivered at the opening of St Philip's Literary Institution, Birmingham.

I(c) GENERAL BACKGROUND

Abbott, E. and Campbell, L. (1897) *The Life and Letters of Benjamin Jowett*, London.

Adams, F. (1882) *The Elementary School Contest*, London, republished with an introduction by Asa Briggs, Harvester Press, Brighton (1972).

Anderson, M. (1971) *Family Structure in Nineteenth Century Lancashire*, Cambridge University Press.

Anderson, O. (1967) *A Liberal State at War: English politics and economics during the Crimean War*, Macmillan, London.

Annan, N. G. (1955) 'The intellectual aristocracy', in Plumb (1955), 243–87.

Archer, M. S. (1979) *Social Origins of Educational Systems*, Sage Publications, London.

Armytage, W. H. G. (1948b) 'A. J. Mundella as Vice-President of the Council, and the schools question, 1880–1885', *English Historical Review*, 63, 62–82.

Armytage, W. H. G. (1951) *A. J. Mundella 1825–97: The Liberal background to the Labour movement*, Ernest Benn, London.

Armytage, W. H. G. (1955b) *Civic Universities: Aspects of a British Tradition*, Ernest Benn, London.

Arnold, M. (1862) 'The Twice Revised Code', reprinted in Sutherland (1973), 27–51.

Arnold, M. (1864) 'A French Eton, or middle-class education and the state', reprinted in Sutherland (1973), 115–64.

Arnold, M. (1869) *Culture and Anarchy*, reprinted in Sutherland (1973), 164–269.

Ashby, E. and Anderson, M. (1974) *Portrait of Haldane at Work on Education*, Macmillan, London.

Austen, J. (1816) *Emma*, London, republished by Penguin, Harmondsworth (1966).

Bamford, T. W. (1967) *The Rise of the Public Schools*, Thomas Nelson, London.

Banks, O. L. (1954) 'Morant and the secondary school regulations of 1904', *British Journal of Educational Studies*, 3, 1, 33–41.

Bateman, J. (1883) *The Great Landowners of Great Britain and Ireland*, London; republished by Leicester University Press (1971).

Beasley, W. G. (1972) *The Meiji Restoration*, Stanford University Press.

Bechhofer, F. and Elliot, B. (1976) 'Persistence and change: The petite bourgeoisie in industrial society', *European Journal of Sociology*, 17, 74–9.

Ben-David, J. (1962) 'Universities and academic systems in modern societies', *European Journal of Sociology*, 3, 45–84.

Ben-David, J. (1963–1964) 'Professions in the class system of present-day societies', *Current Sociology*, 12, 247–77.

Bernal, J. D. (1953) *Science and Industry in the Nineteenth Century*, Routledge & Kegan Paul, London.

Bernstein, B. (1965) 'A Socio-linguistic approach to social learning', in Gould (ed.) (1965), 144–68.

Bernstein, B. (1973a) *Class, Codes and Control Volume One: Theoretical Studies towards a Sociology of Language*, Paladin, London.

Bernstein, B. (1973b) 'On the classification and framing of educational knowledge', in Bernstein (1973a), 227–56.

Binfield, C. (1977) *Sit Down to Prayers: studies in English Nonconformity*, Dent, London.

Bishop, A. S. (1971) *The Rise of a Central Authority for English Education*, Cambridge University Press.

Black, E. C. (1963) *The Association: British Extra-Parliamentary Political Organisation 1769–1793*, Oxford University Press, London.

Bornstein, S. *et al.* (eds) (1982) (forthcoming) *The State in Capitalist Europe*, Centre for European Studies Casebook, Allen & Unwin, London.

Bradley, I. (1976) *The Call to Seriousness: the Evangelical Impact on the Victorians*, Cape, London.

Briggs, A. (1963) *Victorian Cities*, Odhams, London.

Briggs, A. (1972) *Victorian People*, University of Chicago Press.

Browning, O. (1884) 'The training by Universities of the public servants of the state', in Cowper (1884), vol. 3, 191–200.

Brundage, A. (1978) *The Making of the New Poor Law: The Politics of Inquiry, Enactment and Implementation*, Hutchinson, London.

Bunting, T. P. (1859) *Life of Jabez Bunting*, vol. 1, London.

Bunting, T. P. (1887) *Life of Jabez Bunting*, vol. 2, London.

Burgess, H. J. (1958) *Enterprise in Education*, National Society, London.

Burn, W. L. (1964) *The Age of Equipoise: a study of the mid-Victorian generation,* Allen & Unwin, London.

Burns, T. R. and Buckley, W. (1976) *Power and Control: Social Structures and their Transformation,* Sage Publications, London.

Burns, W. (1961) *Charles Reade: A Study in Victorian Authorship,* Bookman Association, New York.

Butterworth, H. (1971) 'South Kensington and Whitehall: a conflict of educational purpose', *Journal of Educational Administration and History,* 4, 1, 9–19.

Cairncross, A. K. (1949) 'Internal migration in Victorian England', *Manchester School,* 17, 67–87.

Cane, B. S. (1959) 'Scientific and technical subjects in the curriculum of English secondary schools at the turn of the century', *British Journal of Educational Studies,* 8, 152–64.

Cannadine, D. N. (1977a) 'Victorian cities: how different?', *Social History,* 2, 457–82.

Cannadine, D. N. (1977b) 'Aristocratic indebtedness in the nineteenth century: the case re-opened', *Economic History Review,* 30, 4, 624–50.

Cannadine, D. N. (1978) 'From "feudal" lords to figureheads: urban landownership and aristocratic influence in nineteenth century towns', *Urban History Yearbook,* 23–35.

Cannadine, D. N. (1980) *Lords and Landlords: The aristocracy and the towns 1774–1967,* Leicester University Press.

Cannon, W. F. (1964) 'Scientists and Broad churchmen: an early Victorian intellectual network', *Journal of British Studies,* 4, 65–88.

Cardwell, D. S. (1972) *The Organisation of Science in England,* Heinemann, London.

Chadwick, O. (1966) *The Victorian Church,* A. & C. Black, London.

Chalkin, C. W. (1974) *Provincial Towns of Georgian England,* Edward Arnold, London.

Chapman, S. D. (1971) *A History of Working-class Housing,* David & Charles, Newton Abbot.

Checkland, S. G. (1964) *The Rise of Industrial Society in England 1815–1885,* Longman, London.

Chester, H. (1861) *The Proper Limits of the State's Interference in Education,* London.

Chichester, Dean of (1866) 'Address on Education', *Trans. NAPSS,* Sheffield Meeting 1865, London.

Clark, G. K. (1973) *Churchmen and the Condition of England 1832–1885,* Methuen, London.

Clarke, J. *et al.* (eds) (1979) *Working Class Culture: Studies in History and Theory,* Hutchinson, London.

Clarke, P. F. (1972) 'Electoral sociology of modern Britain', *History,* 57, 31–55.

Clegg, H. A. *et al.* (1964) *A History of British Trade Unions since 1889–1910,* Clarendon Press, Oxford.

Clements, R. V. (1955) 'Trade unions and emigration, 1840–80', *Population Studies,* 9, 167–273.

Codrington, G. R. (1930) 'Yeoman cavalry', *Journal of Society for Army Historical Research,* 10, 134–42.

Cohen, S. (1967) 'Sir Michael E. Sadler and the socio-political analysis of education', *History of Education Quarterly,* 7, 281–94.

Collins, S. (1976) 'Hobhouse, Bosanquet and the state: philosophical ideas and political argument in England 1880–1918', *Past and Present,* 72, 86–111.

Connell, W. F. (1950) *The Educational Thought and Influence of Matthew Arnold*, Routledge & Kegan Paul, London.

Cornford, J. (1963) 'The transformation of conservatism in the late nineteenth century', *Victorian Studies*, 7, 1, 35–66.

Cottrell, P. L. (1980) *Industrial Finance 1830–1914*, Methuen, London.

Cowper, R. (1884) *Proceedings of the international conference on education*, 4 vols, London.

Crossick, G. C. (1977) *The Lower Middle Class in Britain 1870–1914*, Croom Helm, London.

Crowther, J. G. (1965) *Statesmen of Science*, Cresset Press, London.

Cruickshank, M. (1977) 'A defence of the 1902 Act', *History of Education Society Bulletin*, 19, 2–7.

Cullen, M. J. (1975) *The Statistical Movement in Early Victorian Britain*, Harvester Press, Hassocks.

Currie, R. (1967) 'A Micro-theory of Methodist growth', *Proceedings of Wesley Historical Society*, 36, 65–73.

Currie, R. (1968) *Methodism Divided. A Study in the Sociology of Ecumenicalism*, Faber & Faber, London.

Currie, R. (1977) *Churches and Churchgoers: patterns of church growth in the British Isles since 1700*, Clarendon Press, Oxford.

Dale, R. *et al.* (eds) (1976) *Schooling and Capitalism: A Sociological Reader*, Routledge & Kegan Paul and Open University Press, London.

Davis, R. W. (1976) 'Deference and aristocracy at the time of the Great Reform Act', *American Historical Review*, 81, 3, 532–9.

Deane, P. and Cole, W. A. (1962) *British Economic Growth, 1688–1959*, Cambridge University Press.

De Montmorency, J. E. G. (1909) 'Local universities and national education', *Contemporary Review*, 87, 609–18.

Donajgrodski, A. (ed.) (1977) *Social Control in Nineteenth Century Britain*, Croom Helm, London.

Draper, W. H. (1923) *University Extension: a survey of fifty years 1873–1923*, Cambridge University Press.

Duncan, D. (1911) *Life and Letters of Herbert Spencer*, London.

Durkheim, E. (1949) *The Division of Labour in Society*, Free Press, Chicago.

Durkheim, E. (1970) *Suicide*, Routledge & Kegan Paul, London.

Dyos, H. J. (ed.) (1968) *The Study of Urban History*, Edward Arnold, London.

Dyos, H. J. and Wolff, M. (eds) (1973) *The Victorian City*, 2 vols, Routledge & Kegan Paul, London.

Eaglesham, E. (1956) *From School Board to Local Authority*, Routledge & Kegan Paul, London.

Eaglesham, E. (1967) *The Foundation of Twentieth Century Education in England*, Routledge & Kegan Paul, London.

Eagleton, T. (1976) *Criticism and Ideology*, New Left Books, London.

Elias, N. (1978) *What is Sociology?* Hutchinson, London.

Eliot, G. (1866) *Felix Holt the Radical*, Blackwood, London.

Erickson, C. (1949) 'The encouragement of emigration by British trade unions', *Population Studies*, 3, 248–73.

Erickson, C. (1959) *British Industrialists: Steel and Hosiery, 1850–1950*, Cambridge University Press.

Finlayson, G. B. A. M. (1966) 'The politics of municipal reform, 1835', *English Historical Review*, 81, 673–92.

Foster, J. (1968) 'Nineteenth-century towns – a class dimension', in Dyos (1968), 281–99.

Foster, J. (1974) *Class Struggle and the Industrial Revolution: Early industrial capitalism in three English towns*, Weidenfeld & Nicolson, London.

Fowler, W. S. (1961b) 'The influence of idealism upon state provision of education', *Victorian Studies*, 4, 4, 337–44.

Fraser, D. (1973) 'Areas of urban politics: Leeds 1830–80', in Dyos and Wolff (1973), vol. 2.

Fraser, D. (1976a) *Urban Politics in Victorian England: The Structure of Politics in Victorian cities*, Leicester University Press.

Fraser, D. (1976b) *The New Poor Law in the Nineteenth Century*, Macmillan, London.

Fraser, D. (1979a) *Power and Authority in the Victorian City*, Basil Blackwell, Oxford.

Fraser, D. (1979b) 'Politics and the Victorian city', *Urban History Yearbook*, 32–45.

Gadian, D. S. (1978) 'Class consciousness in Oldham and other North West industrial towns, 1830–50', *Historical Journal*, 21, 161–72.

Garrard, J. (1976) *Leaders and Power in Nineteenth Century Salford: A Historical Analysis of Urban Political Power*, University of Salford Research Series Monograph.

Garrard, J. (1977) 'The history of local political power – some suggestions for analysis', *Political Studies*, 25, 2, 252–69.

Giddens, A. (1973) *The Class Structure of the Advanced Societies*, Hutchinson, London.

Giffen, R. (1878) 'Recent accumulations of capital in the United Kingdom', in Giffen, *Essays in Finance, First Series* (1890), London.

Giffen, R. (1889) *The Growth of Capital*, London.

Gilmour, R. (1967) 'The Gradgrind school: political economy in the classroom', *Victorian Studies*, 9, 2, 207–24.

Glennerster, H. and Pryke, R. (1964) *The Public Schools*, Fabian Society, London.

Goldstrom, J. M. (1972) *The Social Content of Education: a study of the working-class school reader in England and Wales*, Irish University Press, Shannon.

Gordon, P. (1977) 'Commitments and developments in the elementary school curriculum 1870–1907', *History of Education*, 6, 1, 43–52.

Gosden, P. H. J. H. (1966) *The Development of Educational Administration in England and Wales*, Martin Robertson, Oxford.

Gould, J. (ed.) (1965) *Penguin Survey of the Social Sciences*, Penguin, Harmondsworth.

Gray, H. B. (1913) *Public Schools and the Empire*, Williams & Northgate, London.

Gray, R. Q. (1976) *The Labour Aristocracy in Victorian Edinburgh*, Clarendon Press, Oxford.

Griffiths, P. (1976) 'Pressure groups and parties in late Victorian England: the National Education League', *Midland History*, 3, 3, 191–205.

Gutchen, R. M. (1961) 'Local improvement and centralization in nineteenth century England', *English Historical Review*, 4, 1, 85–96.

Guttsmann, W. L. (1951) 'The changing social structure of the British political elite, 1886–1935', *British Journal of Sociology*, 2, 122–34.

Guttsmann, W. L. (1954) 'Aristocracy and the middle classes in the British political elite, 1886–1916', *British Journal of Sociology*, 5, 12–32.

Guttsmann, W. L. (1974) 'The British political elite and the class structure', in Stanworth and Giddens (1974), 22–44.

Halsey, A. H. and Trow, M. A. (1971) *The British Academics*, Faber & Faber, London.

Hamburger, J. (1965) *Intellectuals in Politics: John Stuart Mill and the Philosophical Radicals*, Yale University Press, New Haven.

Hamer, D. A. (1972) *Liberal Politics in the Age of Gladstone and Rosebury: A Study in Leadership and Policy*, Clarendon Press, Oxford.

Hamer, D. A. (1977) *The Politics of Electoral Pressure*, Harvester Press, Brighton.

Hanham, H. J. (1960) 'The sale of honours in late Victorian England', *Victorian Studies*, 3, 3, 277–89.

Harries-Jenkins, G. (1977) *The Army in Victorian Society*, Routledge & Kegan Paul, London.

Harrison, J. F. C. (1961) *Living and Learning: A Study of the English Adult Education Movement*, Routledge & Kegan Paul, London.

Harrison, R. (1972) *Before the Socialists: studies in labour and politics 1861–1881*, Routledge & Kegan Paul, London.

Henderson, W. O. (1966) *J. C. Fischer and his Diary of Industrial England 1814–1851*, Frank Cass, London.

Hennock, E. P. (1963) 'Finance and Politics in urban local government', *Historical Journal*, 6, 2, 212–25.

Hennock, E. P. (1971) 'The sociological premises of the first Reform Act: a critical note', *Victorian Studies*, 14, 321–7.

Hennock, E. P. (1973) *Fit and Proper Persons: Ideal and reality in nineteenth-century urban government*, Edward Arnold, London.

Hennock, E. P. (1976) 'Poverty and social theory in England: the experience of the 1880's', *Social History*, 1, 1, 67–91.

Herrick, F. H. (1945) 'The origins of the National Liberal Federation', *Journal of Modern History*, 17, 2, 116–29.

Hill, A. (ed.) (1857) *Essays Upon Educational Subjects*, London, reprinted by Woburn Books, London.

Hinton, H. (1854) *The Case of the Manchester Educationists*, vol. 2, Manchester.

History of Education Society (1970) *Studies in the Government and Control of Education since 1860*, Methuen, London.

Hobsbawm, E. J. (1964) *Labouring Men*, Weidenfeld & Nicolson, London.

Hollis, P. (ed.) (1974) *Pressure From Without*, Edward Arnold, London.

Holloway, S. W. F. (1964) 'Medical education in England 1830–58: a sociological analysis', *History*, 39, 299–324.

Hook, W. F. (1846) *On the Means of Rendering More Efficient the Education of the People*, A letter to the Lord Bishop of St. David's, London.

Hopkins, T. K. and Wallerstein, I. (1957) 'The comparative study of national societies', *Social Science Information*, 6, 5, 22–58.

Hughes, E. (1952) *North Country Life in the Eighteenth Century*, vol. 1, Oxford University Press.

Hughes, E. (1965) *North Country Life in the Eighteenth Century*, vol. 2, Oxford University Press.

Hughes, K. M. (1960) 'A political party and education. Reflections on the Liberal Party educational policy', *British Journal of Educational Studies*, 8, 2, 112–26.

Hurt, J. S. (1971) 'Professor West on early nineteenth century education', *Economic History Review*, 24, 624–32.

Hurt, J. S. (1972) *Education in Evolution: Church, State and Popular Education 1800–1870*, Paladin, London.

Hurt, J. S. (1979) *Elementary Schooling and the Working Class*, Routledge & Kegan Paul, London.

Jenks, L. H. (1927) *The Migration of British Capital to 1875*, Cape, New York.

Jewson, N. (1974) 'Medical knowledge and the patronage system in eighteenth century England', *Sociology*, 8, 3, 369–85.

Johnson, J. R. B. (1970) 'Educational policy and social control in early Victorian England', *Past and Present*, 49, 96–119.

Johnson, J. R. B. (1972) 'Administrators in education before 1870', in
Sutherland (1972a), 110–38.

Johnson, J. R. B. (1976a) 'Barrington Moore, Perry Anderson and English Social
Development', *Working Papers in Cultural Studies*, Centre of Contemporary
Cultural Studies, University of Birmingham.

Johnson, J. R. B. (1976b) 'Notes on the schooling of the English working class
1780–1950', in R. Dale *et al.* (1976), 44–54.

Johnson, J. R. B. (1977) 'Educating the educators: "experts" and the state
1833–1839', in Donajgrodski (1977), 77–107.

Jones, D. K. (1977) *The Making of the Education System 1851–81*, Routledge &
Kegan Paul, London.

Kamatsu, P. A. (1972) *Meiji 1868: Revolution and Counter-Revolution in Japan*,
Allen & Unwin, London.

Kargon, R. H. (1977) *Science in Victorian Manchester*, Manchester University
Press.

Kearney, H. F. (1970) *Scholars and Gentlemen: Universities and Society 1500–1700*,
Faber & Faber, London.

Kellett, J. R. (1969) *The Impact of Railways on Victorian Cities*, Routledge & Kegan
Paul, London.

Knox, E. A. (1935) *Reminiscences of an Octogenarian, 1847–1934*, Hutchinson,
London.

Lambert, R. (1962) 'Central and local relations in mid-Victorian England: the
Local Government Act office 1858–71', *Victorian Studies*, 6, 121–50.

Laqueur, T. W. and Sanderson, J. M. (1974) 'Literacy and social mobility in the
industrial revolution in England (debate)', *Past and Present*, 64, 96–112.

Laqueur, T. W. (1976) *Religion and Respectability. Sunday Schools and Working-
Class Culture*, Yale University Press, New Haven.

Law, C. M. (1967) 'The growth of urban population in England and Wales,
1801–1911', *Transactions of Institute of British Geographers*, 41, 125–43.

Lawton, R. (1958) 'Population movements in the West Midlands 1841–1861',
Geography, 63, 164–76.

Lawton, R. (1968) 'Population changes in England and Wales in the later
nineteenth century: analysis of trends by registration districts', *Transactions of
Institute of British Geographers*, 44, 55–74.

Layton, D. (1973) *Science for the People: the origins of the school science curriculum in
England*, Allen & Unwin, London.

Lee, J. M. (1963) *Social Leaders and Public Persons: a study of County Government in
Cheshire since 1888*, Clarendon Press, Oxford.

Lees, L. H. (1979) 'Strikes and the urban hierarchy in English industrial towns,
1842–1901', paper presented at Urban History Group, Sheffield.

Lilley, A. L. (1906) *Sir Joshua Fitch: An Account of his Life and Work*, London.

Lockwood, D. (1964) 'Social integration and system integration', in G. K.
Zollschan and W. Hirsch, (1964), 244–56.

London Trades Council (1861) *Trades' Union Directory*, London.

Lyons, N. (1976) 'The clergy in education, career structures in the 1830's',
Journal of Educational Administration and History, 8, 6–10.

McCann, W. P. (1970) 'Trade unionists, artisans and the 1870 Education Act',
British Journal of Educational Studies, 18, 2, 134–50.

McCann, W. P. (ed.) (1977) *Popular Education and Socialization in the Nineteenth
Century*, Methuen, London.

McCarthy, P. J. (1964) *Matthew Arnold and Three Classes*, Columbia University
Press, New York.

McCarthy, P. J. (1971) 'Reading Victorian prose; Arnold's Culture and its
enemies', *University of Toronto Quarterly*, 40, 119–35.

McCloskey, D. N. (1973) *Economic Maturity and Entrepreneurial Decline: British Iron and Steel 1870–1913*, Harvard University Press, Cambridge, Mass.

Macdonald, K. I. (1974) 'The public elementary school pupil within the secondary school system of the 1890's', *Journal of Educational and History Administration*, 6, 1, 19–26.

McHugh, P. (1980) *Prostitution and Victorian Social Reform*, Croom Helm, London.

Mack, E. C. (1938) *Public Schools and British Opinion, 1780–1860*, Methuen, London.

Mack, E. C. (1971) *Public Schools and British Opinion since 1860*, Greenwood Press, Westport, Conn.

MacLeod, R. M. (1972) 'Resources of Science in Victorian England: the endowment of science movement, 1868–1900', in P. Mathias (1972), 111–66.

Maclure, J. S. (1979) *Educational Documents: England and Wales 1816 to the present day*, Methuen, London.

McMenemey, W. H. (1959) *The Life and Times of Sir Charles Hastings, Founder of the British Medical Association*, Livingstone Press, Edinburgh.

Malchow, H. L. (1976) 'Trade unions and emigration in late Victorian England: a national lobby for state aid', *Journal of British Studies*, 15, 2, 92–116.

Mathews, H. F. (1949) *Methodism and the Education of the People 1791–1851*, Epworth Press, London.

Mathias, P. (1969) *The First Industrial Nation: An Economic History of Britain 1700–1914*, Methuen, London.

Mathias, P. (1972) *Science and Society 1600–1900*, Cambridge University Press.

Matthew, H. C. G. (1976) 'The franchise factor in the rise of the Labour Party', *English Historical Review*, 91, 723–52.

Mayer, A. J. (1975) 'The lower middle classes as a historical problem', *Journal of Modern History*, 47, 409–36.

Meller, H. E. (1976) *Leisure and the Changing City 1870–1914*, Routledge & Kegan Paul, London.

Miall, E. (1842) *The Nonconformist's Sketch Book*, London.

Middlemas, K. (1979) *Politics in Industrial Society: The Experience of the British System since 1911*, Andre Deutsch, London.

Miller, F. (1979) 'The British unemployment assistance crisis 1935', *Journal of Contemporary History*, 14, 2, 329–52.

Millerson, G. (1964) *The Qualifying Association: A study in Professionalisation*, Routledge & Kegan Paul, London.

Mitchell, B. R. and Deane, P. (1962) *Abstract of British Historical Statistics*, Cambridge University Press.

Montgomery, R. J. (1965) *Examinations: An Assessment of Their Evolution as Administrative Devices in England*, Longmans, London.

Moore, B. (1969) *Social Origins of Dictatorship and Democracy*, Penguin, Harmondsworth.

Moore, B. (1978) *Injustice: The Social Basis of Obedience and Revolt*, Sharpe, New York.

Moore, D. C. (1966) 'Concession or cure: the sociological premises of the First Reform Act', *Historical Journal*, 9, 1, 39–59.

Moore, D. C. (1971) 'Reply to Hennock (1971)', *Victorian Studies*, 14, 328–37.

Moore, D. C. (1976) *The Politics of Deference*, Harvester Press, Hassocks.

Moorhouse, H. F. (1973) 'The political incorporation of the British working class: an interpretation', *Sociology*, 7, 3, 341–59.

Moorhouse, H. F. (1978) 'The Marxist theory of the labour aristocracy', *Social History*, 3, 1, 61–82.

Moorhouse, H. F. (1979) 'History, sociology and the quiescence of the British working class: a reply to Reid', *Social History*, 4, 3, 481–93.

More, C. (1980) *Skill and the English Working Class 1870–1914*, Croom Helm, London.

Morris, R. J. (1976) 'In search of the urban middle class', *Urban History Yearbook*, 3, 15–20.

Mouzelis, N. (1974) 'Social and system integration: some reflections on a fundamental distinction', *British Journal of Sociology*, 25, 4, 395–409.

Mowat, C. L. (1968) *Britain Between the Wars 1918–1940*, Methuen, London.

Muirhead, J. H. (1942) *Reflections by a Journeyman in Philosophy on the Movements of Thought and Practice in his Time* (ed. J. W. Harvey), Allen & Unwin, London.

Murray, D. (1959) *Steel Curtain: A Biography of the British Iron and Steel Industry*, Pall Mall Press, London.

Musgrave, P. W. (1967) *Technical change, the Labour Force and Education: A Study of the British and German Iron and Steel Industries*, Pergamon Press, Oxford.

Musgrove, F. (1959) 'Middle-class education and employment in the nineteenth century', *Economic History Review*, 12, 99–130.

Musgrove, F. (1961) 'Middle-class education and employment in the nineteenth century: a rejoinder', *Economic History Review*, 14, 320–9.

NAPSS (1860) *Trade Societies and Strikes*, London.

Neale, R. S. (1972) *Class and Ideology in the Nineteenth Century*, Routledge & Kegan Paul, London.

Newman, C. (1957) *The Evolution of Medical Education in England*, Oxford University Press.

Norris, G. M. (1978) 'Industrial paternalist capitalism and local labour markets', *Sociology*, 12, 3, 469–89.

Norris, J. M. (1958) 'Samuel Garbett and the early development of industrial lobbying in Great Britain', *Economic History Review*, 2, 10, 450–60.

Nossiter, T. J. (ed.) (1972a) *Imagination and Precision in the Social Sciences*, Faber & Faber, London.

Nossiter, T. J. (1972b) 'Shopkeeper radicalism in the nineteenth century', in Nossiter (1972a), 407–38.

Nossiter, T. J. (1975) *Influence, Opinion and Political Idioms in Reformed England; case studies from the North East*, Harvester Press, Hassocks.

Parkin, F. (1976) 'System contradiction and political transformation', in Burns and Buckley (1976), 127–46.

Parsons, R. H. (1947) *A History of the Institution of Mechanical Engineers, 1847–1947*, IME, London.

Payne, P. L. (1967) 'The emergence of the large scale company in Great Britain 1870–1914', *Economic History Review*, 20, 519–42.

Payne, P. L. (1974) *British Entrepreneurship in the Nineteenth Century*, Macmillan, London.

Paz, D. G. (1976) 'Working-class education and the state, 1839–1849: the sources of government policy', *Journal of British Studies*, 16, 1, 129–52.

Peel, J. D. Y. (1971) *Herbert Spencer, The Evolution of a Sociologist*, Heinemann, London.

Pelling, H. (1967) *Social Geography of British Elections*, Macmillan, London.

Perkin, H. J. (1961) 'Middle-class education and employment in the nineteenth century: a critical note', *Economic History Review*, 14, 1, 122–30.

Perkin, H. J. (1969) *The Origins of Modern English Society 1780–1880*, Routledge & Kegan Paul, London.

Philips, D. (1975) 'Riots and public order in the Black Country 1835–60', in Quinault and Stevenson (1975), 141–80.

Philips, D. (1977) *Crime and Authority in Victorian England*, Croom Helm, London.

Pickard, O. G. (1948) 'Office work and education 1848–1948', *Vocational Aspect*, 1, 221–43.

Plumb, J. H. (ed.) (1955) *Studies in Social History: A Tribute to G. M. Trevelyan*, Longmans, London.

Pollard, S. (1968) *The Genesis of Modern Management*, Penguin, Harmondsworth.

Pollard, S. and Crossley, D. W. (1968) *The Wealth of Britain 1085–1966*, Batsford, London.

Porter, J. H. (1969) 'Management, competition and industrial relations: the Midlands Manufacturers Iron Trade 1873–1914', *Business History*, 11, 1, 37–47.

Pumphrey, R. E. (1959) 'The introduction of industrialists into the British peerage: a study in adaptation of a social institution', *American Historical Review*, 65, 1, 1–16.

Quinault, R. (1975) 'The Warwickshire county magistracy and public order, c. 1830–1870', in Stevenson and Quinault, (1975).

Quinault, R. and Stevenson, J. (eds) (1975) *Popular Protest and Public Order: Six studies in British History 1790–1910*, Allen & Unwin, London.

Ratcliffe, B. M. and Chaloner, W. H. (1977) *A French Sociologist looks at Britain: Gustave d'Eichthal and British Society in 1828*, Manchester University Press.

Razzel, P. E. and Wainwright, R. W. (1973) *The Victorian Working Class*, Frank Cass, London.

Reade, C. (1857) *It is Never Too Late to Mend*, Bentley, London.

Reade, C. (1911) *Put Yourself in His Place*, Collins, London (originally published in 1870).

Reader, W. J. (1966) *Professional Men*, Weidenfeld & Nicolson, London.

Redford, A. (1964) *Labour Migration in England 1800–1850*, 2nd edn, revised by W. O. Chaloner, Manchester University Press.

Reeder, D. A. (1980) *Educating our Masters*, Leicester University Press.

Reid, A. (1978) 'Politics and economics in the formation of the British working class: a response to H. F. Moorhouse', *Social History*, 3, 3, 347–61.

Reid, D. A. (1976) 'The decline of Saint Monday 1766–1876', *Past and Present*, 71, 76–101.

Reid, W. (1899) *Memoirs and Correspondence of Lyon Playfair*, London.

Richter, M. (1964) *The Politics of Conscience: T. H. Green and His Age*, Weidenfeld & Nicolson, London.

Richter, M. (1966) 'Intellectuals and class alienation', *European Journal of Sociology*, 7, 1–26.

Ringer, F. K. (1979) *Education and Society in Modern Europe*, Indiana University Press, Bloomington and London.

Roach, J. P. C. (1959) 'Victorian universities and the national intelligentsia', *Victorian Studies*, 2, 2, 131–50.

Roach, J. P. C. (1970) *Public Examinations in England 1850–1900*, Cambridge University Press.

Roberts, B. C. (1958) *The Trades Union Congress 1868–1921*, Allen & Unwin, London.

Rothblatt, S. (1968) *The Revolution of the Dons: Cambridge and Society in Victorian England*, Faber & Faber, London.

Rothblatt, S. (1974) 'The student sub-culture and the examination system in early 19th century Oxbridge', in Stone (1974), 247–303.

Rubinstein, W. D. (1974) 'British millionaires, 1809–1949', *Bulletin of the Institute of Historical Research*, 47, 202–23.

Rubinstein, W. D. (1977a) 'Wealth, elites and the class structure of modern Britain', *Past and Present*, 76, 99–126.

Rubinstein, W. D. (1977b) 'The Victorian middle classes: wealth, occupation and geography', *Economic History Review*, 30, 602–23.

Sanderson, M. (1972) *The Universities and British Industry 1850–1970*, Routledge & Kegan Paul, London.

Sanford, J. L. and Townsend, M. (1865) *The Great Governing Families of England*, London.

Seabourne, M. (1971) *The English School: Architecture and Organisation, 1370–1870*, Routledge & Kegan Paul, London.

Shapin, S. and Barnes, B. (1977) 'Science, nature and control: interpreting Mechanics' Institutes', *Social Studies of Science*, 7, 1, 31–74.

Shapin, S. and Thackray, A. (1974) 'Prosography as a research tool in history of science: the British scientific community 1700–1900', *History of Science*, 12, 1–28.

Simon, B. (1974a) *Education and the Labour Movement 1870–1920*, Lawrence & Wishart, London.

Simon, B. (1974b) *The Politics of Educational Reform 1920–1940*, Lawrence & Wishart, London.

Simon, B. (1977) 'The 1902 Education Act – a wrong turning', *History of Education Society Bulletin*, 19, 7–14.

Skeats, H. S. and Miall, C. S. (n.d.) *History of the Free Churches of England, 1688–1891*, London.

Skocpol, T. (1979) *States and Social Revolutions A Comparative Analysis of France, Russia and China*, Cambridge University Press.

Smith, D. (1976) 'Codes, paradigms and folk norms: an approach to educational change with particular reference to the works of Basil Bernstein', *Sociology*, 10, 1, 1–19.

Smith, D. (1977a) 'Social development, the state and education: a structural analysis of Francis Adams's *History of the Elementary School Contest in England*', *Prose Studies*, 1, 1, 19–36.

Smith, D. (1977b) 'Social conflict and urban education in the nineteenth century: a sociological approach to comparative analysis', in Reeder (1980), 95–114.

Smith, D. (1982) (forthcoming) 'Education and the capitalist state: evolution, rationalisation and crisis', in Bornstein *et al.* (1982).

Smith, D. (1982) (forthcoming) *Barrington Moore: Violence, Morality and Political Change*, Macmillan, London.

Smith, J. T. (1851) *Local Self-Government and Centralization*, London.

Smith, P. (1967) *Disraelian Conservatism and Social Reform*, Routledge & Kegan Paul, London.

Spencer, H. (1850) *Social Statics*, London.

Spencer, H. (1861) *Education: Intellectual, Moral and Physical*, London.

Spencer, H. (1873) *The Study of Sociology*, London.

Spring, D. (1951) 'The English landed estate in the age of coal and iron: 1830–80', *Journal of Economic History*, 11, 1, 3–24.

Spring, D. (1954) 'Earl Fitzwilliam and the Corn Laws', *American Historical Review*, 59, 287–304.

Spring, D. (1978) *European Landed Elites in the Nineteenth Century*, Johns Hopkins University Press, Baltimore and London.

Stansky, P. (1962) 'Lyttelton and Thring: a study in nineteenth-century education', *Victorian Studies*, 5, 3, 205–23.

Stanworth, P. and Giddens, A. (1974) *Elites and Power in British Society*, Cambridge University Press.

Stearns, P. N. (1978) *Paths to Authority: the Middle Class and the Labour Force in France, 1820–48*, University of Illinois Press, Urbana.

Stephens, W. B. (1973) *Regional Variations in Education during the Industrial Revolution 1780–1870: the task of the local historian*, Educational Administration and History Monograph No. 1, University of Leeds.

Stephens, W. R. W. (1878) *The Life and Letters of Walter Farquhar Hook*, 2 vols, London.

Stevenson, J. (1977) 'Social control and the prevention of riots in England, 1789–1829', in Donajgrodski (1977), 27–50.

Stone, L. (1971) 'Prosography', *Daedalus*, 100, 46–79.

Stone, L. (1974) *The University in Society, vol. 1: Oxford and Cambridge, from the Fourteenth to the Nineteenth Centuries*, Princeton University Press, New Haven.

Storch, R. D. (1975) 'The plague of the blue locusts: police reform and popular resistance in northern England, 1840–57', *International Review of Social History*, 20, 61–90.

Storch, R. D. (1976) 'The policeman as domestic missionary: urban discipline and popular culture in northern England', *Journal of Social History*, 4, 481–509.

Storch, R. D. (1977) 'Some roots of middle-class moral reform in the industrial north, 1825–50', in Donajgrodski (1977), 138–62.

Stuart, J. (1911) *Reminiscences*, London.

Sturt, M. (1967) *The Education of the People: A history of primary education in England and Wales in the nineteenth century*, Routledge & Kegan Paul, London.

Sutherland, G. (ed.) (1972a) *Studies in the Growth of Nineteenth Century Government*, Routledge & Kegan Paul, London.

Sutherland, G. (1972b) 'Administrators in education after 1870: patronage, professionalism and expertise', in Sutherland (1972a), 263–85.

Sutherland, G. (1973a) *Matthew Arnold on Education*, with an introduction by G. Sutherland, Penguin, Harmondsworth.

Sutherland, G. (1973b) *Policy-making in Elementary Education 1870–1895*, Oxford University Press.

Taylor, A. J. (1972) *Laissez-faire and State Intervention in Nineteenth-Century Britain*, Macmillan, London.

Taylor, A. J. P. (1965) *English History 1914–1945*, Clarendon Press, Oxford.

Taylor, T. (1858) 'On central and local action', *Trans. NAPSS*, Birmingham Meeting 1857.

Teichman, O. (1940) 'The yeomanry as an aid to the civil power', *Journal for Army Historical Research*, 19, 75–91.

Thackray, A. (1974) 'Natural knowledge in cultural context: the Manchester model', *American Historical Review*, 79, 3, 672–709.

Tholfsen, T. R. (1976) *Working-class Radicalism in mid-Victorian England*, Croom Helm, London.

Thompson, E. P. (1966) *The Making of the English Working Class*, Random House, New York.

Thompson, E. P. (1967) 'Time, work-discipline, and industrial capitalism', *Past and Present*, 38, 56–97.

Thompson, E. P. (1974) 'Patrician society, plebian culture', *Journal of Social History*, 7, 4, 382–405.

Thompson, E. P. (1978) 'Eighteenth-century English society: class struggle without class?', *Social History*, 3, 2, 133–65.

Thompson, F. M. L. (1959) 'Whigs and Liberals in the West riding 1830–60', *English Historical Review*, 74, 214–39.

Thompson, F. M. L. (1963) *English Landed Society in the Nineteenth Century*, Routledge & Kegan Paul, London.

Thompson, K. A. (1965) *Bureaucracy and Church Reform: the organisational response of the Church of England to social change 1800–1865*, Oxford University Press.

Tropp, A. (1957) *The School Teachers: The Growth of the Teaching Profession in England and Wales from 1800 to the Present Day*, Heinemann, London.

Turner, R. H. (1960) 'Contest and sponsored mobility and the school system', *American Sociological Review*, 25, 855–67.

Tyack, G. (1972) 'The Victorian country houses of Warwickshire', *Warwickshire History*, 2, 1, 3–19.

Verney, R. G. (1924) *The Passing Years*, Constable, London.

Vigier, F. (1970) *Change and Apathy: Liverpool and Manchester during the Industrial Revolution*, MIT Press, Cambridge, Mass.

Vincent, J. (1967) *Poll books: How Victorians Voted*, Cambridge University Press.

Vincent, J. (1972) *The Formation of the British Liberal Party 1857–68*, Penguin, Harmondsworth.

Ward, D. (1967) 'The Public Schools and Industry in Britain after 1870', *Journal of Contemporary History*, 2, 3, 37–52.

Ward, D. (1975) 'Victorian Cities: how modern?', *Journal of Historical Geography*, 1, 2, 35–51.

Ward, J. T. (1966) 'West Riding landowners and the Corn Laws', *English Historical Review*, 81, 256–72.

Ward, J. T. and Wilson, R. G. (eds) (1971) *Land and Industry: the landed estate and the industrial revolution*, David & Charles, Newton Abbot.

Watts, M. R. (1978) *The Dissenters: From the Reformation to the French Revolution*, Clarendon Press, Oxford.

Webb, B. (1926) *My Apprenticeship*, Longmans Green, London.

Webb, R. K. (1955) *The British Working-class Reader*, Allen & Unwin, London.

Webb, S. & B. (1906) *English Local Government from the Revolution to the Municipal Corporation Act: The Parish and the County*, London.

Webster, C. (1975) *The Great Instauration: Science, Medicine and Reform*, Duckworth, London.

Welton, T. A. (1858) 'On the composition of the population of large towns', in *Trans. NAPSS* Birmingham Meeting, 412–18.

West, E. G. (1978) 'Literacy and the Industrial Revolution', *Economic History Review*, 31, 3, 369–83.

Wilde, O. (1895) *The Importance of Being Earnest* reprinted in *The Works of Oscar Wilde*, Spring Books, London.

Wilkinson, R. and Bishop, T. J. H. (1967) *Winchester and the Public School Elite*, Faber & Faber, London.

Williams, F. C. (1903) *From Journalist to Judge: An Autobiography*, London.

Williams, G. L. (1976) *John Stuart Mill on Politics and Society*, Fontana, London.

Williams, J. E. (1955) 'Paternalism in local government in the nineteenth century', *Public Administration*, 33, 439–46.

Williams, R. (1963) *Culture and Society*, Penguin, Harmondsworth.

Wilson, A. (1974) 'The suffrage movement', in Hollis (1974), 80–104.

Wilson, R. G. (1971) *Gentlemen Merchants*, Manchester University Press.

Wiltshire, D. (1978) *The Social and Political Thought of Herbert Spencer*, Oxford University Press.

Winstanley, D. A. (1960) *Early Victorian Cambridge*, Cambridge University Press.

Woodward, J. and Richards, D. (1977) *Health Care and Popular Medicine in Nineteenth-Century England*, Croom Helm, London.

Zangerl, C. H. E. (1971) 'The social composition of the county magistracy in England and Wales 1831–1887', *Journal of British Studies*, 11, 1, 113–25.

Zollschan, G. K. and Hirsch, W. (eds) (1964) *Explorations in Social Change*, Routledge & Kegan Paul, London.

II. *Other sources*

II(a) UNPUBLISHED THESES AND DISSERTATIONS

Bailey, M. H. (1952) 'The contribution of Quakers to some aspects of local government in Birmingham 1828–1902', MA, Birmingham.

Ball, F. (1971) 'The development of the grammar school in Sheffield', dissertation, Totley Hall College of Education.

Banks, O. (1953) 'The concept and nature of the grammar school in relation to the development of secondary education since 1902', PhD, London.

Baxter, J. L. (1976a) 'The origin of the social war in South Yorkshire – a study of capitalist evolution and labour class realisation in one industrial region c. 1750–1855', PhD, Sheffield.

Blanch, M. D. (1975) 'Nation, empire and the Birmingham working class', PhD, Birmingham.

Board, M. J. (1959) 'A history of the private adventure school in Sheffield', MA, Sheffield.

Bushrod, E. (1954) 'The history of Unitarianism from the middle of the eighteenth century to 1893', MA, Birmingham.

Cannadine, D. N. (1975) 'The aristocracy and the towns in the nineteenth century: a case study of the Calthorpes and Birmingham 1807–1910', D Phil., Oxford.

Clegg, A. P. (1970) 'The residential areas of Sheffield: an analysis of their historical development and current characteristics', MA, Sheffield.

Crawshaw, H. N. (1954) 'Movements for political and social reform in Sheffield, 1792–1832', MA, Sheffield.

Dalvi, M. A. (1957) 'Commercial education in England during 1851–1902: an institutional study', PhD, London.

Dandeker, C. (1977) 'A study of the process of bureaucratisation: the Royal Navy, state and society 1770–1916', PhD, Leicester.

Donnelly, F. K. (1975a) 'The general rising of 1820: a study of social conflict in the industrial revolution', PhD, Sheffield.

Fletcher, D. E. (1972) 'Aspects of Liberalism in Sheffield 1849–1886', PhD, Sheffield.

Foster, C. (1940) 'The influence of science teaching on the development of secondary education with particular reference to the city of Birmingham', PhD, London.

Franklin, R. E. (1950) 'Medical education and the rise of the general practitioner', PhD, Birmingham.

Fraser, D. (1962) 'Newspaper opinion in three Midland cities 1800–1850', MA, Leeds.

Frost, M. B. (1978) 'The development of provided schooling for working-class children in Birmingham 1781–1851', MLitt, Birmingham.

Gammage, M. T. (1972) 'Newspaper opinion and education: a study of the influence of the Birmingham provincial press on developments in education, 1870–1902', MEd, Leicester.

Gaskell, S. M. (1974) 'Housing estate developments, 1840–1918, with particular reference to the Pennine towns', PhD, Sheffield.

Hennock, E. P. (1956) 'The role of religious dissent in the reform of municipal government in Birmingham', 1865–1876, PhD, Cambridge.

Higginbotham, M. (1941) 'The career of A. J. Mundella with special reference to his Sheffield connections', MA, Sheffield.

Jennett, G. D. (1954) 'Thomas Asline Ward: his life and achievements and their effect upon the development of Sheffield', MA, Sheffield.

Johnson, J. R. B. (1968) 'The Education Department 1839–1864: a study in social policy and the growth of government', PhD, Cambridge.

March, K. G. (1966) 'The life and career of Sir William Christopher Leng (1825–1902): a study of the ideas and influence of a prominent Victorian journalist', MA, Sheffield.

Marcham, A. J. (1969) 'The crisis of national education', MEd, Birmingham.

Mathers, H. E. (1979b) 'Sheffield municipal politics 1893–1926: parties, personalities and the rise of Labour', PhD, Sheffield.

Mee, L. G. (1972) 'The Earl Fitzwilliam and the management of the collieries and other industrial enterprises on the Wentworth estate 1795–1857', PhD, Nottingham.

Mole, D. E. H. (1961) 'The Church of England and society in Birmingham, c.1830–1866', PhD, Cambridge.

Parsons, C. (1975) 'Elementary education in the local community: a study of relationships in the Attercliffe area of Sheffield 1870–1940', MEd, Leicester.

Reid, C. O. (1976) 'Middle-class values and working-class culture in nineteenth century Sheffield', PhD, Sheffield.

Richards, P. R. (1975) 'The state and the working class 1833–41: MPs and the making of social policy', PhD, Birmingham.

Salt, J. (1960b) 'Isaac Ironside and education in the Sheffield region in the first half of the nineteenth century', MA, Sheffield.

Scudamore, C. N. J. (1976) 'The social background of pupils at the Bridge St. Higher Grade School, Birmingham', MEd, Birmingham.

Shewell, M. E. J. (1951) 'An historical investigation of the development of a local system of education in the City of Birmingham from 1870–1924', MA, London.

Taylor, A. F. (1955) 'History of the Birmingham School Board 1870–1903', MA, Birmingham.

Taylor, A. F. (1960) 'Birmingham and the movement for national education 1867–1877', PhD, Leicester.

Tunsiri, V. I. (1964) 'The party politics of the Black Country and neighbourhood, 1832–1867', MA, Birmingham.

Tyson, J. C. (1960) 'Elementary education provided by the governors of the Free Grammar Schools of King Edward VI in Birmingham, 1751–1883', MA, Birmingham.

Williams, J. N. (1973) 'A study of the background of the Newcastle commission', MEd, Leicester.

II(b) OFFICIAL PUBLICATIONS

PP 1843, XIV, *Children's Employment Commission, Second Report.*
PP 1852, XXII. *Royal Commission on University of Oxford.*
PP 1852–3, XLIV, *Royal Commission on University of Cambridge.*
PP 1852–3, LIV, *Second Report of the Royal Commission for Exhibition of 1851.*
PP 1852–3, LXXVIII et seq., *1851 Census (England and Wales).*
PP 1861, XXI, *Newcastle Commission.*
PP 1864, XXII, *Children's Employment Commission, Third Report.*
PP 1865, XX, *Children's Employment Commission, Fourth Report.*
PP 1867, XXXII, *Sheffield Outrages Inquiry.*
PP 1867–8, XXVIII, *Schools Inquiry Commission.*

PP 1870, LIV, *Return confined to the municipal boroughs of Birmingham, Leeds, Liverpool and Manchester, of all schools for the poorer classes of children.*
PP 1873, LXXI et seq., *1871 Census (England and Wales).*
PP 1874, LXXII, pts I and II, *Return of Owners of Land 1872–3 (England and Wales).*
PP 1881, LVI, *University of Oxford Commission.*
PP 1884, XXIX et seq., *Royal Commission on Technical Instruction, Second Report.*
PP 1884–5, XXXI, *Royal Commission on Housing of the Working-Classes, First Report.*
PP 1886, XXI, *Royal Commission on Depression of Trade, Second Report.*
PP 1886, XXV, *Cross Commission, First Report.*
PP 1887, XXIX, *Cross Commission, Second Report.*
PP 1888, CCII, *Select Committee on Town Holdings.*
PP 1888, XXXV, *Cross Commission, Final Report.*
PP 1889, LXV, *Report on an Epidemic of Small-pox at Sheffield during 1887–8.*
PP 1893–4, XXXIV, *Royal Commission on Labour.*
PP 1893, CVI et seq., *1891 Census (England and Wales).*
PP 1895, XLIII et seq., *Bryce Commission.*
Committee of Council on Education, *Minutes, 1847–8, 1854–5, 1857–8, 1866–7, 1876–7.*
Science and Art Department, *Seventh Annual Report, 1859.*

II(c) NEWSPAPERS, DIRECTORIES, ANNUAL REPORTS, ETC.

Newspapers, etc.

Aris's Gazette.
Biograph and Review.
Birmingham Daily Gazette.
Birmingham Daily Post.
Birmingham Journal.
Dart.
Edgbastonia.
Gentleman's Magazine.
Morning Chronicle.
Sheffield Independent.
Sheffield Telegraph.

Directories

Robson's Directory of Birmingham and Sheffield, 1839.
Rodgers' Directory of Sheffield and Rotherham, 1841.
White's Directory of Leeds, 1847.
White's Directory of Sheffield, 1849.
White's Directory of Birmingham, 1849.
White's Directory of Warwickshire, 1850.
White's Directory of Sheffield, 1852.
Slater's Directory of Birmingham, 1852–3.
Billing's Directory of Worcestershire, 1855.
White's Directory of Birmingham and the Black Country, 1855.
Corporation Directory of Birmingham, 1861.
White's Directory of Sheffield, 1862.

Annual reports, etc.

Birmingham Education Society, Annual Reports 1868–9.
Birmingham Education Union, report of Birmingham meeting 9 December 1869.
Birmingham Free Industrial School, Annual Reports 1864–76.
Birmingham Higher Education Association, Annual Reports 1875–7.
Birmingham Ladies Educational Association, report of first meeting, 1871.
Birmingham and Midland Institute, Annual Reports 1856–1913.
Birmingham School Board, Reports.
Birmingham School Board, newspaper cuttings, vols 1 and 2, 1870–6.
Birmingham Teachers' Association, Annual Reports 1875–1905.
Central Nonconformist Committee, Annual Report 1874–5.
National Education League, collection of circulars, leaflets, etc., 1869–75.
National Education League, report of first general meeting at Birmingham, 1869.
Sheffield Mechanics' and Apprentices' Library, Minutes 1823–38.
Sheffield Mechanics' Institute, Minutes, vols 1 and 2 (1832–45).
Sheffield Mechanics' Institute, Annual Reports 1835–9.
Sheffield School Board, Annual Reports, 1873–1902.
Wesleyan Proprietary Grammar School, Sheffield, First Report, 1841.

II(d) OTHER MATERIAL

II(d) (i) Birmingham collection

Committee of Dissenters. Statement of facts, arguments and proceedings in opposition to a clause in the Birmingham Free Grammar School Bill, 1830.
Parliamentary Commissioners . . . Report on Birmingham Free Grammar School – Reflections on its Mismanagement, 1830.
The Faithful Pastor Delineated –, 1839.
Memoir of the Rev. John George Breay –, 1841.
Report on the State of Public Health in the Borough of Birmingham by a Committee of Physicians and Surgeons, 1841.
Report of Proceedings of Town Council in relation to the Bill of Governors of the Free Grammar School, 1842.
T. Gutteridge to James Taylor on the Corrupt System of Election of Medical Officers, 1843.
T. Gutteridge to Earl of Dartmouth on Election of Medical Officers at General Hospital, 1844.
General Hospital, Birmingham: proceedings of Annual General Meeting, 20 September 1844.
J. Suckling, The Queen's College, Birmingham: Enquiry by Charity Commissioners. Reply for W. Sands Cox, 1859.
Birmingham School Board, Report on Compulsion as Applied to School Attendance in Birmingham, 1878.
J. O. Bacchus, Letters, accounts, documents, etc. relating to the Union Glass Works, Dartmouth St, Birmingham, 1817–87.
Dawson collection.
G. H. Osborne's *Birmingham Biography* (press cuttings).

II(d) (ii) Sheffield Local History collection

Newspaper cuttings relating to Sheffield.

Newspaper cuttings concerning the nomination of Joseph Chamberlain as
Liberal candidate for Sheffield 1873–4.

Newspaper cuttings relating to the Sheffield Outrages.

Church Congress in Sheffield: report of papers and discussions, Sheffield,
1878.

Wesleyan Methodism in Sheffield and district (newspaper cuttings).

The corrected report of the debates and decisions of the adjourned meeting of
Wesleyan-Methodist delegates held at Sheffield from 30 July to 7 August
1833, London, 1833.

Dr Knight's lecture on national education in reply to the aspersions of the Rev.
T. Best, Sheffield, 1837.

The establishment, principles, discipline and educational course of the
Wesleyan Proprietary Grammar School, Sheffield, 1839.

Proceedings of the Sheffield Town Council 1847–8, Sheffield, 1848.

Cohen, H. (1950) 'George Calvert Holland – Physician Extraordinary to the
Sheffield General Infirmary', Sheffield.

INDEX

Note: Bir denotes Birmingham; Sh denotes Sheffield

Abraham, J. H. (Sh), 40, 114
Acland, T. D., 178
Adams, Francis (Bir), 229–31, 292
Adderley, C. B. (Bir), 92, 97, 100, 135, 261
Addy, S. O. (Sh), 211
adult education: in Bir, 105–6, 137–50, 234; in Sh, 105–6, 137–50
Agenoria works (Sh), 66
Albright, Arthur (Bir), 71, 182
Alcester, 26
All Saints (Bir), 108, 130
Allday, Joseph (Bir), 91, 100–1, 103, 275
Allen, J. R. (Bir), 145
Allen St Sunday School (Sh), 118
Alsop Fields (Sh), 72
Amalgamated Society of Engineers, 244, 246
Andrews, J. H. (Sh), 273
Ansell, W. (Bir), 290
Anti-Corn Law League, 18, 83, 228
Applegarth, Robert, 164
apprenticeship: in Bir, 38, 41, 44, 49, 105, 222, 240; in Sh, 44–5, 54, 105–7, 125, 129, 140, 165, 169, 240, 258
arbitration: in Bir, 38, 239–40; in Sh, 164–6, 175, 245–6
aristocracy, 1, 2, 7–10, 12–14, 17, 90, 153, 192–4, 196, 199, 205, 248–9, 264, 265, 292; in Bir, 28–30, 32–3, 189; in Sh, 27–8, 31–3, 87
armaments, 222, 235, 244
Arnold, J. O. (Sh), 222
Arnold Matthew, 160–1, 189, 196–9, 292
Arnold, Thomas, 284
artisans, 3, 8–9, 11–12, 14, 16, 91, 160, 196, 201–3; in Bir, 38–48, 49–51, 59–60, 64, 93, 95, 97–9, 102–3, 105–6, 111, 134, 143, 146, 151, 158, 162, 175, 186, 213, 219, 232, 234, 238–41, 256, 259, 261; in Sh, 32, 37–46, 50–1, 59–60, 64, 82–3, 89, 97, 103, 105–7, 139, 151, 162, 164, 166–7, 171, 175, 189, 222, 236, 246, 257
artistic occupations: in Bir, 21, 23, 33–4; in Sh, 23, 33–4
Artizan Dwellings Act, 226, 228, 242
Ash family (Bir), 156
Ashley, S. (Sh), 108, 121
Ashley, William (Bir), 222, 223
Ashmead-Bartlett, E. (Sh), 293
Ashton, Harriet (Sh), 116–17
Aston (Bir), 26, 94, 244
Athenaeum (Sh), 142, 146, 209
Athenic Institute (Bir), 144
Atkinson, Charles (Sh), 85, 273
Atkinson, G. B., Rev. (Sh), 115
Atlas works (Sh), 66, 85, 163
Attercliffe (Sh), 32, 63, 66, 69, 71, 85, 87–8, 132, 161–2, 171, 235, 243–5, 257
Attwood, Thomas (Bir), 33–4, 91, 93–4, 100, 144
Austen, Jane, 20
Austin Motor Company (Bir), 234
Avery, Thomas (Bir), 101, 103

Bacchus, J. O. (Bir), 93, 129, 184
Bache, Samuel (Bir), 126
Baden-Powell, Robert, 252
Bagnall family (Bir), 133
Bagshaw, W. J. (Sh), 80
Baker family (Bir), 96
Baker, George (Bir), 285
Baker, T. R. (Sh), 62
Baldwin, James (Bir), 95, 98, 100, 182
Baldwin, Stanley, 221, 295–6
Balliol College, 200, 252
Bantock, Granville (Bir), 218
Baptists: in Bir, 93, 96, 126; in Sh, 244
Barber, J. H. (Sh), 140, 170

327

housing, 228–9; in Bir, 240–1; in Sh, 242
Housing and Planning Act, 241
Howarth, J. (Sh), 273
Howell, George, 170
Hughes, W. R. (Bir), 292
Huxley, T. H., 215

Ibbotson Bros (Sh company), 68, 166
Ibbotson, Alfred (Sh), 37–8, 68
Ibbotson, William (Sh), 83
immigration, 5, 7; in Sh, 67
Imperial College, 195
improvement bills: Bir, 63, 77, 98, 101; Sh, 64, 84, 101
improvement commissioners (Sh), 61, 81, 86
Improvement Scheme (Bir), 226, 232, 240–1, 262
Incorporated Law Society, 152
Independent Labour Party (Sh), 246
India Act, 193
Indian Civil Service, 193
industrial relations, 3, 19; in Bir, 136, 175, 238–40; in Sh, 164, 175; see also arbitration; file strike; trade unions
industrial schools, 100, 104, 127
industrial structure: Bir, 35–8, 39, 69–71, 107, 238–9; Sh, 30, 35–8, 68, 107; see also apprenticeship; armaments; artisans; brass trade; bucklemaking; division of labour; engineering; female labour; file trade; glass industry; grinders; gun trade; jewellery trade; juvenile labour; light trades; machinery; manufacturers; metalworking trades; nail-making; saw-grinders; steel industry; steel-pen trade; sword-making; tool-making
industrialisation, 1–2, 5, 7, 10, 12–16, 191, 236, 257; see also factories; machinery
Inge estate (Bir), 97
Ingleby, Clement (Bir), 34, 151
inns: in Bir, 55; in Sh, 32, 55, 124
Institution of Mechanical Engineers, 16, 33, 145, 155
International, 166
inventions, 40, 238
Irish, 5, 203, 248
Ironside, Isaac (Sh), 19, 74–8, 83–6, 88–9, 101–3, 124, 140–1, 172, 174, 226–7, 247, 257, 285
ironworks: Bir, 26, 37, 43, 147; Sh, 26, 43
Ironworkers' Union (Sh), 167
Islington (Bir), 71
isolation (of Sh), 25–7, 29, 31, 109, 256

Jackson family (Sh), 153, 283
Jackson, Arthur (Sh), 277, 283
Jackson, Robert (Sh), 85, 273, 284
Jackson, Samuel (Sh), 85
Jaffray, John (Bir), 99, 275
James, J. A. (Bir), 100, 126
Japan, 2
Jessop, Thomas (Sh), 85–7, 273, 284, 294
Jessops (Sh steel company), 66, 222, 280
jewellery trade (Bir), 35, 38, 69–71, 162, 222
Johnson, G. J. (Bir), 290
Johnstone family (Bir), 151–2, 156–7
Johnstone, Edward (Bir), 152, 154
Johnstone, John (Bir), 152, 154, 182
joint-stock companies, 17; in Bir, 234; in Sh, 88, 234

Jones, Viriamu, 252
journalism, 20, 167; in Sh, 81, 188, 209; see also Birmingham Argus; Birmingham Daily Gazette; Birmingham Daily Mail; Birmingham Daily Post; Birmingham Journal; Dart; Leader, Robert; Leeds Mercury; Leng, W. C., Manchester Guardian; Morning Chronicle; Nonconformist; Pilot; Saturday Review; Sheffield Courant; Sheffield Free Press; Sheffield Independent; Sheffield Iris; Sheffield Telegraph; The Times
Jowett, B., 200
Jowitt, T. (Sh), 273
justice, administration of, 7, 17, 57–8, 194; in Bir, 58, 62–3, 95, 99, 104, 152, 211; in Sh, 46, 57–9, 61, 63, 80–1, 104, 161, 272; see also crime; legal profession; police; quarter sessions, court of
juvenile labour, 204; in Bir, 40–2, 52–3, 70–1, 105, 120–2, 126, 134, 162, 238; in Sh, 40–2, 53–4, 58, 105, 120–2, 132

Kargon, Richard, 195
Kenrick family (Bir), 96
Kenrick, George (Bir), 218
Kenrick, William (Bir), 235
Kenwood Park Estate (Sh), 86
Kenyon, J. and Sons (Sh manufacturing company), 166
Kidderminster, 18, 26
Kilham, Alexander (Sh), 82
King Edward VI Foundation (Bir), 19, 61, 63–4, 92, 97, 99, 101, 105–6, 108–13, 115, 129, 134, 148, 151, 155–7, 161, 176–82, 184, 192, 212–15, 219–21, 231, 237, 259, 260, 262, 274, 291, 292
King Edward VI Foundation Elementary Schools (Bir), 109–12, 129, 148, 176, 179, 181
King Edward VI Foundation English School (Bir), 111, 180–1
King Edward VII School (Sh), 295
kinship, see family
Knight, Arnold (Sh), 55, 139, 153–4
Knott, J. (Sh), 273
Knowles, Adam (Sh), 85
Knox, E. A. (Bir), 233, 235–6, 241, 244
Kossuth, 77

labour, 7, 10, 14, 17, 45, 202, 254; in Bir, 43; in Sh, 43, 45, 67, 164–5, 169, 246, 256; see also female labour; juvenile labour
Labour Party, 250; in Sh, 243
Labour, Royal Commission on, 244
Labour Representation Committee (Sh), 242, 246, 257
Ladywood (Bir), 71–2
laissez-faire, 197, 231
Lancastrian schools (Sh), 108, 121, 123, 125, 128
land societies: in Bir, 60; in Sh, 60
landowners, 1–2, 7, 172, 192, 235, 249; see also aristocracy; property ownership
Lansdowne, Lord, 197
Lapworth, Charles, 221
Laurie, A. P., 214–15
law courts (Bir), 232
Law, J. T. (Bir), 99, 149–50, 157
Lawrence St. (Bir), 241
Lea, George, Rev. (Bir), 100
Leader, Robert (Sh), 83, 88, 163, 171, 228, 242–3, 275, 277

337